D0554518

ECONOMICS OF INFORMATION SECURITY

Advances in Information Security

Sushil Jajodia
Consulting Editor, Center for Secure Information Systems
George Mason University, Fairfax, VA 22030-4444
email: jajodia@gmu.edu

The goals of Kluwer International Series on ADVANCES IN INFORMATION SECURITY are one, to establish the state of the art of, and set the course for, future research in information security and two, to serve as a central reference source for advanced and timely topics in information security research and development. The scope of this series includes all aspects of computer and network security and related areas such as fault tolerance and software assurance.

ADVANCES IN INFORMATION SECURITY aims to publish thorough and cohesive overviews of specific topics in information security, as well as works that are larger in scope or that contain more detailed background information than can be accommodated in shorter survey articles. The series also serves as a forum for topics that may not have reached a level of maturity to warrant a comprehensive textbook treatment. Researchers as well as developers are encouraged to contact Professor Sushil Jajodia with ideas for books under this series.

Additional titles in the series:

PRIMALITY TESTING AND INTEGER FACTORIZATION IN PUBLIC KEY CRYPTOGRAPHY by Song Y. Yan; ISBN: 1-4020-7649-5
SYNCHRONIZING E-SECURITY by Godfried B. Williams; ISBN: 1-4020-7646-0
INTRUSION DETECTION IN DISTRIBUTED SYSTEMS: ***An Abstraction-Based Approach*** by Peng Ning, Sushil Jajodia and X. Sean Wang ISBN: 1-4020-7624-X
DISSEMINATING SECURITY UPDATES AT INTERNET SCALE by Jun Li, Peter Reiher, Gerald J. Popek; ISBN: 1-4020-7305-4
SECURE ELECTRONIC VOTING by Dimitris A. Gritzalis; ISBN: 1-4020-7301-1
APPLICATIONS OF DATA MINING IN COMPUTER SECURITY, edited by Daniel Barbará, Sushil Jajodia; ISBN: 1-4020-7054-3
MOBILE COMPUTATION WITH FUNCTIONS by Zeliha Dilsun Kırlı, ISBN: 1-4020-7024-1
TRUSTED RECOVERY AND DEFENSIVE INFORMATION WARFARE by Peng Liu and Sushil Jajodia, ISBN: 0-7923-7572-6
RECENT ADVANCES IN RSA CRYPTOGRAPHY by Stefan Katzenbeisser, ISBN: 0-7923-7438-X
E-COMMERCE SECURITY AND PRIVACY by Anup K. Ghosh, ISBN: 0-7923-7399-5
INFORMATION HIDING: Steganography and Watermarking-Attacks and Countermeasures by Neil F. Johnson, Zoran Duric, and Sushil Jajodia, ISBN: 0-7923-7204-2

Additional information about this series can be obtained from
http://www.wkap.nl/prod/s/ADIS

ECONOMICS OF INFORMATION SECURITY

edited by

L. Jean Camp
Harvard University, U.S.A.

Stephen Lewis
University of Cambridge, UK

KLUWER ACADEMIC PUBLISHERS
Boston / Dordrecht / London

Distributors for North, Central and South America:
Kluwer Academic Publishers
101 Philip Drive
Assinippi Park
Norwell, Massachusetts 02061 USA
Telephone (781) 871-6600
Fax (781) 871-6528
E-Mail <kluwer@wkap.com>

Distributors for all other countries:
Kluwer Academic Publishers Group
Post Office Box 322
3300 AH Dordrecht, THE NETHERLANDS
Telephone 31 78 6576 000
Fax 31 78 6576 474
E-Mail <orderdept@wkap.nl>

Electronic Services <http://www.wkap.nl>

Library of Congress Cataloging-in-Publication

ECONOMICS OF INFORMATION SECURITY
edited by L. Jean Camp and Stephen Lewis
Advances in Information Security, Volume 12
ISBN: 1-4020-8089-1
ISBN E-book: 1-4020-8090-5

Printed on acid-free paper.

Printed in the United States of America

Contents

Preface

The security market has failed.

On Tuesday, October 8, 2003 Aaron Caffrey, age nineteen, began his trial. The charge: subverting the operation of the Port of Houston. His prosecution had been a model of international interaction, with the British and American authorities cooperating at every step. Mr. Caffery was to be tried in the United Kingdom.

The Port of Houston took all normal security practices. The Port had developed web-based services for assisting shipping pilots as they moor, in coordinating loading and unloading companies, and in harbor navigation. In a denial of service attack Aaron brought the port to a halt on September 20, 2001. (A denial of service attack consists of repeated initiations of contact, with the attacking machine pretending to be many different machines. An analogous attack would be to repeatedly call someone on the phone and remaining silent until the hearer hangs up, then repeating the process constantly so no work could be completed.) The initial stated reason for the attack? A person from Houston had taunted Aaron about the object of his on-line affections.

Aaron Caffery walked free from that courtroom in October 2003. Security experts explained that there was no way to disprove his assertion that his threats against Houston, his association with a hacker group, and his talents proved nothing. The defense illustrated that there was no way to illustrate beyond a reasonable doubt that Caffery's machine itself was not subverted, so that it acted upon direction other than its owners.

A hacker who can both manipulate code and illustrate that no one is immune to hackers, Aaron Caffrey is an autistic young man.

This is the state of the security of the American information infrastructure.

In July, 2003 a virus, a variant of one originally named SoBig, infected one out of every three computers in China. The virus provides spammers with the processing power and bandwidth of the infected computer in their distribution of unwanted mass email. The virus caused mail server crashes, denial of service attacks, and encouraged the spread of an unrelated virus masquerading as a Microsoft patch for SoBig. SoBig was the most expensive in history – until MyDoom arrived six months later. In the time it takes to publish this work, another even more virulent and expensive virus will undoubtedly appear.

This is the state of the security of the global information infrastructure.

Certainly, the web server at the Port of Houston was economically and politically important enough to warrant sufficient investment in security. Indeed, the Port of Houston is important enough that a single teenager should not be able to single-handedly stop the port from functioning.

Similarly, the investment in personnel, networks, and sheer mass of individual time would argue that a virus such as SoBig would have been more effectively prevented than battled, or tolerated as a chronic insolvable problem, like malaria in the tropics.

Why have market mechanisms thus far failed to create secure networks?

The Internet is critical to all sectors of the economy and integrated into government. Security technologies do exist, and capable programmers can implement secure code. Programming projects and operating systems based on secure design principles populate research databases. Yet the network at the Port of Houston was sabotaged by a creative teenager with limited programming experience.

Why? Clearly the answer to this question must include more than technology. There is a problem in the economics of security, and more broadly in the economics of information control. These problems emerge as security violations, spam, 'private' databases indexed by Google, and products based on practices exposed as snake oil decades before.

Computer viruses and worms are no longer the domains of experts only. Every business experienced infections and disruptions from infected machines in the latest generation of worms. Economics combined with a management, organization theory, and computer security together can address the chronic problems of economic security. Yet the problems of security have not, before now, been systematically examined in economic and management terms. This text, rather than trying to encourage managers and practitioners to become security experts uses the tools of economics to bear on the problems of network security. The result is a narrative about the economic problems of information security, a set of tools for examining appropriate investment in computer security, all embedded in a set of rich metaphors for balancing the various alternative for computer security.

The security market in the case of networked information systems can be thought of in many different ways, and each view suggest a different set of regulatory and economic responses. Yet, for all the metaphors that may apply there is a single potential measure: dollars. Economics offers a powerful lens for understanding the apparently wildly irrational behavior of software providers, companies, home users and even nation states. This text brings all the tools of economics to bear on the individual, corporate, and national problems of computer security. Perverse incentives, lock-in, irrational risk evaluations and bad information all play a role in creating the chronically broken network.

The economics of information security is not a metaphor for computer security, like war or health. Recognizing the economics of information security allow managers to alter incentives and policy makers to better evaluate policies that may be presented under the warfare metaphor.

A simple example of corporate incentives is that of patching vulnerabilities. Individual departments must pay for their own IT services, machines, and employee time. Engaging ITS to support employees and requiring employees to patch creates immediate costs for each manager. Charging each section for vulnerabilities will enhance company wide security, but such a solution comes from consideration of the complexities of the security market. Assuming that security works like all other goods has and will continue to result in the creation of perverse incentives that cause managers to ignore the long term issue of security in favor of goals with more pressing time frames.

While the elephant of computer security emerges piecewise, with the ear and tail and foot, the volume as a whole offers a clear picture of computer and information security. Such clarity could only be obtained by painting the whole picture with the palette provide by economics.

Camp's article discusses the concept of security vulnerabilities as an externality, and the direct implication of such externalities for market construction. Of course the use of economics proposes that security must be some kind of tradable or measurable good. Perhaps security is that canonical economic failure – a public good. In this case one person's security investment is another's gain, therefore no one makes the adequate investment. Or perhaps it is not the value to others but the simple lack of return that means that there is little investment. If security is an externality it can still be subject to measurement. Understanding security as an externality may inform the security debate and, as the chapter concludes, offer some insight in how to manage it in a corporate environment.

Yet perhaps vulnerabilities and externalities is too narrow a description of security. What kind of good exactly is being measured? Hal Varian offers three scenarios.

First, security can be defined by the lowest investment, just as the height of a protective wall is defined by its lowest or weakest point. Even barbarians knew this, as they aimed for the gate and not the towers.

Second, the level of security can be determined by the greatest investment, as when the town is protected by concentric walls. The highest wall provides the greatest protection (or rather, the combination of the strongest gate and highest wall).

Alternatively, the security level can be determined by the average investment. In this case consider the community involved in the construction of the wall – the wall is as high as the combined effort of all participants. Individual effort can raise the average somewhat, but not significantly raise the wall. Consumer behavior reflects the assertion that security and privacy claims are not trustworthy. Few consumers exhibit the understanding of "trusted" computing as trustworthy. Indeed, security is more complex than most goods in that its primary function will be subverted by its users. Passwords written on post-it notes, shared passwords, violations of security policy, and sharing of security information are all common. Why is security both so desirable and so frequently subverted?

Control and verification of information are the critical goal of security and privacy. Yet control of information on an individual machine may be of interest to more then the user. In the most common examples, a remote party with commercial interests will want to constrain the use of information; however, even more common is the desire of en employer to control information use on the employee's machine. One economics of security is needed to analyze remote control of information, whereas distinct economic concepts are required to discuss the protection of a set of machines with a define periphery.

Digital rights management systems are designed by producers with complex commercial interests; these interests are often in conflict with the interests of the user. As a result, the most consistent and highest investment in security has been in the interest of manufacturers, not consumers. Trusted computing has been primarily used to implement bundling. Cell phone companies tie the battery to the phone; automobile companies tie maintenance to the dealership. What would be theoretically prevented in the contract can be prohibited by the code.

Ross Anderson has illustrated this dichotomy in a series of case studies of security as applied in modern technologies. The nature of security as a good is complicated by the fact that it is inherently a bundled good. You cannot purchase security in the abstract. There must be a threat to be considered and the security investment (average, lowest or highest) must be commensurate with and targeted to that threat. In all of these the threat as perceived by the user is the threat of external control; while the threat as perceived by the producer is that of a consumer out of control.

Having acknowledged that producer security is at odds with consumer Desires, it is feasible to examine investment from the perspective of the producer or the consumer. Beginning with the producer, Stephen Lewis asks if producers have accurately and correctly invested in digital rights management technology. Indeed, as shown in the next chapter by Stuart Schechter, investments in encryption against P2P networks are in fact changing the balance. But the balance is being changed in favor of the file traders and against the interests of those who would license the content. Beginning with the argument about the current uses of security technology, observing the incentives in peer to peer systems, the final chapter in this section argues that trusted computing may end up supporting the user and subverting the investors.

Indeed if reliable security information is so difficult to find, the incentives so hard to evaluate, and the results so unreliable, why should anyone share it? What are the economic consequences of sharing information? Esther Gal-or and Anindya Ghose examine the generic question of sharing security information, to find that it is in fact anything but generic. The size of the firm, the nature of the market in which the firm is competing, and even the functional requirements for anti-trust policy. Information sharing among firms and across industries varies widely, and this chapter explains why.

Hussein offers a broad look of the quantitative examinations of computer security economics. The findings are remarkably consistent for a young branch of the dismal science. There are a few discordant findings, illustrating that there is no single unified theory of information security but that a range of possibilities suggests reasons for underinvestment.

If security and confidentiality are primarily targeted at preventing firm loss, then what are the limits to security? If security is primarily a conceptual issue, then attacks on reputation as well as integrity are a security issue. Considering the vast investment in brands, are investments in security rational?

Sharing information may lead to more investment and thus a decrease in losses to security breaches. Beyond direct loss, what is the loss in value of the firm when there are security breaches? Larry Gordon and Marty Loeb illustrate that security breaches by and large have little effect on stock market evaluation of a firm. Yet when confidentiality is lost, then there is a high price to pay. The implicit argument is that the market responds very strongly to losses of privacy and less strongly to losses of security. The security market cannot be extricated from the privacy market, without serious misunderstandings of both.

In rejecting techniques that require effort, users are rejecting investment in the very confidentiality that the market so values. Aquisti argues that is because users share the characteristic so often identified in the stock market itself: extremely high long term discounting. Users value the current convenience offered by privacy violations at current value, and implement extraordinary discounts for the later potential harm.

This observation is validated from an entirely different perspective by Paul Syverson in his examination of the security market. Discounts and probabilities are not well understood when consumers offer information that could be used against them. However that immediate discount is extremely well understood.

Shostack makes a counter observation that it is perhaps not the discounts and risk calculations that make users so casual about protecting their own information. Perhaps users simply have no understanding of the threat. Just as some miners refused to take the accumulation of gas seriously as a threat, and no one understood why workers on the Brooklyn Bridge were dying of the bends, individuals today do not understand the value of privacy. To make an analogy, why would someone buy curtains and then offer details of their home over the Internet? The value of security for the end user is even more difficult to understand than the value of privacy for the consumer. The overall evaluation of the security market when seen from the privacy perspective is not optimistic.

Landwehr argues explicitly that the information flows in the security market are broken. Not only do consumers not understand the issues of privacy and security risks, but even vendors themselves do not understand security. Bill Gates' vaulted commitment to security includes training in security for 7,000 developers, yet there has not been a month without the release of a security patch for Microsoft. Even the considerable financial and technical resources of Microsoft cannot result in coherent application of security research implemented decades ago in a complex computing environment characterized by unpredictable interactions.

If security and privacy policies are "lemons markets", then simple claims of investment in security are far cheaper and easier than actually securing a site. If the claims are security are adequate to insure customer trust (and possibly cause malevolent profit-oriented actors to target others) then there is no reason for investment in security or privacy. Like false claims about a reliable used cars, false claims of secure software and false claims of privacy policy have no costs. Ironically, the lemons argument suggest that the core security failure in the information infrastructure is one of trustworthy information. Vila and Greenstadt argue clearly for this counter-intuitive possibility.

Integrating personal actions in security and privacy is a significant contribution of the next chapter. SoBig, MyDoom, and many other viral variants depend on a large population of unsecured user machines to flourish. Users express great concern for security, and privacy concerns have been monotonically increasing. Given this concern, how can observed user behaviors that illustrate that users share information readily and avoid installing security patches be explained?

Acquisiti uses the issue of on-line and off-line identities to illustrate how economics can shed light on the apparent irrationalities of both individuals and the market, regarding the confidentiality of information.

Odlyzko explains that users are correct in rejecting security designed for them by merchants and providers because the greatest value for merchants in controlling information is to implement price discrimination. Offering information to a merchant who can then charge you more is not in the interest of a consumer, even if the issues of control were not relevant. Security systems that violate privacy are directly opposed to the interest of the user when price discrimination is more likely than personal security loss. In economic terms, users are balancing risks when selecting privacy.

A more detailed discussion of users who reject security is provided in the aptly-titled, "We Want Security But We Hate It: The Foundations of Security Techo-Economics in the Social World". The undercurrents of user resistance to security include economics, as well as being a social and psychological phenomena. Beyond losing money through price discrimination, users seek to maintain control and confidentiality. When much security is implemented in order to best reflect vendor needs (as when security is provided as part of digital rights management) users seek to avoid the "features" offered in mainstream security solutions.

Perhaps users are motivated but misinformed. Certainly, corporate organizations are not discouraged from investing in security because of concerns of control of the desktop - this would be a feature and not a bug. Perhaps the critical problem in the information age is the information flow. Information is calculated and generated. Standards are made. Committees meet. Yet for all the research and effort, homes users do not see themselves at risk. Corporations do not develop appropriate responses.

In fact, manipulation of information and users remains a threat that cannot be addressed through technology alone. Can economics hope to address the problems of manipulation of authorized individuals and naive home users? Economics and markets themselves can be manipulated with the same tools of misinformation. "Cognitive Hacking" can apply to economic systems and information systems.

Yet within the generally bleak picture of information failure, market failure and suspicion there are cases of remarkable success. We end with two of these: secure sockets layer and the cable industry.

Having used economics to extract the distinctions between security and privacy as information control mechanisms in the market, the book closes with some specific examples of security in markets.

The story of the secure sockets layer and secure telnet illustrate that a chronic low level of security need not be an external state of affairs, no matter how long term or ubiquitous the state of affairs. The cable industry illustrates that lock-in need not lock out security, if the incentives are properly aligned. The following examination of the secure shell and the secure sockets layer illustrates that forward movement is possible even in a distributed, chaotic market. However, even the success stories of Larochelle and Rosasco illustrate that history offers as much caution as promise, as each tale offers specific conditions and constraints that enable security diffusion.

Economics offers a powerful lens for the examination of security. This text aims to promote a more sophisticated vision of security in an effort to assist designers in making systems that respect the alignment of incentives, managers in aligning their investments with the most critical security problems, and policy makers in understanding the nature of the chronic, core problem of modern computer security. Bruce Schneier explains better than any how apparently technical failures are in fact economic failures, and his explanation provides the final thoughts in this text.

Incentives in the security market are badly aligned, and the technology is not understood. Ironically in the information age, trustworthy information is increasingly difficult to locate. To paraphrase Mark Twain: A virus can be half way around the world while a patch is still putting its boots on.

L JEAN CAMP

Acknowledgments

Certainly the most obviously deserving of acknowledgement in this volume are the contributors. And indeed they are deserving. We are also in the debt of our editors, Sharon Palleschi and Susan Lagerstrom-Fife. Thank you for your guidance and support.

Individually, Jean Camp has many to acknowledge.

I would like to first and foremost thank my doctoral candidates who have read and discussed this content with much patience. Warigia Bowman and Allan Friedman, I am in your debt. Having now some experience as an advisor makes me far more grateful for those on my own committee. My advisors, Marvin Sirbu and Doug Tygar, were important sources of critical support in my own intellectual path, one that has crossed many disciplinary lines. As for my other committee members, Pamela Samuelson, Mary Shaw and Granger Morgan, the farther I am from them the larger I see that they are. As with so many things, I did not appreciate them then as much as I now know to admire them.

Ross Anderson and Hal Varian have lead the creation of a field by the organizing of interdisciplinary workshops. Before the First and Second workshops on the Economics of Information Security, most of us were breaking down individual barriers in our own corners of the academy: business, mathematics, electrical engineering, economics, business and public policy. With the organization of a series of workshops, and now the publication of this text based loosely on those workshops, an new arena of discourse has formed. We might not have stormed the barricades, but they are certainly sufficiently honey-combed to be highly permeable.

Andrew Odlyzko also deserves unique mention in my own life as a scholar. Ceaselessly a genial academic gentleman, he has offered guidance to more than one junior faculty member and I am lucky to be among them.

Stephen Lewis would like to thank all of his friends and colleagues both within the Computer Laboratory and outside; a special debt of gratitude is owed to Ross Anderson, for his endless support, guidance and patience as a supervisor.

Chapter 1

SYSTEM RELIABILITY AND FREE RIDING

Hal Varian
*School of Information Management and Systems, UC Berkeley**
hal@sims.berkeley.edu

In the total effort case, the agents with the least cost of effort to avoid systems failure should bear all the liability.

System reliability often depends on the effort of many individuals, making reliability a public good. It is well-known that purely voluntary provision of public goods may result in a free rider problem: individuals may tend to shirk, resulting in an inefficient level of the public good.

How much effort each individual exerts will depend on his own benefits and costs, the efforts exerted by the other individuals, and the technology that relates individual effort to outcomes. In the context of system reliability, we can distinguish three prototypical cases.

Total effort. Reliability depends on the sum of the efforts exerted by the individuals.

Weakest link. Reliability depends on the minimum effort.

Best shot. Reliability depends on the maximum effort.

Each of these is a reasonable technology in different circumstances. Suppose that there is one wall defending a city and the probability of successful defense depends on the strength of the wall, which in turn depends on the sum of the efforts of the builders. Alternatively, think of the wall as having varying height, with the probability of success depending on the height at its lowest point. Or, finally, think of a there being several walls, where only the highest one matters. Of course, many systems involve a mixture of these cases.

*First published in *ICEC2003: Fifth International Conference on Electronic Commerce*, N. Sadeh, ed., ACM Press, 2003, pp. 355–366.

1. Literature

[Hirshleifer, 1983] examined how public good provision varied with the three technologies described above. His main results were:

1 With the weakest-link technology, there will be a range of Nash equilibria with equal contributions varying from zero to some maximum, which is determined by the tastes of one of the agents.

2 The degree of under provision of the public good rises as the number of contributors increases in the total effort case, but the efficient amount of the public good and the Nash equilibrium amount will be more-or-less constant as the number of contributors increases.

3 Efficient provision in the best-effort technology generally involves only the agents with the lowest cost of contributing making any contributions at all.

[Cornes, 1993] builds on Hirshleifer's analysis. In particular he examines the impact of changes in income distribution on the equilibrium allocation. [Sandler and Hartley, 2001] provide a comprehensive survey of the work on alliances, starting with the seminal contribution of [Olson and Zeckhauser, 1966]. Their motivating concern is international defense with NATO as a recurring example. In this context, it is natural to emphasize income effects since countries with different incomes may share a greater or lesser degree of the burden of an alliance.

The motivating example for the research reported here is computer system reliability and security where teams of programmers and system administrators create systems whose reliability depends on the effort they expend. In this instance, considerations of costs, benefits, and probability of failure become paramount, with income effects being a secondary concern. This difference in focus gives a different flavor to the analysis, although it still retains points of contact with the earlier work summarized in [Sandler and Hartley, 2001] and the other works cited above.

2. Notation

Let x_i be the effort exerted by agent $i = 1, 2$, and let $P(F(x_1, x_2))$ be the probability of successful operation of the system. Agent i receives value v_i from the successful operation of the system and effort x_i costs the agent $c_i x_i$.

The expected payoff to agent i is taken to be

$$P(F(x_1, x_2))v_i - c_i x_i$$

and the social payoff is

$$P(F(x_1, x_2))[v_1 + v_2] - c_1 x_1 - c_2 x_2.$$

We assume that the function $P(F)$ is differentiable, increasing in F, and is concave, at least in the relevant region.

We examine three specifications for F, motivated by the taxonomy given earlier.

Total effort. $F(x_1, x_2) = x_1 + x_2$.

Weakest link. $F(x_1, x_2) = \min(x_1, x_2)$.

Best shot. $F(x_1, x_2) = \max(x_1, x_2)$.

3. Nash equilibria

We first examine the outcomes where each individual chooses effort unilaterally, and then compare these outcomes to what would happen if the efforts were coordinated so as to maximize social benefits minus costs.

Total effort

Agent 1 chooses x_1 to solve

$$\max_{x_1} v_1 P(x_1 + x_2) - c_1 x_1,$$

which has first-order conditions

$$v_1 P'(x_1 + x_2) = c_1.$$

Letting G be the inverse of the derivative of P', we have

$$x_1 + x_2 = G(c_1/v_1).$$

Defining $\bar{x}_1 = G(c_1/v_1)$ we have the reaction function of agent 1 to agent 2's choice

$$f_1(x_2) = \bar{x}_1 - x_2.$$

Similarly

$$f_2(x_1) = \bar{x}_2 - x_1.$$

These reaction functions are plotted in Figure 1.1. It can easily be seen that the unique equilibrium involves only one agent contributing effort, with the other free riding, except in the degenerate case where each agent has the same benefit/cost ratio: $v_2/c_2 = v_1/c_1$.

Let us suppose that $v_2/c_2 > v_1/c_1$. Then, $\bar{x}_2 > \bar{x}_1$, so agent 2 contributes everything and agent 1 free rides.

FACT 1 *In the case of total effort, system reliability is determined by the agent with the highest benefit-cost ratio. All other agents free ride on this agent.*

The fact that we get this extreme form of free riding when utility takes this quasilinear form is well-known; see, for example, [Varian, 1994] for one exposition.

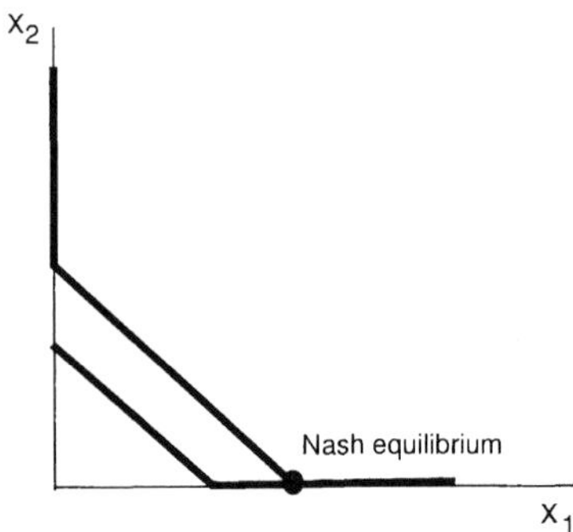

Figure 1.1. Nash equilibrium in total effort case.

Weakest link

Agent 1's problem is now

$$\max_{x_1} v_1 P(\min(x_1, x_2)) - c_1 x_1.$$

It is not hard to see that agent 1 will want to match agent 2's effort if $x_2 < \bar{x}_1$, and otherwise set $x_1 = \bar{x}_1$. The two agents' reaction functions are therefore

$$f_1(x_2) = \min(x_2, \bar{x}_1) \tag{1.1}$$

$$f_2(x_1) = \min(x_1, \bar{x}_2). \tag{1.2}$$

These reaction functions are plotted in Figure 1.2. Note that there will be a whole range of Nash equilibria. The largest of these will be at $\min(\bar{x}_1, \bar{x}_2)$. This Nash equilibrium Pareto dominates the others, so it is natural to think of it as the likely outcome.

FACT 2 *In the weakest-link case, system reliability is determined by the agent with the lowest benefit-cost ratio.*

Best shot

In the weakest link case it is not hard to see that there will always be a Nash equilibrium where the agent with the highest benefit-cost ratio exerts all the effort. What is more surprising is that there will sometimes be a Nash equilibrium where the agent with the lowest benefit-cost ratio exerts all the effort.[2] This can occur when the agent with the highest benefit-cost ratio chooses to exert zero effort, leaving all responsibility to the other agent.

[2] I am grateful to Xiaopeng Xu for pointing this out to me.

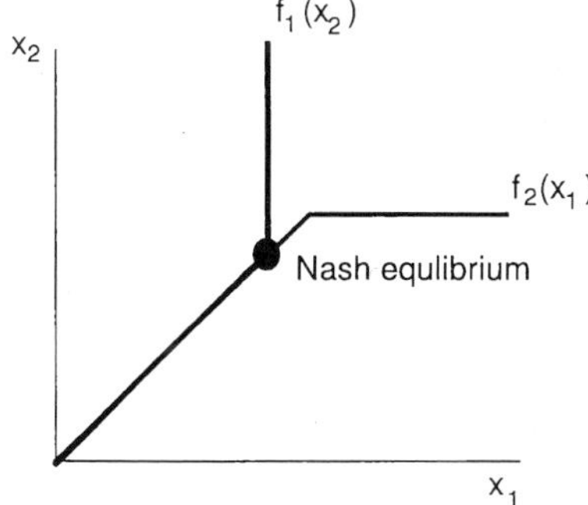

Figure 1.2. Nash equilibrium in weakest link case.

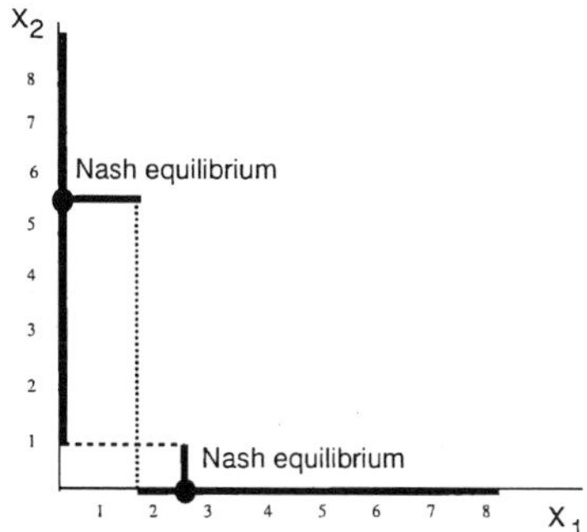

Figure 1.3. Nash equilibria in best-shot case.

To see an example of this, suppose that the agents' utility functions have the form $v_i \ln x - x_i$ where $x = \min(x_1, x_2)$. (True, $\ln x$ is not a probability distribution, but that makes no difference for what follows.)

The first-order condition is $v_i/x = 1$, so $x_1 = v_1$ or 0, depending on whether $v_i \ln v_i - v_i$ is greater or less than $v_i \ln x_2$. Hence $x_1 = v_1$ if $x_2 \leq v_1/e$ and $x_1 = 0$ if $x_2 \geq v_1/e$.

In order to create a simple example, suppose that $v_1 = e$ and $v_2 = 2e$. This gives us $x_1 = e$ for $x_2 \leq 1$ and zero otherwise, while $x_2 = 2e$ for $x_1 \leq 2$ and zero otherwise. These reaction curves are depicted in Figure 1.3. Note that in the case depicted there are two equilibria, with each agent free-riding in one of the equilibria.

The three baseline cases we have studied, total effort, weakest link, and best shot have three different kinds of pure-strategy Nash equilibria: unique, continuum, and (possibly) two discrete equilibria.

4. Social optimum

Total effort

The social problem solves

$$\max_{x_1,x_2} P(x_1+x_2)[v_1+v_2]-c_1x_1-c_2x_2.$$

The first-order conditions

$$P'(x_1+x_2)[v_1+v_2] \leq c_1 \tag{1.3}$$

$$P'(x_1+x_2)[v_1+v_2] \leq c_2. \tag{1.4}$$

At the optimum, the agent with the lowest cost exerts all the effort. Let $c_{min}=\min\{c_1,c_2\}$, so that the optimum is determined by

$$x_1^*+x_2^*=G(c_{min}/(v_1+v_2)). \tag{1.5}$$

Summarizing, we have:

FACT 3 *In the total effort case, there is always too little effort exerted in the Nash equilibrium as compared with the optimum. Furthermore, when $v_2/c_2>v_1/c_1$ but $c_1<c_2$, the "wrong" agent exerts the effort.*

Best shot

The social and private outcomes in this case are the same as in the total effort case.

Weakest link

The social objective is now

$$\max_{x_1,x_2} P(\min(x_1,x_2))[v_1+v_2]-c_1x_1-c_2x_2.$$

At the social optimum, it is obvious that $x_1=x_2$ so we can write this problem as

$$\max_{x} P(x)[v_1+v_2]-[c_1+c_2]x,$$

which has first-order conditions

$$P'(x)[v_1+v_2]=c_1+c_2,$$

or

$$x_1=x_2=x=G((c_1+c_2)/(v_1+v_2)). \tag{1.6}$$

FACT 4 *The probability of success in the socially optimal solution is always lower in the case of weakest link that in the case of total effort.*

This occurs because the weakest link case requires equal effort from all the agents, rather than just effort from any single agent. Hence it is inherently more costly to increase reliability in this case.

5. Identical values, different costs

Let n be the number of agents and, for simplicity, set $v_i = 1$ for all $i = 1, \ldots, n$. In the total-effort case, the social optimum is given by

$$nP'(x) = \min c_i,$$

while the private optimum is determined by

$$P'(x) = \min c_i.$$

In the weakest-link case, the social optimum is determined by

$$nP'(x) = \sum_i c_i,$$

or

$$P'(x) = \bar{c} = \frac{1}{n}\sum_i c_i.$$

while the private optimum is determined by

$$P'(x) = \max c_i.$$

If we think of drawing agents from a distribution, what matters for system reliability are the order statistics—the highest and lowest costs of effort.

FACT 5 *Systems will become increasingly reliable as the number of agents increases in the total efforts case, but increasingly unreliable as the number of agents increases in the weakest link case.*

6. Increasing the number of agents

Let us now suppose that $v_i = c_i = 1$ and that the number of agents is n. In this case, the social optimum in the case of total effort is determined by

$$nP'(\sum_i x_i) = 1,$$

or

$$\sum_i x_i = G1/n).$$

The Nash equilibrium satisfies

$$P'(\sum_i x_i) = 1,$$

or

$$\sum_i x_i = G(1).$$

FACT 6 *In the total efforts case with identical agents, the Nash outcome remains constant as the number of agents is increased, but the socially optimal amount of effort increases.*

In weakest-link case, the social optimum is determined by

$$nP'(x) = n,$$

which means that the socially optimal amount of effort remains constant as n increases. In the Nash equilibrium

$$P'(x) = 1,$$

or

$$x = G(1).$$

FACT 7 *In the weakest-link case with identical agents, the socially optimal reliability and the Nash reliability are identical, regardless of the number of agents.*

7. Fines and liability

Total effort

Let us return to the two-agent case, for ease of exposition, and consider the optimal fine, that is, the fine that induces the socially optimal levels of effort. Let us start with the total effort case, and suppose that agent 1 has the lowest marginal cost of effort. If we impose a cost of v_2 on agent 1 in the event that the system fails, then agent 1 will want to maximize

$$v_1P(x_1 + x_2) + v_2[1 - P(x_1 + x_2)] - c_1x_1.$$

The first order condition is

$$(v_1 + v_2)P'(x_1 + x_2) = c_1,$$

which is precisely the condition for social optimality. This result easily extends to the n-person case, so we have:

FACT 8 *A fine equal to the costs imposed on the other agents should be imposed on the agent who has the lowest cost of reducing the probability of failure.*

Alternatively, we could consider a strict liability rule, in which the amount charged in the case of system failure is paid to the other agent. If the "fine" is paid to agent 2, his optimization problem becomes

$$v_2P(x_1 + x_2) + [1 - P(x_1 + x_2)]v_2 - c_2x_2.$$

Simplifying, we have

$$v_2 - c_2x_2,$$

so agent 2 will want to set $x_2 = 0$. But this is true in the social optimum as well, so there is no distortion. Obviously this result is somewhat delicate; in a more general specification, there would be some distortions from the liability payment since it will, in general, change the behavior of agent 2. If the liability payment is too large, it may induce agent 2 to seek to be injured. This is not merely a theoretical issue, as it seems likely that if liability rules would be imposed, each system failure would give rise to many plaintiffs, each of whom would seek maximal compensation.

The fact that the agents with the least cost of effort to avoid system failure should bear all the liability is a standard result in the economic analysis of tort law, where it is sometimes expressed as the doctrine of the "least-cost avoider." As [Shavell, 1987], page 17-18, points out, this doctrine is correct only in rather special circumstances, of which one is the sum-of-efforts case we are considering.

Weakest link

How does this analysis work in the weakest-link case? Since an incremental increase in reliability requires effort to be exerted by both parties, each agent must take into account the cost of effort of the other.

One way to do this is to make each agent face the other's marginal cost, in addition to facing a fine in case of system failure. Letting $x = \min\{x_1, x_2\}$, the objective function for agent 1, say, would then be:

$$v_1 P(x) - [1 - P(x)]v_2 - c_1 x_1 - c_2 x_1.$$

Agent 1 would want to choose $x = x_1$ determined by

$$(v_1 + v_2)P'(x) = c_1 + c_2,$$

which is the condition for social optimality. Agent 2 would make exactly the same choice.

Let us now examine a liability rule in which *each* must compensate the other in the case of system failure. The objective functions then take the form

$$\max_{x_1} \quad v_1 P(x) - (1 - P(x))v_2 + (1 - P(x))v_1 - c_1 x_1 \tag{1.7}$$
$$\max_{x_2} \quad v_2 P(x) - (1 - P(x))v_1 + (1 - P(x))v_2 - c_2 x_2 \tag{1.8}$$
$$\tag{1.9}$$

Note that when the system fails, each agent compensates the other for their losses, but is in turn compensated.

Simplifying, we can express the optimization problems as

$$\max_{x_1} \quad v_1 - v_2 + v_2 P(x) - c_1 x_1 \tag{1.10}$$
$$\max_{x_2} \quad v_2 - v_1 + v_1 P(x) - c_2 x_2 \tag{1.11}$$

This leads to first order conditions

$$v_2 P'(x) = c_1 \tag{1.12}$$
$$v_1 P'(x) = c_2 \tag{1.13}$$

If we are in the symmetric case where $v_1 = v_2$ and $c_1 = c_2$ (or more generally, where $v_1c_1 = v_2c_2$), then both of these equations can be satisfied and, somewhat surprisingly, the solution is the social optimum. Of course, if all agents are identical, then there is no reason to impose a liability rule, since individual optimization leads to the social optimum anyway, as was shown earlier.

If we are not in the symmetric case, the equilibrium will be determined by $\min\{c_1/v_2, c_2/v_1\}$. In this case, strict liability does not result in the social optimum.

The resolution is to use the negligence rule. Under this doctrine, the court establishes a level of *due care*, $\bar{x}$. In general, this could be different for different parties, but that generality is not necessary for this particular case. If the system fails, there is no liability if the level of care/effort meets or exceeds the due care standard. If the level of care/effort was less than the due care standard, then the party who exerted inadequate care/effort must pay the other the costs of system failure.

Although the traditional analysis of the negligence rule assumes the courts determine the due care standard, an alternative model could involve the insurance companies setting a due care standard. For example, insurance companies could offer a contract specifying that the insured would be reimbursed for the costs of an accident only if he or she had exercised an appropriate standard of due care.

Let x^* be the socially optimal effort level; i.e., the level that solves

$$\max_x \ (v_1 + v_2)P(x) - (c_1 + c_2)x.$$

It therefor satisfies the first-order condition

$$(v_1 + v_2)P'(x^*) = c_1 + c_2.$$

We need to show that if the due care standard is set at $\bar{x} = x^*$, then $x_1 = x_2 = \bar{x}$ is a Nash equilibrium.[3]

To prove this, assume that $x_2 = \bar{x}$. We must show that the optimal choice for agent 1 is $x_1 = \bar{x}_1$. Certainly we will never have $x_1 > \bar{x}$ since choosing x_1 larger than $\bar{x}$ has no impact on the probability of system failure and incurs positive cost. Will agent 1 ever want to choose $x_1 < \bar{x}$? Agent 1's objective function is

$$v_1P(x_1) + (1 - P(x_1))v_2 - c_1x_1.$$

Computing the derivative, and using the concavity of $P(x)$, we find

$$(v_1 + v_2)P'(x_1) - c_1 > (v_1 + v_2)P'(x^*) - c_1 = c_2.$$

[3]Of course, there will be many other Nash equilibria as well, due to the weakest-link technology. The legal due-care standard has the advantage of serving as a focal point to choose the most efficient such equilibrium.

Hence agent 1 will want to increase his level of effort when $x_1 < \bar{x}_1$. Summarizing:

FACT 9 *In the case of weakest link, strict liability is not adequate in general to achieve the socially optimal level of effort, and one must use a negligence rule to induce the optimal effort.*

Again, this is a standard result in liability law, which was first established by [Brown, 1973]; see Proposition 2.2 in [Shavell, 1987], page 40. The argument given here is easily modified to show that the negligence rule induces optimal behavior in the sum-of-efforts case as well, or for that matter, for any other form $P(x_1, x_2)$.

8. Sequential moves

Total effort

Let us now assume that the agents move sequentially, where the agent who moves second can observe the choice of the agent who moves first. The following discussion is based on [Varian, 1994].

We assume that agent 1 moves first. The utility of agent 1 as a function of his effort is given by,

$$U_1(x_1) = v_1 P(x_1 + f_2(x_1)) - c_1 x_1.$$

which can be written as

$$U_1(x_1) = v_1 P(x_1 + \max\{\bar{x}_2 - x_1, 0\}) - c_1 x_1.$$

We can also write this as

$$U_1(x_1) = \begin{cases} v_1 P(\bar{x}_2) - c_1 x_1 & \text{for } x_1 \leq \bar{x}_2 \\ v_1 P(x_1) - c_1 x_1 & \text{for } x_1 \geq \bar{x}_2. \end{cases}$$

It is clear from Figure 1.4 that there are two possible optima: either the first agent exerts zero effort and achieves payoff $v_1 P(\bar{x}_2)$ or he contributes $\bar{x}_1$ and achieves utility $v_1 P(\bar{x}_1) - c_1 \bar{x}_1$.

Case 1. *The agent with the lowest value of v_i/c_i moves first.* In this case the optimal choice by the first player is to choose zero effort. This is true since

$$v_1 P(\bar{x}_2) > v_1 P(\bar{x}_1) > v_1 P(\bar{x}_1) - c_1 \bar{x}_1.$$

Case 2. *The agent with the highest value of v_i/c_i is the first contributor.* In this case, either contributor may free ride. If the agents have tastes that are very similar, then the first contributor will free ride on the second's contribution. However, if the first mover likes the public good *much* more than the second, then the first mover may prefer to contribute the entire amount of the public good himself.

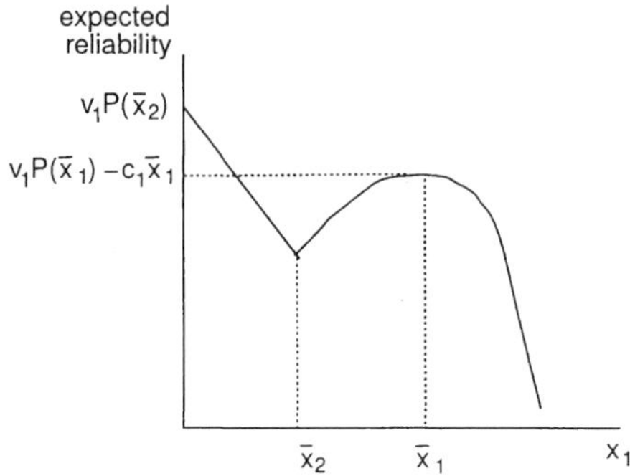

Figure 1.4. Sequential contribution in total efforts case.

Referring to Figure 1.4 we see that there are two possible subgame perfect equilibria: one is the Nash equilibrium, in which the agent who has the highest benefit-cost ratio does everything. The other equilibrium is where the agent who has the *lowest* benefit-cost contributes everything. This equilibrium cannot be a Nash equilibrium since the threat to free ride by the agent who likes the public good most is not credible in the simultaneous-move game.

FACT 10 *The equilibrium in the sequential-move, the total-effort game always involves the same or less reliability than the simultaneous-move game.*

Note that it is always advantageous to move first since there are only two possible outcomes and the first mover gets to pick the one he prefers.

FACT 11 *If you want to ensure the highest level of security in the sequential-move game, then you should make sure that the agent with the lower benefit-cost ratio moves first.*

Best-effort and weakest-link

The best-effort case is the same as the total-effort case. The weakest-link case is a bit more interesting. Since each agent realizes that the other agent will, at most, match his effort, there is no point in choosing a higher level of effort than the agent who cares the least about reliability. On the other hand, there is no need to settle for one of the inefficient Nash equilibria either.

FACT 12 *The unique equilibrium in the sequential-move game will be the Nash equilibrium in the simultaneous-move game that has the highest level of security, namely* $\min(\bar{x}_1, \bar{x}_2)$.

[Hirshleifer, 1983] recognizes this and uses it as an argument for selecting the Nash equilibrium with the highest amount of the public good as the "reasonable" outcome.

9. Adversaries

Let us now briefly consider what happens if there is an adversary who is trying to increase the probability of system failure. First we consider the case of just two players, then we move to looking at what happens with a team on each side.

We let x be the effort of the defender, and y the effort of the attacker. Effort costs the defender c and the attacker d. The defender gets utility v if the system works, and the attacker gets utility w if the system fails. We suppose that the probability of failure depends on "net effort," $x-y$, and that there is a maximal effort $\hat{x}$ and $\hat{y}$ for each player.

The optimization problems for the attacker and defender can be written as

$$\max_x \quad vP(x-y) - cx \tag{1.14}$$
$$\max_y \quad w[1-P(x-y)] - dy. \tag{1.15}$$

The first-order conditions are

$$vP'(x-y) = c \tag{1.16}$$
$$wP'(x-y) = d. \tag{1.17}$$

Let $G(\cdot)$ be the inverse function of $P'(x-y)$. By the second-order condition this has to be locally decreasing, and we will assume it is globally decreasing. We can then apply the inverse function to write the two reaction functions:

$$x-y = G(c/v) \tag{1.18}$$
$$x-y = G(d/w). \tag{1.19}$$

Of course, these are only the reaction functions for *interior* optima. Adding in the boundary conditions gives us:

$$x = \min\{\max\{G(c/v)+y, 0\}, \hat{x}\} \tag{1.20}$$
$$y = \min\{\max\{G(d/w)-x, 0\}, \hat{y}\}. \tag{1.21}$$

We plot these reaction functions in Figure 1.5. Note that there are two possible equilibrium configurations. If $c/v < d/w$, we have $x^* = G(c/v)$ and $y^* = 0$, while if $c/v > d/w$ we have $x^* = \hat{x}$ and $y^* = \hat{x} - G(d/w)$.

Intuitively, if the cost-benefit ratio of the defender is smaller than that of the attacker, the attacker gives up, and the defender does just enough to keep him at bay. If the ratio is reversed, the defender has to go all out, and the attacker pushes to keep him there.

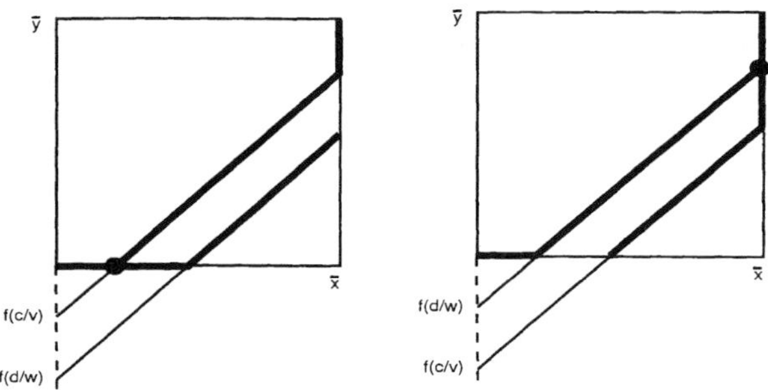

Figure 1.5. Reaction functions in adversarial case.

10. Sum of efforts and weakest link

In the sum-of-efforts case the reaction functions are:

$$\sum_{i=1}^{n} x_i - \sum_{i=1}^{m} y_i = G(c_j/v_j) \tag{1.22}$$

$$\sum_{i=1}^{n} x_i - \sum_{i=1}^{m} y_i = G(d_j/w_j). \tag{1.23}$$

Here the party with the lowest cost/benefit ratio exerts effort, while everyone else free rides. This becomes a "battle between the champions."

In the weakest link case, the conditions for optimality are:

$$\min\{x_1, \ldots, x_n\} - \min\{y_1, \ldots, y_m\} = G(c_j/v_j) \tag{1.24}$$

$$\min\{x_1, \ldots, x_n\} - \min\{y_1, \ldots, y_m\} = G(d_j/w_j). \tag{1.25}$$

As opposed to a "battle of champions" we now have a "battle between the losers," as the outcome is determined by the weakest player on each tam.

Note that when technology is total effort, large teams have an advantage, whereas weakest link technology confers an advantage to small teams.

11. Future work

There are several avenues worth exploring:

- To what extent to these results extend to the more general framework of [Cornes, 1993] and [Sandler and Hartley, 2001]. The possibility of Pareto improving transfers is particularly interesting. Though [Cornes, 1993] examined this in the context of income transfers, knowledge transfers would be particularly interesting in our context.

- One case where transfers are important are when agents can subsidize other agents' actions, as in [Varian, 1994]. The subgame perfect equilibrium of "announce subsidies then choose actions" is Pareto efficient in the case we examine.

- One could look at capacity constraints on the part of the agents. For example, each agent could put in only one unit of effort. Similarly, one could look at increasing marginal cost of effort.

- Imperfect information adds additional phenomena. For example, [Hermalin, 1998] shows that in a model with uncertainty about payoffs, an agent may choose to move first in order to demonstrate to the other agent that a particular choice is worthwhile. Hence "leadership" plays a role of signaling to the other agents.

- [M. and Sandler, 2001] examines how results change when a contribution game's structure moves in the direction of best shot or weakest link. This sort of partial comparative statics exercise could be of interest in our context as well.

- One could examine situations where there were communication costs among the cooperating agents, a la team theory. If, for example, there is imperfect information about what others are doing, it might lead to less free riding.

References

Brown, John (1973). Toward an economic theory of liability. *Journal of Legal Studies*, 2:323–350.

Cornes, Richard (1993). Dyke maintenance and other stories: Some neglected types of public goods. *Quarterly Journal of Economics*, 108(1):259–271.

Hermalin, Benjamin (1998). Towards and economic theory of leadership: Leading by example. *American Economic Review*, 88:1188–1206.

Hirshleifer, Jack (1983). From weakest-link to best-shot: the voluntary provision of public goods. *Public Choice*, 41:371–86.

M., Daniel G. Arce and Sandler, Todd (2001). Transnational public goods: strategies and institutions. *European Journal of Political Economy*, 17:493–516.

Olson, Mancur and Zeckhauser, Richard (1966). An economic theory of alliances. *Review of Economics and Stastistics*, 48(3):266–279.

Sandler, Todd and Hartley, Keith (2001). Economics of alliances: The lessons for collective action. *Journal of Economic Literature*, 34:869–896.

Shavell, Stoeven (1987). *Economic Analysis of Accident Law.* Harvard University Press, Cambridge, MA.

Varian, Hal R. (1994). Sequential provision of public goods. *Journal of Public Economics*, 53:165–186.

Chapter 2

PRICING SECURITY

A Market in Vulnerabilities

L Jean Camp
Harvard University

Catherine Wolfram
University of California, Berkeley

The provision of computer security in a networked environment creates externalities and is subject to market failures.

The Internet and the larger information infrastructure are not secure (e.g., [National Research Council, 1996]). Well known vulnerabilities continue to be exploited long after patches are available. Today too many organizations discover security the day after intruders, interested in attracting attention, have rewritten their Web pages. The recent spread of the increasingly potent viruses clearly illustrates that hackers provide ubiquitous testing of Internet security and find it wanting.

Policies can encourage or prevent the adoption of secure computing. For example, the controls on the export of cryptography have played a significant role in weakening cryptography in general use applications in the United States. The prohibition of cryptography in France has resulted in a nation with a proliferation of short commercial key lengths. Yet while these policies do play a part, they are not responsible for the entire situation. We consider the possibility that a major cause of the lack of security is that software and hardware prices do not reflect their embodied security weaknesses. A supporting observation is that well-documented vulnerabilities with free patches continue to exist on the Internet, including on sites with financial information and electronic transaction capabilities [Farmer, 1999].

The provision of security in a networked computer environment creates positive externalities. Conversely, underprovision creates negative externalities. There are several specific ways in which security, or the lack thereof, on one machine can affect security on another machine.

Users of an insecure network, product or machine do not face the full cost of security violations, and hence the externality.

Current regulatory and market mechanisms for dealing with network security have not provided organizations with sufficient encouragement to respond to potential security threats and vulnerabilities, i.e. the externalities are not adequately addressed. Multiple possible solutions to the underprovision of security are proposed in this text: liability for producers, computer security, and the widespread careful application of tools of finance and accounting. An alternative solution, one that embodies the explicit understanding of security as an externality, is to create a market for security whereby those who neglect to secure their networks, products, and machines can suffer the consequences according to formal pricing mechanisms rather than destructive incidents.

There are a number of analogies between pricing security externalities and pricing pollution. First, for there to be production there must be some pollution, and for there to be connectivity there must be some vulnerabilities. Thus in both cases the there are issues of definition: Is it a feature or a bug? Is it a toxic pollutant or a necessary part of the product? Answering these questions requires determining the socially optimal level of either pollution or network security vulnerabilities. Economists have long relied on markets to determine the efficient level of production. A market coordinates "buyers and sellers" of a product. In other words, those who benefit from more pollution can pay others who want less for the right to pollute. Alternatively, those who want less pollution or vulnerabilities can pay others not to pollute or not to ignore vulnerabilities.

Over the past ten years, a national market for trading permits to emit sulfur dioxide has developed as well as several regional US markets for other pollutants. Market-based approaches to pricing greenhouse gas emissions were discussed as part of the Kyoto Protocol. We draw on the lessons learned from the new markets for pollution to consider the issues raised for a market in network security.

The rest of the paper proceeds as follows. After briefly describing general characteristics of externalities, we describe the externality components of security. We review the strategies currently used to increase network security and note these are not sufficient. We discuss multiple security taxonomies, and draw upon these to develop the definition of a vulnerability necessary for creating a market for vulnerabilities as a commodity. We note the future work necessary to develop a functioning market for security vulnerabilities and close with some thoughts the value of the insight of security as an externality.

1. Security as an externality

Economists define externalities as instances where an individual or firm's actions have economic consequences for others for which there is no compensation. Externalities can be either positive or negative. Pollution is the classic example of a negative externality. For example, a local plant owner may not fully internalize the costs the pollution from his plant inflicts on nearby homeowners. The plant owner will produce pollution until the costs to him outweigh the benefits. If homeowners could pay the plant owner not to pollute or if they could extract payment from the plant owner for every ounce of pollution, the owner's cost of polluting would go up (in the former case, his benefits from not polluting would go up) so there would be less pollution.

Examples of positive externalities are most common in networks, such as communication networks. For instance, the simple act of installing telephone service to an additional customer creates positive externalities on everyone on the telephone network because they can use the telephone to reach one additional person. Externalities created by a network or group of consumers whose choices affect one another are called "network externalities." A recent literature has explored the implications network externalities have for firms competing to provide products that generate them ([Shapiro, Carl and Hal Varian, 1999] provides a non-technical survey of the issues associated with network effects). Coordination on a standard is a classic example.

Another example of a positive externality with useful analogies to computer security is automotive security. When Lojack, the auto theft response system, is introduced in a city, auto theft in general goes down because Lojack is designed so that thieves can't tell whether or not Lojack is installed in a specific car [Ayres and Levitt, 1998]. In other words, people who buy Lojack are providing positive externalities to other car owners in the city.

The most basic conclusion economists draw about externalities is that absent government intervention or other mechanisms to internalize externalities, negative externalities are over-provided and positive externalities are under-provided. There are also several corollaries to the basic conclusion. For instance, products that generate negative externalities will be under-priced. Also, the incentives to invest in technologies that will reduce negative externalities (e.g. incentives to invest in environmentally friendly production processes) will be insufficient.

Several attributes of computer security suggest that it is an externality. Most importantly, the lack of security on one machine can cause adverse effects on another. There are three common ways in which security from one system harms another: shared trust, increased resources, and the ability for the attacker to confuse the trail. Shared trust is a problem when a system is trusted by another, so the subversion of one machine allows the subversion of another. (Unix machines have lists of trusted machines in .rhosts files). A second less obvious shared trust problem is when a user keeps on one machine his or her password and account information for another. The use of cookies to save passwords (as well as the status of a transaction, i.e. state) has made this practice extremely common.

The second issue, increased resources, refers to the fact that attackers can increase resources for attacks by subverting multiple machines. This is most obviously useful in brute force attacks, for example in decryption or in a denial of service attack. Using multiple machines makes denial of service attacks easier to implement, since such attacks may depend on overwhelming the target machine. Multiple machines can simplify attacks on password files, or enable cryptographic brute force attacks by searching for solution in parallel. A commonly used massively parallel search now is the SETI screen saver (`http://www.seti.org/setiathome.html`). In a vein more immediately relevant to this work, parallelism has been essential in the successful attempts at the RSA factoring challenge (`http://www.rsa.com/rsalabs/html/factoring.html`). The SoBig virus family has been used to create a massively parallel system of subverted machine for sending spam; and infected machines are used by criminals who steal information from misdirected users through phishing.

Third, subverting multiple machines makes it difficult to trace an attack from its source. When taking a circuitous route an attacker can hide his or her tracks in the adulterated log files of multiple machines. Clearly this allows the attacker to remain hidden from law enforcement and continue to launch attacks. The third may be the most important as it greatly reduces fear of detection and therefore mitigates the effects of both law enforcement and enforcement of social norms.

The last two points suggest that costs to hackers fall with the number of machines (and so the difference between the benefits of hacking and the costs increases), similar to the way in which benefits to phone users increase with the number of other phones on the network.

Security breaches also may impact users' willingness to transact over the network. For instance, consumers may be less willing to use the Internet for e-commerce if they hear of incidents of credit card theft. This is a rational response if there is no way for consumers to distinguish security levels of different sites.

Because security is an externality, software and hardware prices do not reflect the possibility of and the extent of the damages from associated security failures.

Simply identifying the externalities associated with security is not enough. Many market failures are recognized and continue to persist in the economy simply because the losses associated with them are much smaller than the costs associated with redressing the failure. (The costs of redress could take many forms, for instance, loss of personal freedom, transaction costs, bureaucratic overhead necessary for enforcement, etc.) Before discussing ways to address the fact that security is an externality, it is important to think about the likely economic losses caused by this market failure.

Unfortunately, very little information exists that could help us quantify the externalities, but we will discuss various categories of losses and suggest possible orders of magnitude as a starting point. It is useful to distinguish between losses that are directly tied to one incident (e.g. when a given site is hacked using resources from insecure machines, there are costs associated with lost productivity and administrative costs necessary to get the site back up) and losses that are more indirect (e.g. users losing faith in the security of the network).

On the direct costs, there is information on incidents, for instance, by year in the US, but even counts of the number of incidents vary by orders of magnitude [Howard, 1997]. There have been no attempts to assign economic losses to incidents, even in terms of recording the number of hours a system was down.

There is some aggregate-level information on how much companies are currently spending on network security (e.g. Forrester, 1999). One way of evaluating the extent to which companies are under-spending would involve figuring out whether companies that are spending a lot on security are the same ones that are likely to inflict significant harm on others if their security is lax. For instance, if firms with greater processing and network capabilities invest more than firms with less capacity but also pose a greater potential threat (since hackers can use their machines to stage an attack). If, however, the magnitudes of the individual losses were not proportional to the losses inflicted on the rest of the economy, we would have additional evidence that security externalities are significant.

One potential source of information on indirect costs would be surveys about, for instance, whether people are more reluctant to use credit cards on the Internet after they have heard about security violations.

Externalities and public goods are often discussed in the same sections of economics textbooks. Both identify similar categories of market failures. A common example of a public good is national security, and it might be tempting to analogize national security and computer security. That would be misguided. National security, and public goods in general, are generally single, indivisible goods. (A pure public good is something which is both non-rival – my use of it doesn't affect yours – and non-excludable – once the good is produced, it is hard to exclude people from using it.) Computer security, by comparison, is the sum of a number of individual firms' or peoples' decisions. It is important to distinguish computer security from national security (i.e. externalities from public goods) because the solutions to public goods problem and to externalities differ. The government usually handles the production of public goods, whereas there are a number of examples where simple interventions by the government have created a more efficient market such that trades between private economic parties better reflect the presence of externalities.

A better analogy for computer security is pollution, and a number of market-based approaches have recently been implemented to help achieve a more efficient level of pollution abatement. We consider the newly-created markets for pollution more extensively in the sections that follow.

2. Existing measures

In this section we identify some common ways for addressing externalities, and discuss the extent to which each solution has been successfully implemented in the case of computer security.

There are several ways in which a government body can address externalities: command and control regulation, information provision, standard setting, support for the market and governmental provision of the good, either directly or indirectly through subsidies. In this section we discuss various ongoing attempts to address the issue of network security. Although none of these are explicitly motivated by security externalities, they all address the concern that computer security is not adequately provided by the market.

Information provision

Several federally funded projects have also explored the need for security on the Internet, including The President's Commission on Critical Infrastructure Protection [Critical Foundations, 1997] and The National Academy CRISIS and Trust studies [Computer Science and Telecommunications Board, 1999].

The President's Commission on Critical Infrastructure Protection (PCCIP) [Critical Foundations, 1997] has focused on information sharing. The proposals in the PCCIP report to share information include a suggested exemption from the Freedom of Information Act. The PCCIP also proposes that a select group of public and private organizations cooperate and share information on vulnerabilities. Information on the vulnerabilities, which might serve many computer users, would be held tightly by the select members of this information-sharing organization. Thus, the few selected players would have greater information but the majority of computer users would not only obtain no additional information but would also be barred from seeking Federal information.

The set of proposals in the PCCIP report for best practices is reasonable for a corporate intranet but ill-suited to small businesses, home users, or electronic commerce sites. For example, authenticating every user is not appropriate for browsing customers. Small businesses may be unable to conduct security training for every employee, and certainly cannot establish in-house incident response teams. The PCCIP views the critical elements of the infrastructure as being large intranets, and does not address the many home users, small businesses, academics, and hobbyists.

The Federal Government also encourages the dissemination of information about security breaches by subsidizing incident response teams and computer security research and in its standard setting process. All of these are discussed in the sub-sections that follow.

Setting standards

The National Institute of Standards sets cryptographic standards. The adoption rate of particular Federal Information Processing Standards (FIPS) has varied dramatically. The Data Encryption Standard (DES) as described in FIPS 46 [National Bureau of Standards, 1977] has been widely implemented. DES is the most widely used encryption algorithm in the world. Alternatively the "Clipper" standard, [National Institute of Standards and Technology, 1994] has been subject to wide objections and rarely used.

To set a standard is to provide information. Selected standards are examined by the Federal Government and pronounced trustworthy. The original Clipper FIPS was the first information processing standard based on a classified algorithm. Thus it provided limited information. DES was developed with IBM with the result being an open standard. The Advanced Encryption Standard, to replace DES, was chosen in an international open competitive process. The competitors to the final winning algorithm were examined, with each finalist being a contribution to the larger cryptographic community. Information provision and market coordination in terms of standards-setting has improved network security, but has not proven adequate to address all security vulnerabilities.

Another form of standard setting is classification. The Department of Defense began a decade-long experiment in classifying trustworthy components in 1985. The original proposal was for classifying machine, and commonly called the Orange Book. The Orange Book was followed by a series of books, the Rainbow Series, which defined best practice and classifications for distributed databases, file systems, and other networks. The networks are to be classified by existence of features (e.g. use of passwords), design, and implementation methodology. Together these factors are assumed to illustrate the overall level of security [Department of Defense, 1985]. Although this taxonomy is widely taught in introductory computer security classes for the concepts that it embodies, this effort has arguably failed. There are no major computer systems marketed with a Department of Defense rating.

The National Security Agency has developed a Linux implementation that has been optimized for security, with a set of possible security policies that can be implemented using the free, downloadable Linux. This is both a standard and a subsidy.

The ideals of computer security embodied in the Department of Defense Rainbow Series continues to be popular, with systems built logically from a trusted computing base. However the ratings themselves and the mechanisms are widely ignored by the market.

Subsidies

The government subsidizes the provision of information security in three ways: support for incident response teams, purchase of secure technologies, and support for research in computer security.

A clear subsidy of computer security is the provision of incident response teams. Incident response teams assist in detecting, preventing, defeating, and recovering from attacks on computer systems. Incident response teams provide service free or at subsidized rates. The Federal Government funds the Computer Incident Advisory Capability or CIAC (`http://ciac.llnl.gov/`) through the Department of Energy.

The Computer Emergency Response Team/Coordinating Center was initially a fully federally funded operation. CERT/CC continues to compete for federal research funds, and the organization's stated long term goal is to be self-supporting. Despite the reputedly high quality of services and strong confidentiality CERT/CC has not yet met this goal. The confidentially provided CERT clients is important to clients who would not have their customers, users, or shareholders aware of the breach of security so that there is no corresponding loss of trust. The National Science Foundation has a bi-annual call for proposals on cybertrust.

Military investment in computer security is difficult to judge, as much of it is classified, but it undeniably dwarfs the NSF investment.

The government also provides a market for computer security technologies. In particular, the Department of Defense and the Department of Energy both are large purchasers of computer security technology. In addition federally funded R&D centers (e.g. MITRE and RAND) and DoD contractors and suppliers provide products to the market for cutting-edge security technologies.

Arguably the government support for research in computer security reflects the fact that research is an externality. Computer security can also be seen as a subcategory of national defense, which is a classic public good. Regardless, research support for computer security has proven more effective in finding weaknesses and resulting responses, and less successful in disseminating the results in terms of widespread adoption of optimal security practices.

3. Defining the good

The first step of creating a market is to define the good. In order for a market to function it must be targeted on a definable, discrete good. In the case of computer security, we need to decide whether we want to encourage the provision of more security or the provision of fewer vulnerabilities. An increase in security can involve changes in institutional practices, upgrading platforms, increasing training, removing or adding services, or the removal of vulnerabilities.

In the next section we evaluate a few security taxonomies to determine if there is a need for a new taxonomy when many useful ones are extant. While reviewing this keep in mind that a vulnerability is a flaw which could allow unauthorized access or use. Almost by definition, vulnerabilities are not known until they are exploited. A feature may be considered a vulnerability as soon as its misuse is illustrated. If an organization wants to keep a feature active despite potential for misuse without following good security practice, we propose that this organization face the social cost to the system that such a desire imposes. Simply requiring "no vulnerabilities" is a command and control regulatory solution that is certain to fail.

Characterizing the good: classifying computer security failures

Because of the difficulty identifying a vulnerability ex ante, it is useful to think about using a taxonomy to price security failures. Goods within a certain category would be interchangeable and new vulnerabilities would be assigned to a category once identified. In the context of pollution, characterizing the good is somewhat easier, since a ton of sulfur dioxide is identifiable as such. Nonetheless, the creators of pollution markets needed to think about which existing and prospective polluters would be in the market. For instance, internal combustion engines in vehicles emit small amounts of sulfur dioxide, yet car owners are not required to purchase pollution permits.

Any taxonomy used to price security failures should be deterministic and complete. No security failure should be left unclassified and no security failure should fall into more than one classification. Given this fundamental limitation we now review security taxonomies developed by experts in the field.

An early work on systems [Amoroso, 1994] argued that in addition to being complete and exclusive taxonomies should also be unambiguous, repeatable, acceptable, and useful. Consider how this applies to classifying only vulnerabilities for the purpose of pricing.

First it is most important that the mechanism be mutually exclusive. Any vulnerability must fit into only class in order to be defined. The price must in part be determined by the classification; therefore the classification must also be unambiguous.

A taxonomy of computer security need not be exhaustive for our interests. In particular viruses and worms are not of interest in terms of classification. Malicious actions are not the point of interest here. Rather the effort to price vulnerabilities would remove vulnerabilities from the network, thereby curbing widespread diffusion of viruses and worms.

Clearly the classification system must be repeatable to be unambiguous. However, once a vulnerability is classified there is no need to do so twice. Therefore this condition is less strenuous in this case than in the case of analysis of incidents.

All classifications would meet the last criteria: acceptability and usefulness. According to [Amoroso, 1994], an acceptable taxonomy is logical and intuitive so that the taxonomy might be widely adopted.

A taxonomy is also defined as "useful" by Amoroso if it provides insight into computer security. However, insight into computer security for the purposes of computer security research per se is not our point of interest here. Thus we will discard that requirement as inappropriate for this particular case.

Now consider various security taxonomies.

The most basic classification scheme for security is the original security classification scheme of top secret, secret, and sensitive. This security classification applies to the files that are the subjects of computer security. That is, this classification is based on the material to be protected rather than the mechanisms used for protection. Our entire focus is on the mechanisms for protection so this classification method, and others based upon classification of documents according to content, are not useful.

Consider three attempts to classify security failures, [Aslam, Krsul, and Spafford, 1996], [Landwehr, Bull, McDermott and Choi, 1994], [Howard, 1997]. How applicable are these attempts to pricing?

In his analysis of security incidents on the Internet, Howard focuses exclusively on incidents. An incident is an attack or series of attacks using the same set of tools by a single set of attackers. An attack may begin with a single subverted account and expand to multiple subverted sites over time. Howard focuses upon the exploitation of vulnerabilities rather than the existence of vulnerabilities. This analysis places emphasis on issues of results of attacks and motivations of attackers. Since our work focuses on extant but not necessarily exploited vulnerabilities, any work which focuses on motivation is inappropriate. Clearly the attack is exactly what this work on pricing vulnerabilities would prevent. Thus while complete and unambiguous the taxonomy addresses variables that are not useful for this work.

Motivation is also the reason that the work by Landwehr et al. does not apply. He focuses on genesis, time of introduction, and location. Time of introduction and location are of interest. Landwehr's work is not applicable because of its inclusion of malicious code. His work was reproducible, but not generalizable. In this work we are not interested in the actively malicious attacks, which are the proper realm of law or national security, but of all extant vulnerabilities, which we argue in the previous section is reasonably within the realm of economics.

The work of Aslam, Krsul, and Spafford was an effort to classify security weaknesses and thus is the closet in spirit to this effort. There are four basic types of faults in Spafford's classification.

Synchronization faults and condition validation errors are classified as coding faults. Coding faults are faults which are included in the code. These result from errors in software construction.

Configuration errors and environmental faults are subcategories of emergent faults. Emergent faults can occur when the software performs to specification but the result, when installed in specific environment, is still a security vulnerability.

Defining the good: a vulnerability

We propose that this good, or item which will have a (negative) value, is a vulnerability. The market can then determine the exchange rates of different types of vulnerabilities.

Some vulnerabilities have already been priced because they have been exploited and the destructive use of the vulnerability has placed a cost on the institution subject to the loss. However, the externalities discussed above (shared trust, additional resources and preventing detection) have not been included in this price, and so it is too low.

Another issues is determining what a vulnerability is. We need to distinguish desirable features from vulnerabilities. In order to price vulnerabilities one must classify them. Before classification must come definition. A formal definition from computer security is that a vulnerability is an error which enables unauthorized access. This definition does not clarify the issue of feature versus vulnerability. An error may be an error in judgement and this definition would still hold. Thus we offer the following.

A vulnerability can be defined as follows:

- A technical flaw allowing unauthorized access or use
- Where the relationship between the flaw and access allowed is clear
- Which has been documented to have been used to subvert a machine

For example, the ability to send and receive email can be used for social engineering to obtain passwords. Using email to obtain passwords has been documented to be a useful attack. There is no correcting code or technical procedure available to end social engineering. Social engineering is not inherently a technical problem. The sending and receiving of email may be an error in judgement – one can forbid email from passing through firewalls. Yet the relationship between sending email and obtaining unauthorized access is not clear. Is it allowing passwords to be transmitted? Is it allowing bad judgement? How is this a technical flaw? The option of allowing email to be sent and received in an organization is too broad to fit under our more constrained definition. In other words, social engineering is not a vulnerability because it fails the first bullet point.

A vulnerability could be defined as actionable after it had been posted for some number of days by at least two incident response teams or some days after it has been used to subvert a system. Since some IRTs do not post until a patch is available this would give vendors limited veto power over vulnerabilities. Thus the adoption of the market would require that the existence of the vulnerability be posted immediately, thought certainly not the attack code.

4. Allocating property rights

In an article for which he later won the Nobel Prize, R.H. Coase proposed that an efficient production of goods usually associated with externalities could be achieved if all parties (e.g. the polluters and those harmed by pollution) could get together to make arrangements to internalize the externalities [Coase, 1960]. Coase argued that it did not matter who had the property rights if transactions costs were sufficiently low. In other words, the allocation of property rights and determination of direction of payment does not matter. The Coase Theorem argues that if transactions costs are high then the allocation of the property rights and the law seriously affect the equilibrium.

For the purpose of pricing vulnerabilities to increase security, rights could be assigned in one of two ways. First, computer owners and operators could be charged for having vulnerabilities and coders could be charged for creating them. Second, users of the network could pay others not to use software or engage in practices with known vulnerabilities. The second option would give users heavy incentives to employ vulnerabilities in order to be paid not to use them. We focus on the first option, which allocates the right to a network with less vulnerability to all users and requires those that want to use vulnerabilities to buy that right.

This raises a second issue: who, exactly, should be required to buy the right? One could imagine charging coders for developing software with vulnerabilities. In the case of shrink-wrapped software charging coders could be effective, except perhaps in cases where the software firm ceased to exist, e.g. had gone into bankruptcy, by the time the vulnerability is identified. However, in the critical arena of freeware, shareware, free software and other downloaded software, tracking down the author "responsible" for the vulnerability would involve high transactions costs.

The second alternative, and our preferred, is to allocate certain initial properties, i.e. a set of vulnerability permits, to every machine, (client, server regardless). In the sulfur dioxide emissions market, initial "allowances" (which gave the right to pollute a ton of sulfur dioxide) were allocated to each plant based loosely on the total output of the plant.

With vulnerabilities a comparable approach can be used, by providing vulnerability permits appropriately to each entity using machines, although there are many possible ways to define distinguishing the entities and set their permit level. Here we offer only an alternative. Note that the division of pollution allowances under the Clean Air Amendments was highly political [Schmalensee, R., Joskow, L., Ellerman, A.D., Montero, J.P., and Bailey, E. M., 1998], yet the resulting market still functions.

There are many variables that can be used to determine how many 'machines' are run by an entity (we will discuss what we mean by an entity below, but think of, for instance, a company, university or household). Counting boxes is not a particularly clever approach since boxes have different numbers of processors and different processing power. One web site may have a small fraction of a server, or tens of servers accessing heavy backend hardware.

Counting processing power may then appear reasonable; however, clearly a video processor inserted into a 386 does not make the machine the equivalent of two Pentium III class machines. There is at least a common and recognizable metric in processing power that would recognize that supercomputers are not equivalent to aging dedicated printer servers. Thus we would advocate considering processing power regardless of platform. Notice that this treats implementation and coding errors as equivalent. The hope is that producers of code with well-documented vulnerabilities would see a correcting market response when their code was identified as having many vulnerabilities.

Now having defined 'machines' we consider 'entities'. Defining the distinction between home and work, production and consumption is not trivial with information networks.

Without having home users as part of the market the ability of users to respond to security failures in the computer market as a whole will suffer. By including home users, a successful market for effectively blackmailing users who do not know how to alter their machines will be created. However, we believe that an equivalent market for upgrading home machines would then arise.

Consider again our decision to focus on machines instead of coders. In the pollution context, the total amount of pollution generated by industrial processes is a function both of how polluting the technology used by a given plant is and how much output each plant produces. Pollution levels can be lowered both by giving consumers incentives to purchase products from clean plants and by encouraging plant owners to clean up their plants. Some policies, such as a tax on pollution in a competitive industry, can have both effects. Similarly, with coding, forcing machine owners to acquire more vulnerability permits from the market when they install certain software would create incentives for both those installing the software and those creating it. Assigning the number of vulnerability permits needed for each software product would require some sort of oversight board.

Setting the number of vulnerability permits

The market price for vulnerabilities permits should reflect two factors: the expected severity of damage from vulnerabilities and costs of correcting or working around the vulnerability (e.g. the cost of doing without a particular feature). The first set of factors reflects the demand for reduced vulnerabilities and the second set the cost of supplying vulnerability reductions.

In creating a market for an externality, the government must decide how many permits to create and so think about where the appropriate balance between addressing the externality and hindering economic growth lies. For instance, in choosing the number of sulfur dioxide allowances to issue, the government could have issued so few that power plants that needed them would have bid their price up quite high and a number of coal power plants would have been forced to shutdown rather than purchase expensive permits or install pollution control equipment. On the other hand, if the government created a very large number of permits, for instance, more than enough to cover the existing power plant emission, the market would have had no effect on pollution. In fact, the government did something in the middle and issued enough so that some power plants have taken steps to reduce their sulfur dioxide emissions.

Note that to make a computer perfectly secure it may be necessary, in theory, to disconnect from the network. Thus, just as it must be feasible to continue polluting for production purposes it must be reasonable to continue connectivity despite security vulnerabilities. The government needs to create few enough vulnerability permits to discourage tolerance of known vulnerabilities but not so few as to discourage connectivity.

Consider the factors entering this tradeoff for computer security. The expected severity of damages from a given vulnerability is a function of several things, including the chance that a vulnerability will be exploited, the damage likely given that the vulnerability was exploited, and the increased risk of other machines given that the particular machine was subverted. We have incomplete information on each of these factors.

To determine risk of exploitation would require data that are currently unavailable and unlikely ever to be available. Not only are specific risks to specific machines unknown, there are not public data on the overall pattern of use of vulnerabilities. The validity of extant proprietary data is unknown. Not only can the risk not be known in the specific it cannot be known in the aggregate. One cannot measure ambient crackers in the way one might measure ambient air quality and then extrapolate to cancer risk.

The losses on the exploited machine ideally reflect the investment of the owner of the machine in security. These losses are suffered by the same party that failed to secure the machine, thus are not at issue.

The increased risk to other machines is a function of the connectivity and the processing power of the machine. The connectivity is a function of the topology of the Internet, and so varies based on the location of the machine. By treating all vulnerabilities as identical, we are ignoring this topology, although, in principle, separate types of permits could be created based on the location of the machine. For instance, there could be non-interchangeable "major" permits and "minor" permits. An owner of a machine with a high degree of connectivity (e.g., a T3 ISP versus a DSL home user) would need to purchase a major permit and an owner of a machine with a low degree of connectivity would need to purchase a minor permit. The government could then issue more minor permits than major permits to reflect the higher cost of vulnerabilities on well-connected machines.

We could create more than two permit subclasses, but the problem with creating too many is that the markets for the individual types of permits then become illiquid. These issues are being confronted in deregulated electricity markets, where the tradeoffs between a liquid market for a good with a broad geographic definition (e.g. electricity in Northern California) and an illiquid market for many geographically specific goods, such that the price reflects all of the interactions on the interconnected electric grid (e.g. electricity at the Humboldt substation in Northern California) are being evaluated. In the extreme, the government could create as many permit subclasses as there are Internet connections, but this would amount to regulating individual vulnerability levels and there would be no market. Also, the topology of the Internet is not mapped. Thus this element of price would be highly uncertain and establishing the correct number of permits would be problematic.

Jump starting trading

For a market to allocate goods to those who value them the most, there must be active trading for the good. Creating permits is effectively creating a new good. In the case of pollution permits, building a liquid market has proven possible but not trivial [Schmalensee, R., Joskow, L., Ellerman, A.D., Montero, J.P., and Bailey, E. M., 1998]. There are several factors that can encourage trading in the new good.

First, potential buyers of a permit want to know that a seller in fact has a valid permit to offer. For instance, one could imagine creating physical (e.g. paper) permit "certificates," but, particularly if permits become valuable, there is a strong potential that forgeries will enter circulation. If the number of permits is small enough, the government, or some other officially sanctioned organization (one could imagine the Internet Corporation for the Assignment of Names and Numbers, now in charge of assigning IP addresses and coordinating assignment of domain names, performing this role), could track and validate all existing permits.

Second, there needs to be monitoring of and sanctions for un-permitted vulnerabilities. Otherwise, potential buyers will have little incentive to go to the market to cover their vulnerabilities. A straightforward sanction is a fine, set to exceed the expected permit price. Monitoring for vulnerabilities is more difficult. One solution could be to set up a sort of citizens' militia, and reward finder of a vulnerability. Also, parties that are awarded a lot of permits at the outset will have incentives to find vulnerabilities because it will increase the value of their permit.

With some amount of oversight and enforcement, entities in need of permits will be in search of potential sellers of them. At this point, private firms are likely to step in to help create a market. These market makers serve to bring buyers and sellers together, help publicize information about the market (e.g. by broadcasting market indices) and they often evaluate the credit-worthiness of potential buyers and sellers. For instance, Cantor Fitzgerald has an active brokerage service for environmental permits. They provide advice to potential buyers and sellers, help them structuring deals, and allow them to execute anonymous trades. Alternatively, if market-specific services are of little value, trades could occur at a place like e-Bay.

5. Conclusions

Security is an externality, with vulnerabilities over-produced and secure system under-provisioned. There are a set of strategies currently in use to increase the provision of network security; however these have proven inadequate. Developing a market for vulnerabilities would address the chronic underprovision of security. A mechanism for creating a market for security vulnerabilities based on vulnerability permit is one possible solution. We have provided a broad overview of what a market for vulnerability permits might look like. Obviously, many other issues would need to be addressed to create such a market, but in practice, as in our paper, the experience setting up environmental permit markets would be relevant.

Trading environmental externalities market has been proposed for global market; however, the observations in this paper could be readily applied to individual institutions. Understanding security as en externality can inform charging mechanisms where no department would experience securing their networks as a cost center. Alternatively an internal market could be developed by a firm to encourage managers to invest in mitigating vulnerabilities in their own networks or penalize those who fail to do so.

In theory a market mechanism can address the continued existence of well-documented vulnerabilities. As with any externality, other remedies exist. The government could mandate insurance coverage for security infractions and leave it to potential insurers to aggregate some of the security externalities. The government could set liability for failing to meet minimal security standards. Taxes could sanction owners of machines with exposed vulnerabilities. These other potential remedies, and the overall cost of the under-provision of security, are described in the chapters in this text. The understanding of security as an externality informs much of the following chapters.

References

Amoroso, E. G. (1994), *Fundamentals of Computer Security Technology,* Prentice-Hall PTR, Upper Saddle River, NJ, 1994.

Aslam, Krsul, and Spafford (1996), "A Taxonomy of Security Vulnerabilities", *Proceedings of the 19th National Information Systems Security Conference*, pages 551-560, Baltimore, Maryland, October.

Ayres and Levitt (1998), "Measuring Positive Externalities from Unobservable Victim Precaution: An Empirical Analysis of Lojack", *The Quarterly Journal of Economics,* Vol. 113, p 43-77. February.

Coase, R.H. (1960). "The problem of social cost", *Journal of Law and Economics,* Vol. 3, pp. 1-44.

President's Commission on Critical Infrastructure Protection, *Critical Foundations: Protecting America's Infrastructure: The Report of the President's Commission on Critical Infrastructure Protection,* 1997, President's Commission on Critical Infrastructure Protection, Washington DC.

The Computer Science and Telecommunications Board (1999). *Trust in Cyberspace,* National Academy Press; Washington, DC.

Department of Defense (1985). *Department of Defense Trusted Computer System Evaluation Criteria,* National Computer Security Center, Fort George G. Meade, MD.

Farmer (1999). *Security Survey of Key Internet Hosts & Various Semi-Relevant Reflection,* http://www.fish.com/survey/

Howard, J. (1997). *An Analysis Of Security Incidents On The Internet 1989–1995*, Ph.D. dissertation, Carnegie Mellon University. Available at http://www.cert.org/research/JHThesis/Start.html.

Landwehr, Bull, McDermott and Choi (1994). "A Taxonomy of Computer Program Security Flaws, with Examples", *ACM Computing Surveys,* Vol. 26, Sept. pp. 3–39.

National Bureau of Standards (1977). *Federal Information Processing Publication 46: Specifications for the Digital Encryption Standard,* United States Government Printing Office; Gaithersburg, MA.

National Institute of Standards and Technology (1994). *Federal Information Processing Standards Publications 185: Escrowed Encryption Standard,* United States Government Printing Office; Gaithersburg, MA.

National Research Council (1996). *Cryptography's Role in Securing the Information Society,* National Academy Press, Washington, DC.

Shapiro, Carl and Hal Varian (1999). *Information Rules: A Strategic Guide to the Network Economy,* Harvard Business School Press, Boston, MA.

Schmalensee, R., Joskow, L., Ellerman, A.D. , Montero, J.P., and Bailey, E. M. (1998). "An Interim Evaluation of Sulfur Dioxide Emissions Trading", *Journal of Economic Perspectives.* Vol. 12 (3). p 53–68. Summer.

Tygar and Whitten (1996). "WWW Electronic Commerce and Java Trojan Horses", *Second Usenix Electronic Commerce Workshop*, Berkeley, CA. Also at http://www.cs.cmu.edu/afs/cs/project/decaf/web/usenix96/main.html

Chapter 3

CRYPTOGRAPHY AND COMPETITION POLICY – ISSUES WITH 'TRUSTED COMPUTING'

Ross Anderson
Cambridge University
Ross.Anderson@cl.cam.ac.uk

The most significant strategic development in information technology over the past year has been 'trusted computing'.

Customers of the computing and communications industries are getting increasingly irritated at ever more complex and confusing prices. Products and services are sold both singly and in combinations on a great variety of different contracts. New technology is making 'bundling' and 'tying' strategies ever easier, while IT goods and services markets are developing so as to make them ever more attractive to vendors. These trends are now starting to raise significant issues in competition policy, trade policy, and even environmental policy.

Ink cartridges for computer printers provide a good example. Printer prices are increasingly subsidised by cartridge sales: the combination of cheap printers and expensive cartridges enables vendors to target high-volume business users and price-sensitive home users with the same products. The level of cross-subsidy used to be limited by the availability of refilled cartridges, and cartridges from third-party aftermarket vendors. However, many printer cartridges now come with chips that authenticate them to the printer, a practice that started in 1996 with the Xerox N24 (see [SC2003] for the history of cartridge chips). In a typical system, if the printer senses a third-party cartridge, or a refilled cartridge, it may silently downgrade from 1200 dpi to 300 dpi, or even refuse to work at all. An even more recent development is the use of expiry dates. Cartridges for the HP BusinessJet 2200C expire after being in the printer for 30 months, or 4.5 years after manufacture [Inq] – which has led to consumer outrage [Slashdot-HP].

This development is setting up a trade conflict between the USA and Europe. Printer maker Lexmark has sued Static Control Components, a company making compatible cartridges and components, alleging that their compatible authentication chips breach the Digital Millennium Copyright Act [SC-law; Slashdot-SC]. On February 27, 2003, Judge Karl Forester ordered Static Control to stop selling cartridges with chips that interoperate with Lexmark's printers pending the outcome of the case. "The court has no trouble accepting SCC's claim that public policy generally favors competition," wrote Judge Forester. "The court finds, however, that this general principle only favors legitimate competition. Public policy certainly does not support copyright infringement and violations of the DMCA in the name of competition." So it would now appear that US law protects the right of vendors to use such market barrier technologies to tie products and control aftermarkets[1].

However, the European Parliament has approved a "Directive on waste electrical and electronic equipment" with the opposite effect. It is designed to force member states to outlaw, by 2006, the circumvention of EU recycling rules by companies who design products with chips to ensure that they cannot be recycled [Broersma2002]. The scene looks set for yet another trade war between the USA and Europe. Which side should economists and computer scientists support?

Varian argues that tying printers to cartridges may be not too objectionable from a policy viewpoint [Varian2002]:

> The answer depends on how competitive the markets are. Take the inkjet printer market. If cartridges have a high profit margin but the market for printers is competitive, competition will push down the price of printers to compensate for the high-priced cartridges. Restricting after-purchase use makes the monopoly in cartridges stronger (since it inhibits refills), but that just makes sellers compete more intensely to sell printers, leading to lower prices in that market. This is just the old story of "give away the razor and sell the blades."

However, tying in other industries may well be:

> But if the industry supplying the products isn't very competitive, then controlling after-purchase behavior can be used to extend a monopoly from one market to another. The markets for software operating systems and for music and video content are highly concentrated, so partnerships between these two industries should be viewed with suspicion. Such partnerships could easily be used to benefit incumbents and to restrict potential entrants.

In a growing number of industries, technical tying mechanisms based on cryptography, or at least on software that is tiresome to reverse engineer, are being used to control aftermarkets:

- Mobile phone manufacturers often earn more money on batteries than on the sales of the phones themselves, so have introduced

[1]Since this paper was originally presented at WEIS 2003, SCC has won an appeal. However the problems continue; for example, the recent EU IPR Enforcement Directive seems bound to increase the abuse of IP rights for aftermarket control

authentication chips into the batteries. A mobile phone may refuse to recharge an alien battery, and may turn up the RF transmitter power to drain it as quickly as possible. In Morotola's case, battery authentication was represented as a customer safety measure when it was introduced in 1998 [Mot98];

- Carmakers are using data format lockout to stop their customers getting repairs done by independent mechanics. In the case of the writer's own car, for example, the local garage can do a perfectly adequate 10,000 mile service, but does not have the software to turn off the nagging 'service due' light on the dashboard. Congress is getting upset at such practices [Pickler2002];

- Computer games firms have been using market barrier tricks for years. As with printers, the business strategy is to subsidise sales of the actual consoles with sales of the cartridges (or more recently, CDs) containing the software. Sales of accessories, such as memory cards, are also controlled, and there have been lawsuits invoking the DMCA against unlicensed accessory vendors. As with printers, laws are diverging; for example, it is legal to defeat the Sony Playstation's copy protection and accessory control mechanisms in Australia, but not in Canada [Becker2002].

Up till now, vendors wanting to introduce barrier technologies to control aftermarkets typically had to design them from scratch. It is hard to get security designs right first time – especially when the designers are new to information security technology – so most early designs were easily circumvented [And2001]. The legislative environment is uneven and unpredictable, as the above examples show. There are often major political issues, especially in industries that are already concentrated and exposed to regulation. So there are significant risks and costs associated with these barrier technologies, and they are by no means ubiquitous.

That may be about to change dramatically. The introduction of so-called 'trusted computing' will make it straightforward for all sorts of vendors to tie products to each other, to lock applications and data on different platforms, and to tie down licences for the software components of systems to particular machines. This is likely to usher in a significant change in the way in which many of the information goods and services industries do business, and may spill over into may traditional industries too. First, we need a brief overview of 'trusted computing'. (For more detail, see the Trusted Computing FAQ at [TCPA-FAQ].)

1. Trusted Computing

In June 2002, Microsoft announced Palladium, a version of Windows implementing 'trusted computing' and due for release in 2004. In this context, 'trusted' means that software running on a PC can be trusted by third parties, who can verify that a program running on a machine with which they are communicating has not been modified by the machine's owner. Programs will also be able to communicate securely with each other, and with their authors. This opens up a number of interesting new possibilities.

The obvious application is digital rights management (DRM): Disney will be able to sell you DVDs that will decrypt and run on a Palladium platform, but which you won't be able to copy. The music industry will be able to sell you music downloads that you won't be able to swap. They will be able to sell you CDs that you'll only be able to play three times, or only on your birthday. This will be controversial; other applications will be less so. For example, trusted computing platforms can host games where cheating is much harder, or auction clients which can be trusted to follow a set of agreed rules – which will make it significantly easier to design many types of auction [AM2002].

Palladium built on the work of the Trusted Computing Platform Alliance (TCPA) which included Microsoft, Intel, IBM and HP as founder members. The TCPA specification, version 1.0, was published in 2000, but attracted little attention at the time. Palladium was claimed to use TCPA version 1.1 which supports some extra hardware features, and the next generation of Pentium processors from Intel (the 'LaGrande' series), which offer an extra memory protection mode: the idea is that since many existing untrusted applications run with administrator privilege, that is in ring 0 of the processor, upgrading security without replacing all these applications requires yet another protected memory mode, called 'curtained memory', so that small parts of trusted software can run with extra privilege that gives them access to cryptographic keys. TCPA has recently been formally incorporated and relaunched as the 'Trusted Computing Group' [TCG].

The TCPA/TCG specifications set out the interface between the hardware security component (the 'Fritz chip'), which monitors what software and hardware are running on a machine, and the rest of the system, which includes the higher layers of software and the means by which the Fritz chips in different machines communicate with each other. Fritz's role in the 'trusted' ecology is to assure third parties that your machine is the machine you claim it to be, and that it is running the software that you claim it to be.

Terminology

There is some difficulty in finding a suitable name for the subject matter of this paper. Neither 'TCPA' nor 'Palladium' will really do. For a while, when public criticism of TCPA built up, Microsoft pretended that Palladium and TCPA had nothing to do with each other; this pretence was then abandoned. But as criticism of Palladium has increased in turn, Microsoft renamed it NGSCB, for 'Next Generation Secure Computing Base' [Lettice2002]. Presumably this isn't the final name, and in any case it's a bit of a mouthful. We might refer to the project as 'trusted computing' but that has evoked principled opposition; Richard Stallman, for example, prefers 'treacherous computing' as the real purpose of the technology is to remove effective control of a PC from its owner. It is thus the opposite of trustworthy [Stallman2002].

There is a further twist. In the information security community, the words 'trust' and 'trustworthy' have a more subtle meaning than in common parlance. The following example illustrates the difference. If an NSA employee is observed in a toilet stall at Baltimore Washington International airport selling key material to a Chinese diplomat, then (assuming his operation was not authorized) we can describe him as 'trusted but not trustworthy'. The proper definition is that a *trusted* system or component is one whose failure can break the security policy, while a *trustworthy* system or component is one that won't fail [And2001]. Since this was pointed out, Microsoft has renamed 'trusted computing' as 'trustworthy computing' [WS2003]. (Intel and IBM stick with 'trusted'.)

I will therefore refer to the subject matter as TC, which the reader can pronounce as 'trustworthy computing', 'trusted computing' or 'treacherous computing', according to taste. Perhaps in time we can arrive at a consensus on a more appropriate name (maybe 'controlled computing').

Control and governance

If the owner of a computer is no longer to be in ultimate control of it, then the big question is where the control goes. This is a question on which companies involved in TC have expressed different views at different times. A straightforward reading of the TCPA 1.0 specification suggests that a hierarchy of certification authorities would certify the various hardware and software components that could make up a TC system. The control would thus be exercised centrally by an industry consortium.

After the launch of Palladium, Microsoft took the public stance that there would be no mechanism in Palladium to support such central certification, and it would be up to the vendors of TC applications or of the content used by them to decide what combinations of hardware and operating system software would be acceptable. Thus, in the DRM case, it would be Disney – or perhaps Microsoft as the vendor of Media Player – who would certify particular platforms as being suitable for rendering 'Snow White'.

Further confusion has been created by the recent launch of Windows Server 2003, which contains some of the file locking functions previously ascribed to Palladium. A TC machine may therefore need a number of different layers of hardware and software to collaborate to provide the TC functionality: the curtained-memory CPU, the Fritz chip, the NGSCB software, the Windows 2003 (or later) platform, and the application.

This has enabled Microsoft to reply to early criticisms of TC saying that NGSCB will not do any of the bad things alleged of it; it will not censor your data or take away control of your computer. But Microsoft admits: 'It is true that NGSCB functionality can be used by an application (written by anyone) to enforce a policy that is agreed to by a user and a provider, including policies related to other software that the application can load' [Manfer2003].

So the locus of trust is moved upwards in the stack, but it is not eliminated. This may be thought to make the competition policy issues less acute, but further reflection suggests that a competitor producing a GNU/linux platform running on TCPA hardware, and seeking certification for it, might have to get it approved by a large number of disparate content vendors in multiple jurisdictions, rather than simply bringing suit against a central certification authority run by an industry consortium. This does not imply that there will be no 'TC/linux' – such a product is apparently being worked on by HP and IBM [Erickson2002] – but it suggests that the competition between TC platforms may be less diverse than TC proponents claim. Even if it were a worthy goal to make DRM available on a large variety of platforms, this strategy of fragmenting control and making governance either diffuse or opaque promises to put up the per-platform entry costs to the point that only a small number of popular platforms are ever effectively supported, and that consumers will have little or no real choice.

There is slightly more clarity on the management of policy, by which we mean the rules that a particular application will enforce – such as tags for commercial CDs saying 'never copy' or 'one backup only', or for broadcast movies saying 'recording for time-shifted viewing allowed; copying not allowed'. The primary policy source will be a server at the application vendor, and there will be mechanisms for some policy to be devolved to system owners.

Thus, for example, a TC system used to enforce government-style protective markings for classified information may have a central policy that information may only move upwards, so that part of a 'confidential' file could be cut and pasted into a 'secret' file but not vice versa; there might be a further local policy component that would enable the author of a particular classified document to restrict it to a number of named individuals, or to prevent it from being forwarded, or to prevent it from being printed.

2. Value to corporate and government users

Using TC systems to protect classified government information and corporate secrets is an interesting application, and one being used to promote the TC agenda. "It's a funny thing," said Bill Gates. "We came at this thinking about music, but then we realized that e-mail and documents were far more interesting domains" [Thurrott2002].

Some details about how rights management mechanisms can be applied in this way to the control of confidential information, as opposed to things like music and video, have been released recently in a Microsoft paper on Windows Server 2003 [WS2003]. (This anticipates the release of the full TC platform, but a number of the TC features have already appeared in early form in other Microsoft products; for example, the combination of trusted boot and software copy protection has turned up in the Xbox, albeit using primitive mechanisms that were readily circumvented [Huang]. The early releases of TC component technologies can at least give us some idea of likely mature functionality.)

The new features offered by Windows Server 2003 enable the creator of a document or other file to maintain some control over it regardless of where it may subsequently move. It will be possible to send an email with restrictions, such as that the recipient cannot forward it, or cannot print it, or can read it only if she has a 'secret' clearance, or that the document will only be readable until the end of the month. Apparently the new Windows software on each PC emulates the future role of the Fritz chip. Windows users who wish to use TC functionality can then register, and an online service appears to be involved in deciding whether or not to make an appropriate decryption key available to the application. The details are not entirely clear at the time of writing.

Many government systems already have mandatory access controls that prevent any person or process reading a classified document unless they have an adequate clearance. The implementation of such systems is fraught with surprisingly many practical difficulties, described for example in [And2001]. The complexity of the information flows within real organisations tends to cause all the information to either float up to the highest level of classification, or float down to the lowest level; there is a tendency for the number of compartments in which information is held to become either unmanageably large, or so small as to give little protection against insiders; most applications have to be rewritten to deal with the increased complexity and restricted connectivity; and there are consistency problems when High and Low parts of the system acquire different views of the same data. In general, the experience of mandatory access control systems is that although they can prevent bad things from happening, they prevent even more good things from happening, and provide a poor ratio of benefit to cost. The trend in government systems nowadays is to use more lightweight mechanisms, coupled with procedural controls and disciplinary measures, to achieve the desired results, rather than expecting the technology to do all the work.

So it is unclear what value most of the proposed rights management mechanisms will bring to corporate and government users.

A restricted subset of them may well be adopted widely, though. One of the selling points of the technology is that a corporation can arrange for all internal emails to become unreadable after 90 days. Apparently,

Microsoft already imposes such a discipline internally. Given the increasingly aggressive discovery tactics used in litigation, it is maybe rather attractive to corporate legal officers to make emails behave like telephone calls rather than like letters; whether this is in the public interest is, of course, another question.

Even such a simple application will turn out to be complex to implement, because of established policy conflicts. Export laws in many countries require companies to preserve copies of communications by which software, documentation or know-how on the dual-use list is exported; this may mean keeping all relevant emails for three years. Accounting regulations may require the preservation of relevant emails for six years. One can anticipate widespread tussles between policies mandating destruction, and policies mandating preservation. As with multilevel security policies, it may turn out to be very difficult to implement systems so that just the 'right amount' of data are preserved.

3. Value to content owners

There has been much lobbying by the content industry for stronger digital rights management systems, and for stronger legal protection for the systems that already exist. The argument is made that digital technologies allow free copying, which will destroy content markets. This argument is less widely believed nowadays, as the means for copying CDs have been widely available for several years with no particularly noticeable impact on sales [Lewis2003]. There are many factors from which the content industry can take comfort.

Swapping music informally is not free, because of the time and effort required to build social networks; peer-to-peer systems do not solve the problem, as they are poor at the critical functions of indexing and searching; any organised central index service, such as Napster, can be attacked by legal means; and the existing weak DRM mechanisms, such as those in Media Player, provide a high enough barrier for a number of music subscription services and e-book publishers to flourish. It is not at all clear that a much stronger DRM mechanism, such as that promised by TC, would provide substantial gains for the content owners over the emerging status quo [2].

It is argued by DRM proponents that stronger DRM will extend the reach of DRM solutions [Erickson2002]. However, many of the benefits that have been talked about in this context are unlikely to yield viable business models. Enabling music lending, for example – the idea that you can lend your copy of a CD to a friend, with your own copy becoming unplayable until you get the main copy back – would enable

[2]Since this paper was first published, a major study has shown that file sharing does not in fact have a negative effect on CD sales: see "The Effect of File Sharing on Record Sales – An Empiral Analysis", Felix Oberholzer, Koleman Strumpf, at http://www.unc.edu/~cigar/

people to implement a legal 'Napster' in which members' CD tracks were pooled, and were thus used very much more than the twice a year that an average CD is played. This seems unlikely to be attractive to the music industry. It may well be possible to practice more extreme forms of price discrimination if strong DRM is widely fielded. But it is unclear that most information businesses will get substantial benefit from perfect price discrimination, because of the transaction costs and the negative social externalities such as loss of privacy. In practice, the ability to differentiate three grades of product at three different prices seems to be adequate for most purposes [SV98].

There is also a significant risk – that if TC machines become pervasive, they can be used by the other side just as easily. Users can create 'blacknets' for swapping prohibited material of various kinds, and it will become easier to create peer-to-peer systems like gnutella or mojonation but which are very much more resistant to attack by the music industry – as only genuine clients will be able to participate. The current methods used to attack such systems, involving service denial attacks undertaken by Trojanned clients, will not work any more [Schech]. So when TC is implemented, the law of unintended consequences could well make the music industry a victim rather than a beneficiary.

There is a further risk, in that if Microsoft comes to control the electronic distribution of music and video content through a monopoly built on Media Player, then this could restrict competition in the content industries. For example, a small film producer in a minority language might find it even harder than at present to get effective distribution. The effects of this could be both economic and cultural. Certainly, many of the smaller firms in the content sector may find TC to be at best a mixed blessing.

In any case, if the music industry wants to provide more value for its customers, it is not at all clear that TC is a critical component. New and useful online services such as those supporting indexing, browsing and access to background information seem likely to increase the revenues from subscription as opposed to first-sale income, and thus decrease the industry's likely dependence on strong DRM.

4. Value to hardware vendors

Experience shows that security mechanisms often favour the interests of those who pay for them more than the interests of the customers for whose benefit they were putatively developed [And2001]. For example, the introduction of authentication and encryption into GSM mobile phones was advertised as giving subscribers greater security compared with analogue phones, which were easy to clone and to eavesdrop. However, more mature experience shows that the main beneficiaries were the phone companies who paid for the security development.

With the old analogue phones, people wanting to make free calls, or to defraud the system by calling 900 numbers controlled by associates, would clone phones, which would generally cost the phone companies money. With the GSM system, criminals either buy phones using stolen credit cards (dumping the cost on the banks) or, increasingly, use mobile phones stolen in street robberies (which cost the customers even more). As for privacy, almost all the eavesdropping in the world is performed by police and intelligence agencies, who have access to the clear voice data on the backbone networks anyway.

Such experience suggests that we examine the likely effect of TC on the business of its promoters.

In the case of Intel, the incentive for joining TCPA was strategic. As Intel owns most of the PC microprocessor market, from which it draws most of its profits, it can only grow if the PC market does. Intel has therefore developed a research program to support a 'platform leadership' strategy, in which they lead industry efforts to develop technologies that will make the PC more useful, such as the PCI bus and USB. Their modus operandi is described in [GC2002]: they typically set up a consortium to share the development of the technology, get the founder members put some patents into a pool, publish a standard, get some momentum behind it, then license it to the industry on the condition that licensees in turn cross-license any interfering patents of their own, at zero cost, to all consortium members.

The positive view of this strategy was that Intel grew the overall market for PCs; the dark side was that they prevented any competitor achieving a dominant position in any technology that might have threatened their control of the PC hardware. Thus, Intel could not afford for IBM's microchannel bus to prevail, not just as a competing nexus of the PC hardware platform but also because IBM had no interest in providing the bandwidth needed for the PC to compete with high-end systems. The effect in strategic terms is somewhat similar to the old Roman practice of demolishing all dwellings and cutting down all trees close to their roads or their castles. This approach has evolved into a highly effective way of skirting antitrust law. So far, the authorities do not seem to have been worried about such consortia – so long as the standards are open and accessible to all companies. The authorities may need to become slightly more sophisticated.

5. Value to software vendors

The case of Microsoft is perhaps even more interesting than that of Intel. In its original form, TCPA had the potential to eliminate unlicensed software directly: a trusted platform, reporting to a central authentication structure, could simply refuse to run unlicensed software. The mechanisms currently used to register software could be made very much harder to circumvent: the Fritz chip maintains a list of the hardware and operating system software components of a TC machine, and there is provision for these to be checked against positive and negative authorisation lists. The operating system can then perform a similar service for application programs. Among early TCPA developers, there was an assumption that blacklist mechanisms would extend as far as disabling all documents created using a machine whose software licence fees weren't paid. Having strong mechanisms that embedded machine identifiers in all files they had created or modified would create huge leverage. Following the initial public outcry, Microsoft now denies that such blacklist mechanisms will be introduced – at least at the NGSCB level [Manfer2003][3].

The Palladium/NGSCB/Win2003 system as now presented relies on more subtle mechanisms. Control will not now, we are told, be exerted from the bottom up through the TC hardware, but from the top down through the TC applications. Walt Disney will be free to decide on what terms they will supply content to TC (and other) systems with particular configurations of hardware and software; if they decide to charge $12.99 for a DVD version of 'Snow White', $9.99 for a download for TC/Windows using Media Player, but refuse to to provide content for TC/linux at all, then Microsoft can claim, to the media and the antitrust authorities, that that is their decision rather than Microsoft's.

The resulting incentives run very strongly in Microsoft's favour. Given that TC/Windows will certainly be the dominant TC platform, most developers will make their products available for this platform first, and for others later (if at all) – just as most developers made their products available for Windows first and for Mac later (if at all) once it became clear that the PC market was tipping in the Wintel direction.

So the antitrust concern should now focus not on Microsoft's control of Palladium/NGSCB, but rather on its control of the dominant applications – Media Player and Office.

The importance of applications

In effect, Microsoft is investing in equipping the operating system platform (NGSCB and Windows2003+) with TC mechanisms in order to reap a reward through higher fee income from its applications. This can be direct (such as charging double for Office) or indirect (such as taking a percentage on all the content bought through Media Player). From the competition viewpoint, everything will hinge on how hard it is for other firms to make their applications and their content interwork with Microsoft's applications and content. Where rents can be charged,

[3]It is of course hard to understand how, in the long term, Microsoft will refrain from moving against people who pirate its software, given that it can also do so at the Windows level, the application level, or through controlling interoperability between licensed and unlicensed platforms from the standpoint of licensed platforms.

it is in Microsoft's interest to made this interoperability as difficult as possible.

If popular music subscription services employ Media Player, and Media Player eventually requires a TC platform, then subscribers may be faced with the need to migrate to a TC platform, or lose access to the music they have already stored. Of course, once the use of a TC application becomes widespread, with many users locked in, license compliance mechanisms can be implemented that will be about as hard to evade as the underlying technology is to break. The business model may then follow that pioneered by Nintendo and other game console makers, in which expensive software subsidises cheap hardware. NGSCB/Palladium will then just be a subsidised enabling component, whose real function is to maximise revenue from high-price products such as Office, games and content rental.

If some set of mandatory access controls for email become a popular corporate application under Windows 2003, and mandatory access controls eventually require a TC platform, then corporate users may also have little choice but to migrate. In fact, they may have even less choice than music subscribers. Music fans can always go out and buy new CDs, as they did when CDs replaced vinyl; but if many corporate and official communications and records come to be protected using cryptographic keys that cannot conveniently be extracted from embedded mandatory access control mechanisms, then companies may have no choice at all but to follow the TC mechanisms that protect and control these keys.

Switching costs and lock-in

The role of switching costs in the valuation of information goods and services companies has been recognised over the last few years. In industries dominated by customer lock-in – such as the software industry – the net present value of a company's customer base is equal to the total switching costs involved in their moving to a competitor [SV98]. If it were more than this, it would be worth a competitor's while to bribe them away. If it were less, the company could simply put up its prices.

One effect of TC is to greatly increase the potential for lock-in. Suppose for example that a company information systems manager wants to stop buying Office, and move his staff to OpenOffice running on a GNU/Linux platform. At present, he has to bear the costs of retraining the staff, the cost of installing the new software, and the cost of converting the existing archives of files. There will also be ongoing costs of occasional incompatibility. At present, economic theory suggests that these costs will be roughly equal to the licence fees payable for Office.

However, with TC, the costs of converting files from Office formats to anything else may be hugely increased [Brockmeier2003]. There may simply be no procedure or mechanism for export of TC content to a non-TC platform, even where this is fully authorised by the content owner.

If the means for such export do exist, they are unlikely to be enough on their own if TC mandatory access control mechanisms become at all widely used. This is because much of the data in a company's files may come to be marked as belonging to somebody else.

For example, a law firm may receive confidential client documents marked for the attention of a named set of partners only. The law firm might feel the need to retain access to these documents for six years, in case they had to defend themselves against allegations of malpractice. So they would have to get their client's permission to migrate the document to, say, a TC/linux platform running OpenDRM and OpenOffice. A firm of any size will acquire thousands of business relationships, some of which go sour; even if the logistics and politics of asking counterparties for permission to migrate documents were acceptable, a number of the counterparties would almost certainly be uncooperative for various reasons. Like it or not, the firm would be locked into maintaining a TC/Windows environment as well as the new one[4]. Many similar scenarios can be constructed.

There are soft effects as well as hard ones. For example, controversy surrounding the whole TC initiative can increase uncertainty, which in turn can lead businesses and consumers to take the view 'better the devil you know'. The result can be an increase in switching costs beyond even that following from the technology. (Old-timers will recall the controversies over the 'fear, uncertainty and doubt' element in IBM's marketing when IBM, rather than Microsoft, ruled the roost.)

Antitrust issues

There is thus a clear prospect of TC establishing itself using network effects, and of the leading TC application becoming in practice impossible for a competitor to challenge once it has become dominant in some particular sector.

This will shed a new light on the familiar arguments in information industry antitrust cases. Competition 'for the market' has been accepted by many economists of the information industries as being just as fair as competition 'within the market', especially because of the volatile nature of the industry, and the opportunities created every few years for challengers as progress undermines old standards and whole industry sectors are reinvented. But if the huge and growing quantities of application data that companies and individuals store can be locked down, in ways that make it in practice impossible for the incumbents to be challenged directly, this argument will have to be revisited.

[4]In fact, from the professional practice viewpoint, accepting restricted documents seems to be very hazardous. For example, what if the named partners with access to the documents leave or die?

In any case, the commercial incentive for Microsoft is clear. The value of their company should be roughly equal to the costs incurred – directly or indirectly – if their customers switched to competitors. If switching can be made twice as hard, then the value of Microsoft's software business should logically double.

There are further issues. Varian has already pointed out that TC can reduce innovation, by restricting the technical opportunities to modify existing products [Varian2002]; things will become even worse once application data are locked down. At present, many software startups manage to bootstrap themselves by providing extra ways of using the existing large pools of application data in popular formats. Once the owners of the original applications embrace TC, there will be every incentive for them to charge rentals for access to this data. This looks set to favour large firms over small ones, and incumbents over challengers, and to stifle innovation generally.

Other software application vendors will face not just the threat of being locked out from access to other vendors' application data, but also the prospect that if they can establish their product and get many customers to use it for their data, they can use the TC mechanisms to lock these customers in much more tightly than was ever possible by using the old-fashioned mechanisms of proprietary data formats and restrictive click-wrap contracts. This will open the prospect of much higher company valuations, and so many software vendors will come under strong pressure to adopt TC. The bandwagon could become unstoppable[5].

Some specific industry sectors may be hard hit. Smartcard vendors, for example, face the prospect that many of the applications they had dreamt of colonising with their products will instead run on TC platforms in people's PCs, PDAs and mobile phones. The information security industry in general faces disruption as many products are migrated to TC or abandoned.

The overall economic effects are likely to include a shift of the playing field against small companies and in favour of large ones; a shift against market entrants in favour of incumbents; and greater costs and risks associated with new business startups. One way of looking at this is that the computer and communications industries will become more like traditional industry sectors such as cars or pharmaceuticals. This may turn out to be a decidedly mixed blessing.

6. Conclusion and Scope for Future Work

For many years, security engineers have complained that neither hardware nor software vendors showed much interest in building protection

[5] There does, of course, linger some doubt about the extent to which Microsoft, Intel and the other TC core members may retain some residual control over the TC mechanisms, which might be used to the detriment of a new TC-using company that came to be seen to pose a threat to platform dominance as Netscape did.

into their products. Early work in security economics now suggests why this was so [Ander2001]. The high fixed costs, low marginal costs, high switching costs and network effects experienced by many IT firms lead to dominant-firm industries with strong first-mover advantages. Time-to-market is critical, and so the 1990s Microsoft philosophy of 'we'll ship it on Tuesday and get it right by version 3' was completely rational. Also, when competing to dominate a network market, firms have to appeal to the vendors of complementary goods and services. So operating system vendors have little incentive to offer complex access control mechanisms, as these simply get in the way of application developers. The relative unimportance of the end users, compared to the complementers, lead firms to adopt technologies (such as PKI) which cause application vendors to dump security and administration costs on to end users. Control of the application programming interface is critical to a platform owner, so best make it proprietary, complicated, extensible and thus buggy. It is much more important to facilitate price discrimination than to facilitate privacy. Finally, in the absence of wide knowledge of security, the lemons effect caused bad products to drive out good ones anyway.

What should have suddenly changed Microsoft's mind?

A cynic might argue that the recent Department of Justice antitrust settlement binds Microsoft to sharing information about interfaces and protocols except where security is involved. There is thus an incentive to rebrand everything the company does as being security-sensitive. Microsoft has also argued that recent publicity about network attacks of various kinds was a driver. However, Microsoft has already used obscurity of protocol design from time to time as a competitive tool. There is also a growing consensus that security scaremongering is getting out of hand to the point that average US business may be spending too much on information security rather than too little. Surely a worm or two a year cannot justify a significant change of policy and direction.

This paper argues that another important factor in the recent decision by Microsoft to spend nine-figure sums on information security, after virtually ignoring the issue for decades, is the prospect of increasing customer lock-in. (It should be noted that Intel, AMD, IBM and HP are also making significant investments in TC, despite no immediate antitrust threats.)

There are many other issues raised by TC, from censorship through national sovereignty to the fate of the digital commons and the future of the free and open source software movement [TCPA-FAQ]. But while these issues also merit very serious consideration, they should not altogether deflect regulators and other policymakers from viewing TC developments through the lens of competition policy.

What should legislators and regulators do? Perhaps some useful precedents can be found in patent law. For years, an unlawful tying contract would invalidate a UK patent; if I had a patent on a flour milling process and licensed it to you on condition that you buy all your wheat from me, than by making that contract I made my patent unenforceable against you (or anyone else). At the very least, one might suggest that the legal protection apparently granted by the DMCA and the EUCD to TC mechanisms that claim to be enforcing copyright should be voided in the event that they are used for anti-competitive purposes, such as accessory control or increasing customer lock-in.

But how should a regulator differentiate between 'good' and 'bad' tying? After all, it is a well known proposition in undergraduate economics courses that price discrimination is often efficient.

We would suggest that this question may be one of the more urgent and interesting facing the economics community today. An analysis purely on innovation grounds may not be particularly useful: government-mandated interoperability would reduce the incentives for innovation by incumbents, so regulators would have to balance the costs to incumbents against the benefits to future challengers. As incumbents are more able to lobby than future challengers – who may not even exist yet – this is a difficult balance to manage politically.

As an alternative, we suggest the test for legislators to apply is whether TC mechanisms increase, or decrease, consumer surplus. This is also the test that the literature on abusive patent settlements would suggest [Shapiro2002]. Given the claims by TC supporters that TC will create value for customers, and the clear expectation that it will also create value for the vendors, and all the fog of impassioned argument about the rights and wrongs of digital rights management, perhaps the test of whether the consumers end up better off or worse off may be the most simple and practical way to arrive at a consistent and robust policy direction on TC.

Acknowledgements: I had useful feedback on this paper from Hal Varian, Andrew Odlyzko, Stephen Lewis, Alan Cox, Lucky Green, Richard Clayton and Rupert Gatti; from anonymous reviewers at the Workshop on Economics and Information Security; and from the audience at Johns Hopkins University, where I gave the 2003 Wenk Lecture on this subject. I have also had general discussions on TC issues with hundreds of people since the publication of [TCPA-FAQ].

References

RJ Anderson, *'Security Engineering – a Guide to Building Dependable Distributed Systems'*, Wiley (2001) ISBN 0-471-38922-6

RJ Anderson, "TCPA/Palladium FAQ", at `http://www.cl.cam.ac.uk/users/rja14/tcpa-faq.html`

M Magee, "HP inkjet cartridges have built-in expiry dates – Carly's cunning consumable plan", The Inquirer, 29 April 2003, at `http://www.theinquirer.net/?article=9220`

"Ink Cartridges with Built-In Self-Destruct Dates", Slashdot, at http://slashdot.org/articles/03/04/30/1155250.shtml
"Computer Chip Usage in Toner Cartridges and Impact on the Aftermarket: Past, Current and Future", Static Control, Inc., at http://www.scc-inc.com/special/oemwarfare/whitepaper/default.htm
"Lexmark invokes DMCA in Toner Suit", Slashdot, at http://slashdot.org/article.pl?sid=03/01/09/1228217&mode=thread&tid=123
"Prepared Statements and Press Releases", Static Control, Inc., at http://www.scc-inc.com/special/oemwarfare/lexmark_vs_scc.htm
M Broersma, "Printer makers rapped over refill restrictions", ZDnet Dec 20 2002, at http://news.zdnet.co.uk/story/0,,t269-s2127877,00.html
HR Varian, "New Chips Can Keep a Tight Rein on Customers", New York Times July 4 2002, at http://www.nytimes.com/2002/07/04/business/04SCEN.html
"Motorola Announces Availability of New Wireless Phone Batteries for Increased Performance and Safety, Featuring New Hologram Design", Motorola Press Release, July 23, 1998; pulled after being referenced in [TCPA-FAQ]; now archived at http://www.ftp.cl.cam.ac.uk/ftp/users/rja14/mototola_battery_auth.html
D Becker, "Sony loses Australian copyright case", on CNN.com, July 26 2002, at http://rss.com.com/2100-1040-946640.html?tag=rn
N Pickler, "Mechanics Struggle With Diagnostics", AP, June 24 2002; previously at radicus.net; pulled after being referenced in [TCPA-FAQ]; now archived at http://www.ftp.cl.cam.ac.uk/ftp/users/rja14/car-diagnostics.html
LM Ausubel, P Milgrom, "Ascending Auctions with Package Bidding", 2002, at http://www.ausubel.com/
Trusted Computing Group, http://www.trustedcomputinggroup.org/
J Lettice "Bad publicity, clashes trigger MS Palladium name change", The Register, Jan 27 2003, at http://www.theregister.co.uk/content/4/29039.html
R Stallman, "Can you trust your computer?", at http://newsforge.com/newsforge/02/10/21/1449250.shtml?tid=19
Microsoft Corp., "Windows Server 2003", Feb 20, 2003, at http://www.microsoft.com/windowsserver2003/rm
J Manferdelli, "An Open and Interoperable Foundation for Secure Computing", in Windows Trusted Platform Technologies Information Newsletter March 2003
JS Erickson, "OpenDRM", at http://xml.coverpages.org/EricksonOpenDRM20020902.pdf
A Huang, "Keeping Secrets in Hardware: the Microsoft Xbox Case Study", May 26 2002, at http://web.mit.edu/bunnie/www/proj/anatak/AIM-2002-008.pdf

P Thurrott, "Microsoft's Secret Plan to Secure the PC", WinInfo, June 23, 2002, at http://www.wininformant.com/Articles/Index.cfm?ArticleID=25681

S Lewis, "How Much is Stronger DRM Worth?" at *Second International Workshop on Economics and Information Security*, at http://www.cpppe.umd.edu/rhsmith3/index.html

SE Schechter, RA Greenstadt, MD Smith, "Trusted Computing, Peer-To-Peer Distribution, and the Economics of Pirated Entertainment", at *Second International Workshop on Economics and Information Security*, at http://www.cpppe.umd.edu/rhsmith3/index.html

C Shapiro, H Varian, *'Information Rules'*, Harvard Business School Press (1998), ISBN 0-87584-863-X

A Gawer, MA Cusumano, "Platform Leadership: How Intel, Microsoft, and Cisco Drive Industry Innovation", Harvard Business School Press (2002), ISBN 1-57851-514-9

J Brockmeier, "The Ultimate Lock-In", Yahoo News. Mar 12 2003, at http://story.news.yahoo.com/news?tmpl=story2&cid=75&ncid=738&e=9&u=/nf/20030312/tc_nf/20982

RJ Anderson, "Why Information Security is Hard – An Economic Perspective", in *Proceedings of the Seventeenth Computer Security Applications Conference* IEEE Computer Society Press (2001), ISBN 0-7695-1405-7, pp 358–365, at http://www.cl.cam.ac.uk/ftp/users/rja14/econ.pdf

C Shapiro, "Antitrust Limits to Patent Settlements", preprint, at http://faculty.haas.berkeley.edu/shapiro/settle.pdf

Chapter 4

HOW MUCH IS STRONGER DRM WORTH?

Stephen Lewis
University of Cambridge
Stephen.Lewis@cl.cam.ac.uk

The purpose of DRM systems is to provide rights-holders with the means to control how their copyrighted materials can be used.

There are many stakeholders in the production and use of Digital Rights Management (DRM) systems, and the incentives influencing their behaviour and the interactions between them are complex. In this paper I argue that it may well be more socially efficient to use market mechanisms to protect copyright holders, rather than spending large amounts of money on the development and deployment of stronger DRM mechanisms.

The most publicly visible proponents of DRM systems are those whose economic rights would be protected by them. Of these, the most prominent in the media are the record and movie industry associations. The message that they seem anxious to communicate to the public is that unauthorized duplication of music tracks will destroy the industry. They conflate the effects of commercial and private copying, and most of the messages seem to portray a general nervousness reminiscent of the Y2K 'crisis'.

Within the industry, though, organizations such as the British Phonographic Industry are painting a very different picture. The BPI's 'Market Information' newsletter for February 2003 put 'intense competition from other areas of the entertainment sector', and 'increasing economic uncertainty' before unauthorized copying of recorded music in the list of reasons for a drop in sales. It said further that 'despite the downturn in sales in 2002, UK record companies sustained sales of music at a very high level' and '[the market value] represents the second highest total ever achieved'. The figures also show that 'the volume of CD albums shipped in 2002 reached another all time high: 221.6m units' [BPI, 2003]. Given that the technology to duplicate music has been available to the consumer for many years, this hardly looks like an industry in desperate need of strong DRM protected from circumvention by legislation. A BBC News article in response to the same figures stated that 'the British record industry has experienced its biggest sales decline in decades' and that 'the BPI says piracy is the main factor' [BBC News, 2003a].

The purpose of DRM systems is to provide rights-holders with the means to control how their copyrighted materials can be used. For example, the holder of the copyright in an e-book might be able to time limit a purchaser's ability to read the book, or restrict the amount of material that can be printed out. This paves the way for far more finely grained market segmentation than is currently available in most media, and it is unclear whether having a diversity of licensing restrictions on content, enforced by DRM, will be socially efficient. This possibility for segmentation is already being exploited by some of the subscription services for music, who offer different levels of subscription with a varying number of downloads that can be transferred to permanent media, portable music players etc.

DRM systems are afforded further protection by articles 11 and 12 of the WIPO Copyright Treaty, which is implemented in national legislation such as the Digital Millennium Copyright Act in the US, and in implementations of the EU Copyright Directive in Europe. It states that 'Contracting Parties shall provide adequate legal protection and effective legal remedies against the circumvention of effective technological protection measures [...]' and also states the remedies should be provided against those who 'remove or alter any electronic rights management information without authority' or distribute, broadcast etc. any works from with the protection has been removed.

'Free uses' of copyright material cause significant problems in the implementation of DRM systems, as do the concepts of 'fair use' and 'fair dealing'. 'Free uses' are acts that can be carried out without the authorization of the copyright holder, and without any obligation to compensate him. 'Fair use' and 'fair dealing' can also take into account the 'nature and purpose of the use, including whether it is for commercial purposes' [WIPO]. An example of this is quoting for the purposes of satire: it would be impossible to describe this limitation to protection in any DRM policy. This is a 'problem' that can only be solved at the social level. Furthermore, the circumvention of any DRM mechanism for the purposes of free use and fair use/fair dealing will be illegal under some proposed national legislation implementing the WIPO Copyright Treaty.

Even with the strongest DRM mechanisms we have today, the BORA (break once run anywhere) principle still holds. Once content is retrieved from a DRM system and re-encoded in a non-DRM protected form, the duplication of that content is as easy as moving the bits around. This means that the cost of breaking the DRM on a particular piece of content need only be borne once. The marginal costs of the duplication to the consumer who can obtain the content are near-zero, and furthermore the consumer need not expend any resources in breaking the DRM. Even in the extreme cases where the quality of the content is very low, as with Video CDs encoded from camcorder recordings illicitly made in cinemas, markets are created in these CDs. This suggests the DRM will do nothing at all to prevent the commercial copyright infringment that appears to be hurting the industry the most. Watermarking may go some way towards preventing this, but there are two obstacles to be overcome. The first is the ease with which some contemporary watermarking mechanisms can be defeated in a re-encoding process [Peticolas, Anderson and Kuhn]. The second is that either legislation or market mechanisms must be used to make players that enforce policies on watermarked content ubiquitous. An alternative would be to use watermarking for the purposes of tracing the orginal from which the content was copied, but these watermarks may again be trivially removeable. Only weak DRM is needed to protect against casual copying, and even the strongest DRM systems available are unable to defeat a determined, well-resourced adversary.

A message peddled by the record industry is that they 'can't compete with free', but in fact it is far from clear that the costs of copyright infringement to the consumer of content are zero. Although the costs of exchanging the content once any DRM mechanism has been broken are close to zero, the costs of forming the social networks necessary to support this exchange are far higher. In the case of the film trading 'scene', the amount of time necessary to make oneself a member of the community is high. In the case of most peer-to-peer networks, the costs of forming the networks have initially been borne by companies hoping to make money out of piggy-backing other services. The sunk costs of providing a network the provides the search features that an average consumer wants are high, however, and no company seems to have produced a business model capable of recouping them in any reasonable time.

There are also technical aspects that increase the transaction costs to the consumer of material on which copyright has been infringed. Many companies providing broadband access to consumers have started to put restrictions on the total amount of data that they can transfer in a given time period. To transfer the content on a DVD losslessly would consume nearly five days' quota with one popular UK cable operator [BBC News, 2003]. There is also the issue that most consumer broadband systems are asymmetric, and hence the exchange of large amounts of content between broadband customers is necessarily slower than if they were downloading from a better-connected machine. It may no longer seem worthwhile to a broadband customer to exchange content with a person from whom he has no guarantee of getting anything in return, if the costs to him in terms of the use of his quota and the slowing down of his Internet connection are large.

We therefore see that exchanging content is not by any stretch of the imagination free, as is claimed by many content industry representatives. In obtaining content, we must take into consideration the costs of forming social networks necessary to get access to the material, and the costs in terms of time spent locating and downloading it. The costs in terms of usage of ISP allocated quota also become an issue when dealing with large video files, and people may become less altruistic in exchanging content with each other once these costs become more visible. The use of P2P networks often incurs high search costs in order to find quality content; only a service that offered good indexing and consistent, high-quality content would be a real threat to a content industry run offering.

The presence of these costs suggests that if the industry were willing to compete in supply of content with the 'free' services currently available, market mechanisms could achieve the goals that strong DRM systems were supposed to. Legislation already deals with combating large-scale commercial copyright infringement, although effective enforcement is sometimes lacking. The industry has significant advantages in reducing transaction costs of obtaining content to the consumer, even in the case of 'paid for' services.

The first advantage is that they can build on well-known record industry brands. They also have the necessary bargaining power to negotiate with ISPs for loosening of the quota restrictions for their particular content. This is especially likely given that bandwidth within ISPs is, to a first approximation, free, and the colocation of servers for content within large ISPs is a real possibility. The ISP would have an incentive to participate in such a scheme, as the colocation of industry-provided content might well reduce the usage of expensive, external bandwidth. The industry would also be able to provide easy sampling of audio tracks/film clips before purchase, and much lower search costs. This could well lead to market selection in favour of 'paid for' services, if they are seen to save time and increase convenience in comparison with other systems.

Some companies are already moving in the direction such business models: in the US, Pressplay and MusicNet offer subscription based services, and 'dotmusic ondemand' has recently become available in Europe [Subscription Services]. These services not only allow streaming of an unlimited number of tracks after a subscription is paid; they include a number of downloads that can be transferred to more permanent media such as CDRs. Some DRM is used in delivery of these services, but it is significantly weaker than some of the hardware-based schemes currently under consideration. This signals a shift from the traditional business model of selling music and video recordings as, for example, a book would be sold, to a service-based model where entertainment is provided on a subscription basis.

In conclusion, the evidence suggests that very little should be spent on the development and roll-out of stronger DRM mechanisms. The stated goals of the content owners can, to a large extent, be achieved by entering into competition with the 'free' services, and letting market mechanisms do their work. The lack of incentive for major investment in stronger DRM systems leads us to question if they are being developed solely to increase customer lock-in to specific technologies [Anderson, 2003].

References

RJ Anderson, "Cryptography and Competition Policy – Issues with Trusted Computing", in Second Annual Workshop on Economics and Information Security.

BBC News, 2003. Anger over broadband limits. At `http://news.bbc.co.uk/1/hi/technology/2740621.stm`

BBC News, 2003a. Slump for UK record industry. At `http://news.bbc.co.uk/1/hi/entertainment/music/2743833.stm`

BPI, 2003. BPI Market Information newsletter (February). At `http://www.bpi.co.uk/stats/Trade_Del_Q4-02.pdf`

FAP Peticolas, RJ Anderson, MG Kuhn, "Attacks on copyright marking systems", in David Aucsmith (Ed), Information Hiding, Second International Workshop, IH98, Portland, Oregon, U.S.A., April 15-17, 1998, Proceedings, LNCS 1525, Springer-Verlag, ISBN 3-540-65386-4, pp. 219-239.

Subscription music services:
`http://www.pressplay.com/`
`http://www.musicnet.com/`
`http://www.dotmusic.com/ondemand/`

WIPO: Basic Notions of Copyright and Related Rights. `http://www.wipo.org/copyright/en/activities/pdf/basic_notions.pdf`

Chapter 5

TRUSTED COMPUTING, PEER-TO-PEER DISTRIBUTION, AND THE ECONOMICS OF PIRATED ENTERTAINMENT

Stuart E. Schechter, Rachel A. Greenstadt, and Michael D. Smith
Harvard University
{stuart,greenie,smith}@eecs.harvard.edu

'Trusted computing' technologies promise to enable media players within a PC to execute with the same level of resistance to piracy that one would expect from a proprietary hardware player

The viability of content piracy hinges on the resource costs of and risk from two required steps: extracting content from its protected form and then distributing copies of that content. History demonstrates that advances in technology often reduce these costs. The latest such advance comes in the form of extraction tools and peer-to-peer networks that automate both steps of the piracy process and put them in the hands of the average consumer. In response, the entertainment industry is looking to protect their content using 'trusted computing' technologies, which aims to place content extraction technology back outside the reach of the average consumer. We explore the implications of such technologies and argue that history, against the hopes of the entertainment industry, may continue to repeat itself.

A brief economic history of piracy

The cost of pirated goods is a function of the costs of extracting content and distributing copies. We refer to the one-time extraction cost as e (sometimes called the *first-copy* cost) and the per-copy distribution cost as d. The total per-copy cost of pirating n copies thus equals $\frac{e}{n} + d$, where the cost of extraction is amortized over the number of copies. Using this simple formula as a guide, we briefly review the evolution of the economics of piracy and set a framework for understanding the reasoning behind the anti-piracy techniques used in the past and those being proposed today.

Before the days of consumer-writable media, the cost of piracy was dominated by the per-copy distribution cost d. No effort was expended to make it costly to extract content from media. This one-sided approach makes sense when one considers the components of the distribution cost d: the resource costs related to purchasing and writing media and the legal liability costs associated with the distribution of pirated content in countries that enforce intellectual property laws. The direct effect of high resource costs is to limit the number of pirates. Because the average consumer could not afford to produce pirated media, the entertainment industry could easily afford to pursue legal action against those few with the financial resources for engaging in piracy. Such legal actions had the effect of increasing liability, which ultimately resulted in further increases in per-copy distribution costs.

The advent of audiotape and videotape made recording technology and media available at a reasonable cost, and the widespread acceptance of consumer VCRs created a demand for pirated video content.[1] These technology changes dramatically reduced d, and the entertainment industry reacted by endeavoring to increase e.

In particular, the industry introduced anti-piracy mechanisms into content-players and recorders in order to raise the cost of extraction high enough so that this cost could only be justified if amortized over a large number of copies. Consumer VCRs were built with technology that would refuse to record audio and video signals from sources of copyrighted content [Corporation,]. In parallel, the entertainment industry also employed patent protection and industry license agreements to force manufacturers to include anti-piracy mechanisms in their content players. These legal barriers were meant to exclude from the content-player market any manufacturer not complying with the anti-piracy design requirements. Increasing e made casual piracy prohibitively expensive, and the entertainment industry again kept piracy at bay by investigating and prosecuting only a small number of distributors.

The development of digital content players and cheap digital media again dramatically changed the economics of piracy by driving the resource costs related to purchasing and writing media to near zero.[2] In addition, digital media eliminated the problem of copy degradation and further drove down the costs of distribution. At first, the entertainment industry reacted by delaying the introduction of high-density, writable digital media into the consumer market. However, once personal com-

[1] Even though the proliferation of pirated content was limited by imperfections introduced as copies of copies were made on analog media, these consumer technologies reduced d to the point where the number of potential pirates could increase dramatically.

[2] At the time of this writing, storage costs were approximately 30 cents per gigabyte for removable media, such as DVDs/CDs, and $1 per gigabyte for fixed storage, such as hard disks.

puters (PCs) advanced to the point where compressed audio and video was easy to play and distribute across the Internet, it no longer made economic sense to block the sale of high-density, writable drives to consumers. Writable CD-ROM drives are now standard equipment on PCs, and drives that also write to DVD will soon take their place.

A primary goal of the DVD format was to protect digital video from piracy. As with VCRs, legal barriers and economic incentives were put in place to ensure that manufacturers could only produce a DVD reader if it included anti-piracy mechanisms to thwart content extraction and reverse engineering [Anderson, 2001, page 431]. Once again, the industry's legal efforts would then focus on a smaller set of larger pirate distributors. For these reasons the industry has fiercely protected the DVD format, filing suit under the new Digital Millennium Copyright Act (DMCA) to keep video content extraction tools out of the hands of consumers [Hansen, 2001; Harmon, 2001]. The entertainment industry has also tried, rather unsuccessfully, to retrofit the CD format with similar content-extraction protections [Borland, 2002a].

Napster was the first system to integrate the end user into the distribution process. The reduction in the per-copy cost of pirated content was so significant that the market for pirated music and video content exploded. The market growth was aided by an image of legitimacy resulting from extensive press coverage and professional looking software. Having failed to protect content on CDs, the recording industry attacked the distribution channel, suing Napster as it would any other large distributor of pirated content. Though Napster's centralized infrastructure failed to survive legal attack, newer systems such as Gnutella and Kazaa evolved to use distributed infrastructures more resilient to legal action against individual components. While the Recording Industry Association of America (RIAA) is working to bring makers of piracy applications into US jurisdiction [Borland, 2002b] and break the corporate veil [Olsen, 2002], these piracy networks are designed to live on long after the demise of their creators.

Without an effective way to raise extraction costs or eliminate the current peer-to-peer distribution channels using legal attacks, the entertainment industry has undertaken a two-pronged effort to raise the per-copy distribution cost seen by individual consumers. On the legal front, the industry is using high profile litigation against a few individuals, in hopes of raising in all consumers the perceived liability of using these networks [McCullagh, 2002]. It is a strategy that appears to be having an effect [Harmon, 2003b]. The industry is also learning to use a technical approach to raising distribution costs. In particular, it is attacking the confidentiality, integrity, and availability of peer-to-peer distribution networks.

Enter 'trusted computing'

While attacking channels for distributing pirated content has not been without benefit, it also has costs and limitations. Thus, the entertainment industry continues to explore new ways of protecting the content stored on media and played by software. In particular, 'trusted computing' technologies promise to enable media players within a PC to execute with the same level of resistance to piracy that one would expect from a proprietary hardware player, such as those used to play DVDs. If these technologies succeed, extracting content from the media of the future will be significantly more difficult than ripping a CD is today.

Part of the success of the entertainment industry's anti-piracy effort relies on its ability to make content extraction inconvenient enough to deter the general public. To be successful, the industry must also deter those individuals and defeat those systems that distribute pirated content. In short, the industry would like to return to the days when investigation and legal actions were sufficient to counter a reasonably sized set of professional pirates.

Roadmap

The per-copy cost of piracy, $\frac{e}{n} + d$, is at the heart of the ongoing battle between the entertainment industry and content pirates. In Section 5.1 we explain how 'trusted computing' technologies will be used to protect media players from content-extraction attacks, increasing the pirate's cost of extraction, e. We describe attacks that may be employed against peer-to-peer distribution of pirated content in Section 5.2. If successful, these attacks will increase the pirate's distribution costs, d, and reduce the number of copies, n, that the network is able to distribute. In Section 5.3, we explore a how the 'trusted computing' technologies described in Section 5.1 can be used by pirates to secure their peer-to-peer networks against the attacks of Section 5.2.

1. Protecting Content

To protect their content, owners will encrypt it before writing it to media or otherwise transmitting it to media players. Media players will be required to provide a minimum level of resistance to content-extraction attacks before content-owners will entrust them with the decryption keys. Because the PC platform was not designed to resist such attacks, media players running on today's PCs cannot make such guarantees. Not surprisingly, the leading forces in the PC market formed the Trusted Computing Platform Alliance (TCPA), now succeeded by the Trusted Computing Group (TCG), to introduce technologies that will enable PCs and their applications to obtain the trust of the entertainment industry. Microsoft has also introduced similar technologies as part of its next-generation secure computing base for Windows, formerly known as Palladium.

These efforts introduce into commodity computing hardware a private key of a public key pair, as described in Arbaugh, Farber, and Smith's early work on secure boot processes [Arbaugh et al., 1997]. After placing the private key into the hardware, the manufacturer creates a signed certificate vouching that the hardware into which the key was placed exhibits certain properties, such as tamper-resistance, and that only this hardware was given the public key. The hardware may make claims, or *attest* to statements, to a remote entity by signing these claims with it's private key. Trust in the claims certified by this *remote attestation* [Alliance, 2000] process is only as strong as the trust in the entities that has signed off on the claims. Once claims regarding the identity and anti-piracy properties of the hardware and BIOS have been established, the BIOS may then attest to the identity of the code it will next execute, the operating system. In a final transitive step, an operating system trusted by the remote entity may then attest to the identity and integrity of the application it is running. In order to reduce the number of digital signatures required, hardware registers may be used to collapse these steps into a single claim by the hardware. Alternative approaches place full responsibility for protecting clients in the hardware, removing the need for attestation of the operating system [Lie et al., 2000; Suh et al., 2003].

If each link in the chain is trustworthy then a remote entity may rely upon a client application to behave with the trust properties, such as resistance to content-extraction, for which the application has been certified. Because operating systems rely upon hardware for their correct operation, and applications rely upon operating systems for their correct operation, each attestation step builds on the prior trust layers. If any layer turns out not to be trustworthy, it may subvert all the layers above it.

Once a trust infrastructure is in place, the entertainment industry may protect its content by encrypting it and only transmitting the keys to those platforms built from components (hardware, operating system, and applications) that it trusts. In order to ensure the confidentiality of the keys that protect content and the unencrypted content itself, additional operating services are required to protect them while applications use them. Specifically, the operating system must protect the applications's memory and, if keys are to be stored locally, its file storage. Operating system services will also be required to protect the content on its way to the screen or audio card, lest content be stolen in a digital format on its way to the user. Microsoft's next-generation secure computing base for Windows provides each of these services under the names *curtained memory*, *secure storage*, and *secure input and output.*

However, if humans are to eventually hear the protected audio signals and view the protected video signals, then this protected content can also be recorded. Since video cameras and music recorders can record and store any information perceivable to human eyes and ears, secure output paths all the way from computer to user are therefore impossible. A motivated attacker, who purchases the highest quality viewing or listening equipment and pairs it with equipment that can record the experience, will be able to produce a copy that is good enough to please a vast number of consumers. These limitations are acceptable if the goal is only to increase the cost of extraction enough to deter consumers, not professional pirates, from making copies.

2. Attacking Peer-to-Peer Distribution

Because no level of media protection can raise the cost of extraction beyond the cost of recording the signal presented to the user, a successful anti-piracy effort must also work to maintain a high cost of distributing pirated content. In particular, the entertainment industry must determine how it can deter peer-to-peer distribution of its pirated content.

We explore attacks on peer-to-peer networks and the countermeasures used to defeat them. We consider these attacks with regard to the security assets they target: confidentiality, integrity, and availability.

Confidentiality

Breaches of confidentiality both increase the expected liability cost of distributing content and reveal information that can be used to write programs that attack the system's integrity and availability.

If caught, both senders and receivers of pirated content may face lawsuits or other forms of retaliatory action. Using today's peer-to-peer networks is particularly risky because anyone eavesdropping between the sender and the receiver may observe pirated content in transit. Even if content was transmitted in encrypted form, the eavesdropper could use traffic analysis to determine the network addresses of the sender and the receiver and the size of the files being transferred. These attackers use confidentiality attacks to interrupt file transfers [Borland, 2003], locate pirates in order to send them cease and desist messages [Harmon, 2003a], and gather evidence for litigation.

The first step in protecting the confidentiality of the network is to encrypt the data sent over it so that only the sender and receiver know what was sent. However, there is nothing encryption can do to ensure that the party at the other end of the line, who knows what was transmitted, is not the attacker. For this reason systems that provide anonymity, or at least plausible deniability, are desirable. In such systems, the attacker may know that copyrighted content was transmitted through the network but cannot identify the original sender or final recipient.

A common approach to anonymous networking is to re-route communications through more nodes than can be tracked effectively [Reiter and Rubin, 1998; Syverson et al., 1997]. Attackers may watch the communication as it travels through the network or run routers that expose routing information, but these threats may be mitigated so long as a reasonable fraction of the routers act to keep routing information confidential. At present, there is no way to determine which clients will route traffic through the network with the intent of protecting anonymity.

Attacking the network is not the only way to breach the confidentiality of the peer-to-peer system. By running the peer-to-peer client software and thus controlling a peer, an attacker may look into the peer-to-peer network through the "eyes" of its client software. Client software has no secrets because operating systems make every byte of a program's memory available to the machine's administrator, or root account. The attacker can locate encryption keys, network topology information, or any of the other information required to participate in the peer-to-peer network. Once confidentiality has been breached, the attacker may use the information to write programs to impersonate a genuine peer-to-peer client and attack the network from within. Such programs are invaluable to the attacker as they enable scalable attacks on integrity and availability.

Integrity

The integrity of information in a peer-to-peer system may be attacked through the introduction of degraded-quality content or by misrepresenting the identity of the content. In the context of music, these attacks have included introducing noisy recordings or falsely labelling songs. Attacks on the integrity of information describing the operation of the peer-to-peer network, such as the network's topology and routing information, may disrupt communication or even prevent users from ever accessing the network again. If clients are disconnected from the network, or if content may be misrepresented or its quality decreased, then the user's cost of obtaining pirated content (part of the distribution cost) will increase.

Reputation systems counter corrupt content attacks by enabling users to rate the validity of content and those who provide it. To ensure that all copies of the same content share the same reputation, content may be identified by its fingerprint (or hash). This enables reputations to scale far beyond trust in the user and allows widely duplicated corrupt files to be recalled quickly.

To ensure that an attacker cannot modify or delete its client's reputation information, designers must distribute this information among the other clients using protocols that prevent tampering. Because attackers can delete clients and reinstall new ones, a reputation system should also maintain information for the machines on which clients run. Confounding this problem are virtual machines, in which the few potential unique machine identifiers (e.g. network card addresses) may be modified easily.

While we may construct reputation systems to be resilient to a large number of malicious users, no existing system is immune to attack from an unlimited number of such users [Cornelli et al., 2002; Kamvar et al., 2003]. If the attacker can write programs that impersonate genuine clients, there is no limit to the number of malicious peers that can be introduced into the system.

Availability

More resources are expended performing searches on peer-to-peer networks than are required to request that a search be performed. Attackers may use their client application to issue a large number of search requests, flooding the network with more requests than can be serviced. Alternatively, the attacker may force their client application to drop packets it was meant to route by manipulating the operating system or by simply disconnecting network cables at the right times.

Peers can stem the flood of requests by requiring that requests be accompanied by proof that the requestor had performed computational work, restoring the balance between the computation costs of issuing and responding to requests. This approach was introduced by Dwork and Naor [Dwork and Naor, 1992] to increase the low cost of sending email and make sending spam unprofitable. This concept has been extended to more general settings, such as preventing network level denial of service attacks for TCP [Juels and Brainard, 1999] and TLS [Dean and Stubblefield, 2001]. Requiring clients to solve puzzles before issuing requests could go a long way to prevent flooding attacks on peer-to-peer networks. However, the entertainment industry might be able to harness enough processing power to flood networks if its members can exploit the media players they controls to perform puzzle computations on machines paid for by their users.

An alternative to client puzzles is to use the reputation systems mentioned above to track individual machine's utilization of networks resources. The efficacy of this approach is limited if the attacker can corrupt the reputation system using programs that impersonate genuine clients, or even if a large number of genuine clients can be run on virtual machines and fed scripted input. The payoff to the entertainment industry of scaling such attacks comes in the form of increased barriers between users and pirated content, which in turn increases the per-copy cost of distribution.

3. Defending Peer-to-Peer Distribution

At the time of this writing, Sharman Networks, the makers of Kazaa, claims that well over 200 million copies of its client application had been downloaded. Because these networks contain vast resources, attacks will only be affordable if the cost of attack is many times smaller than the damages inflicted on the distribution network.

The existing countermeasures described in Section 5.2 are sufficient to defend peer-to-peer networks against attacks from individual users running authentic clients on real machines. Attackers still have a leg up in that they may peer into clients running on their own machines, use this information to write programs that impersonate real clients, and run as many copies of these clients as they need to disrupt the network. Alternatively, they may script attack behaviors and feed those behaviors into a large number of authentic clients running in parallel on virtual machines.

Can peer-to-peer networks be made immune from malicious client software written by the attacker? They can if the personal computer industry delivers on its promise of remote attestation. Though this technology was envisioned to thwart pirates, it is exactly what a peer-to-peer system needs to ensure that no client application can enter the network unless that application, and the hardware (not a virtual machine) and operating system it is running on, has been certified by an authority trusted by the existing clients. The trust model may be quite simple: accept only new clients into the network if they are certified by the same authority that vouched for the existing clients.

What's more, if Microsoft delivers on the promises of its next-generation secure computing base for Windows, then clients can also be assured of secure storage and curtained memory. With these technologies, peer-to-peer systems can protect the confidentiality and integrity of the clients' memories, which are collectively the memory of the entire network.

4. Conclusion

To thwart piracy the entertainment industry must keep distribution costs high, reduce the size of distribution networks, and (if possible) raise the cost of extracting content. However, if 'trusted computing' mechanisms deliver on their promises, large peer-to-peer distribution networks will be more robust against attack and trading in pirated entertainment will become safer, more reliable, and thus cheaper. Since it will always be possible for some individuals to extract content from the media on which it is stored, future entertainment may be more vulnerable to piracy than before the introduction of 'trusted computing' technologies.

Acknowledgments

This paper could not have been completed without the advice, comments, and suggestions of Ross Anderson, Kim Hazelwood Cettei, Roger Dingledine, Glenn Holloway, David Molnar, Michael Rabin, and the anonymous reviewers. This research was supported in part by grants from Compaq, HP, IBM, Intel, and Microsoft.

References

Alliance, The Trusted Computing Platform (2000). Building a foundation of trust in the PC. Technical report.

Anderson, Ross J. (2001). *Security Engineering: A Guide to Building Dependable Distributed Systems.* John Wiley & Sons, Inc., first edition.

Arbaugh, William A., Farber, David J., and Smith, Jonathan M. (1997). A secure and reliable bootstrap architecture. In *Proceedings of the IEEE Symposium on Security and Privacy*, pages 65–71.

Borland, John (2002a). Customers put kibosh on anti-copy CD. *CNET News.Com.*

Borland, John (2002b). U.S. liability looms over Kazaa. *CNET News.Com.*

Borland, John (2003). Fingerprinting P2P pirates. *CNET News.Com.*

Cornelli, Fabrizio, Damiani, Ernesto, Capitani di Vimercati, Sabrina De, Paraboschi, Stefano, and Samarati, Pierangela (2002). Choosing reputable servents in a P2P network. In *Proceedings of The Eleventh International World Wide Web Conference.*

Corporation, Macrovision. Solutions > video technology > copy protection. `http://www.macrovision.com/solutions/video/copyprotect/index.php3`.

Dean, Drew and Stubblefield, Adam (2001). Using client puzzles to protect TLS. In *Proceedings of the 10th USENIX Security Symposium.*

Dwork, Cynthia and Naor, Moni (1992). Pricing via processing or combatting junk mail. In *Proceedings of Advances in Cryptology - CRYPTO '92, 12th Annual International Cryptology Conference*, volume 740 of *Lecture Notes in Computer Science*, pages 137–147. Springer.

Hansen, Evan (2001). Ban on DVD-cracking code upheld. *CNET News.Com.*

Harmon, Amy (2001). Judges weigh copyright suit on unlocking DVD shield. *The New York Times.*

Harmon, Amy (2003a). Music swappers get a message on PC screens: Stop it now. *The New York Times.*

Harmon, Amy (2003b). Record concerns sue to end piracy. *The New York Times.*

Juels, Ari and Brainard, John (1999). Client puzzles: A cryptographic countermeasure against connection depletion attacks. In *Proceedings of the 1999 Network and Distributed System Security Symposium.*

Kamvar, Sepandar D., Schlosser, Mario T., and Garcia-Molina, Hector (2003). The EigenTrust algorithm for reputation management in P2P networks. In *Proceedings of The Twelfth International World Wide Web Conference.*

Lie, David, Thekkath, Chandramohan A., Mitchell, Mark, Lincoln, Patrick, Boneh, Dan, Mitchell, John C., and Horowitz, Mark (2000). Architectural support for copy and tamper resistant software. In *ASPLOS-IX Proceedings of the 9th International Conference on Architectural*

Support for Programming Languages and Operating Systems, pages 168–177.

McCullagh, Declan (2002). File-swapping foes exert P2P pressure. *CNET News.Com.*

Olsen, Stefanie (2002). Record labels sue Napster investor. *CNET News.Com.*

Reiter, Michael K. and Rubin, Aviel D. (1998). Crowds: anonymity for Web transactions. *ACM Transactions on Information and System Security*, 1(1):66–92.

Suh, G. Edward, Clarke, Dwaine, Gassend, Blaise, van Dijk, Marten, and Devadas, Srinivas (2003). AEGIS: Architecture for tamper-evident and tamper-resistant processing. In *17th Annual ACM International Conference on Supercomputing.*

Syverson, Paul F., Goldschlag, David M., and Reed, Michael G. (1997). Anonymous connections and onion routing. In *Proceedings of the IEEE Symposium on Security and Privacy*, pages 44–54.

Chapter 6

ECONOMICS OF IT SECURITY MANAGEMENT

Huseyin Cavusoglu
Tulane University

> *The real challenge is determining how much to spend and where to spend. This requires understanding of the economic issues regarding IT security.*

Increased interconnectivity among computers enabled by networking technologies has boosted the scale and scope of information technology (IT) related crimes (Denning 2000). Open access nature of the networked world that facilitates easy exchange of information, goods, and services also presents the biggest impediment in the form of security. Today as the e-commerce continues to grow, so does the cyber crime. IT security, which was once considered an overhead to a company's main operations, is now widely recognized as an important aspect of business operations (Cagnemi 2001). IT Security is no longer purely the concern of the traditional high-risk category organizations such as those in the defense, military, or government sectors. It has become pervasive across all sectors of the economy. While high-risk organizations may adopt security at any price, most commercial organizations have to consider the cost-benefit trade-off of security technologies for effective management of IT security.

The importance of effective management of IT security from an economics perspective has increased in recent years due to increasing frequency and cost of security breaches. A recent survey by Computer Security Institute (CSI) and FBI 2002 found that the ninety percents of respondents detected computer security breaches in the previous twelve months (Power 2002). The number of security breaches reported to Computer Emergency Response Team (CERT) has grown exponentially over the last decade, reaching 82094 incidents in 2002 up from 773 in

1992, even though CERT counted each incident once, irrespective of how widespread the attacks were[1] (CERT/CC Statistics 2003).

The cost of a single security breach can be enormous in terms of monetary damage, corporate liability and credibility and has been increasing at a rapid pace. A global survey conducted by InformationWeek and Pricewaterhouse Coopers LLP estimated that computer viruses and hacking took a $1.6 trillion toll on the worldwide economy and $266 billion in the United States alone (Denning 2000). CSI/FBI 2002 survey revealed that eighty percents of respondents acknowledged financial losses due to security breaches, and forty-four percents were willing or/and able to quantify their financial losses. The total loss from computer crime incidents reported in the 2002 survey was $456 million in contrast to $266 million in 2000 and $124 million in 1999.

Public attention about security breaches increased dramatically when companies like Amazon.com, Ebay, and Yahoo were hit by Denial-Of-Service (DOS) attacks in February 2000. A number of high-profile computer worms and viruses, such as *Code Red*, *Nimda*, and *I Love You*, also heightened the awareness. A fact that attests this increased emphasis is a quote from a recent memo issued by Bill Gates to Microsoft's employees: "(the new emphasis is) more important than any other part of our work. If we don't do this, people simply won't be willing – or able – to take advantage of all the other great work we do. When we face a choice between adding features and resolving security issues, we need to choose security. Our products should emphasize security right out of the box."[2]

In order to combat the computer crime problem the United States government has undertaken several measures. Computer-related crimes are federal offenses under the *Counterfeit Access Device and Computer Fraud and Abuse Law*[3] of 1984, which was expanded by the *Computer Fraud* and *Abuse Act* of 1986 and *National Information Infrastructure Protection Act* of 1996. The law classifies the computer crime and provides guidelines for sentencing provision[4]. The laws and regulations enacted by governments act as a broad deterrent against IT-related crime.

Given that firms have little control on implementation of laws and regulations to deter IT related crime, increased concerns for security breaches have led firms to increase the importance of IT Security man-

[1] CERT considers an incident as any group of activities in which an intruder uses the same tool or exploit. An incident can affect anything from a single computer to computers at numerous locations.

[2] The new emphasis on security includes the unprecedented step of stopping development on new Windows operating system software for the entire month of February 2002 and sending the company's 7,000 systems programmers to a special security-training program.

[3] Computer-related crimes can be charged under at least forty different federal statutes other than Computer Fraud and Abuse Act. These federal statutes include the *Copyright Act, the National Stolen Property Act, the mail and wire fraud statutes, the Electronic Communications Privacy Act, the Communications Decency Act of 1996.*

[4] For a state of art review of computer crimes law, see Nicholson et al. 2000.

agement within firms. Today IT security management seeks to manage the risks associated with IT assets such as loss, disruption, and unauthorized access of information and system resources.

1. An economics perspective to IT security management

While firms seem to realize the importance of security, the assessment of the economic value of security has proved to be challenging. Traditionally, organizations have regarded security as a kind of insurance policy that indemnifies them from losses due to security breaches. Commenting on the current state of affairs, Ron Knode, Computer Sciences Corporation's global director of managed security services stated, "While most IS professionals recognize the benefits of protecting and securing data, the business leadership in the organization still sees security as 'nice to have' rather than 'need to have'. It is not until something goes wrong before perceptions change. The fact is, it costs far less to establish the right security measures at the outset than it does to recover from a breach in security."[5]

In fact, information security should be viewed as a value creator that supports and enables e-business, rather than simply as a cost of doing business. A secure environment for information and transaction flow can create value for the organization as well as its partners and customers. In the same token, security breaches can lead to breach of consumer confidence and trust in addition to lost business and third party liability. In a recent survey by Media Metrix only 12.1 percent of U.S companies with a web presence cite direct financial loss as a concern in a security breach while more than 40 cite consumer trust and confidence (Pastore 2001).

Although the high profile attacks on popular e-commerce sites in recent years have highlighted the importance of security in Internet age, security is still a tough sell to corporate managers. They want to see hard numbers to justify investments in security technologies, which are hard to get because of difficulties in estimating costs and benefits. Even though companies spend more money than ever for the deployment of security technologies, IT security problem is not getting better. Firms need to recognize that even the best technology is not fool proof. Furthermore, even if such a fool proof technology exists, it may not always be desirable for all firms. Firms need to manage security just as any other investment by analyzing the cost-benefit tradeoffs. Today IT security is shifting from what is technically possible to what is economically efficient. As pointed out by Crume (2000) "The first rule of IT security is that you [firms] should never spend more to protect something than thing is actually worth." Firms should carefully consider costs and ben-

[5]CSC News Release, November 19, 2001.

efits before making their security investment decisions. In other words, each firm should strike an appropriate balance between risk and opportunity to reduce the risk through security controls. This balance must be defined within the context the business operates: firm characteristics and hacker characteristics. The ultimate decision is what to protect and how much to protect.

The growing importance of analyzing these tradeoffs is evident from the recent emphasis and discussion on economic aspects of IT security by both academics and practitioners alike. Economics-based research on IT security is a relatively new area where researchers examine IT security-related problems from cost-benefit perspective. Since it is a relatively new area, the literature in this stream is sparse. Researchers have addressed various security issues from an economics perspective, ranging from studies estimating the cost of security breaches and the value of security technologies to studies aiming at determining how much to invest in security and how to design an effective security architecture. Most of these studies basically follow one of the two prominent analysis techniques: Decision theory or game theory. In the next four sections I categorize these studies into four groups based the issues addressed, namely (i) estimation of the total cost of security breaches, (ii) assessment of the value of security technologies, (iii) determination of the optimal level of IT security investment, and (iv) other economics-based security studies.

2. Assessing the total cost of security breaches

The true cost of a security breach is multifaceted, therefore difficult to quantify. The costs of security breaches can be broadly classified into transitory (or short-term) costs that are incurred only in the period in which the breach occurs and permanent (or long-term) costs that are incurred over the long term. The possible transitory costs of security breaches include lost business and worker productivity due to unavailability of the breached information resources, labor and material costs required to detect, contain and repair and reconstitute the breached resources, costs associated with evidence collection and prosecution of the attacker and costs related to providing information to customers and public and other media related costs (D'Amico 2000).

The other group of costs is more permanent in nature and has a long-term affect on the breached firm's future cash flows. These costs include those related to loss of customers that switch to competitors, inability to attract new customers due to perceived poor security, loss of trust of customers and business partners, potential future legal liabilities arising out of the breach and cost of competitor's access to confidential or proprietary information. In addition, the firm may face increased insurance cost and higher capital cost in debt and equity markets because of perceived increase of business risk.

The above costs can further be classified into tangible and intangible costs. It is possible to estimate some of the above costs such as lost sales, material and labor costs, and insurance costs. However, other costs such as those related to trust are difficult to calculate. Nonetheless these costs are extremely important in measuring the true cost of security for business.

For many years, firms have generally relied on the cost estimates from the CSI-FBI surveys. According to the CSI-FBI Computer Crime and Security Survey 2002, which polled 503 respondents from organizations throughout the United States, 80% reported financial losses, but only 44% (223) of them were able to quantify it. The total reported loss was $455,848,000 and the average estimated loss was $2,044,161 per organization across all types of breaches. The highest reported loss was for theft of proprietary information, reported by 41 organizations with an average of $4,166,512 per organization. The sabotage of data networks cost an average of $351,953 while denial-of-service attacks resulted in a $244,940 loss per organization. The reported losses included the firms' estimates of direct and tangible costs associated with security breaches only.

As discussed above, a security breach is multifaceted and can have both tangible and intangible costs. While most tangible costs are immediate or short-term, the intangible costs can have a long-term effect on the firm's expected future cash flows. Therefore, using tangible costs to estimate the total cost of a security breach may be inadequate. However, quantifying intangible costs of a security breach is not easy. Although a direct way of measuring these costs seems difficult, an indirect estimate is possible though capital market valuation of firms. (Cavusoglu et al. 2004a) propose a market valuation-based approach to estimate the true cost of security breaches. Their approach is based on efficient market hypothesis (Fama et al. 1969). In efficient markets, investors are believed to revise their expectations based on new information in announcements. Investors' expectations are reflected in the value of the firm. Security problems may signal to the market a lack of concern for customer privacy and/or poor security practices within the firm. These signals in turn may lead investors to question the long-term performance of the firm. If investors view a security breach negatively, believing that the transitory and long-term costs resulting from the breach will substantially reduce expected future cash flows, then using the change in market value of the breached firms around security breach announcement days can be a proxy to estimate the true cost of security breaches.

Cavusoglu et al. (2004a) show that the announcement of an Internet security breach is negatively associated with the market value of the announcing firm. The breached firm, on average, loses 2.1% of its market value within two days of the announcement. This translates into a $1.65 billion average loss in market capitalization per breach based on the mean market value of firms in their data set. They also found that (i) breach cost is higher for "pure play" or Internet-only firms than for conventional firms, (ii) breach cost has increased over the time of the study period, (iii) security breaches are costlier for smaller firms than larger firms, and (iv) breach cost is not significantly different across breach types. The effects of security breaches are not restricted to breached firms, however. The market values of security technology firms are positively associated with the disclosure of a security breach. Each security firm in their sample, on average, realizes an abnormal return of 1.36% within two days after the announcement. This produces, on average, a total gain for security firms of $1.06 billion over a two-day period.

The average loss estimate obtained through capital markets by Cavusoglu et al. (2004a) is orders of magnitude above the average loss estimate reported in the CSI-FBI surveys. The huge difference in estimates may be explained by the fact that firms in the CSI-FBI surveys estimated only direct costs such as lost productivity or sales, and expenditure on restoring the breached system, whereas the loss estimated through capital markets may also include the investors' expectations about the impact on future cash flows, which requires considerations of intangible costs such as the loss of consumer confidence. Besides, in forming their expectations, investors may also anticipate that the firm may be breached again in the future. The estimates based on capital markets may be noisy because of the uncertainties. However, even if these estimates are discounted, there is an order of magnitude of difference between the firms' reported estimates in the CSI-FBI surveys and the market value loss in Cavusoglu et al (2004a). One possible implication of this finding is that the intangible costs of security breaches can be much larger than the tangible costs, and hence, firms that ignore the intangible costs are perhaps grossly underestimating the loss from security breaches. Since investments in IT security are directly dependent on the extent of potential loss from breaches, firms are likely to underinvest in IT security if they make investment decisions based only on tangible costs.

3. Assessing the Value of Security Controls

Quantifying the value of IT security is not easy because of the difficulties in estimating benefits. This problem is not unique to IT security. The "productivity paradox" literature, which has attempted to quantify the return on IT investments, has grappled with similar problems (Brynjolfsson 1993).

IT security management seeks to establish internal controls to minimize the risk of loss of information and system resources, corruption of data, disruption of access to the data, and unauthorized disclosure of information. These internal mechanisms fall into two major categories:

preventive control and *detective control.* Preventive control mechanisms, e.g. firewalls, aim to develop a "defensive shield" around IT systems to secure them. The detective control mechanisms try to detect the intrusions when they occur. Although preventive control constitutes an important aspect of IT security architecture, it is extremely difficult to build an IT system that is absolutely secure. Detection-based security has become an important element in overall security architecture because IT systems are unprotected without detective controls once intruders manage to break the firewall. Studies have also reported that many of the hackers are employees or outsiders assisted by insiders (Escamilla 1998; Russell and Gangemi 1992). Thus, detection based controls complement the perimeter security by identifying intrusions from both insiders and outsiders.

Intrusion Detection Systems (IDSs) are one of the most common detection approaches used by firms. The goal of these systems is to identify, in real time, unauthorized use, misuse, or abuse of computer systems. Cavusoglu et al. (2002a) investigates the value of IDS within an IT architecture that has firewalls on one side and manual monitoring on the other side surrounding the IDS. They derive the value of IDS by comparing two cases. In the first case, they focus on an architecture that doesn't employ an IDS to detect intrusions. In the second case, they include an IDS within the security architecture to detect security violations. They find that, unlike the common belief, the value of IDS can be negative. They show that the value is positive *only if* the IDS deters hackers from hacking. They also show that firms can deter hackers through IDSs by configurating them effectively. However, irrespective of the value, an IDS reduces the effective manual investigation rate, thus reducing the manual investigation cost, but does not change the effective detection rate. Their results suggest that the value of an IDS arises from deterrence rather than improved detection.

As pointed out by Axellson (2000) "The best effort [security] is often achieved when several security measures are brought to bear together. How should intrusion detection collaborate with other security mechanisms to this synergy effect? How do we ensure that the combination of security measures provides at least the same level of security as each applied singly would provide, or that the combination does in fact lower the overall security of the protected system?" Current practices seem to ignore interaction effect between security technologies in term of value contribution to security when designing a security architecture.

Given the fact that layered security architecture is a necessity for a secure environment, the crucial question to answer is how security controls interact when they are implemented together within the same security architecture. Do they complement each other, for example, is the value of security architecture with both a firewall and an IDS greater than the sum of the values when each control is applied individually?, or do they substitute each other, that is, is the value of security architecture with both a firewall and an IDS less than the sum of the values when each control is applied individually?

This question is important because when a firm sets up its security architecture, it often considers how much value a security control will add to security in isolation with other controls already in place. This presumption is actually a selling point for security developers to sell their products. For instance, the argument that the firewall will reduce hacker attacks by x percent and will result in \$$y$ savings for the firm might be incorrect if there is already an IDS in the firm's security architecture. Hence failing to recognize the interaction between security technologies may lead to security architecture design decisions that are not optimal.

Cavusoglu et al. (2003a) clearly demonstrate that both complementary and substitution effects might exist between security technologies. Since the firm decides whether to install the security control or not based on the cost of security, and its value to security within the firm, it might be the case that the firm justifies investments in some security controls that should have not been justified if it had considered the interaction effect, or the firm disregards investments in some security controls that should have been justified if it had considered the interaction effect. The conclusion is firms should carefully evaluate the value of a security mechanism considering already existing controls before concluding on its return instead of isolation from existing controls.

4. Effective level of investment

The process by which organizations determine their IT security investments is rather blurred because of high degree of uncertainty in estimation of costs and benefits, as described in previous two sections. Fear, uncertainty, and doubt (FUD) (Berinato 2002) has been used for years by security vendors to sell investments in IT security. Although this approach can convince organizations to invest in basic security solutions, e.g. firewalls, anti-virus systems, it does not tell an organization how much to invest to deal with security risks in a cost effective way.

There are basically two approaches to determine the effective IT security investment level. First approach uses the traditional risk or decision analysis framework and quite popular in practice. The idea is to identify the potential risk of security violations in terms of their damage and likelihood. Using this framework Gordon and Loeb (2002) propose a model to analyze investments in IT security. Their economic model determines the optimal amount to invest in security controls to protect a given set of information by considering the vulnerability to a breach and the potential loss associated with a breach. They show that optimal amount to spend on security is far less than the expected loss from a breach in security. Their analysis also reveals that investing in security to mitigate risk from high levels or low levels of vulnerability may not be economically justifiable. Longstaff et al. (2000) propose Hierarchical Holographic

Model (HHM) to assess security risks and provide a model for assessing the efficacy of risk management. They argue that investment in systematic risk assessment can reduce the likelihood of intrusions which yields benefits much higher than the investment. Hoo (2000) provides a decision analytic framework to evaluate different policies for IT security. He develops a risk modeling technique for selection of safeguards which utilizes influence diagrams as a common graphical language that maps relationships between key variables. Instead of comparing all security controls on an individual basis, his model groups controls into baskets of safeguards, or policies. Then he makes the cost-benefit tradeoff for each policy. Different from other two decision theoretic models mentioned above, his model considers not only the cost of security controls and expected loss from security breaches but also additional profits expected from new opportunities associated with the security investment when making cost and benefit calculations.

In essence, all of the above models for IT security investments are not too different from general IT investment models. However, the context of IT security is different from a general IT investment context. In security, organizations are dealing with strategic adversaries who are looking for opportunities to exploit vulnerabilities in systems. While organizations try to cover vulnerabilities in their systems, attackers race with organizations to exploit them. They attack systems that are vulnerable and do not have appropriate controls. To be able to compete, organizations should act strategically when investing in security. IT Security can be treated as a kind of game between organizations and attackers. When choosing security investment level, firms cannot treat the risk environment as static. Security investments not only prevent security breaches by reducing vulnerabilities that attackers can exploit but also act as a deterrent for attackers by making attacks less attractive. Knowing that their attack will not be enough to bypass preventive security mechanisms or will be detected by detective control mechanisms within the system can change the behavior of attackers. As pointed out in the NIST Special Publication on Risk Management 800-30 (Stoneburner et al. 2001), security investment increases the attacker' cost. The deterrent effect comes in when the attacker's cost becomes larger than its benefit, forcing to attacker not to attack the firm in the first place. Hence, looking at security investment problem from decision theoretic perspective might not be appropriate for determining how much to invest in security. Any model that aims to determine IT security investment level must consider the firm's action on attackers' behaviors subsequently and vice versa.

The second approach to determine the effective IT security investment level uses game theory to model such strategic interactions. Cavusoglu et al. (2003b) propose a comprehensive analytical model to evaluate security investment decisions. Their model offers several benefits. First, it captures the individual technologies used in a typical IT security infrastructure. Consequently, managers can evaluate the interaction among different technologies and jointly decide on investments in multiple technologies. Second, the model facilitates managers in understanding the different drivers of return on IT security investment and enables them to conduct sensitivity analysis of return with respect to these drivers. Without referring to specific security controls, Cavusoglu et al. (2004b) extend the model in Gordon and Loeb (2002) using a game theory-based approach for determining the optimal IT security investment level. They show that ignoring the strategic nature of interaction causes a firm to invest either more or less than the required amount. Their results clearly explain that under most circumstances the firm, when faced with a strategic adversary, realizes a lower cost when its uses the game theory as opposed to the decision theory to make security investment decisions.

5. Other economics-based IT security studies

Optimal configuration of IDSs has also attracted attention among security researchers recently, leading to several models for such analysis. Configuration of an IDS involves setting the levels of false positive and false negative rates by calibrating the model used by the IDS. Gaffney and Ulvila (2001) present a decision theoretic approach to determine the best operating point of the IDS for a given environment. Their study integrates cost of dealing with two types of errors and quality profile of the IDS as indicated by Receiving Operating Characteristics (ROC) curve that relates the rate of false positives and rate of false negatives. Since hacker behavior can be influenced by the likelihood that the hacker will be caught, which in turn, depends on the configuration of the IDS, firm can use configuration as a strategic tool in security. Using this idea, Cavusoglu et al. (2002b) present an optimization model based on game theory to determine the optimal configuration of IDSs. They present their results using computational experiments. Cavusoglu and Raghunathan (2003) extends these two previous studies by comparing the effect of the selected methodology – game theory versus decision theory – on configuration and resulting cost. They also provide an analytical solution for configuration problem for both methodologies.

Even technical researchers have begun to incorporate cost elements in design. Lee et al. (2002) propose to build cost-sensitive intrusion detection systems that generate alarms based on various cost elements. They follow a risk analysis procedure to select sensitive assets and create a cost matrix for each intrusion. Then they divide total cost into damage cost, response cost, and operational cost and define those elements for each type of intrusion. They use this cost model and technical effectiveness of the IDS to determine whether it is worthwhile to employ countermeasures to stop an intrusion. To simulate their model they choose an attack taxonomy example from DARPA and verify effectiveness of the model. Using the same attack taxonomy Wei et al. (2001) suggest a similar cost model which considers the cost not only from multiple events but also from multiple hosts, making it more general for a distributed network environment.

Moitra and Konda (2000) analyze CERT Coordination Center incidents data from 1988 to 1995 to understand the underlying process for random occurrence of incidents. Then they develop a simulation model and run it with inputs estimated from the CERT data to observe how well a system survives when it is subjected to a series of attacks. They observe that as cost increases, survivability increases rapidly at first, and then more slowly. They show the tradeoff involved between the cost and expected survivability. So a firm can choose where to be on this curve when the indifference curve is estimated. Although survivability is important for security, their study is related to only one of the security objectives, which is availability.

6. Conclusions and Future Research Directions

In this paper, I overviewed the literature on economics of IT security management. I discussed the issues addressed and methodologies used. Specifically, I categorized the studies into four groups: (i) estimation of the total cost of security breaches, (ii) assessment of the value of security technologies, (iii) determination of the optimal level of IT security investment, and (iv) other economics-based security studies.

Although the recent research on economics of IT security has increased the understanding of important security issues, this new research stream still has many issues to address. There are several directions for future research on economic aspects of IT security. The most prominent one is cyber insurance. Firms can manage security risks against information systems by investing in security technologies and/or buying insurance. The nature and extent of the risk in cyber space, which includes not only the direct risk to a firm but also the risk arising from interconnected partner networks makes insurance different from other contexts. The analysis of conditions under which cyber insurance is a viable option for security is very crucial for effective IT security management. This analysis will shed lights on how firms can use insurance to minimize the cost of security.

Interconnections among IT systems make security levels of individual systems interdependent. Each institution's vulnerability depends not only on the way in which it manages its risk but also the ways in which other entities manage their risks. While investment in IT security reduces a firm's risk exposure and produces positive externalities for others, dependence of the firm's security on the investments of others may negate the payoff the firm receives from its investment in security. It can also diminish the firm's incentive to invest. Therefore, it is critical that firms invest in security after considering the additional risk arising from connected systems. Future research should focus on the effect of liability and litigation on security investment decisions among interconnected systems. It should also investigate the use of subsidy as a way to encourage security investments.

References

Axelsson, S., "The Base-Rate Fallacy and the Difficulty of Intrusion Detection," *ACM Transactions on Information and System Security,* 3(3), August 2000.

Berinato, S. "Finally, A Return on Security Spending," *CIO Magazine,* Feb 15, 2002.

Brynjolfsson, E., "The Productivity Paradox of Information Technology," *Communications of the ACM,* 36(12), pp. 66–77, 1993.

Cagnemi, M. P., "Top Technology Issues," *Information Systems Control Journal,* 4(6), 2001.

Cavusoglu, H., B. K. Mishra and Raghunathan, S., "Assessing the Value of Detective Control in IT Security," *Proceedings of 8th Americas Conference on Information Systems,* pp. 1910–1918, 2002a.

Cavusoglu, H., B. K. Mishra and Raghunathan, S., "Configuration of Intrusion Detection Systems" *Working Paper,* 2002b.

Cavusoglu, H. and Raghunathan, S., "Configuration of Intrusion Detection Systems: A Comparison of Decision and Game Theoretic Approaches," *International Conference on Information Systems (ICIS),* Seattle, Washington, December 2003.

Cavusoglu, H., Mishra, B. K. and Raghunathan, S., "Quantifying the Value of IT Security Mechanisms and Setting Up an Effective Security Architecture," *2nd Annual Workshop on Economics and Information Security,* College Park, Maryland, May 29–30, 2003a.

Cavusoglu, H., B. K. Mishra and Raghunathan, S., "A Model for Evaluating IT Security Investments," *Communications of the ACM,* Forthcoming, 2003b.

Cavusoglu, H., B. K. Mishra and Raghunathan, S., "The Effect of Internet Security Breach Announcements on Market Value of Breached Firms and Internet Security Developers," *International Journal of E-Commerce,* Forthcoming, 2004a.

Cavusoglu H., S. Raghunathan and W. T. Yue, "Decision Theoretic and Game Theoretic Approaches to IT Security Investment," *Working Paper,* 2004b.

CERT/CC Statistics, 2003, available at `http://www.cert.org/stats/cert_stats.html`.

Crume, J., *Inside Internet Security,* Addison Wesley, 2001.

CSC News Release, *CSC Survey Reveals Inadequate Information Security Practices Among Companies Worldwide,* November 19, 2001, available at `http://www.csc.com/newsandevents/news/1584.shtml`.

D'Amico, A. D., *What Does a Computer Security Breach Really Cost?,* Secure Decisions, a Division of Applied Visions, Inc., September 7, 2000.

Denning, D., "Reflections on Cyberweapons Controls," Computer Security Journal, 16(4), pp. 43–53, 2000.

Escamilla, T., *Intrusion Detection: Network Security Beyond the Firewall,* John Wiley & Sons, 1998.

Fama, E., L. Fisher, M. C. Jensen and R. Roll, "The Adjustment of Stock Prices to New Information," International Economic Review, 10(1), pp. 1–21, 1969.

Gaffney, J.E. Jr. and J.W. Ulvila, "Evaluation of Intrusion Detectors: A Decision Theory Approach," *Proceedings of IEEE Symposium on Security and Privacy,* pp. 50–61, 2001.

Gordon, L. A. and M. P. Loeb, "The Economics of Information Security Investment," *ACM Transactions on Information and Systems Security,* pp. 438–457, November 2002.

Lee, W., W. Fan, M. Miller, S. Stolfo and E. Zadok, "Toward Cost-Sensitive Modeling for Intrusion Detection and Response," *Journal of Computer Security,* 10, 1/2, pp. 5–22, 2002.

Longstaff, T. A., C. Chittister, R. Pethia and Y. Y. Haimes, "Are We Forgetting the Risks of Information Technology?," *IEEE Computer,* pp. 43–51, December 2000.

Moitra, S. D. and S. L. Konda, "The Survivability of Network Systems: An Empirical Analysis," *Technical Report,* CMU/SEI-2000-TR-021, December 2000.

Nicholson, L. J., T. F. Shebar and M. R. Weinberg, "Computer Crimes," *The American Criminal Law Review,* Spring 2000.

Pastore, M., Companies Lack Understanding of Information Security Issues, *Internet.Com,* October 10, 2001.

Power, R., "2002 CSI/FBI Computer Crime and Security Survey," *Computer Security Issues and Trends,* 8(1), 2002.

Russell, D. and G. T. Gangemi, *Computer Security Basics,* O'Reilly & Associates, Inc. 1992.

Soo Hoo, K. J., "How Much is Enough? A Risk-Management Approach to Computer Security," *PhD Dissertation,* Stanford University, June 2000.

Stoneburner, G., A. Goguen and A. Feringa, *Risk Management Guide for Information Technology Systems,* NIST Special Publication 800-30, 2001.

Wei, H., D. Frinke, O. Carter and C. Ritter, "Cost-Benefit Analysis for Intrusion Detection Systems," *CSI 28th Annual Computer Security Conference,* 2001.

Chapter 7

EVALUATING DAMAGES CAUSED BY INFORMATION SYSTEMS SECURITY INCIDENTS

Fariborz Farahmand, Shamkant B. Navathe,
Gunter P. Sharp and Philip H. Enslow
Georgia Institute of Technology
{ff,sham,enslow}@cc.gatech.edu, gsharp@isye.gatech.edu

Each threat and vulnerability must be related to one or more of the assets requiring protection and discuss our framework for a classification of threats and countermeasures.

A critical decision security managers must make is the amount to spend on security measures to protect assets of the organization. To arrive at this decision, security mangers need to know explicitly the assets of their organizations, the vulnerability of their information systems to different threats, and potential damages.

1. Cost of Information Security Incidents

Threats and vulnerabilities do not exist in a vacuum. Each threat and vulnerability must be related to one or more assets requiring protection. This means that prior to assessing damages we need to identify assets. Logical and physical information system assets can be grouped into five categories:

1 Information – Documented (paper or electronic) data or intellectual property used to meet the mission of an organization,

2 Software – Software applications and services that process, store, or transmit information,

3 Hardware – Information technology related physical devices considering their replacement costs,

4 People – The people in an organization who possess skills, knowledge, and experience that are difficult to replace and,

5 Systems – Information systems that process and store information (systems being a combination of information, software, and hardware assets and combinations of host, client, or server being considered a system).

The most common metric for these diverse assets is money, which is generally used where the threat is direct financial theft or fraud. Some assets are difficult to measure in absolute terms but can be measured in relative ways, for example, information. The value of information can be measured as a fraction or percentage of total budget, assets, or worth of a business in relative fashion. Assets may also be ranked by sensitivity or importance to an organization in relative ways. The major categories of threats to the information systems are:

1 Destruction of information and/or other resources,

2 Corruption or modification of information,

3 Theft, removal or loss of information and/or other resources,

4 Disclosure of information; and

5 Interruption of services.

The impact of information security incidents may well be financial, in the form of immediate costs and losses of assets. For example, the cost of downtime per hour caused by a denial of service attack can be computed by measuring the loss of:

Productivity (Number of employees impacted) × (hours out) × (burdened hourly rate)

Revenue Direct loss, lost future revenues

Financial Performance Credit rating, stock price

Other Expenses Equipment rental, overtime costs, extra shipping costs, travel expenses, etc.

But, much more serious are difficult to quantify the hidden costs. Consider the example of denial of service attack, where the damaged reputation of the company can have negative impact on the relationship of the company with its customers, suppliers, financial markets, banks, and business partners.

We have chosen to use both qualitative methods (interviews) and a quantitative examination of the damages awarded in cases that have been successfully prosecuted. We have conducted personal interviews with law enforcement agencies dealing with computer crime and with executives from financial institutions dealing with security issues. In addition, we did a literature review of cases prosecuted by the Department of Justice including the evaluation of damages and financial awards. This review illustrates a significant negative market reaction to information security breaches involving unauthorized access to confidential data, but no significant market reaction when the breach does not involve access to confidential data (e.g., Campbell, *et al* 2003). This finding is consistent with the findings from the 2002 CSI/FBI survey, which suggests that among information security breaches, the most serious financial losses were related to the theft of proprietary information (Power 2002). This is also consistent with the recently prosecuted computer cases by the Computer Crime and Intellectual Property Section, CCIPS, of the Criminal Division of the US Department of Justice. According to CCIPS, 91% of cases that have been under the computer crime statute, 18 U.S.C. 1030, are cases that relate to the violation of confidentiality of information. Consider an example of these cases: in November 2001, two former Cisco Systems, Inc., accountants were sentenced to 34 months in prison for "exceeding their authorized access to the computer systems" of Cisco Systems in order to illegally issue almost $8 million in Cisco stock to themselves.

These findings reveal that breaches involving unauthorized access to confidential information are quite different than attacks that do not involve access to confidential information. As an example, we have calculated the tangible cost for break-in using buffer overflow attack against Web servers from real incidents in five different companies as follow:

Total productivity lost

Total downtime; time to access and repair damage: 49 hours

Total productivity lost: 49 hours × 30% time users lost ×500 users = 7,350 hours

Cost of downtime

(Total productivity lost × percentage of staff) × hourly rate

Employees with annual salary of $20,000:

(7,350 hours × 55% of staff) × $10 per hour → $40,425

Employees with annual salary of $30,000:

(7,350 hours × 30% of staff) × $15 per hour → $33,075

Employees with annual salary of $45,000:

(7,350 hours × 15% of staff) × $22.5 per hour → 24,806

Total cost for downtime? $98,306

This total cost for downtime seems to be very low compared with millions of dollars in damage in cases with violation of confidentiality of data.

The literature review also indicates that compromised firms, on average, lose approximately 2.1% of their market values within two days surrounding the events while security vendors gain an average of 1.36% from each such announcement (Cavusoglu, H., *et al* 2002) (These findings are supported by other work included in this text.) Other chapters and the literature more broadly also show the negative average impact associated with announcements decreases with the size of the firm and this suggests that smaller firms are penalized more than larger firms. This result for the managers of small firms serves as a reminder of the importance of security for survivability of these firms. However, the authors do not present detailed data, and thus it is not possible for readers to draw conclusions about the absolute loss of market values. Although the market penalizes all firms for security breaches, Internet firms are penalized more than conventional firms. A possible explanation for this effect is the greater dependency by the firms on Internet to generate revenues. Firms that solely depend on the Internet as a revenue generating mechanism pay higher prices in case of a security breach than firms that have multiple sale channels.

2. Threat-Agent Classification

In their previous works, the authors have presented a subjective analysis and probability assessment approach as a possible solution for vulnerability assessment and damage evaluation of information security incidents (Farahmand et al., 2004). In practical terms, the evaluation of security risks eventually leads to subjective assessment supported by guidelines or some other risk assessment method. In our research, we attempt to provide a generic method by which the process can be made more systematic.

Estimating the probability of attack by human threat actors using subjective evaluation can be complex. One should consider the following factors:

Motive How motivated is the attacker? Is the attacker motivated by political concerns? Is the attacker a disgruntled employee? Is an asset an especially attractive target for attackers?

Means Which attacks can affect the critical assets? How sophisticated are the attacks? Do likely attackers have the skills to execute the attacks?

Building upon this larger factors, the following four variables should be considered.

Opportunity How vulnerable is the computing infrastructure? How vulnerable are specific critical assets. Managers should also be warned about some cognitive biases that stem from the reliance on judgmental heuristics, which may occur in subjective analysis. We classify the origins of these pitfalls into three types:

Representativeness In the representativeness heuristic, the probability that, for example, Bob is a hacker, is assessed by the degree to which he is representative of, or similar to, the stereotype of a hacker. This approach to the judgment of probability can lead to serious errors, because similarity, or representativeness, is not influenced by several factors that should affect judgments of probability.

Availability There are situations in which people access the frequency of a class or the probability of an event by the ease with which instances or occurrences can be brought to mind. For example, one may assess the risk of disclosure of information among financial institutions by recalling such occurrences among one's acquaintances. Availability is a useful clue for assessing frequency or probability, because instances of large classes are usually recalled better and faster than instances of less frequent classes. However, availability is affected by factors other than frequency or probability. Consequently, the reliance on availability can lead to biases.

Adjustment & anchoring In many situations, people make estimates by starting from an initial value that is adjusted to yield the final answer. The initial value, or starting point, may be suggested by the formulation of the problem, or it may be the result of a partial computation. In either case, adjustments are typically insufficient. That is, different starting points yield different estimates, which are biased toward the initial values.

In spite of these pitfalls, the authors believe that subjective analysis can be employed usefully in information security assessment, even when quantitative data is not available or a formal process description is not required.

Among information security experts there appears to be no agreement regarding the best or the most appropriate method to assess the probability of computer security incidents. There does exist, however, a hierarchy of approaches such as checklists and scenario generation techniques that require the user to have only a minimum knowledge of information system security (Wood, et. al., 1987).

To derive an overall likelihood rating that a potential vulnerability may be exploited these governing factors should be considered: threat-source, nature of the vulnerability, and existence and effectiveness of current controls.

The threat-source addresses both motivation and capability. The likelihood that a potential vulnerability could be exploited by a given threat-source can be described as high, medium, or low. In defining these likelihoods we follow the likelihood determination by NIST (Stonebumer, et. al., 2001):

High likelihood The threat-source is highly motivated and sufficiently capable, and controls to against penetration are ineffective

Medium likelihood The threat-source is motivated and capable, but controls are in place that may impede successful exercise of the vulnerability

Low likelihood The threat-source lacks motivation or capability, or controls are in place to prevent, or at least significantly impede, the vulnerability from being exercised.

One can also use these qualitative ratings to assign values for a quantitative evaluation to use in the checklist. Implementing this checklist can extract more easily digestible quantitative data from the information managers' less structured knowledge. Checklists have long been popular in computer security, with proponents including Mercuri (`http://www.notablesoftware.com/checklists.html`).

For example consider a checklist using threat source: High likelihood as 0.9, medium likelihood as 0.5, and low likelihood as 0.1. We can also use a more detailed scale such as: Very high, high, medium, low, and very low, and use 0.9, 0.7, 0.5, 0.3, and 0.1, respectively, for these likelihoods. Yet greater granularity without greater certainty is illusory, and does not provide greater accuracy. The individual who assigns the variables may choose the specificity.

The checklist can be written in an interactive form and should allow a minimum of three possible answers: "yes", "no", or "not relevant". Questions should be asked in a way that a "yes" answer means that the control exists and a "no" answer means that the control does not exist. A control is relevant when both the asset to be protected and the threat exist.

For example, one critical element to evaluate data integrity can be, "Is virus detection and elimination software installed and activated?" A subordinate question for the above question could be, "Are virus scans automatic?" The answer to this question might be "yes", "no", or "not relevant". A metric for this evaluation can be the percentage of systems with automatic virus scanning, which can help gauge the risk exposure caused by known viruses.

We provide below a model of classification of security threats and develop three axes to create a threat space and a scheme for probabilistic evaluation of impact of the security threats (Farahmand et al, 2003). In this classification, threats are considered from both the perspective of the threat agent and the threat technique. A threat is manifested by a threat agent using a specific penetration technique to produce an undesired effect on the network. Threat agents include environmental factors, authorized users, unauthorized users and the threat (penetration) technique could be personnel, physical, hardware, software, or procedural.

3. Threat Agent

The evaluation of the threat agent is dominated by physical environmental failure, insider attacks and external unauthorized access.

Environmental Factors Although it is common sense, one should remember to account for environmental factors. Some areas are more prone to certain environmental influences and natural disasters than others. Some types of disasters, such as fire, are not geographically dependent, while others, such as tornadoes and floods, can be anticipated on a more regular basis in specific areas. In addition to the natural disasters, attention should be paid to the danger of mechanical and electrical equipment failure and the interruption of electrical power.

Authorized users Authorized users and personnel engaged in supporting operations can be considered as potential threats when they exceed their privileges and authorities or commit errors, thus affecting the ability of the system to perform its mission. Personnel granted access to systems or occupying positions of special trust and having the capability or opportunity to abuse their access authorities, privileges, or trusts should be considered as potential threats.

Unauthorized users An unauthorized user can be anyone not engaged in supporting operations that, by design, attempts to interrupt the productivity of the system or operation either overtly or covertly. Overt methods could include outright acts of sabotage affecting hardware and associated equipment, as well as subtle efforts of destruction, which could be accomplished through the manipulation of software, both systems and application.

4. Techniques

We classify techniques into physical, personnel (related), hardware, software, and procedural.

Physical Physical penetration implies use of a physical means to gain entry into restricted areas such as building, compound room, or any other designated area.

Personnel Penetration techniques and methods generally deal with the subverting of personnel authorized some degree of access and privilege regarding a system, either as users or operators (operators would include system-analysts, programmers, input/output schedulers, etc.). They can be recruited by a threat agent and used to penetrate the system, operation or facility, or they themselves can become disaffected or motivated to mount an attack.

Hardware Attacks can be mounted against hardware for the purpose of using the hardware as a means of subverting or denying use of the system. A physical attack against the equipment, a bug implanted within a hardware controller, or an attack against the supporting utilities, are means of subverting the system by using the characteristics of the hardware. Hardware, as used in this category, generally includes any piece of equipment that is part of the system, (i.e., the mainframe, peripherals, communications controllers, or modems). It also includes indirect system support equipment, such as power supplies, air conditioning systems, backup power, etc.

Software Software penetration techniques can be directed against system software, application programs, or utility routines. Software attacks can range from discreet alterations that are subtly imposed for the purpose of compromising the system, to less discreet changes intended to produce results such as destruction of data or other important systems features.

Procedural Authorized or unauthorized users can penetrate the system due to lack or inadequacy of controls, or failure to adhere to existing controls. Examples of procedural penetration include former employees retaining and using valid passwords, unauthorized personnel picking up output, and users browsing without being detected due to failure to diligently check audit trails.

At a more detailed level, the ISO 7498-2 Standard (1989), lists five security control measures to combat these threats: 1) Authentication, 2) Access Control, 3) Data confidentiality, 4) Data integrity, and 5) Non-repudiation. This classification is widely accepted among computer security experts, and the authors also recommend them as good control measures. These security measures along with agents and techniques are shown in Figure 2. One can use this figure to classify threats (agents and the techniques) to e-commerce and security measures to confront these threats. For example, access control is one of the security measures to confront the threats that may be caused by an unauthorized user through software. In total, there are $5 \times 3 \times 5$ combinations of threat technique, agent, and security measure (see Figure 1); however not all of these combinations are applicable. For example, non-repudiation cannot be a security measure for the threats caused by environmental factors or by a procedural technique. We are using this three-dimensional view of threat agents, techniques, and security control measures for a better quantitative assessment and management of security risk.

5. Risk Management System

We believe that the cost of an information system security incident on a company has to be measured in terms of the impact on its business;

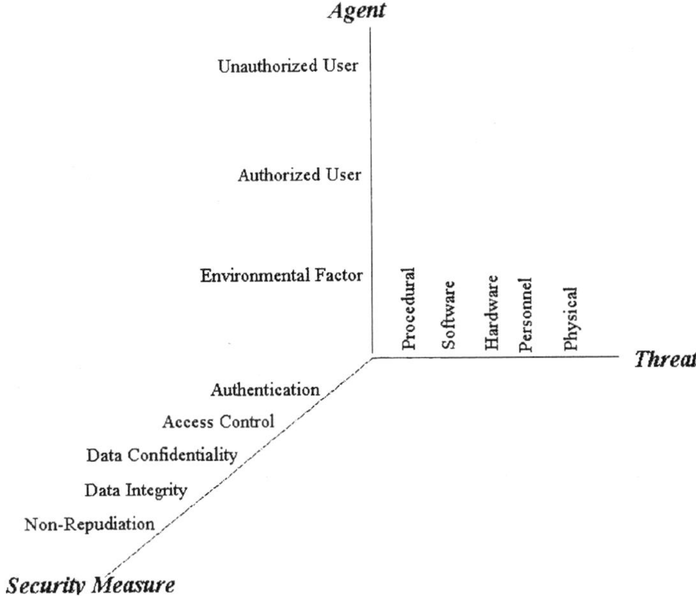

Figure 7.1. Combination of agents, techniques and security measures

hence identical incidents in two different companies could have different costs. To evaluate these costs and measure the impact of a security incident on a company, we need a systematic approach and a comprehensive risk management system. Such a comprehensive security risk evaluation system is currently under development at the College of Computing, Georgia Institute of Technology. This system with five stages is aimed at helping managers to identify the vulnerabilities of their companies and to select the countermeasures and it includes: Resource and application value analysis, Vulnerability and risk analysis, Computation of losses due to threats and benefits of countermeasures, Selection of Countermeasures and Evaluation of implementation alternatives (Farahmand et al. 2004).

References

Campbell, K., Gordon, L. A., Loeb, M. P., Zhou, L. (2003). *The Economic Cost of Publicly Announced Information Security Breaches: Empirical Evidence from the Stock Market*, Journal of Computer Security, Vol. 11, issue 3.

Cavusoglu, H., Mishra B., Raghunthan S. (Feb. 2002). *The Effect of Internet Security Breach Announcements on Market Value of Breached*

Firms and Internet Security Developers, The University of Texas at Dallas.

Farahmand, F., Navathe, S. B., Sharp, G. B, Enslow, P. H. (2004). *A Management Perspective on Risk of Security Threats to Information Systems.* To appear in the *Journal of Information Technology & Management.*

Farahmand, F., Navathe, S. B., Sharp, G. B., Enslow, P. H. (2003). *Managing Vulnerabilities of Information Systems to Security Incidents*", 5th International Conference on Electronic Commerce, ICEC 2003, ACM, Pittsburgh, PA, Sept. 30-Oct. 3, pp. 348-354.

ISO. *(1989). Information Processing Systems – Open Systems Interconnection – Basic Reference Model, Part 2: Security Architecture, ISO 7498-2*

Power, R. (2002). *Computer Security Issues & Trends, 2002 CSI/FBI Computer Crime and Security Survey*, Vol. VIII, No. 1, CSI.

Stonebumer, G., Goguen, A., and Feringa, A. (2001). *Risk Management Guide for Information Technology Systems,* NIST Special Publications 800-30.

Wood, Charles C., et. al. (1987). *Computer Security; A comprehensive Control Checklist*, John Wiley & Sons.

Chapter 8

THE ECONOMIC CONSEQUENCES OF SHARING SECURITY INFORMATION

Esther Gal-Or
University of Pittsburgh
esther@katz.pitt.edu

Anindya Ghose
Carnegie Mellon University
aghose@andrew.cmu.edu

Using a game-theoretic model, we point out how firm and industry characteristics affect the incentives for information sharing amongst competing firms and their impact on firms' profits.

1. Introduction

The increasing pervasiveness and ubiquity of the Internet has provided cyber attackers with more opportunities to misappropriate or corrupt an organization's data resources. As e-commerce continues to grow, so does cyber crime. According to Jupiter Media Metrix, cyber-security issues could potentially cost e-businesses almost $25 billion by 2006 - up from $5.5 billion in 2001.[1] There are many well known examples of cyber-hacking. Citibank lost business when it went public with the news that they had been hacked.[2] Egghead.com faced a massive backlash from its customers after being hacked in 2000 by online intruders which led to its eventual bankruptcy filing. A security breach at Travelocity in 2001 exposed the personal information of thousands of customers who had participated in a promotion. Other victims in the recent past, include Yahoo, AOL and E-Bay. Not just restricted to the online world, this

[1] "Privacy Worries Plague E-Biz", http://cyberatlas.internet.com/markets/retailing/article.html

[2] "Information Sharing-Reactions are Mixed to Government Overtures," http://networking.earthweb.com/netsecur/article, 06/17/02.

trend has been pervasive in the physical world too where Microsoft and NASA, amongst others have been targeted. Hence corporations in many industries have recognized a strong need to beef up their cyber-security against potentially debilitating attacks and to treat computer security like a strategic marketing initiative, rather than a compliance burden.

For a while now, it has been recognized that a key factor required to improve information security is the gathering, analysis and sharing of information related to actual, as well as unsuccessful attempts at, computer security breaches. In this regard, the U.S. federal government has encouraged the establishment of industry-based Information Sharing and Analysis Centers (ISACs). ISACs facilitate sharing of information relating to members' efforts to enhance and to protect the security of the cyber infrastructure. In January 2001, nineteen of the nation's leading high tech companies announced the formation of a new Information Technology Information Sharing and Analysis Center (IT-ISAC) to co-operate on cyber security issues. Using the shared information, the IT-ISAC disseminates an integrated view of relevant information system vulnerabilities, threats, and incidents, to its members. It also shares best security practices and solutions among its members, and thus provides an impetus for continuous improvement in security products. Obviously, such mutual collaboration through information sharing is eventually intended for increases in the demand of security enhancing software and hardware.

Revealing information about security breaches entails both costs and benefits for the disclosing firm. The costs can accrue from loss of market share or stock market value from negative publicity (Campbell, et al. 2003). In a 2002 report by Jupiter Media Metrix, IT executives revealed they were more concerned with the impact of online security problems on consumer confidence and trust in e-business than the actual financial losses of physical infrastructure. Many companies have cited the FOIA (Freedom of Information Sharing Act) as a roadblock to the public-private partnership intended by ISACs. According to firms, the dual role played by the government – customer and regulator, will remain an obstacle to private sector cooperation. Basically, companies are reluctant to give the government information on attacks and vulnerabilities that regulators may use against them later on.

One can think of losses from a scenario in which a competing firm or a third party can leverage the shared information and attempt to hack the databases of the breach reporting firms or malign its reputation by anonymously reporting it to the public. In January 2003, Next Generation Software Services (NGSS) claimed that CERT (Computer Emergency Response Team), the government-sponsored Internet security reporting center passed vulnerability information to third parties uninvolved with a problem about which NGSS had notified CERT.

NGSS felt that this was a direct violation of trust, as the information was leaked to potential competitors of NGSS and it eventually severed ties with CERT.

Other possibilities could include the hacking of the security breach correspondence between an ISAC and its member firms. The recent case of the leakage of a fatal flaw in an Internet software package from Sun Microsystems to a public mailing list proves this. The hacker posted an advisory containing the bug's specifics to the Full-Disclosure security mailing list. He also posted a warning about a separate security flaw discovered by researchers at MIT that wasn't supposed to be published until June. The hacker apparently intercepted both documents from CERT. According to CERT however, intruders may have hacked into systems operated by any of the dozens of affected vendors who received advance copies of the advisories. Irrespective of which party was hacked, the bottomline was that Sun Microsystems took a big hit in reputation.

However there are several positive aspects to reporting and sharing security breaches. The benefit from mutual sharing of actual or attempted security breaches can be partitioned into a private firm specific benefit and an external industry level benefit. This private benefit can be borne either directly by the prevention of further security breach and fraud losses in future (e.g., identifying and repairing vulnerabilities in their information security systems) or indirectly via increased sales emanating from a better security reputation and goodwill amongst consumers (NIPC, 2001). By reporting a security breach to central monitoring or law enforcement agency, a firm can send a strong message to its customers that the company takes information security seriously, is committed to developing rigorous information security procedures designed to protect sensitive information, and upon detection of security breaches can take all necessary steps to mitigate damage from a future breach (Schenk and Schenk, 2002). Such actions can boost the consumer comfort level while dealing with such firms, in terms of alleviating their "perceived security risk".

One can envision a situation in which customers of the ISAC members are many of the big corporations who buy goods or services from other firms, on a regular basis. For instance, in the IT-ISAC, the customers of security vendors like Symantec and Computer Associates include big corporations like Proctor & Gamble, Lockheed Martin and Halliburton and hundreds of other firms. As corporations perceive improvement in the effectiveness of cyber security products – accruing from the information sharing behavior of security vendors (who are members of the IT-ISAC) – the overall customer confidence in stopping or apprehending cyber perpetrators increases, leading to increased demand for IT security products.

Hence, information security investments and sharing of security information can involve spillovers, which result in positive externalities for the industry as a whole. The industry benefits can accrue when enhancement in customers' trust in transacting with a particular firm also expands the overall market size within the industry. A number of industries have experienced positive demand shocks by successful attempts at cross-selling and upselling, as a consequence of mitigating consumers' fears of privacy and information security related issues. These benefits can indeed be significant in the realm of B2C e-commerce. For example, Amazon's pioneering efforts in protecting the integrity of customer data, whether individuals or merchants also has had a positive ripple-effect on the size of potential market of its competitors like Barnes & Nobles and E-Bay. It has led to an increase in online purchases as consumers' confidence in revealing credit card numbers and other personal information has grown considerably. In the online financial services industry, Ameritrade and DLJDirect have been able to reap the benefits of an increase in the customer comfort level in completing financial transactions on the Internet. In this regard, they have acknowledged the increased investment in security and privacy-enhancing technologies made by competitors like Charles Schwab and E-Trade as a potential factor for an increase in the online traffic. As pointed out above, sales of cyber security products have catapulted over the years, as security vendors become increasingly successful in producing an effective arsenal of weapons. One of the main purposes of this paper is to focus on such indirect "demand enhancing" benefits of information sharing alliances.

Research Questions & Prior Literature

For any organizational arrangement focused on the reporting and dissemination of information related to security breaches, there are a number of interesting economic issues that will affect achievement of this goal. We seek to address the following questions in this paper. What are the incentives for competing firms in a given industry, to share information about security breaches through a central organization? Does the degree of competitiveness in an industry hamper the economic incentives to fully reveal information about security breaches? Do smaller firms gain more from information sharing than larger firms? How does industry size impact such sharing behavior amongst competing firms? What is the nature of the relationship between investment in security enhancing technologies and the sharing of information pertaining to cyber-security attacks? Do spillover effects debar firms from sharing information and result in sub-optimal levels of technology investment or do they promote sharing and lead to increased technology investments?

Prior literature which is of relevance includes that of information sharing by (Fried, 1984, Gal-Or, 1985, Shapiro, 1986), the literature on mode of conduct and strategic effects such as (Bulow, Geanakoplos and Klemperer, 1985, Gal-Or, 1986) and extensive economics based literature on joint ventures such as (d' Aspremont and Jacquemin, 1988). Recent papers dealing with the economics of information security include (Anderson, 2001) who discusses various perverse incentives in the information security domain. Varian, 2002 analyzes the free rider problem in the context of system reliability. Gordon and Loeb, 2002 present a framework to determine the optimal amount to invest to protect a given set of information. Gordon, Loeb and Lucyshyn, 2003 raise the issue of the need to study the economic benefits of security information sharing. They show that sharing can benefit firms by reducing the costs incurred in security expenditures. Schecter and Smith, 2003 provide an analysis of the benefits of information sharing to prevent security breaches.

2. Economic Modelling

To answer these questions, we analyze a market consisting of two firms producing a differentiated product in a two-stage non-cooperative game. In the first stage, firms simultaneously choose optimal levels of security technology investment and information sharing levels. In the second stage they choose prices simultaneously. We consider a Subgame perfect equilibrium of this game using backward induction. We normalize the amount of security breach information being shared such that it always lies between 0 and 1. Costs of production are assumed to be symmetric for both firms and are normalized to zero, without loss of generality. We explicitly model "leakage costs" of sharing security information and assume that these costs are increasing and convex in the amount of security information shared. These leakage costs affect demand adversely. The potential costs of security information leakage can have a snowball effect, accruing from the resultant loss of market share and stock market value from negative publicity (Campbell, et al. 2003).

In a scenario where investments in security enhancing technologies by one firm can lead to an overall demand expansion in the industry, thereby benefiting the competing firms as well, one can envision the possibility of "demand side spillover" effects. We account for such spillovers, and subsequently also consider "cost-side spillover" effects which lead to technological cost reductions.

The demand of each firm depends on its own price and the price of its competitor. Each firm obtains information about the level of security investment and information being shared from the central association and uses this in its pricing decision. In this context, we examine how the effect of information on profits depends upon firm and market characteristics. The demand functions for the two firms are assumed to be linear in self and cross-price effects (McGuire and Staelin, 1983). This particular demand model has been used extensively in marketing and economics and there is some research suggesting that comparative statics derived from simpler models may often hold more generally (Milgrom, 1994). We initially assume that the costs of investing in technologies which promote cyber-security are independent of the volume of sales but increasing in the amount of technology invested, and that these costs are increasing and convex. Subsequently, we also consider variable costs of security technologies which increase with the volume of sales.

3. Results

Result 1:
(i) A higher level of security breach information sharing by one firm leads to a higher level of security breach information sharing by the other firm.
(ii) A higher level of information sharing by one firm leads to a higher level of security technology investment by the other firm.
(iii) Technology investment and information sharing act as strategic complements in equilibrium.

Our analysis reveals that the reaction functions are upward sloping, that is, an increase in the investment in security enhancing technologies by one firm induces a higher level of information sharing by the other firm. The two inputs act as strategic complements. This is evident from the fact that increase in profits with increase in technology investment is higher for higher levels of information sharing. Hence one firm responds to less aggressive play by the competing firm, by being less aggressive itself.

We would like to point out that there are two effects here: a direct effect and a strategic effect. The direct effect of increased information sharing results in increased demand (market expansion) for both firms. We can also isolate the strategic effect which promotes higher prices with higher levels of information sharing. Thus, the strategic effect alleviates price competition, allowing firms to increase prices and make higher profits.

Result 2 : *(i) As the degree of product substitutability increases, the extent of information sharing and amount of security technology investment by both firms, increases.*
(ii) A lower level of "demand - side" spillover discourages a higher level of information sharing.
(iii) A lower level of firm loyalty leads to lower levels of security information sharing and security technology investment.

Quite interestingly, to the extent that product substitutability is indicative of the degree of competition in an industry, we find that a higher level of competitiveness in the industry actually leads to higher levels of information sharing about security breaches and increased investment in security enhancing technologies by both firms. Firms generally respond to increased competition with aggressive price cuts. Since increases in security information sharing and security technology investments help in alleviating price competition, in equilibrium both firms raise their investment and sharing levels as competition intensifies.

We also find that a higher spillover effect between the two firms is not detrimental to the firms since it promotes a higher level of information sharing. Increased spillover shifts the demand curve out which enables the other firm to increase its price. This facilitates less aggressive pricing by the technology investing firm.

We highlight that a steeper demand schedule, lowers a firm's propensity to invest in security technology and share security information. A steeper slope implies that each firm sells fewer units of the product for a given level of the equilibrium prices, i.e. consumers are more price sensitive. Smaller quantities imply, in turn, that the marginal return to any kind of technology investment is more limited. As a result, the firms have reduced incentives to invest in enhanced security technology. Further, the strategic complementarity between technology investment and information sharing implies also that the extent of sharing declines when demand schedules are steeper.

Result 3 : *Security breach information sharing and security technology investment levels increases with firm size and with industry size.*

This suggests that sharing information is more valuable to larger firms and in bigger industries. Note, however, that whether or not a firm is large is measured not in absolute terms, but how large it is relative to the other firms in its industry. Our analysis suggests that larger firms may in fact assign a higher value to such information because the marginal benefit-cost ratio of sharing information, is higher for them than for smaller firms. This is similar to the intuition that a monopolist benefits more from cost-reducing innovations in R&D than a firm competing in a duopoly, because it can extract a higher proportion of the surplus from the market.

How critical is the nature of the cost function? Of late, organizations of all types and sizes are considering outsourcing the management of their security infrastructure. If there is managed security firm that is doing it as an outsourced contract, for different levels of service or for a larger number of machines etc., once could imagine a scenario where the firm also incurs some additional costs which are affected by the volume of sales. As the demand grows and firms' IT infrastructure grows, so would costs like those incurred for additional servers, software license fees, service agreements and importantly for associated security weapons like firewalls, intrusion detection systems, access control systems etc. In an extension of the basic model, we analyze the impact of volume dependent costs of technology on firms' optimal profits and strategies.

Having analyzed the impact of spillovers on the demand side, we now also consider spillover effects on the cost side.[3] Consider a situation in which a spillover in cost reduction occurs as a result of the knowledge accruing from the competitor's information sharing. This can happen when disclosure of vulnerabilities in a particular security technology by one firm leads the other firm to invest less in that technology. A direct consequence of such information sharing would be preemptive cost savings. Suppose the impact of sharing information by one firm is that spillover effects lead to a reduction in marginal costs for the other firm. Hence the possibility of free riding or under investment becomes plausible in this situation.

Result 4: *When the costs of security technology investment are affected by the volume of sales, and there are "cost side spillovers" , an increase in the spillover parameter has ambiguous implications on the propensity to share security information or invest in security technology for both firms.*

Basically, changes in the spillover parameter introduce two countervailing effects. An increase in the parameter serves the purpose of making a firm's competitor more efficient by reducing its cost coefficient. This enables the competitor to price more aggressively. If a given firm increases its level of information shared, it further increases the cost efficiency of the competitor, which acts to the disadvantage of the firm. Since the improved cost efficiency precipitates further price competition, both firms respond strategically by reducing their levels of information sharing. On the other hand, an increase in the parameter also increases the profit margin of each firm, thus providing greater incentives for increased investment in technology and information sharing.

4. Conclusion

The U.S. federal government has encouraged the formation of Information Sharing & Analysis Centers (ISACs), with the goal of helping to protect critical infrastructure assets that are largely owned and operated by the private sector. This has been witnessed in industries such as banking & finance, IT, chemicals, oil & gas, electricity, etc. The underlying assumption is that such centrally coordinated information sharing organizations would facilitate the alignment of goals for both the private sector and the federal government, which in turn would improve the security of cyber-infrastructure assets. However, all sectors do not have a fully established ISAC, and in those sectors that do, there is mixed participation. Specifically, five recently reviewed ISACs showed differ-

[3]Introducing cost-side spillovers when the cost of the technology is independent of the volume of sales does not affect our main results.

ent levels of progress in implementing the PDD 63 suggested activities. These were the IT, Telecommunications, Energy, Water and Electricity ISACs. Hence, the government felt it important to identify economic incentives to encourage the desired information sharing behavior in IT security (Dacey, 2003a).

Our results point out that there are indeed some very strong economic incentives for firms to indulge in such security breach information sharing. These incentives, become stronger with increases in the firm size, industry size and degree of competition. Importantly we point out that the nature of the cost function plays a pivotal role in determining whether spillovers are beneficial or detrimental to the firms' interests. It is important to note that while firms might gain unambiguously by sharing higher levels of information and investing more in information-security related technologies, the resultant increase in prices might have an adverse effect on consumer surplus. This can have important implications for anti-trust issues and form a potential legal hurdle to information sharing. ISACs are not intended to restrain trade by restricting output, increasing prices, or otherwise inhibiting competition, on which the antitrust laws generally focus. We are exploring some of these issues in our ongoing research. In addition, empirical studies could address the role of government intervention at some stage in the form of optimal incentives or subsidies to prevent firms from increasing prices.

References

Anderson, Ross. (2001). *Why Information Security is Hard : An Economic Perspective*, Proceedings of 17th Annual Computer Security Applications Conference, Dec. 10-14.

Bulow, J., J. Geanakoplos and P. Klemperer. (1985). *Multimarket Oligopoly: Strategic Substitutes and Complements*,The Journal of Political Economy, Vol 93, Issue 3,pp 488-511.

Campbell,K., L. Gordon, M. Loeb and L. Zhou. (2003). *The Economic Cost of Publicly Announced Information Security Breaches: Empirical Evidence from the Stock Market* forthcoming, Journal of Computer Security.

d'Aspremont, C. and A. Jacquemin. (1988). *Cooperative and Non-cooperative R&D in a Duopoly with Spillovers*, American Economic Review, 78: 1133-1137.

Fried, D. (1984). *Incentives for Information Production and Disclosure in a Duopolistic Environment*, The Quarterly Journal of Economics, Vol. 99, pp. 367-381.

Gal-Or, E. (1985).*Information Sharing in Oligopoly*, Econometrica, Vol. 3, pp. 329-343.

Gal-Or, E. (1986). *First mover and second mover advantages*, International Economic Review, 26 (3) pp. 649653.

Gordon, L.A. and M. P. Loeb. (2002). *The Economics of Investment in Information Security*, ACM Transactions on Information and System Security, Vol. 5, (4) November, pp. 438-457.

Gordon, L. A., M. P. Loeb, and W. Lucyshyn. (2003). *Sharing Information on Computer Systems Security: An Economic Analysis*, Journal of Accounting and Public Policy, Vol 22, (6).

McGuire, Timothy M., Richard P. Staelin. (1983). *An industry equilibrium analysis of downstream vertical integration*, Marketing Science, Vol. 2, pp. 161192.

Milgrom, P. (1994). *Comparing optima: Do simplifying assumptions affect conclusions?*, Journal of Political Economy, 102(June), pp. 607 615.

(NIPC) National Infrastructure Protection Center (2001). *Information Sharing & Analysis Centers*, May 15th.

Schecter, Stuart E., and Michael D. Smith. (2003). *How Much Security is Enough to Stop a Thief? The Economics of Outsider Theft via Computer Systems Networks*, Proceedings of the Financial Cryptography Conference, Guadeloupe, January 27-30.

Schenk, M. and M. Schenk. (2002). *Defining the Value of Strategic Security*, Secure Busines Quarterly, Vol. 1(1), pp 1-6.

Shapiro, C. (1986). *Exchange of Cost Information in Oligopoly*, Review of Economic Studies, Vol. 53 (1986), pp. 433-446.

Varian, H. (2002). *System Reliability and Free Riding*, Proceedings of the First WEIS, UC Berkeley, May 16-17.

Chapter 9

THE ECONOMICS OF INFORMATION SECURITY INVESTMENT

Lawrence A. Gordon and Martin P. Loeb
University of Maryland

To maximize the expected benefit from investment to protect information, a firm should spend only a small fraction of the expected loss due to a security breach.

Security of a computer-based information system should, by design, protect the confidentiality, integrity, and availability of the system (e.g., see NIST 1995, p.5). Given the information-intense characteristics of a modern economy (e.g., the Internet and World Wide Web), it should be no surprise to learn that information security is a growing spending priority among most companies. This growth in spending is occurring in a variety of areas including software to detect viruses, firewalls, sophisticated encryption techniques, intrusion detection systems, automated data backup, and hardware devices (Larsen 1999). The above not withstanding, a recent study by the Computer Security Institute, with the participation of the Federal Bureau of Investigation, reported that "Ninety-one percent of respondents... detected computer security breaches within the last twelve months" (Power 2001, p. 33). Moreover, the study found that (for those organizations that provided loss estimates) the losses averaged over $2 million per organization (Power 2001, p.33). Hence, it would appear that many firms are not adequately investing in information security. In this regard, based on a large information security survey, KPMG (2000, p. 1) concluded that, "Our overall finding is that information security requirements are not being adequately addressed, especially in the new fast moving, global, e-business environment. This will leave some organizations critically exposed."

The importance of information security in a computer-based environment has resulted in a large stream of research that focuses on the technical defenses (e.g., encryption, access control, and firewalls) associated with protecting information (e.g., Anderson, 1972; Wiseman, 1986; Simmons, 1994; Muralidhar, et al., 1995; Denning and Branstad, 1996; Sandhu, et al., 1996; Schneier, 1996; Pfleeger, 1997; Larsen, 1999; and

Peyravian et al., 1999;Sandhu, et al., 1999; Osborn, et al., 2000) and intrusion detection systems (Denning, 1987; Daniels and Spafford, 1999; Vigna and Kemmerer, 1999; Axelsson, 2000; and Frincke, 2000). In addition, research has been rapidly developing which focuses on the behavioral aspects of reducing information security breaches (e.g., Straub, 1990; Loch et al., 1992; Straub and Welke, 1998). In contrast, research focusing on the economic aspects of information security is rather sparse. The work that does exist on, or related to economic aspects of information security provides little generic guidance on how to derive the proper amount to invest on such security (e.g., see Millen, 1992; Luotonen, 1993; McKnight et al., 1997; and Finne, 1998; Jones, 1998; Buzzard, 1999; Hoo, 2000; Anderson, 2001; Meadows, 2001; Powers, 2001).

The purpose of this paper is to derive an economic model that determines the optimal amount to invest in information security. Accordingly, information security in our model may be broadly interpreted. Our model is applicable to investments related to various information security goals, such as protecting the confidentiality, availability, authenticity, non-repudiation, and integrity of information[1]. Although there is often a conflict among these goals, the model we present does not address this conflict. Rather, we construct a model that specifically considers how the vulnerability of information and the potential loss from such vulnerability affect the optimal amount of resources that should be devoted to securing that information. Without a careful analysis of the effect of vulnerability on information security, intuition might suggest that, for a given potential loss and a given threat level, the optimal amount to spend on such security is an increasing function of the information's vulnerability. Our analysis demonstrates that this may, or may not, be the case[2]. We demonstrate that under certain sets of assumptions concerning the relationship between vulnerability and the marginal productivity of the security investment, the optimal investment in information security may either be strictly increasing or first increase and then decrease as vulnerability increases. Thus, under plausible assumptions, investment in information security may well be justified only for a midrange of information vulnerabilities. That is, little or no information security

[1]Moreover, our model could be used to gain insights for the optimal protection of assets other than information

[2]2. This is in contrast with earlier literature, such as Pfleeger (1997, Chapter 10), which discuss the importance of vulnerability in the decision to invest in information security, but does not examine the effects of changes in vulnerability on the optimal investment in information security. Previous papers on information security usually combine vulnerability with the potential dollar loss associated with such vulnerability, to come up with the notion of risk (e.g., Straub and Welke, 1998; Finne, 1999). Thus, earlier literature entangles the relationship between information vulnerability and the proper amount to spend on preventing such vulnerability

is economically justified for extremely high, as well as extremely low, levels of vulnerability.

Our analysis also indicates that, even within the range of justifiable investments in information security, the maximum amount a risk-neutral[3] firm should spend is only a fraction of the expected loss due to security breaches. For two broad classes of security breach probability functions, this fraction never exceeds 37% of the expected loss. For most cases, however, this fraction is substantially below the 37% level. Given that organizations possess limited resources, our analysis provides managers with a framework for considering decisions regarding the allocation of scarce information security dollars.

The remainder of the paper is organized as follows. In the second section, vulnerability is formally defined and the general model is presented. The third section contains an analysis of how vulnerability affects the optimal level of investment in information security, given the potential loss associated with such vulnerability. The fourth, and final, section of the paper offers some concluding comments.

1. The Model

We consider a one-period model[4] of a firm contemplating the provision of additional security to protect a given information set. The information set could take many forms, such as a list of customers, an accounts payable ledger, a strategic plan, or company website. The increased security could be with respect to protecting the confidentiality, integrity, authenticity, non-repudiation or availability, to authorized users of the information set. An information set is characterized by three parameters: λ, t, and v, representing, respectively, the loss conditioned on a breach occurring, the probability of a threat occurring, and the vulnerability, defined in the model as the probability that a threat once realized (i.e., an attack) would be successful.

The parameter λ represents the monetary loss to the firm caused by a breach of security of the information set. This loss could be due to a security breach related to confidentiality (e.g., the loss due to the strategic information becoming available to competitors or the fraudulent use of credit card information by hackers), integrity (e.g., the loss due to

[3]If someone is risk-neutral, it means that they are indifferent to investments that have the same expected value, even though the investments may have varying amounts of risk. Thus, a risk-neutral decision-maker would be indifferent to Investment #1 that generates either a net return of $200,000 or a net loss of $100,000 each with probability of.5, and Investment #2 that generates a net return of either $40,000 or $60,000 each with probability of.5, as both investments have an expected net return of $50,000. Notice that Investment #1 has more risk (i.e., larger standard deviation around the expected value) than Investment # 2, and yet the two investments are being considered equal. Someone who is risk averse would require a higher expected value for an investment with a higher risk.

[4]In one-period economic models, all decisions and outcomes occur in a simultaneous instant. Thus, dynamic aspects, such as a first-mover advantage or the time value of money, are not considered

the firm making faulty decisions based on data altered by an intruder), or denial of services (e.g., loss due to missed sales from authorized users who were denied legitimate access). Although λ would normally depend on the use of the information (by the firm itself, by competitors, or by hackers) and would change over time, for simplicity we take λ to be a fixed amount as estimated by the firm (e.g., the present value of lost profits from current and future lost sales). Even though we initially assume that this loss is a fixed value, we will investigate how changes in the value of the loss affect the firm's security investment decision. However, we assume λ is finite and less than some very large number, say M[5]. Thus, the model is not intended to cover protection of national/public assets or other circumstances where a loss could be catastrophic.

The probability of an attempted breach of the given information set is denoted by $t \in [0, 1]$, and we call t the threat probability. We make the simplifying assumption that there is a single threat to an information set[6]. The parameter v is used to denote the information set's vulnerability, by which we mean the probability that without additional security, a threat that is realized will result in the information set being breached and the loss, λ, occurring. Our view of threats and vulnerabilities is consistent with the argument of Littlewood et al. (1993, p. 228) concerning "the desirability of a probability-based framework for operational security measurement." Since v is a probability, $v \in [0, 1]$.

Typically, the threat to an information set and the information set's vulnerability would lie in the interior (i.e., $0 < t < 1$ and $0 < v < 1$). Note that the information is completely invulnerable when $v = 0$. One can consider an information set on a computer buried in concrete thirty feet underground to be completely invulnerable. Of course this state of invulnerability (and perfect confidentiality) is achieved at the cost of having the information set become completely inaccessible[7]. Similarly, if $v = 1$, the information set is completely vulnerable. Such information sets, like last quarter's statement of earnings (for a publicly traded firm) or the retail price of a specific product, may be viewed as public information. For a given information set, the probability of the loss occurring (sometimes called the risk of the loss) is the product of the vulnerability and the threat probabilities. Thus, the product $vt\lambda$ represents the expected loss (conditioned on no investment in information security) as-

[5]5. For a catastrophic loss, *lambda* $\geq M$, the assumption of risk-neutrality becomes unrealistic. In the language of economics, the disutility of a catastrophic loss is so large that decision makers would prefer the expected value of the gamble rather than risking a loss of λ.

[6]Allowing multiple threats significantly increases the complexity of the model. However, there is no reason to believe that a more complex economic model would yield additional insights. In fact, it is often argued that clearer insights are provided by models that are less rather than more complex. In this vein, Varian (1997, p. 4) writes, "A model is supposed to reveal the essence of what is going on: your model should be reduced to just those pieces that are required to make it work."

[7]Hence, this is one illustration of the trade-offs among the goals of confidentiality, integrity, and availability referred to earlier

sociated with the given information set[8]. Thus, for any positive threat $t > 0$, the expected loss increases with the vulnerability.

Of course, firms can and do invest in information security[9]. In general, one would expect a firm to have more influence over an information set's vulnerability than over the threats to the information set[10]. For the purposes of our model, we make the simplifying assumption that firms can influence the vulnerability of an information set by investing in information security, but the firm cannot invest to reduce the threat. We therefore fix the threat probability at $t > 0$, and focus on the firm's choice of the level of investment to reduce the vulnerability of their information[11]. Since the threat probability is held constant, for notational simplicity we define $L = t\lambda$. For expositional ease, we will refer to L as the loss or potential loss associated with the information set.

Let $z > 0$ denote the monetary (e.g., dollar) investment in security to protect the given information set. Thus, z is measured in the same units (i.e., dollars) used to measure the potential loss L. The purpose of the investment z is to lower the probability that the information set will be breached. Let $S(z, v)$ denote the probability that an information set with vulnerability v will be breached, conditional on the realization of a threat and given that the firm has made an information security investment of z to protect that information. We refer to the function $S(z, v)$ as the security breach probability function and to its value at a particular level of z and v as the security breach probability.

As is common with nearly all economic models, we abstract from reality and assume that postulated functions are sufficiently smooth and well behaved. This is done so that an optimization problem, which can be solved with basic tools of calculus, can be used to represent the economic phenomenon. In our model, we assume that the function $S(z, v)$ is continuously twice differentiable. Of course, in reality, discrete investments in new security technologies are often necessary to get any incremental result. Such discrete investments result in discontinuities. However, even though the commitment to invest in security may be made in discrete

[8] As noted in the previous footnote, the calculation of the expected loss becomes more complicated when multiple threats are considered. Assume for simplicity that a threat that results in a breach causes a loss of λ, but that there can be no additional losses from a second breach (once your shot dead, additional threats are irrelevant). Now suppose there are two (independent) threats occurring with probability $t_1 = 0.8$ and $t_2 = 0.9$ and suppose the vulnerability probability is $v = 0.1$. Then, the probability of a loss (calculated using a simple decision tree) will be $0.1628 < vt_1 + vt_2$.

[9] Investments in information security have many of the same characteristics of what firms usually consider capital expenditures. This fact notwithstanding, firms usually treat an inordinate portion of the costs of information security as operating expenditures. Although beyond the scope of this paper, such treatment raises its own set of interesting question.

[10] Of course, this may not always be the case. For example, if each employee having access to an information set is viewed as a threat, the threat can be reduced by restricting employee access.

[11] Although we hold t fixed, our model allows us to see how changes in the value of the parameter t (and the parameter λ) would change the optimal security investment decision.

pieces, the actual expenditures can often be broken down into small increments. Furthermore, some information investments can be reversed (e.g., additional security personnel can be fired and purchased equipment and software can be sold). Thus, a smooth approximation of the security investment represents a reasonable first approach to gaining insights into the problem of determining the optimal investment in information security[12].

The nature of information vulnerability and information security leads us to consider the following assumptions concerning $S(z,v)$:

> **A1.** $S(z,0) = 0$ for all z. That is, if the information set is completely invulnerable, then it will remain perfectly protected for any amount of information security investment, including a zero investment.
>
> **A2.** For all v, $S(0,v) = v$. That is, if there is no investment in information security, the probability of a security breach, conditioned on the realization of a threat, is the information set's inherent vulnerability, v.
>
> **A3.** For all $v \in (0,1)$, and all z, $S_z(z,v) < 0$ and $S_{zz}(z,v) > 0$, where S_z denotes the partial derivative with respect to z and S_{zz} denotes the partial derivative of S_z with respect to z. That is, as the investment in security increases, the information is made more secure, but at a decreasing rate. Furthermore, we assume that for all $v \in (0,1)$, $\lim_{z\to\infty} S(z,v) \to 0$, as $z \to \infty$, so by investing sufficiently in security, the probability of a security breach, t times $S(z,v)$, can be made to be arbitrarily close to zero.

Note that from A3 that even a very small expenditure for information security will reduce the probability of a security breach. This may be due to the fact that there are no fixed costs of information security. An alternative interpretation of the model views the investment in information security as an incremental investment beyond security measures already in place. A firm may have an Information Technology Director and other IT staff who devote limited time to security issues. By allocating a bit more time (and hence money) to security issues, it would be reasonable to expect some decrease in the probability of a breach. Similarly, most firms have some security measures (e.g., firewalls, intrusion detection systems, anti-virus software) in place and are considering incremental expenditures to enhance or supplement these measures. Also, note that A3 implies that no finite investment in information security can make a vulnerable ($v > 0$) information set perfectly secure. The analysis

[12]By making such simplifying assumptions, economists have been able to gain powerful insights that have proven valid in more general settings.

that follows assumes that the security breach probability functions meet assumptions A1–A3.

In order to determine the amount to invest in information security, a risk-neutral firm would compare the expected benefits of the investment with cost of the investment[13]. The expected benefits of an investment in information security, denoted as EBIS, are equal to the reduction in the firm's expected loss attributable to the extra security. That is:

$$EBIS(z) = [v - S(z, v)]L \tag{9.1}$$

EBIS is written above as a function of z, since the investment in information security is the firm's only decision variable (v and L are parameters of the information set). The expected net benefits from an investment in information security, denoted *ENBIS* equal *EBIS* less the cost of the investment, or:

$$ENBIS(z) = [v - S(z, v)]L - z \tag{9.2}$$

To focus on the effect of vulnerability, we denote the optimal investment as $z^*(v)$. Observe that from A1, if an information set is completely invulnerable, the optimal investment in information security is set equal to zero, i.e., $z^*(0) = 0$. For now, we assume that the information set is neither completely vulnerable nor completely invulnerable, i.e., $0 < v < 1$.

From assumption A3, $S(z, v)$ is strictly convex in z, thus *ENBIS* is strictly concave in z. Hence, an interior maximum $z^* > 0$ is characterized by the first-order condition:

$$-S_x(z^*, v)L = 1 \tag{9.3}$$

where the left hand side of (9.3) represents the marginal benefits from the security investment and the right hand side of (9.3) represents the marginal cost of investment[14]. One should invest in security only up to the point where marginal benefit equals marginal cost.

[13]We believe risk-neutrality is a reasonable assumption for most security related issues. Of course, if the loss associated with a security breach were of an immense magnitude, a more realistic assumption may well be that of risk-aversion. By implicitly restricting the magnitude of the potential loss, we concur with Littlewood et. al. (1993, p. 217), who write, "in these initial stages of attempting to model operational security, we should restrict ourselves to systems for which the security requirements are also modest." Under a risk-averse assumption, the level of expenditure on information security would depend on the specific nature and degree of the decision-maker's risk aversion (modeled by economists as the decision-maker's utility function), and the optimal investment in information security would increase with the level or risk-aversion. Such an analysis, however, is beyond the scope of this paper

[14]Recall that z measures information security investment in dollars (or other monetary units). Hence, by definition, the price of a unit of z equals one. Thus, the marginal cost of investment (i.e., the cost of increasing z by one unit) equals one.

Recall that the value of an information set is measured by the potential loss associated with the information set. It follows from equation (9.3), as one would expect, that for a given level of vulnerability, the optimal amount to be invested in information security, z^*, increases with increases in the value of the information set (i.e., with increases in the threat t or the loss λ)[15].

This optimal level of investment in information security is illustrated in Figure 9.1. From equation (9.1), A1, and A2, the benefits of an investment in information security, $EBIS(z)$, starts out at zero and approach vL as the investment level increases. The costs of the investment are given by z, the 45° line in Figure 9.1. The optimal investment, z^*, is where the difference between benefits and costs are maximized, and at that point the tangent to $EBIS(z^*)$, has a slope, representing the marginal benefits, equal to the marginal cost of one. Observe that the optimal amount to be invested in information security, z^*, is less than vL, the loss that would be expected in the absence of any investment in security[16].

This can be seen by noting in equation (9.2) that the expected benefits will always be less than vL. In Figure 9.1, this can be seen by noting that the benefits of an investment in information security, $EBIS(z)$, crosses the 45° line below vL. In section three, for two broad classes of security breach probability functions, we will show that the optimal amount to be invested in information security is only a small fraction of the expected loss, vL.

The optimal level of investment in information security equals zero if the marginal benefits at $z = 0$ are less than or equal to the marginal costs of such investment. This condition can be rewritten as:

$$L \leq \frac{1}{-S_x(0, v)} \tag{9.4}$$

Since our focus is on the effects of vulnerability, we are interested in determining the levels of v that cause the optimal level of investment in

[15]This can be seen by first rewriting (9.3) as:

$$-S_z(z^*, v) = \frac{1}{L}$$

and taking the total differential to get:

$$S_{zz}(z^*, v)dz^* = \frac{dL}{L^2}.$$

This yields:

$$\frac{dz^*}{dL} = \frac{1}{L^2 S_{zz}(z^*, v)}.$$

Thus, as $S_{zz}(z^*, v)$ is positive from assumption A3, we have $dz^*/dL > 0$, giving the desired result.

[16]To see this formally, note that $0 < vL - S(z^*, v)L - z^* < vL - z^*$, so $z^* < vL$.

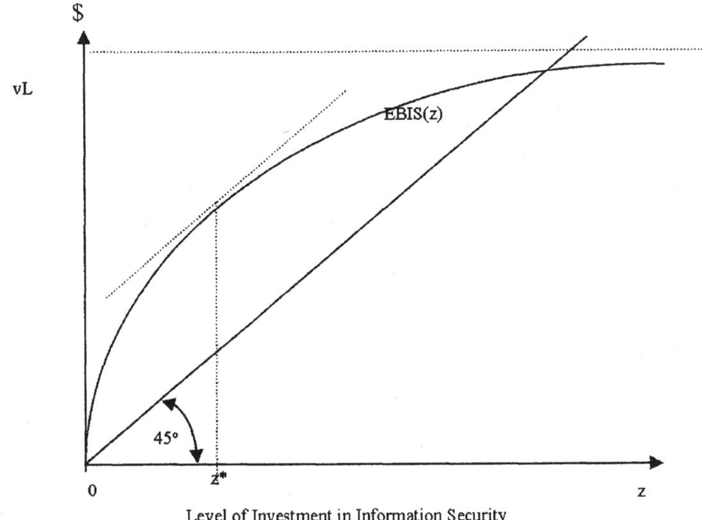

Figure 9.1. The benefits and cost of investment in information security

information security to become zero, holding L constant[17]. For a given L, $z^*(v) = 0$ whenever $-S_z(0, v)$, a positive number, is sufficiently small.

2. How Vulnerability Affects the Optimal Level of Investment in information security

We now investigate the properties of z^*v to see how vulnerability affects the optimal level of investment in information security. From the first-order condition given in equation (9.3), we see that vulnerability affects the optimal level of investment by affecting the partial derivative of the security breach function with respect to z. This partial derivative, $S_z(z, v)$, may be interpreted as the marginal productivity of security investment, as it measures the rate at which the probability of a security breach decreases with an increase in security investment. Thus, the change in the optimal level of information security investment in response to a change in vulnerability is determined by the cross partial derivative $S_{zv}(z, v)$, which may be interpreted as the change in the marginal productivity of the investment with respect to a change in vulnerability.

[17] Clearly, if one were to hold v constant and let L vary, the optimal investment in information security will be zero for sufficiently small L. That is, if the loss conditional on a security breach is very small, a positive investment in information security is not justified

If the information set were perfectly invulnerable ($v = 0$), then no investment in information security would be made (i.e., $z^*(0) = 0$). At some sufficiently larger level of vulnerability, it would be optimal to make a positive investment in information security in order to reduce the probability of the loss (and, therefore the expected loss). Hence, in some range, an increase in vulnerability leads to an increase in investment in information security. This observation is stated in the following proposition (a formal proof appears in the appendix).

> **Proposition 1:** For all security breach probability functions for which A1-A3 hold, there exists a loss, L, and a range of v in which increases in vulnerability result in an increase in the optimal investment in information security.

In order to be able to calculate a closed form solution for $z^*(v)$ and gain further insights into the relationship between vulnerability and optimal security investment, we examine two broad classes of security breach probability functions. The first class of security breach probability functions, denoted by $S^I(z, v)$, is given by:

$$S^I(z, v) = \frac{v}{(\alpha z + 1)^\beta} \tag{9.5}$$

where the parameters $\alpha > 0$, β are measures of the productivity of information security (i.e., for a given (v, z), the probability of a security breach is decreasing in both α and β). As is easily verified, each member of this class of security breach probability functions satisfies conditions A1–A3, and was selected because of its relatively simple functional form. In particular, the security breach probability functions in this class is linear in vulnerability. Figure 9.2 shows how increases in the amount of investment in information security, z, reduce the expected loss from an information security breach. The top line, $S(0, v)L$ in Figure 9.2, equals vL, the expected loss without increased investment in information security. The straight line below it represents $S(z_1, v)L$, which is the expected loss when z_1 is invested in information security. Thus, for an information set with vulnerability v, the difference between the lines at v represents *EBIS* (i.e., the expected benefit of investing z_1 in information security gross of the costs of the investment).

For security breach probability functions belonging to this first class, an expression for an interior optimal level of investment in information security can be found by solving for z^* in the first-order condition given by equation (9.3). Letting $z^{I*}(v)$ denote this optimal yields:

$$z^{I*}(v) = \frac{(v\beta\alpha L)^{1/(\beta+1)} - 1}{\alpha} \tag{9.6}$$

For this first class of security breach probability functions, condition (9.4) yields that $z^{I*}(v) = 0$ for $0 \leq v \leq 1/(\alpha\beta L)$. Thus, for the first class

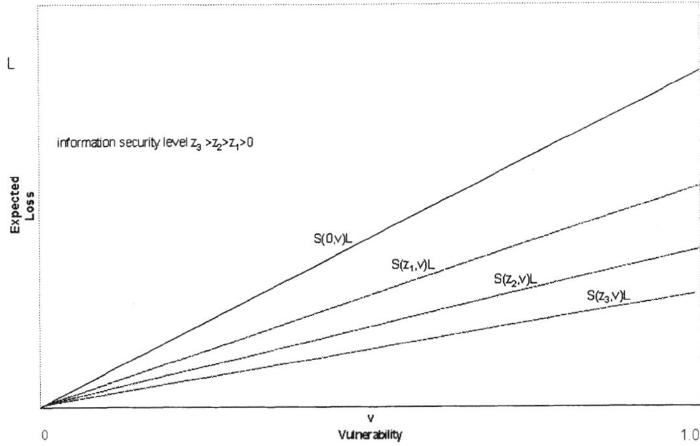

Figure 9.2. Expected value of information loss, $S(z,v)L$, as vulnerability increases at different levels of investments in information security (for Class I)

of security breach functions, the optimal investment in security equals zero until $v = 1/(\alpha\beta L)$, and then, based on equation (9.6), increases at a decreasing rate (see Figure 9.3). As $z^{I*}(v)$ is strictly increasing in v over the high range of vulnerabilities, Figure 9.3 illustrates that, at least for security breach probability functions belonging to $S^I(z,v)$, for a given potential loss, a firm can be better off concentrating its resources on high vulnerability information sets.

We now examine a second broad class of security breach probability functions which also meets assumptions A1–A3, yet demonstrates that a firm is not always better off concentrating its resources on high vulnerability information sets. Consider the second class of security breach probability functions is given by:

$$S^{II}(z,v) = v^{\alpha z+1} \tag{9.7}$$

where the parameter $\alpha > 0$, is a measure of the productivity of information security. Each curved lines in Figure 9.4 represents a particular member of the class $S^{II}(z,v)$, parameterized by varying values of $z > 0$, for a fixed level of α. At any level of vulnerability, v, the difference between one of the curved lines and the straight line (representing vL) gives the *EBIS* for the given investment, z, in securing the confidentiality of the information set. This class of security breach probability functions has the property that the cost of protecting highly vulnerable

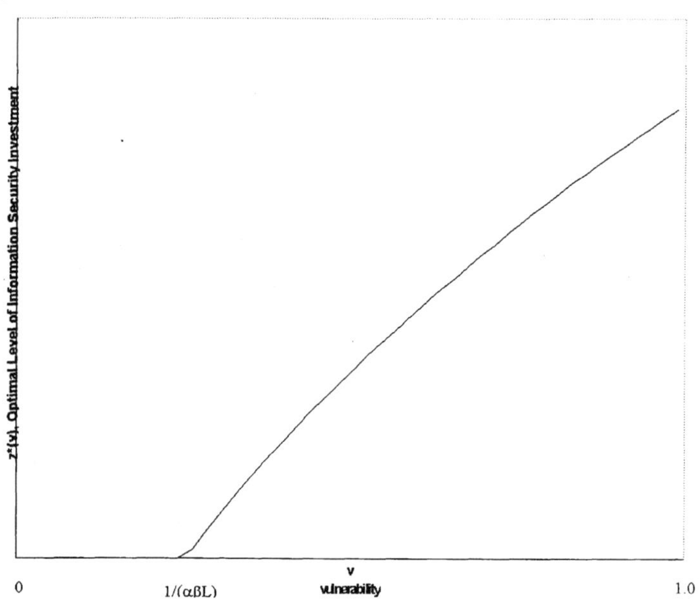

Figure 9.3. Optimal value of security investments as a function of vulnerability, $z^*(v)$ for Class I

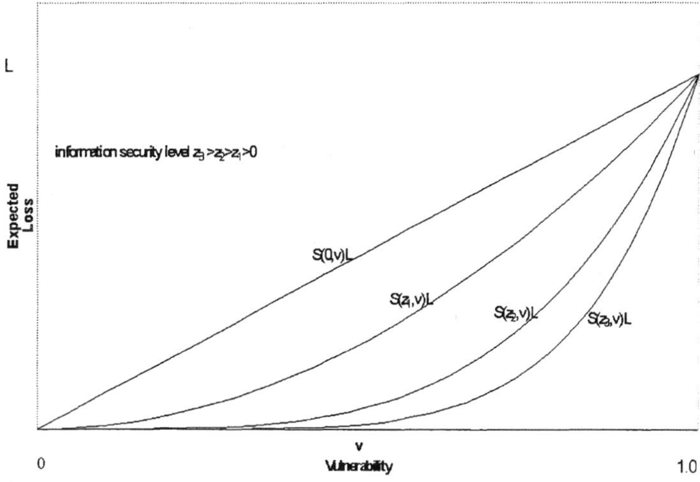

Figure 9.4. Expected value of information loss, $S(z,v)L$, as vulnerability increases at different levels of investment in information security (for Class II)

information sets becomes extremely expensive as the vulnerability of the information set becomes very large[18].

Using the first-order condition given in equation (9.3), the expression for the interior optimal level of investment in information security for $S^{II}(z,v)$ is found to be:

$$z^{II*}(v) = \frac{\ln(1/ - \alpha v L(\ln v))}{\alpha \ln v} \tag{9.8}$$

For this second class of security breach probability functions, condition (9.4) can be rewritten (after rearranging terms) as $1/L > -\alpha v \ln v$. Note that $-\alpha v \ln v > 0$ for $0 < v < 1$, and takes on a maximum at $v = 1/e \approx 0.3679$, and gets sufficiently close to 0 for v sufficiently close to either 0 or 1. Thus, for a given L, there exists a lower limit, $\underline{V}(L)$, and an upper limit $\overline{V}(L)$ with $0 < \underline{V}(L) < \overline{V}(L) < 1$, such that $z^{II*}(v) = 0$, when $0 < v < \underline{V}(L)$ or $\overline{V}(L) < v < 1$ and $z^{II*}(v) > 0$ when $\underline{V}(L) < v < \overline{V}(L)$. Although one cannot find a closed form expression for $\underline{V}(L)$ and $\overline{V}(L)$, by plotting $z^{II*}(v)$, numerical values for

[18]The class of security breach function $S^{II}(z,v)$ given in equation (9.7) is not the only class of security breach functions that has this property and could be used to demonstrate the propositions that are given later in this section. For example, the class of security breach probability functions given by $S^{III}(z,v) = ve^{\alpha z(v-1)}$, where $\alpha > 0$ could have been used instead of $S^{II}(z,v)$. The class $S^{II}(z,v)$ was selected for presentation because of its slightly simpler form.

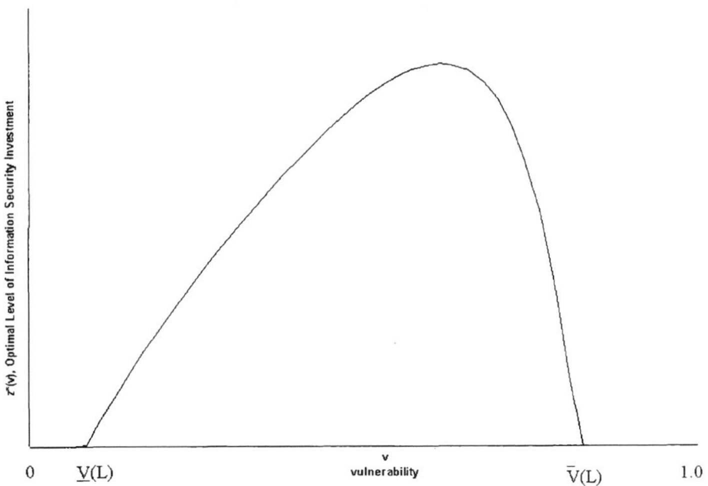

Figure 9.5. Optimal value of security investments as a function of vulnerability, $z^*(v)$ for Class II

these points can easily be approximated[19]. The regions of extremely low and extremely high vulnerability are shown in the graph of $z^*(v)$ for $S^{II}(z,v) = v^{\alpha z+1}$ in Figure 9.5.

While our earlier Proposition (and the analysis of the first class of security breach probability functions) left open the possibility that the optimal investment in information security is always (weakly) increasing in vulnerability, the analysis of the second class of security breach probability functions shows that this is not the case. We have seen that the class of security breach probability functions $S^{II}(z,v) = v^{\alpha z+1}$ meets conditions A1–A3 and results in the optimal security investment first increasing and then decreasing in the vulnerability. Thus, the demonstration and analysis of the second class of security breach probability functions provides a counterexample that is sufficient to prove the following:

> **Proposition 2:** Suppose a security breach probability function meets conditions A1–A3, then it is not necessarily the case that the optimal level of investment in information security, $z^*(v)$, is weakly increasing in vulnerability, v.

Proposition 2 indicates that a firm should be careful in deciding where to concentrate information security resources. Figures 9.3 and 9.5 illus-

[19]For example, when $\alpha = 0.00001$, and $L = \$400,000$, then $\underline{V} \approx 0.1$ and $\overline{V} \approx 0.7$.

trate that for a given potential loss, a firm may be better off concentrating its resources on high vulnerability information sets (as demonstrated by the fact that for the first class of security breach probability functions, $z^{I*}(v)$ is strictly increasing in v over the high range of vulnerabilities), or on information sets with midrange vulnerabilities (as demonstrated by $z^{II*}(v)$ for $S^{II}(z,v)$). In other words, for the second class of security breach probability functions (which meets assumption A4), the area of zero investment, for a given L, should be two tailed rather than one tailed. For security breach functions in class II, as well as in class I, the marginal benefit from investment in information security for low vulnerability information sets does not justify the investment since the security of such information is already good. For security breach functions in class II, when an information set is extremely vulnerable, the benefit of spending a given amount for increased information security of the information (as measured by the decrease in expected loss from the extra security) is very small. For example, for the case where the security issue is that of confidentiality, knowledge that a firm is trying to sell a particular business unit may become nearly public information. In such a case, because of the multiple sources of potential information leakage, it may well be too expensive to monitor employees and business contacts to provide even a mild level of information security. Hence, the key in analyzing information security decisions is not the vulnerability (or the expected loss without the investment), but the reduction in expected loss with the investment.

The next proposition provides insight into the relationship between the optimal level of investment in security and the loss that would be expected in the absence of any investment in security when the security probability breach functions belong to class I or class II.

> **Proposition 3:** Suppose the security breach probability function belongs to class I (i.e., it can be expressed as $S^I(z,v) = v/(\alpha z+1)^\beta$ for some $\alpha > 0$, β) or to class II (i.e., it can be expressed as $S^{II}(z,v) = v^{\alpha z+1}$ for some $\alpha > 0$), then $z^*(v) < (1/e)vL$. (See Appendix for proof.)

Proposition 3 shows that, for the two broad classes of information security breach probability functions, the optimal investment in information security is always less than or equal to 36.79% of the loss that would be expected in the absence of any investment in security[20]. The restriction that the security breach probability functions have one of two specific functional forms warrants a discussion of the robustness of the proposition. First, note that the two classes of security breach probability functions appear unrelated, other than the fact that functions in

[20]As indicated in the footnote above, Proposition 3 extends beyond the two classes of information security breach functions

both classes satisfy conditions A1–A3. Functions belonging to class I are linear in vulnerability and those belonging to class II are strictly concave (for $\alpha > 0$). Moreover, the result holds for all values of $\alpha > 0$, β, i.e., the productivity of information security is unrestricted[21]. Second, the proposition critically depends on the assumption that the firm already has some information security infrastructure in place (e.g., an IT officer devoting some time to security issues, access controls, etc.) so that there are no incremental fixed costs associated with new security investments[22].

The practical import of Proposition 3 as guidance for decision-making is enhanced when one considers that the 36.79% figure is a maximum, and for a wide range of security breach probability functions belonging to class I and II, the optimal amount to be invested in information security is considerably less. For example, for class I security breach probability functions with $\beta = 1$, the maximum percent to be invested is 25% of vL (as can be seen by examining equation (9.A.4) in the Appendix) and only occurs when $\alpha vL = 4$. Thus, when $\beta = 1$, $\alpha = 0.00001$, $L = \$400,000$ and $v = 1$, the 25% limit will hold, but at lower values of v, the optimal level of investment is less than the 25% of vL[23].

The findings discussed in this section of the paper can be summarized as follows. The optimal expenditures for protecting a given information set do not always increase with increases in the information set's vulnerability. Furthermore, for two broad classes of security breach probability functions, the optimal amount to invest in information security should not exceed 37% ($\approx 1/e$) of the expected loss due to a security breach. The analysis presented is not without limitations. First, our result giving the maximum amount of the optimal investment in information security depended on the specific functional forms of the security breach functions and assumed no lumpiness in expenditures for information security. While the assumption that incremental fixed costs of information security investment is zero clearly played a crucial role in our demonstration, it is an open question as to whether or not our result extends to all continuous security breach functions meeting assumptions A1–A3. Second, there is no simple procedure to determine the probabilities of the threat and the vulnerability associated with an information set. Third, in a similar vein, procedures for deriving and considering the potential loss

[21]Also note that some simple perturbations of the two classes of security probability functions do not affect the conclusion of proposition 3. Specifically, suppose A3 is generalized so that $v - w$ of the probability of breach is due to sources that cannot be reduced through investment in security, i.e., $\lim z \rightarrow \infty S(z, v) \rightarrow v - w$, where $0 \leq w \leq v$. Letting $S(z, v) = v - w + S^i(z, w)$, for $i = I$, one can easily verify that the conclusion of proposition still holds

[22]Of course, if there were incremental fixed costs of F, in addition to variable costs z, then (for the two classes of breach functions), the optimal total amount spent on information security as a fraction of the expected loss in the absence of additional security would increase by F/vL. As F increases, the lower range of vulnerabilities in which investment is uneconomical increases. Clearly, if F were sufficiently large, no investment would take place.

[23]For example, when $v = 0.52$, the optimal investment is \$41,421 or 20.7% of vL.

from an information security breach, especially for a huge loss (as would likely be the case for the protection of many national/public assets), is also problematic. A fourth limitation of this research is that we have not modeled how conflicts of interest between senior management and the firm's chief information security officer would affect the derivation of the optimal amount to invest in information security[24]. Finally, we have not modeled the case where a single investment in information security is used to protect the security of multiple information sets having correlated security risks[25].

3. Concluding Comments

The new computer-based information age has changed the way organizations operate, as well as the way they need to look at information security. Indeed, information security has become at least as important to modern corporations as is the protection of tangible physical assets. Not surprisingly, a rapidly growing body of research addresses the issue of information security. This research has focused primarily on the technical aspects of protecting information in a computer-based system (i.e., encryption, data and software controls, and hardware controls). The behavioral aspects of preventing information security breaches have also been attracting much recent attention among researchers. In contrast, very little work has been done which addresses the economic aspects of information security. In particular, given the amount of resources currently being devoted by organizations to shore up information security, what is needed is a conceptual framework to help derive an optimal level of information security spending. This paper helps to fill this void in the literature by presenting such a framework, in the form of an economic model for information security investment decisions. An economics perspective naturally recognizes that while some investment in information security is good, more security is not always worth the cost. The model given in this paper specifically considers how the vulnerability of information, and the loss associated with such vulnerability, affect the optimal level of resources that should be devoted to securing information.

[24]In another context, Hann and Weber (1996) model the conflict of interest between senior management and the CIO. The cost of the conflict of interest between a principal (e.g., a senior manager) and an agent (e.g., the CIO) is known in economics as an agency cost. Agency costs arise in a variety of other situations where the decision making authority is delegated by a principal (e.g., an owner) to an agent (e.g., a senior manager).

[25]Similarly, our paper does not address the joint protection of information sets along with tangible assets such as desks, printers, and personnel. For example, fire protection adds to the security of non-information assets along with information assets. Of course, if we bundle all assets together as a single set, we could still use our model for guidance in determining a joint level of (information plus non-information) security investment. However our model, does not give guidance on how the total investment in security should be allocated between information security investments and security investments for other assets.

The analysis contained in this paper has shown that, for a broad class of security breach probability functions, the optimal amount to spend on information security is an increasing function of the level of vulnerability of such information. Our analysis also shows that, for a second broad class of security breach probability functions, the optimal amount to spend on information security does not always increase with the level of vulnerability of such information. For this second class, the optimal amount to spend on information security initially increases, but ultimately decreases with the level of vulnerability of such information. Thus, the second class of security breach probability functions also shows that managers allocating an information security budget should normally focus on information that falls into the midrange of vulnerability to security breaches. Hence, a meaningful endeavor for managers may be to partition information sets into low, middle, and high levels of security breach vulnerability. Some information sets may be so difficult to protect to a very high level of security, that one may be best off defending them only at a moderate level.

Information security vendors and consultants will naturally focus on huge potential losses from security breaches in order to sell their products and services. Astute information security managers no doubt are aware that expected losses are typically an order of magnitude smaller than such potential losses. Our analysis shows that for two broad classes of security breach probability functions, the optimal amount to spend on information security never exceeds 37% of the expected loss resulting from a security breach (and is typically much less that 37%). Hence, the optimal amount to spend on information security would typically be far less than even the expected loss from a security breach.

Our findings for the two classes of security breach probability functions shed significant light on the much overlooked issue of determining how much to invest in information security. While our analysis provides new insights, a number of important aspects of the information security investment decisions are not addressed by our model, and therefore represent opportunities for extending the line of research pursued in this paper. One aspect that our model does not address is the various perverse economic incentives (e.g., externalities arising when decisions of one party affects those of others) affecting investment in information security. The nature and effects of perverse economic incentives is the principle focus of a stimulating paper by Anderson (2001), and it would be interesting to examine how these incentives affect the analysis resulting from our model. As a model of a single-decision maker, our analysis does not take into account how potential attackers of an information system change strategies in reaction to an additional security investment. That is, our analysis does not consider the game theoretic aspects of information security, although such consideration would enrich our analysis[26]. While our single-period model allows us to see the effects of changes in the model's parameters (e.g., the loss associated with a security breach), it would be interesting to extend our model to include dynamic issues.

In addition to extending our model as suggested above, future research could, and should, empirically assess whether or not organizations invest in information security in a manner which is consistent with the findings of this paper. Of course, the differences between the empirical evidence and the analytical findings of this paper would need to be explained. In this regard, particular attention should be given to determining how firms estimate the potential loss and the probabilities associated with the threats and vulnerabilities of information. The above notwithstanding, the analysis contained in this paper provides a framework for future research addressing issues related to the economics of investment in information security.

Acknowledgements

This paper is reprinted from ACM Transactions on Information and System Security, Vol. 5, No. 4, November 2002, pp 438–457, with the permission from ACM. The authors wish to thank Mike Ball, John Hughes, Jon Millen, Ravi Sandhu, Tashfeen Sohail, Gene Spafford, Zheng Wang and the participants at the accounting and finance workshop at the London School of Economics and Political Science for comments on an earlier version of this paper. This research was partially supported by The Robert H. Smith School of Business, University of Maryland and the Laboratory for Telecommunications Sciences (within the Department of Defense) through a grant with the University of Maryland Institute for Advanced Computer Studies.

References

Anderson, J. 1972. Computer security technology planning study. U. S. Air Force Electronic Systems Division Technical Report. (Oct.), 73–51.

Anderson, R. 2001. Why information security is hard - an economic perspective. In Proceeding of 17th Annual Computer Security Applications Conference (ACSAC) (New Orleans, Louisiana. December 10–14).

Axelsson, S. 2000.The base-rate fallacy and the difficulty of intrusion detection. ACM Transactions on Information and Systems Security. 3,3 (Aug.), 186–205.

[26]This game-theoretic aspect is noted by Jajodia and Millen (1993, p.85), "Computer security is a kind of game between two parties, the designer of a secure system, and a potential attacker." The game-theoretic aspect of information security is also highlighted by Gordon and Loeb (2001).

Buzzard, K. 1999. Computer security – what should you spend your money on. Computers & Security. 18,4, 322–334.

Daniels, T.E. and Spafford, E. H. 1999. Identification of host audit data to detect attacks on low-level IP. Journal of Computer Security. 7,1, 3–35.

Denning, D. 1987. An intrusion-detection model. IEEE Transactions on Software Engineering. 13,2 (Feb.), 222–226.

Denning, D., and Branstad, D. 1996. A taxonomy of key escrow encryption systems. Communications of the ACM. 39,3(Mar.), 34–40.

Finne, T. 1998. A conceptual framework for information security management. Computers & Security. 17,4, 303–307.

Frincke, D. 2000. Balancing cooperation and risk in intrusion detection. ACM Transactions on Information and Systems Security. 3,1(Feb.), 1–29.

Hann, J., and Weber, R. 1996. Information systems planning: a model and empirical tests. Management Science. 42,7(Jul.), 1043–1064.

Gordon, L. and Loeb, M. 2001. A Framework for using information security as a response to competitor analysis systems. Communications of the ACM, Vol. 44. No. 9 (Sept.) 70–75

Hoo, K. 2000. How much is enough? A risk-management approach to computer security. Consortium for Research on Information Security Policy (CRISP) Working Paper. Stanford University. (June).

Jajodia, S., and J. Millen. 1993. Editors' preface. Journal of Computer Security. 2,2/3, 85.

Jones, A. 1997. Penetration testing and system audit. Computers & Security.16, 595–602.

Kpmg. 2000. Information Security Survey 2000. `http://www.kpmg.co.uk/services/audit/pubs/ISS`, (Apr.), 1–4

Larsen, A. 1999. Global security survey: virus attack. `InformationWeek.Com`. `http://www.informationweek.com/743/security.htm` (Jul.12).

Littlewood, B., Broclehurst, S., Fenton, N., Mellor, P., Page, S., Wright, D., Dobson, J., Mcdermid, J., and Gollman, D. 1993. Towards operational measures of security. Journal of Computer Security. 2,2, 211–229.

Loch, K. D., Carr, H. H., and Warkentin, M. E. 1992. Threats to information systems: today's reality, yesterday's understanding. MIS Quarterly. 17,2, 173–186.

Luotonen, O. 1993. Risk management and insurances. Painatuskeskus Oy. Helsinki.

Mcknight, L., R. Solomon, J. Reagle, D. Carver, C. Johnson, B. Gerovac, and Gingold, D. 1997. Information security of internet commerce. In Internet Economics, ed. L. McKnight and J. Bailey. Cambridge, Mass.: MIT Press, 435-452.

Meadows, C. 2001. A cost-based framework for analysis of denial of service in networks, Journal of Computer Security. 9,1/2, 143–164.

Millen, J. 1992. A resource allocation model for denial of service. Proceedings of the 1992 IEEE Symposium on Security & Privacy. IEEE Comp Soc Press, 137–147.

Muralidhar, K., Batra, D., and kirs, P. 1995. Accessibility, security, and accuracy in statistical databases: the case for the multiplicative fixed data perturbation approach. Management Science. 41,9 (Sep.), 1549–1564.

NIST (National Institute of Standards and Technology). 1995. An Introduction to Computer Security: The NIST Handbook. (Special Publication 800–12).

Osborn, S., Sandhu, R., and Munawer, Q. 2000. Configuring role-based access control to enforce mandatory and discretionary access control policies. ACM Transactions of Information and Systems Security. 3,2(May), 85–106.

Peyravian, M., Roginsky, A., Zunic, N. 1999. Hash-based encryption. Computers & Security. 18,4, 345–350.

Pfleeger, C. 1997. , Security in Computing (2nd ed.), Prentice-Hall, N.J.

Power, R. 2001. 2001 CSI/FBI computer crime and security survey. Computer Security Journal. 17,2 (Spring), 29-51.

Sandhu, R. S., Bhamidipati, V., and Munawer, Q. 1999. The ARBAC97 model for role-based administration of roles. ACM Transactions on Information and Systems Security. 1,2 (Feb.), 105–135.

Sandhu, R. S., Coyne, E. J., Feinstein, H. L., and Youman, C. E. 1996. Role-based access control models. IEEE Computer. 29,2 (Feb.), 38–47.

Schneier, B. 1996. Applied Cryptography (2nd ed.), Wiley. New York, NY.

Simmons, G. 1994. Cryptanalysis and protocol failures. Communications of the ACM. 37,11(Nov.), 56–64.

Straub, D. W. and Welke, R. J. 1998. Coping with systems risk: security planning models for management decision making. MIS Quarterly. 23,4, 441–469.

Straub, D. W. 1990. Effective IS security: an empirical study. Information Systems Research. 1,3, 255–276.

Varian, H.R. 1997. How to Build an Economic Model in Your Spare Time. It is part of a collection titled Passion and Craft: Economists at Work, edited by Michael Szenberg, University of Michigan Press, available at `http://www.sims.berkeley.edu/~hal/Papers/how.pdf`

Vigna, G. and Kemmeerer, R. A. 1999. NetSTAT: a network-based intrusion detection system. Journal of Computer Security.7,1, 37–71.

Wiseman, S. 1986. A secure capability computer system. Proceedings of the IEEE Symposium on Security & Privacy. IEEE Comp Soc Press, 86–94.

Appendix

Proof of Proposition 1:
Observe from A1, $S_z(z,0) = 0$ for all $z > 0$ and from A3, $S_z(z,v) < 0$, for all $z > 0$ and $0 < v < 1$. Therefore, at least over some range, $S_z(z,v)$ is decreasing in v. Consider the pair $(\underline{z}, v)$ which is in the range where $S_z(z,v)$ is decreasing in v. There exists an L such that $-S_z(z,v)L = 1$, so for that L, $z^*(v) = \underline{z}$. Then for all sufficiently small but positive ϵ, $-S_z(z^*(\underline{v}), \underline{v}+\epsilon)$, $L > 1$. From A3, $S_{zz} > 0$, so there exists $\delta > 0$ such that $-S_z(z^*(\underline{v}) + \delta, \underline{v} + \epsilon)L = 1, i.e., z^*(\underline{v}+\epsilon) = z^*(v) + \delta$. Hence, z^* is increasing at v.

Proof of Proposition 3:
Suppose the security breach probability function belongs to class I. Then using equation (9.6), we have:

$$\frac{z^{I*}(v)}{vL} = \frac{(\beta\alpha vL)^{1/(\beta+1)} - 1}{\alpha vL} \tag{9.A.1}$$

Letting $x = \alpha vL$, equation (9.A.1) can be rewritten as:

$$\frac{z^{I*}(v)}{vL} = \frac{(\beta\alpha vL)^{1/(\beta+1)} - 1}{\alpha vL} \tag{9.A.2}$$

The right hand side of (9.A.2) reaches its maximum at:

$$x = (\beta+1)^{\beta+1}\beta^{-2-\beta} \tag{9.A.3}$$

and substituting this (9.A.3) into (9.A.2) we get:

$$\frac{Z^{I*}}{vL} = \left(\frac{\beta}{\beta+1}\right)^{\beta+1} \tag{9.A.4}$$

The right hand side of (9.A.4) is increasing in β. Applying L'Hospital's rule, we have:

$$\lim_{\beta\to\infty}\left(\frac{\beta}{\beta+1}\right)^{\beta+1} = \frac{1}{e} \tag{9.A.5}$$

Hence, the right hand side of (9.A.4) is less than $(1/e)$ and $z^*(v) < (1/e)vL$ for the first class of security breach probability functions.

Now suppose the security breach probability function belongs to class II. Using equation (9.8) we have:

$$\frac{z^{II*}(v)}{vL} = \frac{\ln(1/-\alpha vL(\ln v))}{\alpha vL\ln v} \tag{9.A.6}$$

Letting $x = -\alpha vL\ln v$, equation (9.A.6) can be rewritten as:

$$\frac{z^{II*}(v)}{vL} = \frac{\ln(1/x)}{-x} \tag{9.A.7}$$

The first-order condition for maximum of the right hand side is:

$$\frac{1+\ln(1/x)}{x^2} = 0 \tag{9.A.8}$$

Condition (9.8) is satisfied at the point $x = e$, as is the second-order condition:

$$\frac{-3 - 2\ln(1/x)}{x^3} < 0 \tag{9.A.9}$$

Thus, the right hand side of (9.A.7) is maximized at $x = e$, taking on a maximum value of $1/e$ at this point. Hence, $z^{II*}(v)/vL < 1/e$. Hence, $z*(v) < (1/e)vL$ also holds for the second class of security breach probability functions.

Chapter 10

WHAT PRICE PRIVACY?

(and why identity theft is about neither identity nor theft)

Adam Shostack
adam@homeport.org

Paul Syverson
Naval Research Laboratory
syverson@itd.nrl.navy.mil

> *The cost of the discomfort felt at the collection of information is especially difficult to quantify.*

It is commonplace to note that in surveys people claim to place a high value on privacy while they paradoxically throw away their privacy in exchange for a free hamburger or a two dollar discount on groceries. The usual conclusion is that people do not really value their privacy as they claim to or that they are irrational about the risks they are taking. Similarly it is generally claimed that people will not pay for privacy; the failure of various ventures focused on selling privacy is offered as evidence of this. In this chapter we will debunk these myths. Another myth we will debunk is that identity theft is a privacy problem. In fact it is an authentication problem and a problem of misplaced liability and cost. When these are allocated to those who create them, the problem does not exist. Finally we consider the oft asked question of how much privacy should be given up for security. We find this to be the wrong question. Security of institutions may decrease and infrastructure costs may be increased by a reduction in privacy.

[†]This chapter is an expanded and revised version of both "The Paradoxical Value of Privacy" by Paul Syverson and " 'People Won't Pay For Privacy,' Reconsidered" by Adam Shostack. Both of these were presented at the 2nd Annual Workshop on Economics and Information Security, College Park MD, USA, May 2003.

1. The Meanings of Privacy

The word 'privacy' is heavily loaded with hard-to-disentangle meanings. It can mean anything from email confidentiality (PGP), to controlling who emails you (SPAM), to who sees your credit report (identity theft) to the ability of a woman to have an abortion (Roe v. Wade). The many meanings of 'privacy' contribute to the confusion which surrounds it, and some of the apparent contradictions may be resolved simply by paying close attention to them. Other work that has examined privacy and economics has chosen to focus on a single definition ([Varian, 1996]). By pointing out a rational way to behave in the context of a single definition of privacy, these analyses may actually contribute to the idea that people are acting irrationally.

Therefore, for clarity, we will try to use following words in place of 'privacy':

Unobservability is when you can not be observed. For example, shutting the door to the bathroom offers unobservability.

To Be Left Alone is a classic definition from Justice Brandeis. There is some subtlety in his writing, which we ignore, because the phrase is so powerful.

Untraceability is when you can not be traced from one identity to another. For example, "John, who we play softball with, but don't know his last name" is untraceable; you can't track down a phone number for him.

Informational self-determination is when you are confident that information you provide will be used only in ways you understand and approve. Giving your mother your new phone number probably qualifies.

Anonymity is when you are without any identifiers.

Many of these terms are based on other uses within the technical and legal privacy literature, and we believe that their uses here are very close to their understood meanings.

Each of these terms captures a meaningful aspect of privacy, and each of them is a goal which people pursue. There is also a measure of how important privacy is to people, which Westin breaks down into the "fundamentalists," "pragmatists" and "Don't cares" ([Westin, 2001]). It is the last group often cited as willing to trade away their privacy for a free hamburger.

Given these meanings, we will examine how people pay for them. From there, we will examine a number of areas where people don't pay for privacy. We will then explore what lessons can be learned from this.

2. Privacy People Pay For

The most obvious way people pay for privacy is in banking services, paying for informational self-determination, in the form of a guarantee that information about them won't be provided to some set of tax authorities, family members, or others. This is a business estimated at many billions of dollars per year.

In the realm of unobservability, privacy is one component of what drives purchases on curtains and drapes, as well as large shrubbery and fences. This statement is based on the easily observed fact that privacy is listed in most advertising for "window treatments" in home decoration magazines. We use advertising as a proxy for what people value because advertisers won't include things which they don't believe will sell their product, and they won't put in things which they expect will cause their audience to shake their heads. Drapery and curtains, whose sales are motivated not only by unobservability, but also by aesthetics and economics of insulation, were approximately 1.8 billion dollars in 1997 ([US Census Bureau, 1999]). We do not attempt to break down these numbers as to which motivator leads. We do note that see-through or lace curtains seem relatively rare. (Speaking of homes, privacy or distance from neighbors is often a reason to move to the suburbs or country.) On January 27, 2003, the New York Times published a story on college dormitories and private rooms. The story teaser on the web site was "With more students demanding – and paying for – privacy, the roommate is no longer the staple of college life it once was." Students at Boston University are paying an extra $1,400 per year, or about 4% extra for a private room.

Unobservability also drives mailboxes, private mail boxes, and mail receiving services in two ways. Some of this is unobservability with respect to the sender: one's real physical location is not revealed. Some of it is unobservability with respect to one's house-mates or family, who don't know what mail a person is getting. The post office rents more than 18 million post office boxes, for nearly 500 million dollars per year. It is unclear how many of these are personal or small business/sole proprietor sorts of rentals ([USPS, 2001]). Privacy is explicitly listed by both the US Postal Service and Mailboxes, Etc. as a motivator for renting of post-office boxes ([USPS, 1998], and [Mailboxes, Etc. web page]).

Another area where the right to be left alone matters to people is their telephones. Some people find unwanted calls to be enormously annoying and intrusive. To address this concern, there are caller-ID, caller-ID blocking, voice mail services, and unlisted numbers. We consider both caller ID and the blocking service to be privacy driven. Caller ID is a desire to be left alone by unknown callers, a function of which is also served by answering machines with a call-screening function. Caller ID blocking is an untraceability feature, where the caller desires privacy. Voice mail services regularly advertise themselves as a unobservability services, where roommates and others don't know what calls you're receiving. Unlisted numbers reflect a desire to be left alone; in California over half of all home phone lines are unlisted. (A perhaps interesting aside is that one of the authors no longer calls directory assistance to try to find people, only businesses, because he assumes that all of his friends have unlisted numbers.)

It might be interesting to add up the numbers above, but that presents several substantial difficulties. First, and most easily solved, the numbers are not for the same years. Secondly, many of the products are "tied", where privacy is bundled into a complex product, rather than a feature for which one can choose to pay. Some of this might be separable; for example, in the curtain example, We could pursue average sizing of curtains per dwelling, find the lowest cost option to block the view, and assign that as the privacy component. However, this strikes us as potentially misleading: Are all curtains purchased for privacy? If privacy were the only concern, would people re-use more older curtains? Similarly, with a post-office box, some portion of the rental may be to obtain a "professional appearance" or to avoid mail-theft issues. How to separate that out is not clear. Thirdly, we have not attempted to assemble a comprehensive list of markets where privacy is a factor. Lastly, and most importantly, its unclear what such numbers would mean, and thus they could not be used correctly. Therefore, we make no effort to add up these numbers. We simply point out that privacy is an important component of what people are paying for, refuting the claim that "people won't pay for privacy."

3. The Irrational Privacy Consumer: Selling your virtual self for a hamburger

Austin Hill has observed that people will tell you that privacy is very important to them, but then give you a DNA sample in exchange for a Big Mac. While there is clearly a bit of bemused (or frustrated) hyperbole in this statement, the thrust appears correct. But is it really so irrational to exchange private information for something of relatively little economic value?

We claim that there need be no inconsistency inherent in such behavior. Suppose a hamburger is worth two dollars, a full blown identity theft costs an average of 100K dollars, and the probability of such identity theft from giving name, address, and phone number to the hamburger vendor is 10^{-10}. In this case, the rational action is to trade the information for the hamburger. Expected value of such a transaction is still effectively two dollars.

But even assuming these numbers are reasonable, this example reflects a short-sighted consumer. Suppose the incremental probability given a previous history of such transactions is on average slightly higher, say 10^{-9} A thousand such transactions reduce the long term average expected value to a dollar. Thus even in the relatively long run, the consumer made no mistakes.

This is a very simplistic example. It overlooks the cost of discomfort the individual feels from her information being held by the vendor, the inconvenience from receiving resulting unwanted junk mail or the positive value if the consumer actually desires, e.g., the resulting coupons she receives, etc.

The cost of the discomfort felt at the collection of information is especially difficult to quantify. But, it may be reasonable to completely remove it from any analysis. For it is the expectation of how that information will be used that is significant. If such data were collected such that the individual felt genuinely sure that it would simply be filed away and never accessed, never correlated with any other actions of hers, never used in any way, it is unclear that she would care. Of course there is always some expectation that if an effort is made to collect the data, then someone intends to use it in some way. In any case, even adding such costs as the increase in junkmail, the expectation of unpleasant inferences about her by marketers, financial institutions, etc. it is at best unclear that the expected cost exceeds the value of the hamburger.

This is not to say that people are more *or less* rational with respect to privacy than any other aspect of their lives. They still understate or ignore risks in the temptation of immediate gratification, and there have even been some economic models of this in the privacy context ([Acquisti, 2004]). While quite insightful, such analysis can at best be hypothetical at this point, as we shall see presently. However, the point of the example is that while the consumer may violate some ideal rationality of an economic model, it is indeed hyperbole to claim obvious and extreme irrationality in such actions.

So, what is going on? Are privacy advocates just fanatics, themselves irrational about such things? Some have concluded as much with less justification. But there are other aspects to this issue.

First, the above numbers, however plausible, are made up. A shift of a few orders of magnitude could change things drastically. Second, real numbers are very difficult to come by and virtually impossible to justify. It might be possible to collect data on occurrence of identity theft correlated with consumer behavior so that probabilities of at least such clear privacy problems could be assigned to some actions. However, this is at best unclear and has not been done yet. And even this would ignore the other types of privacy cost, a few of which we have mentioned. Also, limiting ourselves to identity theft for the moment, any data collected would be of limited predictive value. According to the US FTC, the rate of identity theft is doubling every year. Obviously if true, that cannot continue for long. The situation is just too dynamic right now for there to be any empirically accurate analysis of current trends. Plus, the market typically needs to learn from experience, so consumer behavior is likely to lag behind any current reality. So one answer is that the expected cost of privacy compromise, both large and small, is increasing. Privacy advocates (along with economic privacy modelers) are just ahead of their time.

Third, the example we have been considering is one involving the assessment of low probability but high value events. This is difficult enough for those who have good numbers and good understanding. Individuals may be somewhat polar in response to these circumstances. Horror stories of lost livelihood are met with sympathy but an expectation that it won't happen to me. And historically that has been statistically accurate. But, there may come a tipping threshold that will make this a major issue not just in polls but in individual behavior and in individual demands of government and business Alternatively, the right sort of individual soundbite may resonate through society. A recent story in MSNBC recounts the plight of Malcolm Byrd who besides economic suffering, job loss, etc. has been arrested many times and spent time in jail more than once as the result of an identity theft ([Sullivan, 2003]). These stories may also desensitize people or leave them feeling helpless, since they have no meaningful way to respond. We will return to the advice people are currently given below. For now we note with trepidation that, while identity theft in general continues to rise exponentially, so-called *criminal* identity theft (as in this story) has increased as a percentage of the total, from 1.7% in 2001 to 2.1% in 2003 ([FTC, 2004]). On the other hand, the Anonymizer (the self-proclaimed "Kleenex" brand name in Internet privacy) claims a 500% increase in subscriber base from 2002 to 2003. Perhaps a tipping point is being approached.

Another indicator of privacy attitudes frequently cited is that people don't click through to read privacy policies. This is often cited in support of the assertion that people don't actually care about their privacy. We believe that it is more accurate to state that privacy policies rarely reveal anything in comprehensible language, and even more rarely give meaningful choices. Additionally, companies rarely distinguish themselves in their actual privacy commitments, so it is hard to choose a company for its privacy policies. (Initiatives such as the World Wide Web Consortium's P3P may help to change that, but it is still early to see.) Finally, most companies reserve the right to change their privacy policies at any time, and many exercise that right, meaning that even if a consumer chooses a company for its current privacy policies, he is unlikely to feel that he will have informational self-determination, or control over how information about him is used. As such, consumer decisions to not waste time with them reflect more on their utility than on consumer's privacy desires. Consumers failure to read, understand, and respond to bank privacy notices required under recent US laws may be understood the same way. However, in the case of those laws, the presence of the weasel word "affiliate" make it hard to determine if one would actually be left alone if one did bother to fill out the card.

Again, what appears to be insensitivity to privacy is actually a rational decision about the effect of investing time and energy in understanding a policy, and the expected value of that investment.

4. Analysis

Privacy is often a component of some other sale—home decoration or convenience. This makes it hard to place solid numbers on "The privacy market," although those would be quite interesting.

Consumers seem to spend money when there is a comprehensible threat, with an understandable solution, for example, with curtains. The concern of people looking in through windows is easily understood, and the solution is easily comprehended. In newer, or less transparent situations, understanding may be harder to come by. An example would be http cookies. It is not trivial to understand what an http cookie is, as this requires some understanding of the idea of a protocol, a server, and statefulness. Understanding the interaction of cookies with traceability and linkability is even more complicated, as it requires understanding of web page construction, cookie regeneration, and non-cookie tracking mechanisms. So, understanding the technical nature of the threat has a high threshold. From there, understanding the impact of the threat is complicated. What does it matter if all my browsing can be linked together to my real identity? What impressions or notes may be made when one goes to a pharmaceutical (or illegal) drug site, a gay rights site, or the web site of an accused terrorist organization? In contrast, understanding that anyone driving by can see in your windows if you don't have curtains is trivial. Protecting against threats too difficult for the average current consumer to grasp is a hard sell. A potential example is iPrivacy, a company that began five years ago offering comprehensive protection of consumer name, credit card information, and even address for physical delivery of goods. But it has never taken off. It does not help that vendors may try to convince consumers that it is in their best interest to provide personal information, whether or not this is true.

Businesses spend time and energy to present their activity in the best possible light, sometimes to the point of misdirection. For example, warranty cards which state they must be filled out completely to "ensure the best possible service" also ask for demographic information. Understanding what will be done with the information may take more effort than the result is worth.

Even if one does take the time to learn about and understand how different organizations will handle one's personal information, there may be little difference between them. In the financial services world the difference in actual policy may be very slim. In addition, information important for understanding what privacy an offer really entails may be lacking. Alternately, a choice may appear to be a marketing ploy, not one based on real distinctions. As such, there may not be a real choice that can be made on privacy.

A recurring feature of the privacy world is that new issues are raised. New ways of invading privacy are suggested, people are outraged, studies are written, and the new technology succeeds or fails without apparent correlation to privacy issues. This is a phenomenon worth exploring. Those new technologies which succeed do so in one of two ways: First, they succeed in the marketplace. The benefits that they offer are so substantial that people are willing to give up their privacy for the benefits gained. It is worth asking in this instance, is this an informed choice? Will they regret it later? However, it is a choice which is sometimes freely made; for example, the capability to track cell phones deters very few people from carrying them. Concerns are raised more regularly about cancer risks. The second way new technologies succeed is that they are mandated. For example, cell phones will soon come with new and enhanced tracking technology, courtesy of the so called "Enhanced-911" mandate from the FCC. In this instance, the new privacy invasion is mandated, paid for, and only later will it be discovered what secondary uses are made of it. Then there are the technologies which fail. These generally have their failures attributed to non-privacy factors.

5. Default States

In making a purchase, sometimes there is an exchange of information that the buyer sees as needed for the transaction. A good example of this is the provision of credit card information online. It obviously needs to happen to make the purchase happen (absent such services as iPrivacy, which would make this relation more subtle), but what happens to the data afterwards? The consumer, if s/he has considered the issue at all, often believes that nothing should be done other than what needs to be done. The merchant, having considered things at great length, would like to be able to monetize the data in every way possible. As we discuss in the analysis section above, there is currently no easy way to find a merchant who will offer this choice, or to confirm that they are offering the choice that is want. (Again widespread adoption of P3P or related initiatives could change this.)

Informally, consumers feel strongly that they should not have to pay extra for their privacy to be protected. They feel taken advantage of if the basic transaction as they see it is not respected.

The only time we know of that this has been tested in a vote, the people of North Dakota voted to require banks to get permission to re-sell data, rather than offer them the choice of opting-out. This vote demonstrates that when offered the choice about their privacy (in the form of the right to be left alone), those voters chose to make the default that information be used for the purpose for which it was provided.

Of course, this was a small vote: 128,206 ballots were cast, of which 119,028 voted on the question—the most votes cast on any question, compared to 113,182 on the other constitutional ballot question, or 108,747 votes cast in the US Congressional race. It would be incorrect to draw too many conclusions from the vote, as only twenty six percent of voters turned out. However, it is useful to note that the voters acted in a manner consistent with what they have told pollsters, that is, that their privacy matters to them, and to note that more voters who voted voted on this issue than on any other.

6. Why Identity Theft is Not About Identity or Theft

Why have we focused so much of this chapter identity theft? In addition to the above points, it illustrates how the allocation of the costs in protecting privacy do not currently reflect the value and incentives of those with control over its protection.

Malcolm Byrd, introduced in section 10.3 above, ended up in jail because the primary cost of misidentifying him was not born by the criminal who used his name, nor by the police who misidentified the criminal as Byrd, nor by any of the police, prosecutors, employers, credit issuers or others who continue to misattribute crimes to Byrd and act accordingly. The cost has been primarily born by Byrd. In our society while individuals are primarily legally responsible for their reputation, the actions of others (government entities, businesses, etc.) are increasingly causally responsible for how that reputation is constituted. This absurdity has absurd implications.

Current advice to protect oneself against identity theft includes checking one's credit record twice a year (up from once a year only a few years ago). Though prudent in the current US socio-economic environment, making individuals responsible for protecting their identity and reputation by such means is akin to requiring them to leave their homes unlocked while suggesting they check with the local pawn shop to see if any of their things are fenced as stolen. It is not a tremendous comfort that the 'pawn shop' in identity theft is larger, more centralized, and has in recent years made some efforts to return goods to their owners, i.e., correct credit records. Worse, as the far from unique case of Malcolm Byrd illustrates, it may only be a short time before one is well advised to check one's criminal record twice a year as well. In fact, Privacy Rights recommends that you "periodically obtain a copy of your driver's license record from your local DMV" for just such reasons ([Privacy Rights Clearinghouse, 2002]). For criminal identity theft, there is currently no centralized place to clear your record.

A longterm solution better than prosecuting the identity "thief" while leaving the victim to clean up the mess would be to structure the incentives in collecting, attributing, and dissemination information to accurately reflect costs. We have been looking at criminal records, but the same applies to other areas. If the sending of preapproved credit offers required that the senders bear the expected cost not just of duly reported fraudulent charges but of the resultant reputation damage, such offers might not be worth sending. Similarly if the expected damage caused by sharing of personal financial data were figured into the value of such sharing, there would be no need to push for legislation to allow people to opt in rather than opt out of such sharing. It would not be worthwhile for institutions to share; indeed the amount of data that is even worth collecting would probably greatly diminish as the responsibility not just the benefit for the correct value of that data were accounted.

How might this more accurate accounting be instituted? This is hard to say. Litigation is an easy answer. Another possibility is government reform of standards of evidence, not just for criminal trial but also for arrest, for attributions in best practice business accounting, etc. Many activities such as misdemeanor crimes and small value economic transactions might better be handled without affecting reputation at all. Any suggestion here would be very speculative; however, that some such change may be coming is reflected both in recent legislation in North America and Europe, and more importantly in corporate practice. Companies both large (IBM) and less large (Zero Knowledge) have made a substantial commitment to providing enterprise policy management service to corporations that would attempt to properly manage the data they have. If the proposal we suggest is followed, the potential exists to simplify the problem since less data are likely to be held. And certain types of data currently viewed as private might no longer need to be treated as such.

So far, this proposal still somewhat reflects the squishy worldview that treats Social Security numbers, credit card numbers, and such as quasi-private. This view relies on a notion that these are somehow secrets known only to the bearer of those numbers and those s/he trusts—as if one could have meaningful personal trust with thousands, indeed millions, of others. It also runs together these artificially private numbers with the actually private information associated with them: employment history, purchase history, etc. It is in their capacity to authorize transactions that such data acquire their need for privacy. If one could not use them to gain access to truly personal information, if one could not use them to create attributions of properties or behavior to the person assigned to them, then there would be no need to view them as private

Much of the modern consumer economy is built on the offering of credit with minimal authentication. While the direct costs for bad authentication of credit card transaction may be primarily born by the credit card industry (assuming the consumer notices them in a timely manner *and* follows all the measures necessary to remove false charges from their accounts), indirect costs of cleaning credit records, jobs lost or not offered, loans lost, time, psychological effects, etc. are primarily born by the party whose identity is spoofed. If these costs were born by the parties that authenticate improperly *and* by any party that propagates such information it would be financially infeasible for them to continue the cavalier authorization of transactions that have been a hallmark of current practice.

This could be taken to mean that every action we take should be scrutinized and properly bound to us. However, the costs of such an approach, both literal and intangible are astronomical. Alternatively, our responsibility for any action could (at minimum) be proportional to the degree of authentication associating us with that action. Criminal and other personal records are currently reputation management systems with no probabilities (in compiling the entries). However, building such probabilities in is a daunting, perhaps hopeless, task especially given the dynamics of how reliable identifications of various types are.

An even more direct approach may be more viable. For example, suppose that a loan is denied or a job application turned down due to errors in a credit report. Currently the reporting agency is obligated to correct errors documented as such, but it is not liable for any effects of the denied loan, particularly if it is simply passing on information that it acquired in good faith; thus it may be appropriate for the agency to similarly pass on its liability. However, if the agency were responsible for any such losses and required to cover any losses it could not pass on, then it would be much more careful about the data it stores, the supporting documentation of it, the reputation and indemnification of the source of the information, but also it would be more cautious in its sharing of such information with others. This has the advantage that, e.g., preapproved credit cards are not themselves a liability for issuers in this sense. But, pursuing someone to pay for charges on such a credit card might be. The burden of proof that a charge is legitimate would of course be on the card issuer and the merchant, but the cost of rectifying errors, the time and any expense of the consumer in rectifying the errors should also be on the issuer (more strictly the authenticator of the transaction). The same approach applies as well in criminal cases. If someone is arrested based on a misauthentication of outstanding charges, this should count as the false arrest that it is rather than as an unfortunate side effect of due process. And associated liability may propagate from the arresting law enforcement agency through the source of its information.

Identity theft as a privacy problem simply goes away on this approach, to be replaced by the problem of properly authenticating transactions that affect the reputation and/or economic and social freedoms of individuals. This is not without large social and infrastructural costs. For example, it may become much harder to obtain unsecured loans in such a society, and the trend away from cash transactions may reverse. However, it moves costs and incentives to those responsible for authorizations rather than those on whose behalf such authorizations are usurped.

7. Infrastructure Cost

We have already noted how accurate reflection of the costs of assigning, storing, and disseminating reputation would affect the incentives and behavior of infrastructure elements such as businesses and the components of the justice system. However, even without such reallocation, a more accurate assessment of infrastructure costs might lead to an increased emphasis on privacy.

Spam is a large privacy issue. (This is more from the right-to-be-let-alone aspect of privacy than the self-determination of reputation aspect we discussed in the last section.) But, it is not just an issue of personal inconvenience. Recent estimates of spam put it at approaching half of all email traffic in the US ([Krim, 2003]). This is a tremendous overhead born by business, government, and individuals. And, part of it comes from the distribution of email addresses without the consent of those who hold the addresses. Recent focus on SPAM as a major public thrust of some of the largest ISPs and software vendors, in addition to recent legislation, is evidence that this invasion of privacy is also recognized as a major cost to business.

Note that kneejerk 'solutions' to such problems, for example, wholesale automatic identification of mail senders, especially by the communications infrastructure, may actually cause more harm than good. This is not likely to deter spammers who have access to large numbers of zombie machines that will count as legitimate senders by protocols and who have easy access to jurisdictions from which sending spam is not a problem. In fact, such solutions provide an incentive for spammers to break into systems or otherwise steal accounts to send spam. Schneier notes, " anti-spam security that relies on positive identification isn't likely to work. It'll mean that more spam will rely on stolen accounts. It'll change the tactics of spammers, but not the amount of spam" ([Schneier, 2004]).

Thus, such approaches are likely to primarily hamper the private actions of the honest while at the same time making it more likely that they will be attacked and framed for sending spam rather than merely receiving it. For spam and for more directed communications, criminals already know how to communicate anonymously and privately. Another example, they can just steal cell phones for brief use, then toss them and steal more. Still another technique noted in the general press is to compromise a web host and leave files there for others to retrieve. Thus, monitoring communication primarily eavesdrops only on the law abiding.

One counterargument to this is that such activity by criminals involves transactional risk ([Schechter and Smith, 2003]). Thus, providing general private and anonymous Internet communication removes a disincentive to crime. True enough, but the analysis by Schechter and Smith does not account for the cost of privacy loss. If incorporated, an anonymous communications infrastructure may be more cost effective for the infrastructure providers.

Reduction in privacy also has a cost to security. A commonplace in recent polls is to ask how much privacy people would exchange for increased security. However, it is assumed rather than argued that decreasing privacy increases security. Just the opposite may be true. Law enforcement has made use of anonymous tips for years with the recognition that much of the information so gathered would not have been given without a plausible expectation of anonymity. Very shortly after September 11th, the Anonymizer set up an Web interface "providing anonymous access to the FBI's Terrorism Activity tip page to over 26,000 individuals around the world" ([CNN, 2001]). They have since added anonymous interface to the Utility Consumer's Action Network. Similarly, the Witness Protection Program relies on the ability to assign people a new identity. In an environment in which all commercial and public actions by individuals is monitored, this possibility becomes far less plausible. To effectively monitor to the degree necessary for effective authentication as discussed in section 10.6, the creation of a new identity would likely be noticed in a commercial database (whose entries would be shared without disincentives to do so). The person who recently turned in Khalid Sheikh Mohammed and received a new identity might not have risked doing so without a plausible new identity possible.

8. Conclusion

We have argued in this chapter that assumptions about privacy are not empirically justified. Contra that people will not pay for privacy we have found that when privacy is offered in a clear and comprehensible fashion, it sells well. Complex technologies offered for sale in response to nebulous threats don't sell well, even when those threats are against important targets. We also found that people are not wildly irrational in their dealings with privacy, especially when the cost of examining and understanding privacy policies and practices themselves is taken into account. Privacy is often a complex topic. Different people use the word to mean different things. What one person considers their deepest secret, another may announce to the world. For example, HIV-positive status is something that many people consider to be very private, but there are activists who make it the core of their public personas. That it is difficult to create products that address these complex needs should come as no surprise.

Finally, we observed that the cost of protecting privacy is not allocated in an accurate way. Reallocating appropriately and properly placing costs with those whose actions create them would remove identity theft as a privacy issue. A correct reallocation would also provide government and business with incentives to increase rather than decrease protection of individual privacy.

References

Acquisti, Alessandro (2004). Privacy in electronic commerce and the economics of immediate gratification. In Feigenbaum, Joan, editor, *ACM Conference on Electronic Commerce (EC'04)*. ACM Press.

CNN (Sept. 14, 2001). Web site passes anonymous tips to FBI. www.cnn.com/2001/TECH/internet/09/14/anonymous.tips/. Cf. also Secure Tips Online Program. www.anonymizer.com/tips/.

Mailboxes, Etc. Mailbox services. www.mbe.com/ps/ms.html.

FTC (2004). National and State Trends in Fraud & Identity Theft: January - December 2003. Federal Trade Commission Report. www.consumer.gov/sentinel/pubs/Top10Fraud2003.pdf.

Krim, Jonathan (March 13, 2003). Spam's Cost to Business Escalates. *The Washington Post*, page A01.

Privacy Rights Clearinghouse (2002). Fact Sheet 17(g): Criminal Identity Theft. www.privacyrights.org/fs/fs17g-CrimIdTheft.htm.

Schechter, Stuart E. and Smith, Michael D. (2003). How much security is enough to stop a thief? In Wright, Rebecca N., editor, *Financial Cryptography*, pages 122–137. Springer-Verlag, LNCS 2742.

Schneier, Bruce (Feb 15, 2004). The economics of spam. *Cryptogram Newsletter* www.schneier.com/crypto-gram-0402.html

Sullivan, Bob (March 9, 2003). The darkest side of ID theft. www.msnbc.com/news/877978.asp?0si=-&cp1=1.

US Census Bureau (1999). Curtain and Drapery Mills, Economic Census Manufacturing Industry Series. Report EC97M-3141B, US Census Bureau.

US Postal Service (1998). Pub. 201 - Consumer's Guide to Postal Services & Products. www.usps.com/cpim/ftp/pubs/pub201/pub201.htm#H1.

US Postal Service (2001). Comprehensive Statement on Postal Operations. wwwusps.com/financials/

Varian, Hal R. (1997). Economic Aspects of Personal Privacy. In *PRIVACY AND SELF-REGULATION IN THE INFORMATION AGE*. National Telecommunications and Information Administration, Washington, DC.

Westin, Alan (May 8, 2001). Opinion surveys: What consumers have to say about information privacy. Prepared Witness Testimony, The House Committee on Energy and Commerce.

Chapter 11

WHY WE CAN'T BE BOTHERED TO READ PRIVACY POLICIES

Models of Privacy Economics as a Lemons Market

Tony Vila
Harvard University
avila@fas.harvard.edu

Rachel Greenstadt
Harvard University
greenie@eecs.harvard.edu

David Molnar
University of California, Berkeley
dmolnar@hcs.harvard.edu

> *If we believe that people value privacy, why is there not an efficient market for it?*

People generally equate e-commerce with violations of their personal property. They are concerned that buying online will result in unwanted spam email, their personal information being sold to marketing organizations and possibly even their identity or credit card information stolen. Recent survey data indicated that 92% of consumers are concerned about the misuse of their personal information online,[Center for Democracy and Technology, 2002] and privacy concerns are the number one reason why individuals choose to stay off the Internet[Green et al., 2000]. Others simply decide that loss of privacy is an inevitable consequence of doing business these days. If we believe that people value privacy, why is there not an efficient market for it? This is the question that this paper seeks to address.

For the purposes of this paper, we will define "protecting privacy" as following the fair information practices principles as delineated by the FTC[Commission, 2000]. These principles are:

- Notice - Web sites provide consumers with clear and conspicuous notice of their information practices. This would include what information they collect, how they collect it, whether they provide the other properties, whether they disclose this information to other entities, and whether other entities are collecting information through the site.

- Choice - Web sites offer consumers choices as to how their personal information is used beyond the use for which the information was provided.

- Access - Web sites offer consumers reasonable access to the information a site has collected about them, and an opportunity to delete it, or correct inaccuracies.

- Security - Web sites take reasonable steps to protect the security of the information collected from consumers.

In 2000, the FTC found that that only 20% of randomly sampled web sites partially implemented all four fair information practices. The percentage was higher (42%) for the most popular web sites. There had been hope that privacy on the internet could be improved through seal programs[TrustE, 2003] or P3P[Mulligan et al., 2000], but by 2000 these programs had not seen wide adoption[Commission, 2000; EPIC, 1999].

Recently, however, things are looking up for privacy protection. A similar study to the FTC report was done in 2002 by the Progress and Freedom Foundation[Jr et al., 2002]. The survey found that web sites are collecting less information, notice is more prevalent, prominent and complete. Choice also increased, with the percentage of the most popular sites offering consumers a choice about sharing information with third parties jumped from 77% to 93%. With the introduction of P3P enabled browsers, P3P adoption was growing (5% in the random domain and 25% in the most popular domain). On the other hand, sites displaying seals were still a very small proportion of the sites (12%).

We attempt to explain these trends and understand where privacy protection and violations may go in future. In section 2, we present a simplified model of privacy as a lemons market with signaling. In section 3 we complicate the model by adding a cost to the consumer to search for a signal. We conclude with discussion of the model and future directions.

1. Related Work

Varian defines "privacy rights" as "the right not to be annoyed" and focuses on assignment of property rights in privacy as a means to establish a market[Varian, 1996]. Our work shows that this market may not be efficient in the presence of asymmetric information.

Acquisti has a general discussion of economic incentives for and against privacy-enhancing technologies, such as anonymizing web proxies; his paper also describes work on how information sharing between vendors in the presence of a strategic consumer leads naturally to a privacy-protecting regime[Acquisti, 2002]. One example of such sharing is the work on privacy policies by Calzolari and Pavan, in which buyers are allowed to choose between a contract whose terms are public(shared with all vendors) or private(shared only with a single vendor); they show that in this case buyers choose the appropriate contract to maximize their privacy[Calzolari and Pavan,]. Our work, in contrast, focuses on the information available to the consumer about the vendor.

2. Privacy as a Lemons Market

The "lemons market" was introduced by Akerlof as an example of asymmetric information [Akerlof, 1970]. Sellers present "peach" or "lemon" cars to buyers who cannot tell which is which. As a result, buyers pay only what they would pay for a lemon and no peach cars are sold.

Online, a consumer chooses among web sites that may respect her privacy ("Respecting" sites) or may not ("Defecting") with no way to determine beforehand which is which. Then privacy in web sites looks like the lemons market. As a result, we would expect all web sites to not respect privacy.

In the context of web sites, we can make this more formal as follows. Suppose web sites fall into two categories: Respecting(R) sites that do not sell private information and Defecting(D) sites that do sell such information. A customer may choose to buy or not buy with a site. If the customer buys from a Respecting site, it gains B. If it buys from a Defecting site, it obtains $B - V$, where V is the cost to the customer of a privacy violation. The resulting payoff matrix is

$$\begin{pmatrix} & Respects & Defects \\ Buys & B & B - V \\ Doesn't & 0 & 0 \end{pmatrix}$$

3. Privacy Signals

The lemons market for privacy motivates the introduction of privacy *signals*. For instance, a web site may adopt a strict privacy policy to demonstrate its commitment to keeping customer information private. In general, a signal is a means by which privacy-respecting sites can differentiate themselves from their defecting competitors.

Signalling is well studied in the context of a lemons market; if a signal is low cost for "good" players and high cost for "lemon" players, then consumers can reliably use the signal to separate good players from lemons[Spence, 1973]. Assuming that such a signal exists, we can show a separation in the web site privacy market.

Web sites now fall fall into four classes: Respecting who do not signal, Respecting who do signal, Defecting who do not signal, and Defecting sites who do signal. Consumers now fall into three classes: Buy from a site, Don't buy from a site, Only buy from a site that presents the signal that they follow fair information practices.
B = the benefit the consumer gets from a transaction
V = the cost for the consumer of having their privacy violated
P = the benefit the firm gets from the transaction
S_R, S_D = the cost to the respectful or defecting firm to send the signal guaranteeing privacy
I = the benefit the firm gets from selling the consumer's personal information.

The payoff matrix is then

$$\begin{pmatrix} & Respects-NS & Respects-S & Defects-NS & Defects-S \\ Buys & B,P & B,P-S_R & B-V,P+I & B-V,P+I-S_D \\ Doesn't & 0,0 & 0,-S_R & 0,0 & 0,-S_D \\ BuysSignal & 0,0 & B,P-S_R & 0,0 & B-V,P+I-S_D \end{pmatrix}$$

Now the rational choice of each player depends on the relationship between S_R, P, and $S_D - I$. In particular, if $S_R < P < S_D - I$, then all and only the respecting web sites will send the signal, and the rational consumer will only make transactions with these signalling web sites. This is the desired separation of the market. The separation requires that the signal be high cost for Defecting sites and low cost for Respecting sites, i.e. $S_D - S_R$ must be at least I.

Do signals with high cost for Defecting sites and low cost for Respecting sites exist in the real world? Privacy policies are the most obvious candidates for such a signal. The P3P standard provides a way for sites to mechanically codify privacy policies [Mulligan et al., 2000]. User interfaces such as the AT&T P3P Privacy Bird give customers easy ways to tell whether a site's P3P policy matches their individual preferences [AT&T,]. Implementing a P3P policy costs a significant amount of time and effort, demonstrating a commitment on the part of the web site to privacy.

At the same time, relying on privacy policies alone is problematic. What prevents a site from publicizing a strict policy but then reneging on the policy and selling information anyway? Put another way, where does the cost differential between Respecting and Defecting sites come from for privacy policies? One answer may lie in the legal and public relations exposure to a Defecting site that collects information despite the presence of a privacy policy. For example, Real Networks suffered public criticism when its software was found to gather and report information[McWilliams,]. Unfortunately, this sort of discovery happens rarely, and may not provide enough of an incentive against violating the policy.

Reputations offer a potential alternative. There is empirical evidence that reputations can work in electronic commerce to differentiate sellers. Resnick, Zeckhauser, Swanson, and Lockwood show that reputation on eBay does lead consumers to pay an average of 7.6% higher prices to sellers with high reputation over others with low reputations[Resnick et al., 2002]. Yamagichi and Matsuda show experimentally that reputation can alleviate a lemons market [Yamagichi and Matsuda, 2002]. Unfortunately, unlike eBay, no centralized, often-updated repository of web site privacy reputations exists. We cannot depend on a customer having knowledge of the web site's previous actions, or even other customer's reports of the web site's actions.

These issues cause us to take a different approach. Instead of focusing on the difference in cost to the web sites of sending a signal, we suggest focusing on the cost to the consumer of *testing* whether the web site is privacy-respecting. The resulting privacy market with testing is the focus of the next section.

4. Testing in the Lemons Market

We now introduce a factor T, the cost for a consumer to check if a firm is sending the a signal in the lemons market. This is analogous to hiring your own mechanic to check if a car is a lemon or not before buying it. For every signal a firm would create to represent its attitude towards your personal information, there are costs associated with it such as:

- Read the rather long privacy policy
- Check consumer responses and e-trust web sites
- Install the P3P bird program

Of course these are extremely heterogeneous actions and costs that we are looking at. Different firms would require different amounts of effort in checking on these signals, and each type of checking would take a different effort. Reading a click-through contract is not the same thing as researching in Consumer Reports. Different sectors will definitely have a different T associated for each. For the purposes of simplicity, we assume that consumers a priori assume the cost of T, based on their experience and conventional wisdom; they perceive T as the average of all firms, T_a.

So what happens when this cost T enters the traditional signaling payoff matrix?

Let us define variables representing:
B = the benefit the consumer gets from a transaction
T = the cost to test for the consumer

V = the cost for the consumer of having their privacy violated
P = the benefit the firm gets from the transaction
S = the cost to the firm to send the signal guaranteeing privacy
I = the benefit the firm gets from selling the consumer's personal information.

$$\begin{pmatrix} & Respects & Defects \\ Tests & B-T, P-S & -T, 0 \\ Doesn't & B, P-S & B-V, P+I \end{pmatrix}$$

Let us label p as the portion of firms that respect privacy and send the signal, with $(1-p)$ as the portion of firms that sell information and don't send the signal appropriately. We can then find the relative utility of deciding to test a site instead of buying without being aware.

$$\begin{aligned} (Tests) &= p(B-T)+(1-p)(-T) \\ &= pB-T \\ U(Doesn't) &= p(B)+(1-p)(B-V) \\ &= B-V+pV \\ U(Tests)-U(Doesn't) &= pB-T-(B-V+pV) \\ U(Tests)-U(Doesn't) &= pB-T-B+V-pV \\ U(Tests)-U(Doesn't) &= -(1-p)(B-V)-T \end{aligned}$$

When p approaches 1, and all firms respect privacy, then the consumer has great incentive to not test web sites, since the only difference is that he is paying T. As long as the system is making firms behave, then free riders emerge who dont want to take the cost of testing. When p approaches 0, and all firms sell personal information, than the consumer has great incentive to test web sites. Since we assume the cost of someone's privacy being violated to be higher than the benefit of the transaction and the cost of testing, $-(B-V)-T$ is positive. Similarly, let q be the proportion of the consumers who test, and $(1-q)$ as the portion of consumers who don't bother to test privacy policies. Checking the relative benefits reveals such:

$$\begin{aligned} U(Respects) &= q(P-S)+(1-q)(P-S) \\ &= P-S \\ U(Defects) &= q(0)+(1-q)(P+I) \\ &= P+I-qP-qI \\ U(Respects)-U(Defects) &= P-S-(P+I-qP-qI) \\ U(Respects)-U(Defects) &= -S-I+qP+qI \\ U(Respects)-U(Defects) &= -(S+I)+qP+qI \end{aligned}$$

When q approaches 1, and all consumers test web sites, then the firm has significant incentive to create a respectful privacy market, by P-S. When p approaches 0, and no consumers test web sites, then the firm is very likely to not respect privacy or send the signal, and stands to gain S+I.

This suggests a dramatic instability in the privacy market:

1 When all firms respect privacy, no consumers test.

2 When no consumers test for signals, all firms will sell.

3 When most firms sell personal information, consumers begin to test.

4 When all consumers test for signals, all firms will establish commitments to respect privacy (which is where the data suggests the market is headed).

5 Return to step 1 ad infinitum.

These broad trends will continue to revolve around various values of p and q as time moves on. Any attempt to reach a perfect market where all firms respect personal information, and consumers knowingly pay the premium for that, will dissolve, with firms leaping to take advantage of pauses in testing. What will eventually emerge are stable middle ground values for p and q: p* and q*.

$$\begin{aligned}
U(Tests) - U(Doesn't) &= 0 \\
-(1-p)(B-V) - T &= 0 \\
p^* &= \frac{B-V-T}{B-V} \\
U(Respects) - U(Defects) &= 0 \\
-(S+I) + q^*P + q^*I &= 0 \\
q^* &= \frac{S+I}{P+I}
\end{aligned}$$

If testing and non-testing consumers reach the right balance, then firms are indifferent between deciding to respect or not to respect privacy. Similarly, if a certain mix of firms signal and don't signal, then consumer's loss to testing equals how much they lose from having their information violated on average. This is the only Nash equilibrium in the payoff matrix, although it is not the most stable situation, since individual consumers or firms will only be indirectly and slowly affected by any change they make strategy, and not immediately drawn back to the equilibrium.

5. Conclusions and Future Directions

Our models explain previous trends in the web site privacy market. In the Introduction, we saw that despite the fact that more web sites follow the Fair Information Practices today than in 2000, the number of web sites with privacy seals has not increased proportionally. Through our analysis of privacy seals as a signal, we showed that this non-adoption can be explained because a privacy seal does not have a lower cost for privacy-respecting sites than for privacy-defecting sites.

Our models also give insight into the structure and future of privacy for web sites. Recall that our model for testing yielded a single equilibrium point, namely

$$(p^*, q^*) \quad = \quad (\frac{B-V-T}{B-V}, \frac{S+I}{P+I})$$

We now show that the market does not move directly to that equilibrium point. The continuing progression of privacy policies and consumer protection software, and fluctuating statistics regarding privacy protection, and the conclusions of our model both agree that instead the market oscillates around the equilibrium point. We suggest three reasons why.

1) Time to reach equilibrium is large. The simplest model is where every player is shortsighted, has perfect information, and can costlessly change their strategy each turn. We found a cycling through the four possible absolutes, of consumers testing or not testing, and companies signaling and not signaling. In this state, no one will ever reach the equilibrium point. Instead, assume that actors take a certain amount of time to find out information (like the proportion of their opposites who are following certain strategies) and to time. Each turn, only a certain portion of each actors will switch their strategy if switching benefits them. Even more, assume that this speed is directly proportional to the utility difference between one strategy and another, ie., the greater the benefit their is to switch to the other strategy, the more people will switch each turn. A system of two parametric equations could now be used to calculate how many people will test or how many firms will signal at any given turn. In this sub-model, the proportion of consumers and companies will frequently meet their part of the equilibrium point, but will "overshoot" the point, because their opposite number (the companies or consumers) are not in the correct proportion similarly. These should spiral around, until they eventually come to a stand still with both portions at the equilibrium point.

This is an interesting approach, because the velocity at which people change strategy is not actually equivalent to how fast the market reaches the equilibrium point. Too slow a speed, would mean no change at all from the present situation. Too fast a speed, guarantees more over shoots, the extreme of which would be eternal cycling between the four absolutes. Velocity, and changes in it, would only have second order effects. So consumer protection companies (or business consultants) who endeavor to spread information regarding and abilities to switch strategies, may either be irrelevant, or even preventing the market from reaching the equilibrium point, the most efficient position that the market can reach.

2) The point is not self-reinforcing and stable. Ideal equilibria are defined by recursive and supporting factors. A ball at rest in a valley is stable because if it starts to go to either side, gravity will pull it back down. This equilibrium point does not have immediate reinforcements. If there is a sudden shock that changes the portion of consumers who test, no consumers are directly affected and encouraged to restore the ideal portion. Instead, companies will have some incentive to deviate, and from that consumers will have incentive to deviate again, slowly oscillating once more around the equilibrium point.

3) The equilibrium point may change. The internet environment is such that benefits from purchases, benefits for consumer information, and signaling and testing costs may change. But even if they are all relatively static, there are changes.

In particular, the expected testing cost, T_a, can be viewed as an endogenous variable that is dependent on respectful firms trying to lower the cost of testing (they present T_1), and privacy violators who want to make testing a hassle to consumers by writing purposefully obtuse policies (they present T_2). Since we have

$$T_a = pT_1 + (1 - p)T_2$$

the actual equilibrium point for p is affected by, and changes with, the different firms out there. As more non-respectful firms enter the market, they raise the cost of T_a, changing the incentives for consumers, so that they are less likely to bother testing. This aspect reduces even further the effectiveness of possible reductions in T (like the P3P bird), since defecting firms can foil that by not adhering to those improvements, and in fact making them more difficult. A "one-armed bandit" approach to finding a firms true testing cost could also greatly change the landscape. By gradually estimating the cost and possible signal that a firm is sending, some interesting dynamics might affect the ways people should test sites[Burnetas and Katehakis, 2002].

These reasons suggest new directions if one wants to achieve an efficient and reliable marketplace. Simply making consumers more aware of the cost of privacy violations, or trying to decrease the cost of testing (via programs like the P3P bird) cannot make an absolutely efficient market. They can reduce the eventual ratios of testing consumers and respectful firms, or speed the arrival to the equilibrium point, but only that.

Even grouping all firms under one trusted intermediary has drawbacks, because as soon as all consumers trust that intermediary and no longer test it, it has every incentive to abuse its resources, this time with complete market power, making even an exact mixed-strategy equilibrium unlikely. The traditional "free market" approaches are in general unwieldy, given the problems for free-riding and interference from defectors.

Instead, our model suggests that one needs to provide firms with direct incentives to respect personal information. Permanent and enforced laws against certain uses of such information, or absolute reductions of T to 0 (such as by the government taking on the testing itself) are the only methods at the moment that can raise p and q to 1 in a stable solution (ie., making all consumers test and all companies respect fair information practices). Future research could focus on whether these conclusions are preserved even after augmenting our model by the previous complications.

Acknowledgements

We thank Professor Ed Glaeser and Professor Richard Zeckhauser for advice and suggestions on directions of research. We also thank Stuart Schecter for helpful discussions. We are also indebted to Hal Varian and the other attendees of the Workshop on Economics and Information Security for their constructive comments.

References

Acquisti, Alessandro (2002). Protecting privacy with economics: Economic incentives for preventive technologies in ubiquitous computing environments. In *Workshop on Socially-informed Design of Privacy-enhancing Solutions, 4th International Conference on Ubiquitous Computing (UBICOMP 02)*. `http://guir.berkeley.edu/privacyworkshop2002/papers/acquisti-ubicomp-09-19-02.pdf`.

Akerlof, George A. (1970). The market for lemons: Quality uncertainty and the market mechanism. *Quarterly Journal of Economics*, pages 488–500.

AT&T. P3p privacy bird. `http://www.privacybird.com`.

Burnetas, A.N. and Katehakis, M. N. (2002). Asymptotic bayes analysis for the finite horizon one armed bandit problem. *Probability in the Engineering and Informational Sciences*. to appear.

Calzolari, Giacomo and Pavan, Alessandro. Optimal design of privacy policies. `http://faculty.nwu.edu/faculty/pava/ODPP.pdf`.

Commission, Federal Trade (2000). Privacy online: Fair information practices in the electronic marketplace. `http://www.ftc.gov/reports/privacy2000/privacy2000.pdf`.

EPIC (1999). Pretty poor privacy. `http://www.epic.org`.

Center for Democracya and Technology (2002). Surveys main page. http://www.cdt.org/privacy/guide/introduction/surveyinfo.html.

Green, Heather, France, Mike, Stepanek, Marcia, and Borrus, Amy (2000). Our four-point plan. *Business Week Online.*

Jr, William F. Adkinson, Eisenach, Jeffrey A., and Lenard, Thomas M. (2002). Privacy online: A report on the information practices and policies of commercial web sites. http://www.pff.org/publications/privacyonlinefinalael.pdf.

McWilliams, Brian. Real networks hit with privacy lawsuit. http://www.internetnews.com/bus-news/article.php/8161_235141.

Mulligan, Dierdre, Cavoukian, Ann, Schwartz, Ari, and Gurski, Michael (2000). P3p and privacy: An update for the privacy community. http://www.cdt.org/privacy/pet/p3pprivacy/shtml.

Resnick, Paul, Zeckhauser, Richard, Swanson, John, and Lockwood, Kate (2002). The value of reputation on ebay: A controlled experiment. http://www.si.umich.edu/~presnick/papers/postcards/.

Spence, Michael (1973). Job market signalling. *The Quarterly Journal of Economics*, pages 355–74.

TrustE (2003). Truste statistics. http://www.truste.org/bus/pub_bottom.html.

Varian, Hal (1996). Economic aspects of personal privacy. http://www.sims.berkeley.edu/~hal/Papers/privacy/.

Yamagichi, Toshio and Matsuda, Masafumi (2002). Improving the lemons market with a reputation system. Technical report, University of Hokkaido.

Chapter 12

IMPROVING INFORMATION FLOW IN THE INFORMATION SECURITY MARKET

DoD Experience and Future Directions

Carl E. Landwehr
University of Maryland

> *Caveat Emptor! Let the buyer beware... Information is the best defense against purchasing defective products or falling victim to fraudulent practices.*
>
> *– from the website of the Morris County, New Jersey Public Library*

The market for information security has long been seen as dysfunctional [National Research Council, 1991]. Although there have been significant investments in research in techniques to improve information security (under various names, including computer security, information assurance, network defense, and so on), relatively little of that research is reflected in the products found in the marketplace or in the methods used to develop them. Why?

First, simply defining what "secure" means for some application or system is not an easy task. An intuitive notion of how a system is expected to behave, and not behave, rarely provides a sufficient basis to make any strong statement about the relative security or insecurity of a system.

Even if they have a clear understanding of the security they expect from a product, customers have a hard time knowing if they are getting it when they make purchase decisions. The features of a product are relatively easy to see and test; assessing the ability of the product to resist attack or abuse is much harder. Secure and insecure versions of the similar systems may behave indistinguishably except under attack.

Security properties are also unstable under system change. Even a small change in a system can make a big difference in its vulnerability, particularly if the system has not been constructed with security requirements in mind. Imagine a system in which a single bit may disable or enable a protection mechanism such as a virus scanner: flipping that bit clearly makes a major difference in vulnerability but little difference in observable behavior. The changes made in a typical software patch or system upgrade are of course much more substantial.

Security is also a system property. Two secure components connected inappropriately will make an insecure system. Assessing the security of individual components is hard enough; reasoning about entire digital systems, unless they are structured for this purpose, is extremely difficult.

Finally, system security depends on more than technology. Even systems in which significant resources have been devoted to security engineering may be abused by operators or users who are too trusting of others or too untrustworthy themselves.

Faced with these difficulties, and offered the choice between a system displaying a rich set of features, though cobbled together under the surface, and a system that provides only a few functions, albeit solidly implemented, is it surprising that for many years buyers have chosen sizzle security?

1. U.S. Defense Efforts to bring security information to the marketplace

Early Years

Security was a strong factor in the early history of electronic computers – the computations that motivated their development, such as decrypting intercepted messages, generating gunnery tables and developing weapons, had military applications. But the computers themselves were so big and so few that their computations were relatively easy to protect simply by limiting physical access to the machines. Further, users often shared these early machines sequentially, so there was relatively little opportunity for one user's computation to affect another's.

As multiprocessing and then timesharing of computers was developed in the 1960's, assuring the separation of different users' computations became more important, so that a single user could not bring down a system or steal another user's data. In this period, commercial and military concerns about computer security diverged. Commercial concerns naturally focused on the flow and protection of financial assets. The desire to prevent, detect, and prosecute commercial fraud motivated both security policy and technology development in this area and typically led to controls on application-level programs, so that only authorized individuals could invoke certain operations, and to the generation and preservation of audit trails so that potential fraud could be identified and the perpetrators identified, prosecuted, and convicted.

Military information security concerns at this time focused primarily on preserving the confidentiality of sensitive information. Computers were few, large, and expensive; it made economic sense to share them among users and applications. Yet leakage of sensitive information from a highly classified application to uncleared users might compromise an expensive intelligence collection system or a particular military operation and have a tremendous cost in dollars and lives; further, the compromise might not be detected.

These facts dictated a focus on preventive measures that would withstand a determined attack by a capable opponent. The notion of building systems that could protect sensitive information from a Trojan horse program – one which had full access to sensitive data and would try to export it without arousing suspicion – arose in this context. Although computer and software vendors sometimes asserted their systems could provide the kind of isolation desired by the military, when subjected to attack, their systems failed the test.

Military investment subsequently fueled much of the research and development in this area, though perhaps a declining fraction over the past decade or so, as computers have become critical to so many functions throughout society. The focus of this research, particularly in the early years was most often on securing the lower levels of the infrastructure – the operating systems, for example, rather than the applications, both because of the diversity of military applications and the belief that securing the applications without securing the infrastructure would be like building on a foundation of sand.

The DoD Strategy for Improving Computer Security through the Market

In the early years, the U.S. Department of Defense (DoD) often built its own computers and operating systems to suit its particular needs. By the late 1970's and early 1980's, U.S. government officials, and in particular, Stephen Walker of DoD, correctly recognized that, for cost reasons, the military would increasingly be driven to base its information systems on commercial, off-the-shelf, computers and software. These systems clearly lacked the properties sought by DoD to enforce its security policies. Yet the research already conducted under DoD sponsorship seemed to indicate that if vendors could be persuaded to pay more attention to security issues as they developed their systems, providing the structure and "hooks" needed for more secure modes of operation, commercial platforms might in fact provide an adequately secure base for DoD applications. Then DoD might simply acquire a high-security version of a commonly available product, taking advantage of the economies of scale. But how could DoD bring about this happy state of affairs in the commercial marketplace?

The strategy that Walker played the key role in developing was, in effect, one of trying to make better information about product security available to consumers. A set of criteria would be developed that could be used to evaluate the security of commercially offered computer systems. Products would be evaluated against these criteria and the results published. Once consumers (and in particular DoD acquisition program managers) could easily understand which systems had stronger security and which had weaker, they could make intelligent choices about which to buy for systems with security requirements. DoD could also make it a policy to purchase systems that achieved higher security ratings. The potential for increased sales in the defense market would give vendors the needed incentive to invest the presumably marginal added development cost needed to provide a base for higher security versions of their systems. In the best case, even non-defense sales would improve for systems with higher ratings and the market would produce better quality products for everyone.

This seemed a rational strategy, one based on improving the information available to the marketplace. It offered both the carrot of increased sales for systems with good evaluations, and the stick of an impartial, *Consumer Reports*-like mechanism to evaluate product security. The government had also followed a somewhat similar strategy in identifying equipment that met other kinds of security requirements in its TEMPEST Preferred Products List, an Endorsed Crypto Products List, and a Deguasser Qualified Products List.

Implementing the Strategy

Major investments were needed to implement this strategy. The evaluation criteria had to be developed, a major effort in itself. The National Computer Security Evaluation Center (originally planned by Walker to be at the National Bureau of Standards, but ultimately created at the National Security Agency in 1981) was created to draft the criteria and subsequently evaluate products against it. The criteria became a book length document, the Trusted Computer System Evaluation Criteria (TCSEC), first published in 1983. Its cover color soon supplanted its lengthy title, and it was universally known as "The Orange Book." It defined seven ordered classes of overall product security ranging from level A1 (highest) through B3, B2, B1, C2, C1, to D (lowest). To meet the criteria for a given level, a product had to provide both an increasing set of security features such as audit functions, access control functions, information labels, and an increasing amount of evidence that the system correctly implemented the specified functions. This assurance came both from system documentation and increasing test requirements. Evaluators were required to review specified documentation and, depending on the evaluation class sought, assure that it corresponded accurately to the system as implemented. At the highest class specified (A1), no additional functions were required over the prior class (B3), but formal methods of specification and verification were to be applied to increase assurance that the system would behave as intended.

As added carrots to developers, the government agreed to bear the cost of evaluations (though the developer was responsible for developing the needed documentation), to evaluate only products submitted to it, and to conduct evaluations under nondisclosure agreements that would prevent detailed evaluation information from flowing to other parts of the government. The criteria took a good deal of expertise to apply, so the government also had to develop and train a workforce that was up to the job.

Experience

The first Orange Book evaluations were completed in 1984. Two business-oriented add-on access control packages, RACF-MVS and ACF2-MVS/SP achieved ratings of C1 and C2 respectively, and Honeywell's Secure Communications Processor (SCOMP) achieved an A1 rating. The SCOMP had been specifically developed in response to DoD requirements and its evaluation was actually underway as the Orange Book was being written. In 2000, the final TCSEC evaluation was complete: Sybase Adaptive Server Anywhere v. 7.0 achieved a C2 rating. In the 16 years from 1984-2000, a total of 85 evaluation certificates were issued; 29 more evaluations were initiated but not completed. The profile of systems evaluated over the period is shown in Figures N-1 and N-2. In many cases, after a system is evaluated, it is changed or updated, and the changed system must be re-evaluated; this is the basis for the distinction between number of certificates issues and number of distinct systems. Evaluations are now conducted under the international Common Criteria framework by a set of private, government-certified laboratories, addressed later in this paper.

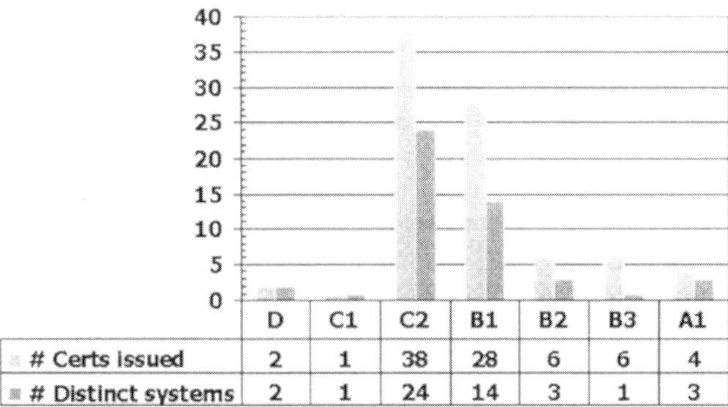

	D	C1	C2	B1	B2	B3	A1
# Certs issued	2	1	38	28	6	6	4
# Distinct systems	2	1	24	14	3	1	3

Figure 12.1. TCSEC evaluations completed 1984–2000. Data from `http://www.radium.ncsc.mil/tpep/epl`

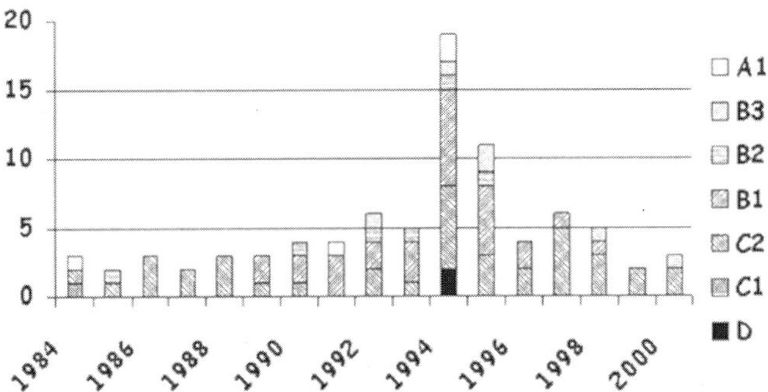

Figure 12.2. TCSEC evaluations completed by year and class 1984–2000. Data from `http://www.radium.ncsc.mil/tpep/epl`

This attempt to leverage market forces had some successes, but failed ultimately to have the effect its creators intended, for several reasons.

The evaluation process proved expensive and time-consuming. As noted, evaluations required expertise on the part of evaluators and developers. They were expensive for both the government and the developers, requiring substantial documentation to be generated by the developer and reviewed by the evaluators. Neither party felt in control of the resulting delays: because the process was voluntary, neither side could impose a schedule on the other.

The evaluation criteria were relatively abstract and interpretations had to be developed for different kinds of components. These generated a "case law" of interpretations that sometimes led to protracted discussions over "criteria creep" when vendors felt they were being subjected to more stringent interpretations than had been applied to earlier systems. Because the evaluation classes bundled assurance and features, they didn't apply well to high assurance devices with simple, specific functions.

There were significant startup problems in enforcing the intended procurement policy. In general, government procurements are required to be competitive. Initially, there were few evaluated products available. So, a procurement that required a product meeting, say, the B1 evaluation class might effectively designate a single supplier, thereby violating government procurement rules for open competition. Instead of having an advantage, the vendor to first achieve an evaluated product might be penalized, in effect, for having invested the resources needed to obtain it. Ultimately, officials controlling the procurements demanded the latest operating systems and features as long as there was some evidence of intention to have the product evaluated eventually; this gave vendors an incentive to start the evaluation process, but not necessarily to complete it.

Product changes and upgrades were difficult to accommodate. To keep up with advancing technology and competing products, and even to correct flaws, vendors need to update their systems regularly. Any change to a system would require its re-evaluation. In the end, a "ratings maintenance program" (RAMP) was developed to deal with this problem.

Systems, rather than products, are frequently the significant unit of procurement. Governments often procure systems, not single products. The evaluation criteria proved difficult or impossible to apply to systems – yet security is fundamentally a system property. During this time period, networking of systems became increasingly important, both to system function and to system security. Although a "network interpretation" of the criteria was developed, it was not effective.

The government's market leverage declined. As the commercial market for computers boomed, the government's share of that market declined substantially, reducing government leverage overall, and private purchasers did not in general perceive similar security needs.

In the end, the promised the carrot of lucrative government procurements of evaluated systems never really materialized for most of the vendors who participated in the program. The investment required of the vendors in order to meet the evaluation criteria, in dollars but more importantly in development time, proved more than they could justify economically.

2. Globalization

A few years after the Orange Book was published, Canada, the UK, and several European countries began developing and adapting their own evaluation criteria and mechanisms. These related efforts eventually led to the Common Criteria that are in use today. These criteria provide a flexible means for specifying security functions and levels of assurance relatively independently. This flexibility imposes a corresponding specification burden, however. An independent laboratory, paid by the developer, performs the evaluation (and in many cases, a separate part of the same laboratory is paid by the same developer to produce the documentation to be evaluated). Government participation, though at a much lower level, is still required to certify the evaluation practices of the commercial laboratories. Although this process has shifted the financial burden of evaluations from government to industry and accelerated the speed of evaluations, it is not clear that it is contributing greatly to improved security in delivered products, particularly at the lower assurance levels.

3. Conclusions and future directions

Rational market decisions depend on good information. All of the attempts to provide security evaluation criteria and to evaluate products can be seen as efforts to improve the flow of information in the market for secure computer systems.

The slow rate at which information about the security properties of products is generated impedes improvements in security of deployed systems. More precisely, the lack of specific information about the ability of specific components and system architectures to preserve information availability, integrity, and confidentiality in the face of failures and attacks, and the difficulty of developing this information quickly, is a strong factor in the current generally poor state of computer system security in many widely distributed computer systems.

Experience shows that information about computer security properties is hard to obtain. The properties are not only difficult to specify and quantify, they are time-consuming to evaluate. Though asymmetric information may be a factor in this market, in that a seller may know more about the security properties of his product than the buyer can, in many cases even the vendor lacks full knowledge of his product. Because it takes significant time and energy to extract the information needed to support rational decisions, the buyer commonly faces a choice between new, unevaluated products or systems using the fastest hardware and providing the latest features, but with uncertain security properties, and older products with better known properties but poorer performance.

One way to improve the flow of this kind of information would be to seek measures and assessments of product security that can be obtained quickly and easily. Perhaps security could be viewed as a "hidden variable" and researchers might look for related exposed variables that could be assessed more quickly. For example, a developer might be able to certify that a piece of software is not subject to buffer overflow problems. The concept of proof-carrying code also help: some basic properties of the code can be certified immediately before it is executed.

One might also consider providing tools to help evaluate open source software. Security information about proprietary software can take longer to develop because only the proprietor has unrestricted access to the code and so the decision of whether to apply resources to security analysis of it is constrained. Opening source permits anyone who cares to apply resources to this task to do so [Witten, Landwehr and Caloyannides, 2001]. DARPA's Composable High Assurance Trusted Software (CHATS) program funded some efforts to encourage security review of open source software [Sardonix].

Other kinds of information, beyond the internal properties of components or systems, are lacking from the security marketplace as well. These include reliable information on actual system behavior, actual security incidents, and actual losses. Other mechanisms are needed to foster bringing this kind of information, which is often considered sensitive by the parties who control it, to the marketplace, but may be releasable in aggregate form [Geer, 2003].

Market pressures can indeed influence vendor behavior. In January 2002, the dominant company in the software industry changed course significantly by announcing an initiative in "Trustworthy Computing" and, according to its own statements, has since invested hundreds of millions of dollars in trying to improve the security engineering in its software development processes and its products. This behavior was apparently triggered by a perception that the continuing stream of security incidents facilitated by features and flaws in their products would eventually deter buyers. Nevertheless, it remains difficult for their customers to make valid comparisons among different products.

Better information will make a better market for computer security. We need to explore how to bring that information to decision makers efficiently.

References

National Research Council, System Security Study Committee, CSTB, *Computers at Risk*, National Academy Press, 1991. Chapter 6, "Why the Security Market Has Not Worked Well", pp.143–178. Also available at `http://www.nap.edu`.

B. Witten., C. Landwehr, and M. Caloyannides. Does open source improve security? *IEEE Software 18*, 5, (Sept. 2001), 57–61.

Sardonix website: `http://www.sardonix.org`

D. Geer. Information security: why the future belongs to the quants. *IEEE Security & Privacy* (July/August 2003), 24-32.

Chapter 13

PRIVACY ATTITUDES AND PRIVACY BEHAVIOR

Losses, Gains, and Hyperbolic Discounting

Alessandro Acquisti
H. John Heinz III School of Public Policy and Management
Carnegie Mellon University
acquisti@andrew.cmu.edu

Jens Grossklags
School of Information Management and Systems
University of California at Berkeley
jensg@sims.berkeley.edu

We discuss which factors play a role in the decision process of individuals with respect to their privacy and information security concerns

Several surveys have identified personal information security and privacy as some of the most pressing concerns of those using new information technology. On the Internet, sales for billions of dollars are said to be lost every year because of information security fears.[1] At the same time, several technologies have been made available to protect individuals' personal information and privacy in almost any conceivable scenario - from browsing the Internet to purchasing on- and off-line. With some notable exceptions, very few of these technologies have been successful in the marketplace. There is apparently a demand, and there is an offer. So, why does market clearing seem to be absent?

In this paper we discuss which factors play a role in the decision process of individuals with respect to their privacy and information security concerns, and advance hypotheses about why individuals' information security attitudes seem inconsistent with their behavior.

[1]See, for example, [Commission, 2000].

Understanding this dichotomy is important for the formulation of information policies and for the design of information technologies for personal information security and privacy. Technically efficient technologies have gained only lackluster results in the marketplace. This should be a signal that we need to incorporate more accurate models of users' behavior into the formulation of both policy and technology. In this chapter we try to offer insights on such models. Although in the rest of this chapter we will mostly focus on privacy concerns, most of the analysis can also be applied with minor modifications to personal information security concerns.

1. Personal Information Security and Privacy: Attitudes versus Behavior

Advancements in information technology have often created new opportunities for use and risks for misuse of personal information. Recently, digital technologies and the diffusion of the Internet have have caused both popular concerns and market-based offerings of protective technologies to grow.

Rising concerns have been documented by several surveys and over time. In a Jupiter survey conducted in Spring 1999, forty percent of the 2,403 respondents said that they would have shopped on-line more often if more security of personal information could be guaranteed. A PriceWaterhouseCoopers study in 2000 showed that nearly two thirds of the consumers surveyed abandoned more than once an on-line purchase because of privacy concerns. A Federal Trade Commission (FTC) study reported in 2000 that sixty-seven percent of consumers were "very concerned" about the privacy of the personal information provided on-line ([Commission, 2000]). A February 2002 Harris Interactive Survey ([Harris Interactive, 2002]) stated that the three biggest consumer concerns in the area of on-line personal information security were: companies trading personal data without permission, the consequences of insecure transactions, and theft of personal data. According to a Jupiter study in 2002, "$24.5 billion in on-line sales will be lost by 2006 - up from $5.5 billion in 2001. On-line retail sales would be approximately twenty-four percent higher in 2006 if consumers' fears about privacy and security were addressed effectively." ([Jupiter Research, 2002]).

In addition, some of the numerous surveys in this field not only reveal that individuals are concerned about the privacy and security of their personal information. They also document that certain individuals *claim* they would be willing to take steps to protect their own information - including, in some cases, paying for it.[2]

[2]See Truste-Boston Consulting Group 1997 privacy survey, quoted by the Center for Democracy and Technology, www.cdt.org.

However, more recent surveys, anecdotal evidence, and experiments have painted a different picture. [Chellappa and Sin, 2002], [Harn et al., 2002], [Spiekermann et al., 2002], and [Jupiter Research, 2002] have found evidence that even privacy concerned individuals are willing to trade-off privacy for convenience or to bargain the release of very personal information in exchange of relatively small rewards. In addition, the failure of several online services aimed to provide anonymizing services to Internet users [3] provides indirect anecdotal evidence of the reluctance of most individuals to pay to protect their personal information.

Comparing these apparently conflicting data raises three related questions:

1 Are the two sets of evidence (attitudes revealed in surveys and behavior exposed in experiments) *truly* in contradiction? In other words, is there an actual dichotomy between attitudes and behavior with regard to privacy and security of personal information - or, rather, those apparent discrepancies can be attributed to wrongful measurements and procedures?

2 If a dichotomy actually exists, can we characterize its causes? For example, can we find a relationship between how informed an individual is about privacy and personal information security issues and her attitudes and behavior in this area? What are the relations between her market behavior as an economic agent and her behavior in terms of privacy and information security? What are the psychological factors and economically driving variables that ultimately determine the behavior of information security concerned individuals?

3 Does an observed difference between actual behavior and reported attitudes actually represent a conflict with the economic assumption of rationality and the economic agent's search for an economic optimum? For example, are individuals acting against or in their best interest when they choose *not* to shield themselves from possible information intrusions, or when they accept to give away personal data in exchange for small rewards?

In the rest of this chapter we will comment on questions 1 and 3, but we will focus on question 2. In particular, we will discuss possible heuristics applied by individuals facing privacy and information security-related decisions.

[3] See [Brunk, 2002].

2. Exploring the Dichotomy

The first question to address is whether, in fact, we should be at all surprised by the comparison of results from privacy surveys (such as [Commission, 2000]) and experiments (such as [Spiekermann et al., 2002]).

The apparent dichotomy could simply be explained by observing that different people act in different ways, and those who claim that their privacy is important are not those who fail to take actions to protect themselves.

However, that this unlikely is the case should be evident from the magnitudes of the results reported by both experimental and survey data. Although in different setups, the vast majority of subjects (both those interviewed for surveys and those tested during experiments) expressed privacy concerns *and* still traded-off privacy for other advantages (rewards, convenience, etc.). In addition, in their experiment, [Spiekermann et al., 2002] controlled for individual behavior and attitudes for each participant. They found that also those individuals classified as privacy advocates would in fact reveal personal information in exchange of small rewards.

Another argument brought forward to refute the existence of a dichotomy relies on the difference between the two following concepts: 1) protecting one's privacy and information security, and 2) offering personal information in exchange of some reward. This argument emphasizes that the markets for protecting and for trading personal information may be related, but not interchangeable.

We agree with the observation that these two markets should not be confused. However, this argument cannot discount the evidence that many privacy-concerned individuals explicitly *claimed*, in surveys, to be willing to pay to protect their privacy - but then acted otherwise. In such case a dichotomy appears *within* the market for information protection. Furthermore, if the two markets for information protection and information trading are distinct (as well as the decision processes of the individuals in each market), then it remains to be explained where the differences lie and what are their causes. Both protecting and revealing personal information imply material and immaterial (perceived) costs and benefits. Our goal in this chapter is precisely to explore the heuristics through which individuals weight these costs and benefits. it could be that analyzing the differences between the market for information hiding and the market for information sharing, we can also understand better the dichotomy between attitudes towards information hiding and behavior in terms of information sharing.

An additional argument against the existence of a dichotomy is that many individuals may in fact be endorsing a defensive strategy by *not completing* at all certain transactions. Again, many individuals have certainly adopted this strategy to address their privacy concern. Simply observing this, however, does not explain why such approach is also adopted in presence of protective technologies available at low monetary or immaterial costs in the market.

Our analysis instead aims to understanding why individuals decide to take different actions - such as completing a certain transaction without protecting their information, completing the transaction under the umbrella of some technology or policy that protects their information, or not completing the transaction at all. Why privacy concerned individuals can and do react in so many different ways is precisely what we attempt to understand by addressing question 2).

In doing so, we will touch also upon the related question 3): which individual behavior is optimal when her personal information security and privacy are at stake? However, we will only comment briefly on this point. We refer the reader to other (current, e.g., [Acquisti, 2002a], and forthcoming) research for more in depth analysis of the existence and efficiency of an equilibrium in the market for personal information.

Attitudes, Behavior, and Privacy

Individuals who claim they are concerned about their personal information act in various, different ways when an information-sensitive situation actually arises. Some complete transactions anyway, without actually protecting personal information. Some give away information for small rewards. Some falsify the information they provide to other parties.[4] Some other avoid information risks altogether by aborting ongoing transactions (and ignoring protecting technologies).

What influences these choices? Are there common, underlying factors which can explain the variety of forms that the attitudes/behavior dichotomy takes? In this section we address this question by analyzing the individual's decision process with regards to privacy issues.

The lack of correspondence between expressed attitudes and subsequent behavior has been detected in several aspects of human behavior and studied in the social psychology literature since [LaPiere, 1934] and [Corey, 1937]. On the other side, evidence of attitudes *causing* a particular behavior has been provided by [Ajzen, 1988], [Eagly and Chaiken, 1993], and [Fazio, 1990]; evidence of *behavior influencing attitudes* has been also described by [Festinger, 1957], [Festinger and Carlsmith, 1959] and [Aronson and Mills, 1959]. These nuances may make the reader sensitive to the intricacies involved in conducting empirical work on human

[4]See the 8th annual poll of the Graphics, Visualization, and Usability Center at the Georgia Institute of Technology, www.gvu.gatech.edu.

attitudes and behavior, and aware of the particular challenges involved in interpreting privacy surveys and privacy experiments.

Experimental research work in psychology must always be carefully controlled for other sources of observed differences - in particular those that can be attributed to the research procedures. During interviews or questionnaire sessions, for example, people might feel a pressure to comply to a norm or a need to satisfy the researcher or interviewer; they might report a better version of themselves to avoid embarrassment or to strive for approval. The researcher may influence the results of a study by modifying details in the design: for example, phrasing of questions can induce question-order effect, while in behavioral experiments, the "experimenter effect" may bias participants when they are imposed *surveillance* in a controlled laboratory environment.

Careful research into the attitudes-behavior relationship has highlighted many explaining factors (see, e.g., [Fazio, 1990] for a review): *situational* variables (including normative constraints, inducements, and the individual's vested interest in the issue), personality factors (such as self-monitoring, self-consciousness, and the individual's level of moral reasoning), and attitudinal qualities (such as the confidence with which an attitude is held, and the process and time the attitude was formed).

In particular, privacy is a concept interwoven to many aspects of an individual's psychology and personal life, and confronts the individual with many demanding trade-off decisions. Therefore, in our analysis we must expect the existence of several factors affecting the decision process of the individual. As researchers, we are faced with the task to evaluate how those factors are affecting differently the individual at the forecasting (survey) and operative (behavior) phases, thus leading to the variety of adopted privacy strategies quoted above. It may well be that many of the parameters influencing the privacy decision process of the individual are perceived differently at the forecasting (survey) and operative (behavior) phases, thus leading to the variety of adopted strategies quoted above. The following sections are devoted to discuss those further parameters that we believe add to the understanding of the concept of privacy and the individual decision process in front of information-sensitive decisions.

3. Factors Affecting the Rational Decision Process

Elsewhere, one of the authors (see [Acquisti, 2002b]) formalizes the abstract economic trade-offs faced by an idealized rational agent who were to decide between information release and information protection. As we move from abstract representations to actual observations, we note that real human beings will face an intricate web of trade-offs dominated by subjective evaluations and uncertainties when attempting to "solve" for the best privacy decision. Because of uncertainties, complexities, and psychological nuances that we describe below, many genuinely privacy sensitive individuals may decide against protecting their own personal information. The decision process considered by an individual therefore does not reduce to (just) an issue of different privacy sensitivities. Several other factors may be playing a role, and their relevance may be realized by the individual only when she is facing an actual decision rather than a fictional survey. The factors that we have observed through surveys, user studies, and analysis that could influence the individual are listed below:

1 Limited information, and, in particular, limited information about benefits and costs.

2 Bounded rationality.

3 Psychological distortions.

4 Ideology and personal attitudes.

5 Market behavior.

If the above factors impact the decision process of the individual, and if their perception during an experiment or survey is different from their perception when an actual decision has to be taken, then these factors may also cause the dichotomy between abstractly stated attitudes and actual behavior. (Of course, the residual dichotomy between attitude and behavior may also be due, as discussed above, to the artificial nature of the survey environment.) Hence we discuss them in more detail below.

Limited information. The amount of information the individual has access to: Is she aware of information security risks and what is her knowledge of the existence of protective technology?

The individual may not be at all aware of information security risks during certain transactions, or may ignore the existence of protective technologies, in which case the consideration of the parameters in an otherwise fully rational model would be distorted.

Gathering full information on every aspect of life is impossible. As a result individuals have to decide based upon incomplete or asymmetric information. Both concepts are well known in the economic literature: asymmetric information was scholarly first analyzed by Akerlof in his famous market for lemons ([Akerlof, 1970]). Varian discusses similar concepts in the privacy scenario ([Varian, 1996]). Incomplete information becomes a problem for the individual when she has to commit to an action without a full assessment of the associated privacy-risks. In our scenario, the individual may be ignorant about the risks she incurs by not protecting her personal information or about ways to protect herself. People may assume that institutions and governmental organizations are providing a secure platform for their actions.

Benefits and costs. In particular, information may be limited about benefits and costs related to privacy issues. Obviously, there are several benefits and costs associated to using (or not using) protective technologies. Only some of the costs are monetary (and they could be either fixed - such as adoption costs, or variable - such as usage costs). Other costs may be immaterial: learning costs, switching costs, usability costs, and social stigma when using anonymizing technologies, and may only be discovered through actual usage (see, for example, the difficulties in using privacy and encrypting technologies described in [Whitten and Tygar, 1999]). A survey participant may not be considering or realizing the existence of all these possible benefits and costs when answering abstract questionnaires.

One example of these hard to assess costs is stigma. Goffman [Goffman, 1963] defined stigma as an "attribute that is deeply discrediting" that reduces the bearer "from a whole and usual person to a tainted, discounted one." Consider, for example, the uneasiness of using stronger anonymizing or privacy enhancing technology, like encryption or onion-routing networks, which arises from the fear of judgement of others about what information or practices should be hidden from them. For example, personalized anonymization may be regarded as suspicious by governmental as well as by more community-based organizations. On the other side, *not* using security technologies might represent a psychological cost. For example, an individual might fear embarrassment when requesting that content filters on a public library computer should be shut down in order to be able to acquire information about topics that overlap with restricted content.

Bounded rationality. Is the individual able to calculate the various parameters relevant to her choice, or is she rather limited by bounded rationality? Is she able to quantify costs and benefits of revealing or hiding information?

Bounded rationality refers to both the inability to calculate probabilities and amounts for risks and related costs for the various possible individual strategies, but also to the inability to process all the uncertain and stochastic information related to information security costs and benefits. Classic economic literature assumes humans to be rational in all aspects of life. However, even in situations with full information humans are not always capable of processing all data and deriving correct conclusions. As one of the first Herbert Simon incorporated constraints on the information-processing capacities of the individuals or entities (see [Berger, 1982]). Economic theories of bounded rationality can be constructed by modifying classical or perfect rationality assumptions in various ways: (i) by introducing risk and uncertainty into demand and/or cost functions, (ii) by assuming that the entity has only incomplete information about alternatives, or (iii) by assuming complexity in the cost function or other environmental constraints so great as to prevent the actor from calculating the best course of action. The relation to the privacy notion discussed here is obvious. Individuals would collapse under the task of calculating their best strategies to minimize privacy risks for all possible interactions.

In the scenario we consider, when an individual is providing personal information to other parties, she loses control of her personal information. That loss of control propagates and persists for an unpredictable span of time. Hence, the individual is in a position of information asymmetry with respect to the party with whom she is transacting, and the value of the factors to be considered are very difficult to calculate correctly. In other words, the negative utility coming from future potential misuses of somebody's personal information is a random shock whose probability and scope are extremely variable, and the individual is likely in a condition of bounded rationality. For example, a small and apparently innocuous piece of information might become a crucial asset in the right context. Furthermore, an individual who is facing potential privacy intrusions is actually facing risks whose amounts are distributed between zero and possibly large (but mostly uncertain) amounts according to mostly unknown functions. Hence, the individual may not be able to quantify or calculate risks and benefits (see also [Noam ,1996]). In other words, individuals might decide not to protect themselves because the material and immaterial costs of protection, given the current technologies, are actually higher than the expected losses from privacy intrusions. Thus, the decision not to protect oneself paradoxically may be considered as a rational way to react to these uncertainties: the "discrepancies" between privacy attitudes and privacy behavior may reflect what could at most be called a "rational ignorance."[5]

Psychological distortions. Are the individual's calculations affected by psychological distortions such as self-control problems, hyperbolic discounting, underinsurance? Literature in psychology and behavioral economics has identified numerous factors that can lead to substantial, however, predictable deviations from behavior one would expect from an agent acting according to the classical rational model (see, for example, [Rabin and O'Donoghue, 2000]).

Individuals might impose constraints on their future behavior even if these constraints limit them in achieving maximum utility. This concept is incorporated into the literature as the self-control problem (sometimes also titled as changing tastes). McIntosh ([McIntosh, 1969]) tried to approach this puzzling problem in the following way: "The idea of self-control is paradoxical unless it is assumed that the psyche contains more than one energy system, and that these energy systems have some degree of independence from each other." According to this idea, some economists now model individuals as multi-sided personalities, e.g. one

[5] See, in a different context, [Lemley, 2000].

personality as a farsighted planner and another one as a myopic doer ([Thaler and Shefrin, 1981]).

The protection against one's future lack of own willpower could be a crucial aspect in providing a link between information security attitudes and actual behavior. People do want to protect themselves before information losses, but similarly to the attempt to stop smoking or the realization of planned consumption behavior, they might fail. One of the experiments reported in an earlier section of this paper already provided evidence for missing self-control (see, for details, [Spiekermann et al., 2002]).

Furthermore, evidence of psychological experiments and observations suggest that human discounting is dynamically inconsistent. [Ainslie, 1975] found that discount functions are approximately hyperbolic. Hyperbolic discount functions are characterized by a relatively high discount rate over short horizons and a relatively low discount rate over long horizons. This discount structure sets up a conflict between today's preferences, and the preferences that will be held in the future ([Laibson, 1997]). One can also relax from the assumption of a concrete functional form that is hyperbolic. However, it is generally agreed that intertemporal preferences take on the following form of time inconsistency: a person's relative preference for well-being at an earlier date over a later date gets stronger as the earlier date gets closer (present-biased preferences) ([O'Donoghue and Rabin, 2001]).

Thus, individuals tend to under-discount long-term risks and losses while acting in privacy-sensitive situations. Note again the anecdotal finding of Jupiters' survey ([Jupiter Research, 2002]) that: "82 per-cent of online consumers are willing to provide various forms of information to shopping Websites from which they have yet to make purchases in exchange for something as modest as a 100 USD sweepstakes entry."

This is an interesting phenomenon, which can lead to consumer's exploitation by marketers who can design shopping sites benefitting from the immediate gratification and discounting failures of humans.

A related concept is underinsurance, the situation where an individual or entity has not arranged adequate insurance cover for the financial value of the property insured. Some researchers have already addressed this topic in detail, here also behavioral aspects where discussed. For example, Coate showed that simple altruism can lead to underinsurance by assigned recipients of donations if collective action among donors is only possible before risks are realized ([Coate, 1995]).

An individual's propensity to underinsure herself against future losses that might incur with low probability but may impose a high risk emerges in the scenario we analyze. Consider, for example, the case of identity theft, where individuals' lack of carefulness can lead (with small probability) to the loss of important personal information like the Social Security Number that can then be used to create a false second identity to impose substantial financial harm on the individual.

Ideology and personal attitudes. Different individuals differ in their sensitivity to privacy. In addition, is the individual considering other ideological factors that affect her attitude towards privacy? For example, does the individual believe that information protection is a right that the government should protect?

People might have the general belief that privacy is an enforced right, which should be guaranteed and not paid for. In this case, the individual is not adopting an utilitarian decision process based on monetary rewards, but is considering a different source of utility and personal satisfaction, based on the advocacy of personal information rights. Hence, this is another possible psychological factor that may affect the behavior of information security-concerned individuals.

Market behavior. Is market behavior (such as propensity to risk, to gains or losses, and to bargaining) affecting her choice?

There may be a relation between the attitudes of a individual with respect to (for example) pricing and bargaining, and her attitude and behavior with respect to information security and privacy. In other words, market behavior may also affect the decision process of individuals who face information related issues. For example, do individuals who bargain a lot also profess more interest in privacy? Are they more or less likely to conform to those attitudes with their behavior?

In particular, let us define a "market-strategic" individual as one that knows that her actions will in turn impact the actions of another party (for example, a merchant) as in a game theoretical setup. So, for example, a strategic individual might refuse a good at a certain price in order to obtain a lesser price in a second offer (see [Acquisti and Varian, 2002]). A "market-myopic" individual on the other side will not be so forward-looking and will act following short-term interest. Similarly, a "privacy-strategic" individual is one that calculates privacy benefits and risks and acts accordingly; a "privacy-myopic" individual on the other side will be the one who, even if she professes to appreciate privacy, does not take actions to protect herself (because of rational ignorance, as defined above, or because she only considers short-term factors).

4. An Experimental Design

In the previous section we have discussed which factors likely influence the individual's decision process when it comes to privacy issues. Several hypotheses can be advanced to explain individual decision processes. Only an experimental setup under controlled conditions can determine which factors play a dominant role.

While researchers may not able to determine whether the parameters discussed above are perceived differently at the forecasting (survey) and actually operative (behavior) phases, an experimental approach may address related issues:

- Correlate personal information attitudes and behavior to the factors discussed above.
- Isolate the factors that affect the decision process of individuals with respect to their privacy and information security concerns.
- Explain the attitudes/behavior dichotomy through those factors.

So far, in this chapter we have discussed economic aspects of the market for personal information security and privacy. Our analysis was motivated by the observation that many privacy-enhancing technologies are available but few have succeeded in the market. Using economic reasoning we have discussed which factors may affect (and possibly distort) the decision process of the individual and why privacy attitudes apparently differ from privacy behavior: limited information, self-control problems, other behavioral distortions, bounded rationality.

Our future work aims to provide empirical evidence and experimental results that should enable us to differentiate between the different hypotheses and factors brought forward in this paper and to disentangle the causes of the dichotomy between personal information attitudes and behavior. Such a comparison would require data about the subjects' information security and privacy attitudes and knowledge; data about their market behavior; and data about their actual personal information behavior.

The mixed results met in the marketplace by personal information security technologies is evidence of the need to incorporate more accurate models of user's behavior into the formulation of policy and technology guidelines. We hope that our ongoing analysis can be useful to the design of information policies and information technologies.

References

Acquisti, Alessandro (2002a). Privacy and security of personal information: Economic incentives and technological solutions. In *1st SIMS Workshop on Economics and Information Security.*

Acquisti, Alessandro (2002b). Protecting privacy with economics: Economic incentives for preventive technologies in ubiquitous computing environments. In *Workshop on Socially-informed Design of Privacy-enhancing Solutions, 4th International Conference on Ubiquitous Computing - UBICOMP '02.*

Acquisti, Alessandro and Varian, Hal R. (2002). Conditioning prices on purchase history. Technical report, University of California, Berkeley. First draft: 2001. Presented at the European Economic Association Conference, Venice, IT, August 2002.

Ainslie, George W. (1975). Specious reward: A behavioral theory of impulsiveness and impulsive control. *Psychological Bulletin*, 82:463–496.

Ajzen, Icek (1988). *Attitudes, personality, and behavior*, chapter 6. Open University Press, Milton-Keynes, England.

Akerlof, George A. (1970). The market for "lemons": Quality uncertainty and the market mechanism. *The Quarterly Journal of Economics*, 84:488–500.

Aronson, Elliot and Mills, Judson (1959). The effect of severity of initiation on the devaluation of forbidden behavior. *Journal of Abnormal and Social Psychology*, 59:177–181.

Berger, Peter L. (1982). *Models of bounded rationality, Vol. I-III.* The MIT Press, Cambridge, MA.

Brunk, Benjamin D. (2002). Understanding the privacy space. *First Monday*, 7. "http://firstmonday.org/issues/issue7_10/brunk/index.html.

Chellappa, Ramnath K. and Sin, Raymong (2002). Personalization versus privacy: An empirical examination of the online consumer's dilemma. In *2002 Informs Meeting*.

Coate, Stephen (1995). Altruism, the samaritan's dilemna, and government transfer policy. *American Economic Review*, 85(1):46–57.

Commission, Federal Trade (2000). Privacy online: Fair information practices in the electronic marketplace. http://www.ftc.gov/reports/privacy2000/privacy2000.pdf.

Corey, S.M. (1937). Professional attitudes and actual behavior. *Journal of educational psychology*, 28(1):271 – 280.

Eagly, Alice H. and Chaiken, Shelly (1993). *The Psychology of Attitudes*, chapter 4. Harcourt Brace Jovanovich College Publishers, Fort Worth, TX.

Fazio, Russell H. (1990). Multiple processes by which attitudes guide behavior: The mode model as an integrative framework. *Advances in experimental social psychology*, 23:75–109.

Festinger, Leōn (1957). *A theory of cognitive dissonance.* Row Peterson, Evanston, IL.

Festinger, Leon and Carlsmith, James M. (1959). Cognitive consequences of forced compliance. *Journal of Abnormal and Social Psychology*, 58:203–210.

Goffman, Erving (1963). *Stigma: Notes on the Management of Spoiled Identity.* Prentice-Hall, Englewood Cliffs, NJ.

Harn, Il-Horn, Hui, Kai-Lung, Lee, Tom S., and Png, Ivan P. L. (2002). Online information privacy: Measuring the cost-benefit trade-off. In *23rd International Conference on Information Systems.*

Harris Interactive (2002). First major post-9-11 privacy survey finds consumers demanding companies do more to protect privacy; public wants company privacy policies to be independently verified. http://www.harrisinteractive.com/news/allnewsbydate.asp?NewsID=429.

Jupiter Research (2002). Seventy percent of US consumers worry about online privacy, but few take protective action. http://www.jmm.com/xp/jmm/press/2002/pr_060302.xml.

Laibson, David (1997). Golden eggs and hyperbolic discounting. *Quarterly Journal of Economics*, 62(2):443–477.

LaPiere, Robert (1934). Attitudes versus actions. *Social Forces*, 13:230–237.

Lemley, Mark (2000). Rational ignorance at the patent office. Technical report, Berkeley Olin Program in Law and Economics, Working Paper Series.

McIntosh, Donald (1969). *The Foundations of Human Society*. The University of Chicago Press, Chicago, IL.

O'Donoghue, Ted and Rabin, Matthew (2001). Choice and procrastination. *Quarterly Journal of Economics*, 116(1):121–160.

Rabin, Matthew and O'Donoghue, Ted (2000). The economics of immediate gratification. *Journal of Behavioral Decision Making*, 13(2):233–250.

Spiekermann, Sarah, Grossklags, Jens, and Berendt, Bettina (2002). E-privacy in 2nd generation e-commerce: Privacy preferences versus actual behavior. In *3rd ACM Conference on Electronic Commerce - EC '01*, pages 38–47.

Thaler, Richard and Shefrin, Hersh M. (1981). An economic theory of self-control. *The Journal of Political Economy*, 89:392–406.

Varian, Hal R. (1996). Economic aspects of personal privacy. In *Privacy and Self-Regulation in the Information Age*. National Telecommunications and Information Administration.

Whitten, Alma and Tygar, J. D. (1999). Why Johnny can't encrypt: A usability evaluation of PGP 5.0. In *8th USENIX Security Symposium*. `citeseer.nj.nec.com/whitten99why.html`.

Chapter 14

PRIVACY AND SECURITY OF PERSONAL INFORMATION

Economic Incentives and Technological Solutions

Alessandro Acquisti
H. John Heinz III School of Public Policy and Management
Carnegie Mellon University
acquisti@andrew.cmu.edu

> *In the majority of real life instances the off-line and on-line identities of a same individual are linkable (or, in fact, linked) together*

Several technological approaches have been proposed to solve the problem of personal privacy. In almost any conceivable scenario - when making purchases, browsing the Internet, responding to surveys, or completing medical tests - the identity of an individual can be dissociated from the rest of the information revealed during the transaction. The companies based on those technologies, however, have struggled to balance the differing needs of the various parties in the privacy equation, eventually failing to gain widespread adoption. While privacy and security of personal information remain a concern for many, the economic incentives have not generated widespread adoption, and government intervention has increased the responsibilities for companies to collect personal information, without determining their liabilities for misuses of those data. Privacy, so it seems, is more difficult to "sell" than to protect.

One of the causes of these difficulties lies in the ambiguity of the very concept of privacy. Privacy means different things to different people, including the scholars who study it, and raises different concerns at different levels. Hence "protecting privacy" is a vague concept. Not only different parties might have opposite interests and views about the amount of information to disclose during a certain transaction, but also the same individual might face trade-offs between her need to reveal and her need to conceal different types of personal information.

But trade-offs are the domain of economics - even when not all dimensions of a problem are economically measurable. [Posner, 1978], [Posner, 1981], and [Stigler, 1980] (as well other contributors to the Spring 1978 issue of the *Georgia Law Review* and the December 1980 issue of the *Journal of Legal Studies*) were among the first to discuss privacy from an explicitly economic perspective. The orthodox economic view suggested that market forces and economic laws, if left alone, would eventually result in the most efficient amount of personal information being exchanged. Individuals and entities interested in information about individuals would converge to that equilibrium regardless of the initial allocation of privacy rights.

After a long silence, economic analysis focused again on privacy at a moment (roughly, the second half of the 1990s) when both privacy intrusions and technologies for privacy protection were dramatically expanding. Concepts such as encryption, National Information Markets, and secondary use of personal information appeared in the analysis. While some (like [Noam, 1996]) maintained that technology such as encryption would "not create privacy," but simply cause consumers to be paid more to give it up, others started noticing the emergence of externalities [Varian, 1996] and even the possibility of market failures [Laudon, 1996].

The panorama today, with both anecdotal evidence of growing privacy costs and intrusions [Gellman, 2002] and reports of scarce adoption and success of privacy technologies and initiatives, offer arguments to all sides: those who believe that individuals act rationally when they choose not to adopt privacy technologies; and those who consider individual customers stuck in an impasse they are unable to cope with alone. At the same time, however, a *new* economics of privacy has emerged, its novelty being the application of formal micro-economic modelling to various privacy considerations [Acquisti and Varian, 2002; Calzolari and Pavan, 2001; Taylor, 2002], and a growing literature thereafter). In what follows I will consider the insights offered by these recent economic approaches to discuss the market for the technological protection of individual information.

1. On-line and Off-line Identities

While my analysis is not restricted to privacy and personal information security issues that arise in e-commerce or Internet transactions, I find it useful to draw from the cryptographic literature on pseudonyms and (un)linkability and distinguish between the "on-line" and "off-line" identities of an individual. The on-line identity might carry information about an individual's tastes, her evaluation of a certain good, her browsing behavior, her purchase history, etc.: the on-line identity is what in an economic model would be called the customer "type." In e-commerce transactions the on-line identity is often associated to cookies or IP addresses used to track customer behavior during and across sessions. On the other side, the off-line identity represents the actual identity of an individual, as revealed by identifiers such as credit card numbers and social security numbers. When I login to Amazon.com with a Hotmail.com email address, for example, I am revealing my on-line identity. When I complete a purchase at Amazon.com with my personal credit card, I am revealing my off-line identity.

Of course, this distinction has several gray areas. In the majority of real life instances the off-line and on-line identities of a same individual are linkable (or, in fact, linked) together because of legacy applications and existing infrastructures. Re-identification or "trail" attacks can expose an otherwise anonymized identity by matching data from different sources. In the Amazon case, I might login with a certain unidentifiable email address and then receive a certain cookie on my computer (two items potentially representing on-line identities). The cookie and the email address could then be linked to my credit card information (the off-line identity) released when I check-out. Now not only Amazon, but possibly also other third parties may be able to link my on-line behavior to my real identity.

Information technology, however, can be used not only to track, analyze and link vast amounts of data, but also to split and un-link pieces of data and keep on-line and off-line information separate in ways that are both effective (in the sense that matching, linking back, or re-identifying information becomes either technically impossible or just costly enough to be no longer profitable) and efficient (in the sense that the transaction can be regularly completed with no additional costs for the parties involved). A purchase history at a merchant site, for example, can be associated to an on-line account whose balance is paid through one of many anonymous payment technologies. Or, information sharing between merchants can be realized through coupons and referrals that do not reveal the identity of the customer. Or, individuals can share files and recommendations in ways that hide their personal identities and yet track their contributions to the system. And so on.

While I will not discuss here the many privacy enhancing technologies that can be used to ensure anonymity and protect individual privacy in several scenarios, I will analyze the economic incentives of the various parties to adopt such technologies.

2. The Economics of On-line Identities

Some recent economic studies [Acquisti and Varian, 2002; Calzolari and Pavan, 2001; Taylor, 2002] have shown something interesting about the economics of privacy in relation to purchase transactions: when information about customers' tastes and purchase history is available and can be shared among sellers, market laws alone might produce Pareto-optimal outcomes. For example, in [Acquisti and Varian, 2002], under general conditions allowing firms to use cookies make society better off, because the buyer can benefit from the seller knowing him better and thereby providing him targeted services. In [Calzolari and Pavan, 2001], sharing information between sellers reduces the distortions associated to asymmetric information between buyer and seller. In [Taylor, 2002], when the seller is facing strategic customers, she will autonomously tend to adopt a policy that protects the privacy of her customers. In a more abstract framework, [Friedman and Resnick, 2001] have found that "the distrust of newcomers is an inherent social cost of easy identity changes," but persistent pseudonyms can help both the society and the individual. Do these results then support the 1980s economic view of an eventually self-regulating market for privacy? Something must be noted: what these papers have in common is that they all deal with individuals as (economic) agents whose profiles might include information on taste, purchase histories, price sensitivity or risk aversion, etc., but not necessarily information about those individuals' off-line identities. This literature shows that, while distortionary forces might also be in action, for several types of transactions market laws tend towards fair use of on-line information. To put it another way, this literature tells us that there might be economic benefits from sharing and increasing the use of on-line information, and that these benefits would not be harmed by the protection of the off-line information.

Existing information systems, however, are built in ways that link on-line and off-line identities of their users. With the growth of e-commerce and the diffusion of the Internet these linkages have caused increasing concerns about the practices and protection that other parties (such as merchants) will adopt for an individual's off-line, personal information. At the peak of the privacy scare in the late 1990s, several surveys found that identity thefts and credit card frauds were the main concerns of individuals using new information technology, and that billions of dollars were lost in missed sales because of these concerns. These surveys supported the view that there are in fact economic reasons to protect the off-line identity of individuals.

On the other side, a number of more recent surveys, anecdotic evidence, and experiments (see [Spiekermann et al., 2002]), have also shown that individuals are actually less concerned about privacy than what they claim to be: many are willing to provide very personal information, in exchange for small rewards. From an economic perspective, one could make the argument that those individuals who demand privacy but take no action to protect theirs, are actually acting rationally. They discount the potential losses from losing control of their personal information (uncertain, but possibly large) with the probability that such an outcome will take place (uncertain, but perceived as low). Then, they compare the resulting value with the implicit or explicit costs of using an anonymizing technology, which are certain and immediate. All things considered, most individuals will therefore decide not to go through the hassle of hiding their off-line information. Some might simply decide not to purchase on-line (or not to use credit cards). Only a few will choose the anonymizing technology.

So: personal preferences respected and market equilibrium re-established even in absence of wide protection of the off-line information? Well, not necessarily. As progresses in information technology make the dissemination and use of information so inexpensive, new complexities arise.

3. The Economics of Off-line Identities

First, given that the individual loses control of her personal information and that information multiplies, propagates, and persists for an unpredictable span of time, the individual is in a position of information asymmetry with respect to the party she is completing transaction with. Hence, the negative utility coming from future potential misuses of off-line personal information is a random shock practically impossible to calculate. Because of identity theft, for example, an individual might be denied a small loan, a lucrative job, or a crucial mortgage.

In addition, even if the expected negative utility could be estimated, I put forward the following hypothesis: when it comes to security of personal information, individuals tend to look for immediate gratification, discounting hyperbolically the future risks (for example of being subject to identity theft), and choosing to ignore the danger. Hence, they act myopically when it comes to their off-line identity even when they might be acting strategically for what relates to their on-line identity.

If individuals are myopic about the future potential risks related to their off-line identities, and do not act optimally, the other parties they interact with have little incentive to take the burden of protecting the personal data of those individuals. The database of a merchant, for example, might be hacked and the credit card numbers stored there might be stolen and then illegally re-used, without the individuals being able to know where the "leak" took place and without the merchant (in almost all occasions) having to pay for it. This implies that without liability for misuse, abuse, or negligence in handling personal information, moral hazard ensues on the side of the other parties.

Finally, since the market of privacy conscious individuals willing to pay for their protection is small, it ends up not being satisfied. The economic rationale can be described in the following way. Since the only economic interest in protecting personal information seems to belong to the owner of that information, who is also subject to "immediate gratification," the profit margins in this area of business are low. Since few people are so conscious about their information security needs to be willing to pay for it, the size of the market is in addition very small. Low margins and small demand make it very hard for any technology to succeed - except in niche (and possibly disagreeable) markets. Now: while actual usage costs of privacy enhancing technologies are low once adopted, their adoption fees are high because they involve significant switching costs. Hence, as merchants decide against offering anonymizing technologies to their customers, the privacy concerned customers choose not to purchase on-line, or to purchase less. A latent, potentially large market demand remains therefore unsatisfied.

4. Economics and Technology of Privacy

While market forces might ensure fair use of data connected to the on-line identity of individuals, they do not guarantee optimal use and appropriate protection of the off-line identity. In fact, the evaluation of current dominant practices in the handling of privacy and personal information (on-line and off-line) shows that self-regulation has not provided the results expected by the Federal Trade Commission (2000). Information technology, on the other side, can be used to split on-line and off-line identities or make the linkages between the identities of an individual too costly for any practical application. But without economic incentives no technology reaches widespread adoption.

So, what can economics do?

Firstly, in specific instances, economics can be used to define mechanisms which are privacy enhancing. For example, in anonymous protocols based on the interaction of many agents (see, e.g. [Acquisti et al., 2003]), economics can assist in the design process of mechanisms to solve the impasse when no party alone would have the incentive to perform certain actions (for example, sending dummy traffic to other parties in order to increase the level of anonymity in the system). Under an appropriate incentive compatible contract, different parties might be induced to support each other and therefore the anonymity of the system. Secondly, and more generally, in the framework of socially-informed design of privacy technologies economics can be used to define what information should be shared, and what protected.

Thereafter economics will need to be assisted by law and technology to actually achieve the balances it proposes. Market forces might ensure fair use of data connected to some pseudo identities of individuals. However, because of the adoption costs and trade-offs analyzed in the previous section, they do not guarantee optimal use and appropriate protection of her legal identity. In these cases, legal intervention, on the model of the EU directive on data protection, or as proposed in [Samuelson, 2000], should place constraints and liabilities on the side of the parties receiving private information, calibrating them in order to compensate the moral hazard and asymmetric information in the market of personal data, and combining them with information technology as a "commitment" device in the system.

By generating incentives to handle personal information in a new way, appropriate legal intervention can allow the growth of the market for third parties providing solutions that anonymize off-line information but make it possible to share on-line profiles. By designing the appropriate liabilities, that intervention can also fight the tendency of "trust-me" or self-regulatory solutions to fail under pressure. If privacy is a holistic concept [Scoglio, 1998], only a holistic approach can provide its adequate protection: economic tools to identify the areas of information to share and those to protect; law to signal the directions the market should thereby take; and technology to make those directions viable.

References

Acquisti, Alessandro, Dingledine, Roger, and Syverson, Paul (2003). On the economics of anonymity. In *Financial Cryptography - FC '03*, pages 84–102. Springer Verlag, LNCS 2742.

Acquisti, Alessandro and Varian, Hal R. (2002). Conditioning prices on purchase history. Technical report, University of California, Berkeley. First draft: 2001. Presented at the European Economic Association Conference, Venice, IT, August 2002.

Calzolari, Giacomo and Pavan, Alessandro (2001). Optimal design of privacy policies. Technical report, Gremaq, University of Toulouse.

Friedman, Eric J. and Resnick, Paul (2001). The social cost of cheap pseudonyms. *Journal of Economics and Management Strategy*, 10(2):173–199.

Gellman, Robert (2002). Privacy, consumers, and costs - how the lack of privacy costs consumers and why business studies of privacy costs are biased and incomplete. `http://www.epic.org/reports/dmfprivacy.html`.

Laudon, Kenneth C. (1996). Markets and privacy. *Communications of the ACM*, 39(9):92–104.

Noam, Eli M. (1996). Privacy and self-regulation: Markets for electronic privacy. In *Privacy and Self-Regulation in the Information Age*. National Telecommunications and Information Administration.

Posner, Richard A. (1978). An economic theory of privacy. *Regulation*, pages 19–26.

Posner, Richard A. (1981). The economics of privacy. *American Economic Review*, 71(2):405–409.

Samuelson, Pam (2000). Privacy as intellectual property. *Stanford Law Review*, 52(1125).

Scoglio, Stefano (1998). *Transforming Privacy: A Transpersonal Philosophy of Rights*. Praeger, Westport.

Spiekermann, Sarah, Grossklags, Jens, and Berendt, Bettina (2002). E-privacy in 2nd generation e-commerce: Privacy preferences versus actual behavior. In *3rd ACM Conference on Electronic Commerce - EC '01*, pages 38–47.

Stigler, George J. (1980). An introduction to privacy in economics and politics. *Journal of Legal Studies*, 9:623–644.

Taylor, Curtis R. (2002). Private demands and demands for privacy: Dynamic pricing and the market for customer information. Technical report, Department of Economics, Duke University.

Varian, Hal R. (1996). Economic aspects of personal privacy. In *Privacy and Self-Regulation in the Information Age*. National Telecommunications and Information Administration.

Chapter 15

PRIVACY, ECONOMICS, AND PRICE DISCRIMINATION ON THE INTERNET

Andrew Odlyzko
Digital Technology Center
*University of Minnesota**
odlyzko@umn.edu

> *The incentives to price discriminate and the increasing ability to do so are among the key factors in the evolution of our economy.*

The Internet offers the possibility of unprecedented privacy. According to the famous 1993 Pat Steiner cartoon in *The New Yorker*, "On the Internet, nobody knows you're a dog." But in practice, there are many who not only know you are a dog, but are familiar with your age, breed, illnesses, and tastes in dogfood. The Internet offers not only the possibility of unprecedented privacy, but also of unprecedented loss of privacy, and so far privacy has been losing.

The steady erosion of privacy and prospects for the continuation of this trend have been well documented (cf. [Garfinkel, 2000]). Many observers, such as Scott McNealy of Sun Microsystems, say that privacy is irretrievably lost, and we should "get over" our hangups about it. However, the public is unwilling to "get over it," and concerns about collection and dissemination of information about our lives rate highly in opinion polls. Laws and regulations to protect privacy enjoy broad support. There are also novel technologies that attract public attention that can protect and enhance privacy (cf. [Lester, 2001]). However, the technologies that are developed and deployed most intensively are those that reduce privacy.

One of the many privacy puzzles is that even though the public shows intense concerns about loss of privacy, it is not doing much to protect itself. Privacy-protecting technologies have not fared well in the marketplace, and very minor rewards are enough to persuade people to sign

*First published in *ICEC2003: Fifth International Conference on Electronic Commerce*, N. Sadeh, ed., ACM Press, 2003, pp. 355–366.

up for grocery store loyalty programs. So are people being irrationally paranoid, or is there something else that the loss of privacy might bring, that they instinctively fear?

Another puzzle is that so many commercial organizations are actively working to erode privacy. Governments often decrease privacy in attempting to combat terrorism, or tax evasion, or to increase their political control. Criminals invade privacy to make money by using other people's credit cards. Employers monitor their employees to increase productivity. And ordinary citizens, armed with an array of increasingly powerful and versatile tools, such as cameras in cell phones, are beginning to collect massive amounts of information that, if combined and analyzed, could lead to dramatic decreases in privacy (cf. [Brin, 1998]). However, most of the data collection efforts so far have come from private enterprises, and are the ones that attract most of the concern and publicity. These efforts are often extremely intrusive, and are extremely widespread. Moreover, they persist in spite of intense public opposition, even though there have not been too many commercially successful exploitations of the information that is gathered. Are the enterprises that engage in these practices irrational?

Many privacy advocates are concerned about the dangers of government control, limitations on freedom of speech, and related political factors. However, most of the pervasive privacy erosion is coming from the private sector, which is interested primarily in its customers' money, not control of their behavior. The standard explanation is that better information allows merchants to target ads better, thereby saving expense for the merchants and the trouble of discarding unwanted material for the customers. However, that explanation does not seem to be sufficient. For one thing, the effectiveness of ads is limited, and in particular online ads' response rates have been dropping recently. Advertising spending has been a fairly stable fraction of the economy for many decades, and is not likely to change.

The thesis of this paper is that the powerful movement to reduce privacy that is coming from the private sector is motivated by the incentives to price discriminate, to charge different prices to various customers for the same goods or services. Erosion of privacy allows for learning more about customers' willingness to pay, and also to control arbitrage in which somebody who might face a high price from a seller buys instead from an intermediary who manages to get a low price. The key point is that price discrimination offers a much higher payoff to sellers than any targeted marketing campaign. Adjacent seats on an airplane flight can bring in revenues of $200 or $2,000, depending on conditions under which tickets were purchased. It is the potential of extending such practices to other areas that is likely to be the "Holy Grail" of ecommerce and the inspiration for the privacy erosion we see. For it is the privacy intrusion represented by airplane tickets being non-transferable contracts with named individuals that enables airlines to practice yield management in the extreme form it has reached. (The requirement that passengers show government-issued identification cards before boarding, another privacy-eroding measure, plays a key role in making this effective.) When the sellers have less information about buyers, and less control over resale, possibilities for differential pricing are more limited, but even so, they are increasingly being exploited. For example, Dell Computer is doing this extensively [McWilliams, 2001]:

> One day recently, the Dell Latitude L400 ultralight laptop was listed at $2,307 on the company's Web page catering to small businesses. On the Web page for sales to health-care companies, the same machine was listed at $2,228, or 3% less. For state and local governments, it was priced at $2,072.04, or 10% less than the price for small businesses.

The dynamic pricing practiced by Dell has many more components, and it is indeed making the economy more efficient. As is described in [McWilliams, 2001], Dell has record low overhead costs, is a consistent leader in price cutting, and can satisfy customer demands with record speed and flexibility. Yet price discrimination appears to be a substantial part of the Dell success story. It is easy to understand why. Dell operates in a commodity market, with low net margins. Obtaining an extra 10% from a particular buyer is likely to be much more important for the bottom line than better targeted advertising.

In general, discrimination has a very negative connotation in our society, and various forms of it, in particular those based on age, gender, race, and religion, are illegal. However, price discrimination is an ancient technique that is widespread in the economy, although it is often disguised to avoid negative public reactions. It is frequently supported by government as a matter of public policy, sometimes explicitly, more often implicitly. The underlying reason is that standard economic arguments show that "generally, discriminatory prices [are] required for an optimal allocation of resources in real life situations" (p. 1 of [Phlips, 1983]). Moreover, price discrimination is likely to play an increasing role in the future, for two main reasons. One is that an increasing fraction of the costs of producing goods and services consists of fixed one-time charges, with low marginal costs. (As an example, a software program might cost hundreds of millions of dollars to develop, but can be distributed at practically zero cost over the Internet.) The other reason is that modern technology is making it possible to price discriminate. For example, Coca Cola was discovered in 2000 to be experimenting with soda vending machines that would raise prices when temperatures were high. It might have wanted to do this in the past, but the technology was not available. Similarly, booksellers were in general not able to tell much about their customers in the past, while Amazon.com can.

The thesis of this paper is that the incentives to price discriminate and the increasing ability to do so are among the key factors in the evolution of our economy. The arguments in favor of this thesis are supported by a variety of examples. Some are recent, such as the evolution of yield management techniques in the airline industry. Some are older, such as the evolution of 19th century railroad pricing.

19th century railways will be cited extensively in this paper. They have often been compared to the Internet, usually as examples of revolutionary technologies that led to booms and crashes. There are indeed striking similarities in these areas, as discussed in [Odlyzko, 2004a]. However, the most relevant comparison between the Internet and railways is likely to be in the area of pricing, a comparison that apparently has not been made before. The railways, like much of modern economy, especially that related to the Internet, faced very high fixed costs and low marginal costs. This produced strong incentives to price discriminate. The information technology of the 19th century allowed railways less freedom to price discriminate than airlines have today, though. Still, they did manage to price discriminate on a grand scale. The way society reacted then to such discriminatory practices may allow us to predict how our society will react to the spread and intensification of price discrimination that the Internet facilitates.

The incentives to price discriminate are likely to overcome the trend towards the type of dynamic pricing that is normally associated with claims of the "New Economy." The standard predictions there (cf. [Bayers, 2000]) are of widespread use of auctions, shopping agents, and related techniques. Priceline.com, eBay, and the myriad of B2B and B2C exchanges were supposed to be the forerunners of the new future. They were expected to bring back the art of haggling, and by better matching of supply and demand, as well as by lower transaction costs, to produce a significantly more efficient economy. They are growing, but their progress has been disappointing to their early proponents. The drive for price discrimination offers a partial explanation. If transactions are conducted anonymously, it is hard to tell how much a buyer is willing to pay. One can try to set up auction mechanisms to do that, but it is hard. It is easier and more productive to just charge more to those able to pay more, if one can. Note that governments do not collect taxes by sending their software agents to negotiate with those of the taxpayers. Instead, tax agencies use their coercive power to find out how much people earn, and then extract a large share.

That privacy-reducing measures are induced by the drive to price discriminate does not imply that the people designing or implementing those measures think of their work this way. Enterprises generally try to optimize their state by making small incremental changes within the confines of their technological, economic, and legal environment. It is usually only when we step back that we can say it was the social and economic advantages of price discrimination that shaped the choices faced by the decision makers. 19th century railroad managers who set freight rates and late 20th century American college administrators who decided on tuition fees were not aiming to price discriminate. They did what seemed best for their institutions, it's just that their decisions led to increasing price discrimination. The managers who today invest in privacy eroding data collection systems are likely also often not thinking consciously about price discrimination. Instead, they are acting on the hope that the information they gather can be used to increase their enterprises' profits. Usually what they have in mind for early applications are relatively mild departures from traditional business practices [Shabi, 2003]. As they gain experience, better tools are developed, and general business practices change, their methods will evolve. The logic of price discrimination is likely to lead them eventually to techniques that will be much more overtly discriminatory.

The "New Economy" visions of [Bayers, 2000] represent fairly small departures from the usual practices in the current "Old Economy." Auctions and automated shopping bots are well known, and fit well the standard economic models. Their spread, predicted in [Bayers, 2000], does not require any major revisions of the economic canon. On the other hand, spread and intensification of price discrimination are likely to lead to major changes in thinking about economics, law, and public policy. "First degree" price discrimination, in which the buyer is charged his maximal willingness to pay, has long been treated in the literature as an unattainable ideal. Erosion of privacy and improved IT systems will enable a close approximation to this ideal to be achieved. Further, the presence of price discrimination in a market traditionally has been seen as a sign of monopoly power on the part of sellers. More competition has been regarded almost universally as a cure. However, there have always been some contrary examples, in which intensification of competition led to an increase in differential charging. As such examples proliferate, major revisions in the doctrine governing actions of courts and regulators will be required.

The logic of price discrimination suggests a future drastically different from the anonymous shopping agents of [Bayers, 2000]. Instead, it leads to an Orwellian economy in which a package of aspirin at a drugstore might cost the purchaser $1 if he could prove he was indigent, but $1,000 if he was Bill Gates or simply wanted to preserve his privacy. Such a future would justify the efforts that enterprises are putting into destroying privacy. It would also show that the public's concerns about privacy are well-founded, since current and historical precedents strongly suggest such a future would be resented. In practice, we are not likely to see this future any time soon. However, we will be catching an increasing number of glimpses of it, as enterprises move to exploit the opportunities that differential pricing offers.

The notion of a market price is very powerful, and underlies much of the theoretical framework of economics. Prices that depend on the buyer would require a complete rethinking of that framework. All those nice intersecting supply and demand curves would have to be replaced by more complicated constructs.

While the incentives to price discriminate are likely to be among the most powerful forces shaping our economy, the extreme Orwellian forms outlined above are not likely to appear, at least not soon. There are strong countervailing factors which are likely to slow the spread of overt price discrimination and push it into concealed forms. One such factor is arbitrage, in which buyers who secure low prices sell to those who are faced with high prices. For effective price discrimination, that method has to be circumvented. Airline yield management is as effective as it is because a ticket is a contract for carriage of a specific person, and is not transferable. In other areas, accepted practices and often laws have to be changed. That, however, requires time.

Another, even more important factor slowing the spread of price discrimination comes from behavioral economics. People do not like being subjected to dynamic pricing. There is abundant evidence of this, as shown, for example, in reactions to airline yield management and the moves to extend such practices to other areas. Yet more evidence can be found in the reactions to 19th century railroad pricing, reactions that dominated politics at the end of that century in the U.S.. Even in the days when racial, age, gender, and other types of discrimination were not just widely practiced, but respectable, price discrimination aroused strong opposition. Such reactions are still common.

The public's dislike of price discrimination will be combined with new tools for detecting price discrimination. These tools are products of the same technologies that enable sellers to practice differential pricing. (The recent Amazon.com experiments with variable pricing were noticed and publicized almost immediately.)

The result is likely to be that price discrimination will grow, but in a concealed form. Stress will be on tactics such as bundling and loyalty programs, which tend to disguise the actual price that is charged. This means that auction mechanisms and micropayments are likely to be used in very limited situations. On the other hand, there will be continued pressure to erode privacy in order to find out just what the willingness to pay is, as well as to control how products and services are used. Thus privacy will continue to erode.

Price discrimination is often just one of many factors that lead to deployment of new technologies or business models. Thus it is often hard to tell just how important differential pricing is in various situations. However, it is likely to be among the most important motives in the growth in Digital Rights Management (DRM) schemes, as well as in the spread of licensing as opposed to outright sales, and in tying arrangements, such as security techniques that enable a printer to work effectively only with cartridges from that printer's manufacturer, as discussed in [Anderson, 2003]. Price discrimination is clearly the main (although usually hidden) issue in the discussions of the future of the Internet, including the prospects for retaining the "end-to-end" principle. The debates about open access and peering are really about the extent to which differential pricings should be allowed. (The issue there, as it had been on the telephone network, on railways, and even on canals before that, is whether the carrier should be entitled to charge twice as much for transmission of a hit movie as for an obscure one.)

Governments are often expected and pressured to act to preserve privacy. Of course, governments are among the main privacy violators, in pursuit of either tax revenues or criminals. Still, those incentives are well understood, and at least in democratic societies can be controlled by the public. Thus there is still widespread hope that governments can be persuaded to limit privacy intrusions by the private sector. However, government roles in this area have been and likely will continue to be ambiguous. The problem is that price discrimination often does provide real measurable gains for social and economic welfare. It is not just a measure for increasing profits of sellers, as is often suspected (e.g., [Albrecht, 2003]). Increased price discrimination is often associated with increased competition as well as increased economic activity, and works to decrease profits. That is what happened in the 19th century, and induced the railroads to welcome regulation. This profit-decreasing but welfare-increasing effect of price discrimination is likely to keep regulators and legislators from interfering too much with the privacy-eroding measures that facilitate it.

This paper is just an extended abstract. Because of space and time limitations, only the basic outlines of the evidence and arguments for the main thesis are presented here. For more details, see [Odlyzko, 2004c; Odlyzko, 2004a; Odlyzko, 2004b]. Those papers also contain acknowledgements to the many people who have helped me with comments and references.

There are many recent papers related to the work that summarized in this paper. Here I mention just a few, with fuller references in [Odlyzko, 2004c; Odlyzko, 2004a; Odlyzko, 2004b]. In particular, the main thesis about the importance of price discrimination and its relation to privacy erosion was already mentioned in [Odlyzko, 1996], although only briefly. Many of the general points about the desirability of price discrimination have been made, for example in [DeLong and Froomkin, 2000; Huber, 1993; Shapiro and Varian, 1998; Varian, 1996]. That privacy erosion is leading to differential pricing is also increasingly recognized, cf. [Albrecht, 2003]. That price discrimination can arise in a competitive environment is also becoming recognized in the literature, for example in [Levine, 2002]. The most novel element in this paper appears to be the connection with 19th century railroad pricing.

1. The important role and prevalence of price discrimination

Price discrimination is one of the basic concepts in microeconomics. For comprehensive surveys of the literature, see [Phlips, 1983; Varian,

1989]. A shorter and easier to obtain treatment is available in [Varian, 1996]. Here I just present a simple example which explains why price discrimination is economically and socially desirable. Suppose that Charlie is a consultant, and two potential customers, Alice and Bob, are interested in getting him to write a report on implementing digital cash. Suppose also that Alice is willing to pay $700 for such a report, while Bob is willing to pay $1,000. Suppose also that Charlie's cost (which is likely to be the opportunity cost, for example the price that will persuade him to write the report as opposed to going to the beach) is $1,500. If Charlie has to charge the same price to both Alice and Bob, the report will not get written. Any price up to $700 per copy will persuade both Alice and Bob to buy, but will bring in at most $1,400, which will not be enough to get Charlie to do the work. Any price between $700 and $1,000 will only attract Bob as a buyer, and again will not bring in the required $1,500, and any price above $1,000 will find no buyers at all. On the other hand, if Charlie can sell the report to Alice for $650 and to Bob for $950, then by conventional economic arguments everybody should be happy. Charlie will collect $1,600, more than the $1,500 that makes him indifferent between writing the report and surfing, and so should be satisfied. Alice and Bob will each get the report for $50 less than they are willing to pay, and so both should also be happy. Thus a transaction with differential pricing will make everybody better off.

The example shown above does suffer from the usual limitations of toy economic models, but it does demonstrate the essential features of differential pricing, and how it can make everybody better off, at least in the standard economic model. In particular, Charlie has to have at least some idea of what Alice and Bob are willing to pay (so no anonymous shopping agents, please), and a way to keep Alice from reselling the report. Thus privacy and first-sale doctrine have to be limited.

In practice, sellers have usually solved the problem of determining customers' willingness to pay and at the same time avoided the fairness issue through versioning. Almost identical products are sold at differing prices, although production costs are almost the same. A standard example is that of hardcover versus paperback editions of books. Such versioning will be treated in the next section. Here I just present some examples of essentially pure price discrimination.

Senior citizen and student discounts are a well known type of price discrimination. A much less obvious form is that of periodic sales in stores, which serve to discriminate between informed and patient buyers and the rest, as shown in [Varian, 1980]. Price-matching offers (in which a store promises to match any competitor's price) play a similar role, see [Corts, 1996].

Another visible example of price discrimination is in scholarly journal publishing. For several decades, both commercial and nonprofit publishers have been charging libraries far more than individuals for the same journal. Usually, though, all libraries were charged the same rate. As scholarly journals move online, the incentive to price discriminate and the ability to do so are both growing. As a result, we are seeing dramatic growth in differential pricing. For example, unlimited usage site licenses for the online edition of the *Proceedings of the National Academy of Sciences* for 2004 will range from $250 to $6,600 per year, depending on the size and nature of the subscribing institution.

An example of the evolution of scholarly publishing is offered by the JSTOR project, `http://www.jstor.org`. It is a nonprofit organization that makes available electronic versions of old issues of scholarly journals. The pricing for U.S. educational institution varies by a factor of more than four. For non-U.S. educational institutions, the pricing is more involved. It is worth quoting from the description on the JSTOR Web page:

> There is no equivalent to the Carnegie Classification for grouping academic institutions outside of the United States. Nevertheless, just as we have done with the U.S. fee structure, we aim to match the contributions non-U.S. institutions make to the value they derive from participation. Through analysis of JSTOR usage and collecting patterns at participating libraries, we have developed a methodology for setting value-based fees for libraries around the world. Institutions are first placed into JSTOR classes ranging from Very Large to Very Small. Fee levels are then set taking into account the relative value of the JSTOR journal titles to the higher education community in the country as well as the local availability of fiscal and technological resources.

Note the explicit statement of the goal to charge in proportion to the value received. Note also that the estimation of this value is done partly based on studies of JSTOR usage patterns. Such usage data was simply not available in the print world. Thus more information about customers (less privacy) provided by modern technologies leads to more price discrimination.

JSTOR is a monopolist in that its content is usually available electronically only from JSTOR. However, it does compete in the information delivery market with the print journal copies that its client libraries often have available on their shelves, with commercial information systems, and with other publishers offering content that is not identical, but which often can be used instead of that in JSTOR. The result is that the scholarly information system is becoming more efficient, with costs going down, and quality and quantity of available material increasing. In the process, though, price discrimination is becoming more important and also more explicit.

Profit-making enterprises have the same incentives to price discriminate that non-profits like JSTOR do. However, they essentially never explain in detail the rationale for their pricing decisions the way JSTOR does. Thus it is necessary to infer their goals from the price and volume information that one can obtain. There is an extensive literature in economics on this subject. In most cases enterprises in the past did not have the detailed usage information that JSTOR is collecting. Still, that did not prevent some sophisticated schemes from being developed. Many examples are presented in [Phlips, 1983; Varian, 1989]. Here I note a few additional and interesting ones.

Some instances of price discrimination are not visible to the public, except through indirect effects. For example, gasoline wholesalers in the U.S. charge gas stations prices that depend on the "zones" where the stations are located, zones that often contain just a single station [Barrionuevo, 2000]. The price differences within a single state approach 15%, far exceeding differences in distribution costs. They help explain why the car-owning inhabitants of New York City (who are on average more affluent than those in the rest of the country) pay far more for gas than those in rural areas of New York State. While it is not known publicly how prices for different zones are derived, one can expect that they are based on prior experience, presence of competition, and demographics of a zone, the last provided in great detail by U.S. Census Bureau.

The last few examples underline the important role that information about customers plays in making price discrimination effective. At an extreme, income tax relies on taxpayers providing detailed financial information, and is enforced by the coercive power of the government.

A very interesting example is that of U.S. private colleges. These educational institutions have high tuition and fees, typically around $25,000 per year in 2001 among the more selective schools. (Room and board costs are additional.) However, all these schools offer financial aid to students, and in some of them, the amount spent on aid (which is determined overwhelmingly on need) comes to about half of the tuition revenues. In essence these institutions are practicing price discrimination on a massive scale, charging according to their estimates of what the students' parents can afford. Parents can preserve their full financial privacy, but at the cost of paying the full tuition.

There are several important features to this system. One is that competing colleges are all driven by the incentives to price discriminate towards very similar pricing policies. Another important factor is that the massive privacy violation involved in allocating student aid is abetted by the government. Parents usually have to fill out federal forms to obtain aid for their children. Fraudulent filings are subject to federal criminal penalties, and are not just a matter of a civil dispute between the college and the parents. Thus the government assists educational institutions in price discrimination. This is, of course, done in the interests of social welfare. However, much of the price discrimination by private institutions furthers social welfare. That is why we can expect governments' role to be ambiguous. They will be trying to respond to citizens' demands for privacy protection, and at the same time trying to facilitate sellers' price discrimination.

Public universities are also being drawn towards greater price discrimination. A widely noted article, [Yudof, 2002], explained how demographic and other trends are leading to decreased state support for higher education. At the same time, the costs of supporting educational and research activities are rising, and so is their value to society. The likely response, predicted by [Yudof, 2002] and observed in recent rounds of budgeting, is a continued push to raise tuition. However, to continue fulfilling their core mission of educating the states' youth, financial aid will have to be provided for the needy. Thus without aiming to do so, public universities are also being pulled into increasingly discriminatory pricing.

Incentives to price discriminate are just one element that goes into price setting, and it is often hard to determine their role. For example, airlines charge extremely high fares for passengers who buy tickets just before departure. On the other hand, they offer considerably reduced "bereavement fares" for trips to funerals (at a cost in privacy, since passengers taking advantage of such fares usually have to tell who is being buried, where, and so on). Are they being charitable, are they trying to get good publicity, or are they price discriminating (since many of the funeral attendees are likely not to be too closely associated with the deceased, and so might be quite price sensitive)? We don't know, and it is possible that the airlines themselves do not know precisely how much various of these factors enter into their calculations. In economic analyses of price discrimination, a particularly sticky issue is that of "joint costs." Space constraints prevent a thorough treatment here, but it should be noted that joint costs can be used to explain many instances of what seems to be price discrimination. However, as differential pricing intensifies, it becomes clearer that price discrimination is usually the main motive. As an example, on February 27, 2002, I obtained the following prices from the Web site of Continental Airlines for advance purchase round trip tickets:

- from Minneapolis to Newark, NJ on Wednesday, March 20, returning Friday, March 22: $772.50
- from Minneapolis to Newark, NJ on Wednesday, March 20, returning Wednesday, March 27: $226.50
- from Newark, NJ to Minneapolis on Friday, March 22, returning on Wednesday, March 27: $246.50

By buying the second and third tickets, and using just the first half of each, I could have saved almost 40% compared with the cost of the first ticket. Pricing structures that make such maneuvers possible are easiest to explain as coming from the desire to obtain more revenue from business travelers who are the ones most likely to make short mid-week trips. Any explanation in terms of joint costs would be very artificial.

The purchase of the second and third tickets would have violated the conditions of the Continental contract, but it is hard for the airline to enforce it. One ticket could have been bought by A. Odlyzko, the other by Andrew M. Odlyzko. As long as separate credit cards were used, and frequent flyer information was not provided on one of the purchases, Continental would not have had a way to prevent this. However, in the post-9/11 era, there is talk of setting up a unified database of travelers. Such a database, perhaps with biometric elements, probably would not do much to stop terrorism. However, if made available for commercial use, it could enable airlines to enforce their contracts. Again, a decline in privacy would enable more intensive price discrimination.

In this brief note I will not discuss legal issues, except to note that various types of price discrimination are legal. "Zone pricing" for gasoline has been upheld repeatedly by the courts, and landlords have won lawsuits filed by lawyers they refused to rent apartments to. (Thus it is legal to discriminate against lawyers!) On the other hand, many cities in the U.S. have enacted ordinances making it illegal for dry-cleaning establishments to charge more for laundering women's shirts than for men's shirts. This shows the danger in practicing price discrimination. Pigou already noted that a monopolist has to be careful in setting a pricing policy (p. 250 of [Pigou, 1924]): "... since a hostile public opinion might lead to legislative intervention, [the monopolist's] choice must not be such as to outrage the popular sense of justice." Price discrimination is extremely tempting, and increasingly feasible, but it is like playing with fire.

2. Versioning and damaged goods

The practical problem is how to price discriminate effectively. Buyers are naturally reluctant to say how much they are willing to pay. In the past, technology for price discrimination was very limited, as purchasers had effective privacy. The standard way of overcoming this problem is through versioning, as is done with books. Hardcover books sell for more than paperbacks, far more than the cost difference justifies, and are usually available a year or so earlier. This induces the readers who are impatient or who care about nice hardcover volumes to pay more. Such versioning has been going on for ages, but it became much more noticeable and was first studied systematically in the middle of the 19th century, in connection with railroads. There is a memorable and oft-quoted 1849 passage on this subject by Jules Dupuit (translation from [Ekelund, 1970]):

> It is not because of the few thousand francs which would have to be spent to put a roof over the third-class carriages or to upholster the third-class seats that some company or other has open carriages with wooden benches. What the company is trying to do is to prevent the passengers who can pay the second class fare from traveling third class; it hits the poor, not because it wants to hurt them, but to frighten the rich. And it is again for the same reason that the companies, having proved almost cruel to the third-class passengers and mean to the second-class ones,

> become lavish in dealing with first-class passengers. Having refused the poor what is necessary, they give the rich what is superfluous.

Railroads did indeed behave literally the way Dupuit describes. They even put third class carriages in front of the train. The expectation was that anyone willing to deal with cinders in his hair and eyes was indeed so desperately poor that he could not be induced to pay more than third-class fare. And that is the inefficiency induced by versioning. It would have been much more efficient as well as kinder for railroads to provide better seats and simply charge passengers according to their willingness to pay. However, railroads did not have any way to determine that willingness in those days.

The incentive to price discriminate leads even to extreme versions of versioning, in which extra costs are incurred in order to make a product less serviceable. This is known as the "damaged goods" approach, and appears to be used with increasing frequency, as documented by [Deneckere and McAfee, 1966]. A classic example is provided by the IBM Laser Printer and Laser Printer E of 1990. The latter cost less, printed at half the speed of the former, and differed from it in having an extra chip that slowed down processing.

Versioning, and especially "damaged goods" practices, incurs costs for buyers, or sellers, or both. One of the big gains from price discrimination would be the reduction of such waste. Instead of being cruel, mean, or lavish to various customers, sellers could just charge them what they are willing to pay. Daimler could save itself the expense of designing, manufacturing, and marketing the Maybach at $300,000 each. Instead, it could simply charge that much for a much more modest Mercedes for the folks with really deep pockets. Of course, that would upset not just the basic pricing paradigm, but the bases of our social order, where expensive toys like the Maybach car play an important role in determining status. But the savings would be immense!

Even greater savings, in both money and lives, could be achieved through increased price discrimination in medicine.

3. The convergence of capitalism and communism

The most contentious pricing issue today is that of pharmaceuticals. Health care spending as a whole is rising rapidly, and spending on drugs is rising even more rapidly. There are complaints about Big Pharma's profits, about marketing of expensive drugs directly to the public, about special deals with physicians, etc. However, the most contentious issue is that prescription drugs tend to sell for far more in the U.S. than in other countries. Although no pharmaceutical company has admitted this publicly, the obvious rationale for this is that Americans are more affluent than inhabitants of most other countries, and able to pay more. This might appear fair to many, but unfortunately there is no consensus on what is fair. In particular, a defense of drug pricing in the business weekly *Barron's* elicited the following rejoinder from Congressman Bernie Sanders of Vermont [Sanders, 2000]:

> On average, for each dollar American consumers pay for prescription drugs, the Germans are paying 71 cents; the Swedes, 68 cents; the British, 65 cents; the French, 57 cents, and the Italians, 51 cents. Unfortunately, U.S. policy allows the pharmaceutical industry to maintain that price disparity. ... It's a moral outrage that Congress continues to allow millions of elderly and chronically ill Americans to suffer and die because they cannot afford the inflated prices charged for pharmaceuticals.

Thus we have the irony that the one declared Socialist in the United States Congress complains when pharmaceutical companies engage in one of the most socialist activities possible!

Bernie Sanders does have a point in that wealthy inhabitants outside the U.S. benefit from prices lower than those charged to his poor constituents. His concern about fairness and the industry's desire to maximize revenues could both be satisfied if pricing could be tailored to each individual, instead of being decided country by country. Thus the substantial erosion of privacy that would be involved in individualized pricing, depending on a person's ability to pay, could satisfy several goals.

The first part of the Communist motto, "from each according to his ability" applies exactly to what unfettered capitalism attempts to do. It tries to extract more from the rich because that is where the money is. (The goal is not the same as of the second part of the Communist motto, "to each according to his needs," though.) Moreover, both capitalism and Communism need to destroy privacy to achieve their aims. Now Communism has failed, and gone to the scrapheap of history. It simply could not deliver on its promises. Capitalism, on the other hand, survives and is generally thriving. However, it is not the unfettered capitalism of the late 19th century. While that capitalism did deliver the goods, it did so in ways that the public was not willing to tolerate. In particular, what really incensed the population was the price discrimination on railways. It offended the public sense of fairness. As a result, capitalism was tamed through government action.

4. Fairness, behavioral economics, and railroads

The example in Section 2 shows the advantages of price discrimination in the standard economic model. Unfortunately this model ignores how people behave in practice.

As a simple example, consider Coca Cola and its experiments with vending machines that would vary prices depending on the temperature. When those experiments became public, they aroused an intensely negative reaction, and Coca Cola was forced to cancel them. In retrospect, Coca Cola's main problem was that news coverage always referred to its work as leading to vending machines that would raise prices in warm weather. Had it managed to control publicity and present its work as leading to machines that would lower prices in cold weather, it might have avoided the entire controversy. To an economist trained in the standard model, it is clear that it does not matter whether one sets a low reference price and raises it on special occasions, or whether one sets a high reference price and lowers it the rest of the time. However, for the public, there is a tremendous difference. That is why discounts are ubiquitous, while surcharges are rare.

Some of the most striking results in behavioral economics involve the sense of fairness, as in the "ultimatum game," in which human subjects tend to act against their own best interests, and attempt to be fair to others in a zero-sum situation. The importance of fairness for public policy was brought out initially and very convincingly in [Zajac, 1995]. Fairness turns out to have been the key reason that railroad price discrimination was limited through political action a century ago. The next three sections deal with this experience.

The key reason for carefully studying 19th century railroads is that they represent a large scale experiment with price discrimination. Technology changes rapidly, but human nature does not. Thus we should be able to pick up hints on how the public will react to an intensive dose of differential pricing by looking at how their ancestors reacted.

We can also hope to learn how price discrimination might develop by observing how it developed on railroads. Researchers in economics and marketing have come up with models which show that even when price discrimination is feasible, it might not be to the advantage of the sellers to engage in it, since it could lead to more intense competition. However, those are the usual theoretical models, and so one has to worry about their applicability. As it turns out, railroads did not want to engage in price discrimination, but could not help getting drawn into it. That is likely to happen again in our future.

5. 19th century railroad pricing revolution

The impact of the Internet on the economy has been compared to that of railroads in the 19th century (cf. [Gordon, 2000; Odlyzko, 2004a]). There are certainly many intriguing analogies. There are also noticeable differences. Perhaps the most important was that railroads were far larger (in comparison to the whole economy) than the Internet. Therefore in looking at the impact on society, it is better to compare railroads to all of IT [Odlyzko, 2004a].

Railroads were the dominant industry in the second half of the 19th century. By 1880, about $4.6 billion had been invested in American railroads. This investment (accumulated over decades) came to about 40% of that year's GDP. (The comparable percentage of today's GDP would come to $4 trillion.)

The railroad revolution led to a pricing revolution. The stimulus came from the incentives for price discrimination that railroad economics generated. Railroads required investments that were huge for that time. On the other hand, marginal costs were comparatively small. Even most of the operational costs (such as track maintenance) were largely independent of traffic volumes. Hence it was inexpensive to run extra trains or longer trains, with most of the additional revenue dropping straight to the bottom line. As an illustration of railroad economics in the early years of the industry, consider the statistics for British railroads for 1842 that are presented on p. 51 of [Galt, 1844]. The 55 lines in operation at that time cost almost $300 million to build (compared to a national budget of about $250 million per year, and a GDP of about $2,500 million). Annual revenues of these railroads were $35 million, of which $10.6 million went to operating expenses, leaving $24.4 as the operating margin. The financial margin of safety was not very high. Small changes in revenues produced large changes in profits. Of the 55 lines in operation, 7 were in bankruptcy or had been taken over by others after failing.

A major innovation that railroads introduced was to provide not just the basic network of rails, but a complete transportation service, involving their own stations, locomotives, and cars. This allowed them to price discriminate effectively. Because of the scale of investment that was required, they had enough market power to do this. Interestingly enough, the early expectations for railroads were that they would operate the way turnpikes did, with customers providing their own cars and locomotives. There were technical reasons for such a change, as was predicted by some early observers (see [Locklin, 1972]). However, it appears that the possibilities for price discrimination were also very important in inducing this transition, as is discussed in [Odlyzko, 2004c]. Certainly price discrimination became one of the most noticeable features of railroad pricing.

19th century railroads did not have the information technologies that would allow for "frequent rider" programs. Neither did they have a "positive passenger identification" system, complete with government-issued identification cards, that would allow them to sell non-transferable advance purchase tickets with Saturday night stay-over restrictions. What they did have were a variety of other tools for price discrimination, and they used them with abandon. Versioning was one of the main ones, as shown in the quote from Jules Dupuit earlier. There was also extensive personal discrimination. Passenger tickets in the U.S. were commonly bought from brokers, and varied widely in price.

While versioning worked reasonably well for passengers, it could not work for freight. Hence explicit price discrimination was the rule for freight from early days. This was carried out through complicated freight classifications, leading to confusion and complaints. There was plenty of scope for discriminatory dealing, with special deals for particular shippers. Charging more for short haul than long haul along the same line was prevalent. In some periods, cargo from New York to Salt Lake City was sent to San Francisco on trains that went through Salt Lake City, and then was shipped back to Salt Lake City as this saved money. Fans of "dynamic pricing" will find many of the features they advocate in 19th century freight rates, as well as others that are likely to be less appealing. The latter included rebates, including the infamous rebates that John D. Rockefeller, Sr., was able to collect even on his competitors' shipments. The market was dynamic, did not generate outsized profits, and, as discussed below, appeared to work very efficiently. However, it aroused great controversy.

6. 19th century railroad pricing counterrevolution

The pricing revolution that accompanied the railroad era generated a counterrevolution. This counterrevolution appears to have been most intense in the United States, although there was a similar movement in Britain [Odlyzko, 2004a]. (Other countries were affected much less, because of heavy government involvement in their railroads.)

Railroads were initially welcomed very warmly. However, with time they became probably the most hated institutions in the country. Their popular image is conveyed by a quote from the conclusion of Frank Norris' famous novel, *The Octopus: A Story of California*:

> The drama was over. The fight of Ranch and Railroad had been wrought out to its dreadful close. ... Yes, the Railroad had prevailed. The ranchers had been seized in the tentacles of the octopus; the iniquitous burden of extortionate freight rates had been imposed like a yoke of iron.

It is only a slight exaggeration to say that in the United States, the politics of the last third of the 19th century were dominated by a revolt against railroad pricing. That was certainly the focus of the Grange and other populist movements. Moreover, it was not just the farmers and the poor who were rebelling. The Chicago Board of Trade, for example, was concerned about its city being handicapped by rates for transport to New York that were higher than those from Milwaukee, even though trains from Milwaukee went through Chicago [Stevens et al. 1876]. Many other powerful commercial interests were also interested in controlling railroad pricing. After intense agitation and unsuccessful attempts at regulating railroads at the state level, political action moved to the federal government. It eventually resulted in the Interstate Commerce Act of 1887, the first serious federal regulation of private business. It took many years of court cases for this act and the Interstate Commerce Commission (ICC) that it set up to become effective. In the end, though, it did revamp railroad pricing. What caused it to be set up, and what was its mission? In the words of Alfred Chandler, Jr., the preeminent business historian of the railroads [Chandler, 1965],

> The demands that brought the first permanent regulatory commission to the United States resulted directly from the railroads' discriminatory pricing policies.

An earlier writer explained in more detail what the objections were [Hadley, 1885]:

> But the fact that the charges are so low does not make *differences* in charge bear any less severely upon business. A difference of five cents per bushel in the charge for transporting wheat a thousand miles is a small matter, taken by itself. It would be weeks before it would make a difference of one cent to the individual consumer of bread. But if a railroad makes this reduction for one miller, and not another, it will be enough to drive the latter out of business.

The pervasive price discrimination by railroads was undermining the moral legitimacy of capitalism. Unequal treatment in an opaque environment raised questions whether success was being achieved by one's merit, or through corrupt deals (as in the "crony capitalism" that many countries are accused of harboring today).

Congress did eventually respond to these concerns. The initial (and most important) sections of the Interstate Commerce Act of 1887 can be summarized as follows:

(1) Rates to be "just and reasonable'

(2) Personal discrimination forbidden

(3) "Undue or unreasonable preference" forbidden

(4) Charging more for short than long haul on same line forbidden

(5) Pooling forbidden

(6) Rates to be published

(7) Impediments to continuous travel of freight forbidden

The remaining dozen or so sections were concerned primarily with administrative matters (setting up the ICC, determining procedures and penalties, and so on).

There are several remarkable features to the above summary of the Interstate Commerce Act. Only one section deals with the level of pricing. Moreover, it is vague, and basically just restates what was already an obligation of railroads as common carriers under common law, ordinary statutes, as well as the railroad charters. Of the other 6 main sections, all but one limit discrimination and "dynamic pricing."

It is now widely accepted that the passage of the Interstate Commerce Act of 1887 was not a pure triumph of the populist movement and its allies in the anti-railroad camp. The railway industry largely decided that regulation was in its best interests and acquiesed in and even encouraged government involvement. This is often portrayed as the insidious capture of the regulators by the industry they regulate (see, for example, [Kolko, 1965]). There is certainly much evidence to support this view. For example, a modern description of the Elkins Act of 1903 says that [Locklin, 1972]

> By 1903 it had become apparent that the law relating to personal discrimination and rebating needed strengthening. The carriers themselves sponsored legislation of this sort because they were losing revenue as a result of the widespread discrimination and departure from published rates. Yet they were unable to stop the practice without the aid of the government.

(Many more examples from contemporary sources are cited in [Parsons, 1906].) The railroads were clearly using regulation to limit competition. Before, even while they were exploiting their customers, they were also engaged in cutthroat competition that brought many of them to ruin. Government intervention stabilized the industry. Yet this was not a simple subversion of the regulatory process. Railroads' customers did get something they cared deeply about. To be more precise, those customers got much of half of what they had been asking for, namely reasonably simple, predictable, and seemingly fair prices. What they did not get was their other demand, namely lower prices. Figure 1-1 on p. 12 of [Locklin, 1972] and the graphs in [Odlyzko, 2004a] show the average revenue collected by U.S. railroads per ton-mile of freight carried. This average was dropping rapidly in the 1870s and 1880s, during the period of most intense anti-railroad agitation, and then levelled off in the late 1890s, when regulation was at last becoming most effective.

Although average prices stopped decreasing, anti-railroad agitation decreased. As often happens, it was not the level of charges, but how those charges were imposed, that mattered.

7. Transportation regulation and deregulation and general observations on pricing

Regulation did not reduce average prices, and may even have served to raise them. On the other hand, it did lead to simpler pricing. However, it was not truly simple pricing. The economic logic of price discrimination was too powerful to overcome. Some 19th century reformers argued that it might be acceptable to allow railroads to gouge passengers any way they wished, but that freight fares should be simple and fair, since those were crucial to the smooth functioning of the economy. Yet, ironically, it was only passenger fares that were truly simplified. Most countries settled on a fixed rate per mile (or kilometer, ...), different for each class, with some special excursion, weekend, commuter, and other fares.

While simple passenger pricing did emerge from the protest movements, price discrimination for freight remained. Personal discrimination (charging different prices for the same service to different customers) was greatly reduced, although there remained various vestiges of it, for example in different charges for different localities. However, the incentives to charge more for transport of more valuable cargo were apparently too strong to be ignored. The difference was that this practice was codified, and was subject to extensive government regulation. Political attacks on railroads were replaced by regulatory and judicial hearings, with millions of pages of filings.

The rigidities and inefficiencies of the railroad regulatory regime (which was extended to truck transportation in the U.S.) grew to an absurd extent. By one estimate there were over 43 trillion rates on file with the Interstate Commerce Commission in the 1960s. It was almost a miracle when two rate clerks would come up with the same prices for any complicated quotes. A large body of experts in setting, verifying, and challenging transportation rates developed, and they found plenty of jobs at carriers, customers, and specialized consulting firms. The inefficiencies of the system (which included fleets of trucks running empty half of the time, and transportation companies whose only substantial assets were federal trucking licenses) led to push for reform, and a freeing of the markets. The deregulation of the late 1970s and early 1980s swept most of the regulatory system away. The government, prodded by reformers, decided that there was enough competition between railroads, trucks, airlines, pipelines, barge lines, and other carriers to let a relatively free market operate. There is still some government oversight (through the Surface Transportation Board) to prevent extreme cases of carriers exercising market power, but it is far more limited than before.

The general assessment among experts who have studied the effects of deregulation is that it has been a great success. Average prices have fallen in all industries. For example, inflation-adjusted rail rates are down 45% since 1984 [StPierre, 2001]. Yet not everybody is happy. The public sense of fairness is offended by findings such as that on railroads, "captive shippers commonly pay rates 20% higher than shippers with competitive alternatives" [StPierre, 2001].

Railroad freight rates are invisible to the general population. On the other hand, airline fares are a frequent topic for conversation and complaints. There is extensive statistical evidence that deregulation has been a success. Even though technological progress is slow, average fares are down, planes are flying fuller than before, and seats are usually available even at the last minute. However, what the public talks about is unhappiness with the bewildering variety of constantly changing fares, travel restrictions, fares to an intermediate city costing more than to a more distant one (even when one flies on the same plane), and so on.

Airline yield management is spreading to trains, hotels, and even golf courses. This is not applauded by the public. A story about the privatization of British railroads spent as much time discussing the annoying pricing structure that is evolving as the lower quality of service [Cowell, 2000]:

> But perhaps the most baffling aspect of British rail travel is the price. ... Fare structures have become a tangle of elusive discounts and incentives for early booking that have widened the gap between standard and first class passengers – but probably united them in complaining about poor service.

8. Overt or covert price discrimination?

The incentives to price discriminate are growing, while the means to price discriminate are exploding, as technologies erode privacy and enable more sophisticated controls. Therefore enterprises will likely be pulled towards differential pricing. It may not lead to greater profits, but the experience of the railroads in the 19th century suggests that the competitive dynamic of the marketplace will not allow them to refrain from trying. Will their customers accept overt price discrimination? The business world operates that way, with extensive use of differential pricing. Perhaps individuals in their private lives will also learn to live with it. As the economy evolves, our discretionary incomes grow, and people may accept that purchasing is a game. Harrah's casino has developed an advanced information system it uses to motivate its customers to spend at Harrah's. It relies on detailed information about each customer, and incentives tailored to each one, as described in [Binkley, 2000]. At least some customers appear to accept this well:

> [One customer] says she's not put off by Harrah's "Pavlovian" marketing. "A gimmick to get me to spend more money?" she asks rhetorically. "Why of course it is."

However, it is more likely that, when subjected to a constant barrage of differential pricing, people would do what they did a century ago, and rebel. Certainly their reactions to variable pricing by Amazon.com or Coca Cola do not suggest any greater tolerance than their ancestors had shown. Pigou's warning (Section 2) to sellers about legislative intervention is likely to be still valid. Therefore the best strategy for sellers will be to hide their differential pricing.

9. The many ways to skin a cat, or how to hide price discrimination

How does one conceal price discrimination? The basic way is to avoid simple cash pricing. Make an offer where the price is a combination of cash and frequent flyer miles, say. Make individualized offers that supposedly reflect the prospective purchasers' past dealings with you. There are many variations, and they are already being tried in the marketplace.

There are also several systematic ways to practice hidden forms of price discrimination, based on bundling. The main reason bundling is practiced so widely is that it allows sellers to take advantage of uneven preferences among buyers for the goods in the bundle. (For references to the extensive literature on bundling, see [Fishburn, Odlyzko, and Siders, 1997].) Thus bundling serves the same purpose as explicit price discrimination in reducing consumer surplus. Consider an example of site licensing, which is really a form of bundling. Suppose Alice has a software package to sell, and a company she would like to sell it to. Of the company's 1000 employees, 900 have no interest in Alice's program, 10 of them are willing (or their bosses are willing) to pay $10 apiece, 10 are willing to pay $20 apiece, and so on at each $10 price break, up to 10 who are willing to pay $100 apiece for the program. If Alice knows these valuations, and has to sell to individuals at a fixed price, the optimal choice for her is to charge either $50 or $60 for her package. In either case she will get $3,000. However, the collective valuation of all the employees in this company is $5,500, so she should be able to sell the package for unlimited use by every one of the 1,000 employees for $5,500. Thus by selling a site license, Alice will actually do as well as if she could charge each individual that person's valuation for her package. At the same time, she will appear to be offering the company a bargain. The package, which might sell to individuals outside for $50 per copy or more, will be available at a cost per eligible employee of just $5.50.

The conclusion is that there are ways to achieve the same ends as explicit price discrimination without appearing to do so. Furthermore, methods such as site licensing have additional advantages, such as increased usage and network effects. A brief summary is given in [Odlyzko, 2003].

10. Conclusions

The general conclusion is that in the Internet environment, the incentives towards price discrimination and the ability to price discriminate will be growing. Sellers will be increasingly tempted to engage in differential pricing. However, such practices are fraught with danger, since the public is likely to resent them intensely. Therefore the stress is likely to be on finding ways to hide price discrimination. This means that techniques such as DRM are likely to be used only in mild forms, and instead preference will be given for various bundling strategies, especially personalized bundles. However, privacy will continue to erode, since intimate knowledge of consumer preferences and willingness to pay will be of advantage in creating those bundles, and will often provide crucial competitive advantage to sellers.

Governments are likely to play an increasing role in pricing. The temptation for companies to push their differential pricing to the extremes of public acceptability is likely to lead to sufficiently negative reactions from time to time that governments will get involved in setting rules. Moreover, since prices in an an environment of low marginal costs will be seen to be almost completely arbitrary, there will be a temptation for the public to demand regulation. Governments are also likely to continue playing an ambiguous role, in order to protect the welfare-enhancing effects of price discrimination. Thus on balance we should not expect governments to protect privacy. The most they are likely to do is to set rules on how private information can be used in setting differential prices (as they already do in insurance, for example).

In general, the economic advantages of price discrimination are and are likely to remain in direct conflict with public dislike of such practices. Hence it is not likely that there will be an easy resolution to the problem, and privacy erosion and differential pricing will continue to be contentious public issues.

References

Albrecht, K. (2003). *CASPIAN: Consumers Against Supermarket Privacy Invasion and Numbering,* Web site, `http://www.nocards.org`.

Anderson, R. (2003). "Cryptology and competition policy - Issues with 'Trusted Computing"'.
Available at `http://www.cpppe.umd.edu/rhsmith3/agenda.htm`.

Barrionuevo, A. (2000). "Secret formulas set the prices for gasoline," *Wall Street J.*, March 20.

Bayers, C. (2000). "Capitalist Econstruction," *Wired,* March. Available at `http://www.wired.com/wired/archive/8.03/markets.html`.

Binkley, A. (2000). "Casino chain mines data on gamblers, and strikes pay dirt with low-rollers," *Wall Street J.*, May 4.

Brin, D. (1998). *The Transparent Society.* Perseus Publishing.

Chandler, Jr., A. (1965). *The Railroads, the Nation's First Big Business: Sources and Readings.* Harcourt, Brace, & World.

Corts, K. S. (1996). "On the competitive effects of price-matching policies," *Intern. J. Industrial Organization,* vol. 15, pp. 283-299.

Cowell, A. (2000). "Service slips, fares baffle on British trains," *New York Times*, May 28.

DeLong, J. B. and Froomkin, A. M. (2000). "Speculative microeconomics for tomorrow's economy," in *Internet Publishing and Beyond: The Economics of Digital Information and Intellectual Property,* Kahin, B. and Varian, H. R., eds., MIT Press, pp. 6-44. A 1997 draft, entitled "The next economy?", is available at `http://www.law.miami.edu/~froomkin/articles/newecon.htm`.

Deneckere, R. J. and McAfee, R. P. (1996). "Damaged goods," *J. Economics and Management Strategy,* vol. 5, no. 2, pp. 149-174.

Ekelund, R. B. (1970). "Price discrimination and product differentiation in economic theory: an early analysis," *Quarterly Journal of Economics,* vol. 84, pp. 268-278.

Fishburn, P. C., Odlyzko, A. M., and Siders, R. C. (1997). "Fixed fee versus unit pricing for information goods: competition, equilibria, and price wars," *First Monday,* vol. 2, no. 7, http://www.firstmonday.org/.

Galt, W. (1844). *Railway Reform: Its Expediency and Practicality Considered. With a Copious Appendix, ...,* Pelham Richardson, 3rd ed.

Garfinkel, S. (2000). *Database Nation: The Death of Privacy in the 21st Century.* O'Reilly & Associates.

Gordon, J. S. (2000). "The golden spike," *Forbes ASAP,* February 21. Available at http://www.forbes.com/asap/2000/0221/118.html.

Hadley, A. T. (1885). *Railroad Transportation: Its History and its Laws.* G. P. Putnam's Sons.

Huber, P. (1993). "Two cheers for price discrimination," *Forbes,* September 27.
Available at http://www.phuber.com/huber/forbes/092793.html.

Kolko, G. (1965). *Railroads and Regulation, 1877-1916.* Princeton Univ. Press.

Lester, T. (2001). "The reinvention of privacy," *The Atlantic Monthly,* vol. 287, no. 3, March, pp. 27-39. Available at http://www.theatlantic.com/issues/2001/03/lester-p1.htm.

Levine, M. E. (2002). "Price discrimination without market power," *Yale Journal on Regulation,* vol. 19, no. 1, Winter, pp. 1-36. Preliminary version available at http://www.law.harvard.edu/programs/olin_center/papers/276_levine.htm.

Locklin, D. P. (1972). *Economics of Transportation.* 7th ed., Richard D. Irwin.

McWilliams, G. (2001). "Dell fine-tunes its PC pricing to gain an edge in slow market," *Wall Street J.,* June 8.

Odlyzko, A. M. (1996). "The bumpy road of electronic commerce," in *WebNet 96 - World Conf. Web Soc. Proc.,* H. Maurer, ed., AACE, pp. 378-389. Available at http://www.dtc.umn.edu/~odlyzko.

Odlyzko, A. M. (2003). "The case against micropayments," in *Financial Cryptography: 7th International Conference, FC 2003,* R. N. Wright, ed., Springer, pp. 182-189. Available at http://www.dtc.umn.edu/~odlyzko.

Odlyzko, A. M. (2004a). "The Internet and 19th century railways," in preparation.

Odlyzko, A. M. (2004b). "Privacy, price discrimination, and the future of ecommerce," in preparation.

Odlyzko, A. M. (2004c). "Fairness and price discrimination on the Internet and on 19th century railroads," in preparation.

Parsons, F. (1906). *The Heart of the Railroad Problem: The History of Railway Discrimination in the United States, the Chief Efforts at Control and the Remedies Proposed, with Hints from Other Countries.* Little, Brown, and Company.

Phlips, L. (1983). *The Economics of Price Discrimination.* Cambridge Univ. Press.

Pigou, A. C. (1924). *The Economics of Welfare,* 2nd ed. Macmillan. First edition published in 1920.

Sanders, B. (2000). "Letter to the editor," *Barron's,* February 28.

Shabi, R. (2003). "The card up their sleeve," *The Guardian,* July 19. Available at `http://www.guardian.co.uk/Print/0,3858,4714196,00.html`.

Shapiro, C. and Varian, H. (1998). *Information Rules: A Strategic Guide to the Network Economy.* Harvard Business School Press.

Stevens, E. B., Baker, Wm. T., Pope, W. J., Stiles, J., and Dater, P.W. (1876). *Report of Committee of Chicago Board of Trade on Railroad Discrimination, submitted February 7, 1876.* Knight & Leonard.

St. Pierre, N. (2001). "Railroads: Asleep at the switch: Lousy service is driving away freight customers," *Business Week,* April 2.

Varian, H. R. (1980). "A model of sales," *Am. Economic Review,* vol. 70, pp. 651-659. Erratum on p. 517 of vol. 71 (1981).

Varian, H. R. (1989). "Price discrimination," in *Handbook of Industrial Organization,* R. Schmalensee and R. D. Willig, eds.. Elsevier, pp. 597-654.

Varian, H. R. (1996). "Differential pricing and efficiency," *First Monday,* vol. 1, no. 2, August, `http://firstmonday.org/`.

Yudof, M. G. (2002). "Is the public research university dead?," *The Chronicle of Higher Education,* Jan. 11. Available to subscribers at `http://chronicle.com/weekly/v48/i18/18b02401.htm`.

Zajac, E. E. (1995). *Political Economy of Fairness.* MIT Press.

Chapter 16

WE WANT SECURITY BUT WE HATE IT

The Foundations of security technoeconomics in the social worldfrom Control to Surveillance

Mauro Sandrini
Teramo University, Italy
msandrini@complessita.it

Ferdinando Cerbone
President of Ass. Coevoluzione, Reichian Studies Center, Italy
radhaolmo@libero.it

> *The issue, then, is how will technology* embed *the social values?*

The Internet Operating System does not yet exist[1]. But we are in the process of building it [Buckendorff, 2002]. In the upcoming phase of this transition we will go toward a network operating system that will be a fundamental layer of human society's communications system.

The first signs of what is happening are already visible, thanks to tools like e-mail, joint productivity and social software, chat lines etc. As a result there is an enormous increase in the number of messages that each of us receives every day. It may seem as if we are evolving into *human message-processing machines* [Ozzie, 2003]. The designers' aim is to avoid this, leaving the mechanical work to automatic software systems [Betts, 2003]. The contradiction related to this approach is that we are fighting the environment's complexity by introducing technologies that increase the global system entropy. What we need, instead, are solutions capable of reducing this complexity.

Up to now, faith is what humanity has used to pursue this aim [Luhmann, 2000]:

> 'Faith reduces social complexity and therefore simplifies life by taking a risk'

Faith as an embedded value does not seem to belong to the emerging technological infrastructure. Security, on the other hand, is at the root of this developing network operating system. The aim is to build a world of 'trustworthy computing' [Anderson, 2003] which will be part of a social environment, where the main value will be mistrust. The issue, then, is how will technology *embed* the social values [Carboni, 2002]? Now the security concept core is entwined with that of fear. But fear of what?

Fear arises at several levels but we will concentrate on the two most important ones for our analysis:

The first level of fear concerns losing control of the profits obtained by the knowledge economy to date. Here the DRM (Digital Rights Management) issue becomes paradigmatic. Historically, copyright laws have worked rather well, to protect the owners of these rights[2] (who more often than not, are not the authors themselves [Lessig, 2001]). However, the conflict arises when the contents start to reproduce themselves thanks to an evolutionary process based on the widespread possibility of sharing and communicating knowledge as never before. Here is where the copyright owners lose control and conflicts arise.

Open Source is the most well known case. Despite the fact that it is being taken into consideration in some business contexts (for example Oracle and IBM) it has just started to contaminate the old-new-economy. For example try to imagine what will happen if [Betts, 2003]:

> In early 2004, some bored geek starts an open-source OLAP [On Line Analytical Processing] initiative. Suddenly, Oracle doesn't think that Linux and its ilk are that cool any more
> *Gerald Boyd, Director of research,*
> *NCS Technologies Inc., Piscataway, N.J.*

This is exactly the fear that lies below the surface of the 'Controlled Computing' strategies and policies in its various forms and evolutions[3].

Trying to capture knowledge is like trying to capture air. You can lock it up but it will fly away as soon as the first crack appears. On the contrary, to be successful in locking up this knowledge will mean producing stale air that, in the end, will poison us.

When goods were made mostly of 'hardware' and contained small quantities of knowledge, the market barriers were made mainly of high investments in fixed assets and that was all. Now the competition borders are defined by the will of some 'bored geek' who wants to launch a new challenge. Therefore, the borders are completely different. But with the rising of 'Controlled Computing' this will definitely stop.

> The 'Controlled Computing' core issue is just this: the erection of economic entry barriers in the high intensity knowledge sectors through embedding software in the hardware.

The entry barriers will rise enormously as a result of the high capital investments that this innovation will require to newcomers. The fear is to lose control of a knowledge economy that is growing, and in the meantime it is sharing the value it is generating more and more.

The second level of fear concerns controlling the contents.. There exists only one way to feed a knowledge economy: by sharing the knowledge itself in a learning social system [Capra, 2002; Maturana, Varela, 1992].

In the short term, an economy which controls knowledge to gain profits, may live with another, sharing based economic model[4]. This phenomenon may continue until the former model is able to extract profits from the latter. This is an important aspect of what is happening today with Open Source economics[5]. However, the process upon which this is based is non linear and evolving. It is in contrast with a linear based profit generation model which will become stable when market saturation arises (most of the time this is a monopolistic market when dealing with information goods). This stabilization may correspond to the opening of a new market, with the monopolist's death or with its complete transformation. If this occurs in too many markets at the same time this may mean the end of the global economic system.

On the other hand we have another evolutionary *Open* process that generates value through knowledge production, without the primary aim of pursuing a profit. This occurs, furthermore, without the markets' saturation but, on the contrary, without preventing the opening of new economic horizons. On one hand, the traditional market process reduces breathable air[6], on the other, it is possible to continuously discover new lands. Forces which are promoting the former economic model are based on mistrust and fear, the forces which feed the latter are curiosity, knowledge eagerness, desire for life[7]. The Open Source case is the most well known but the real interest of it lies in being paradigmatic of how knowledge can evolve and generate value. In a knowledge economy content is everything: software, music, video, books. Ever since DNA has been sequenced, even we ourselves have become 'itinerant code carriers'; in other words each of us is a content carrier. If the final aim of 'Controlled Computing' is content control then the richest content to take possession of is ourselves. Each of us for his or her genetic code.

Are we claiming that the Internet Operating System is not to be founded on security? No, what we are saying is that it must not be founded on the present security concept. It is this security concept that finds its true implementation on the 'Controlled Computing' trend. Another security model may emerge if we consider this as a true human and social need, instead of a gasping corporation system's last chance to avoid change [Locke,2001]. Another way to face this idea of security/control may germinate only by embedding faith as a value in the network operating system. Perhaps the way to pursue this resides in the shadow line path that exists between surveillance and security without being dazzled by the preconceived ideas that these words very often trigger off.

We will now try to follow this path.

1. Security and Society

Society's role in producing a security system has been underestimated in the past. This is not restricted to some social engineering techniques as it may seem from some media over exposure[8] but it emerges from a simple reality: attacks are based more and more on human system weakness instead of on technological weaknesses. If, as Ross Anderson says [Anderson, 2003]:

> 'The complexity of the information flows within the real organizations tends to cause all the information to either float up to the highest level of classification, or float down to the lowest level'

then in today's organizations it is not possible to be positioned in the highest levels of classified information. This is why in a complex unstable economic environment, in which flexibility and adaptability are at the root of organizational behaviour [Wood, 2000], sharing knowledge is necessary. The highest levels of classification contradict flexibility and adaptability in a complex system. It is possible to compete only at certain levels of sharing or, that is, of faith. And faith, as we have already seen, brings with it some risks. This is why the lowest level of security is so widespread, and why it makes room for human based attacks. Today that security is becoming an important layer of the network operating system, and is no longer related to small organizationally closed entities, it becomes evident that security is a process and not a solution. A process, furthermore, that is strongly related to today's society evolution. Recognizing this may help us build safer systems, as they will become more closely related to how real organizations are.

With security technoeconomics we are laying the foundations of our actions and lives out there. Until we accept that we are looking for both security and surveillance in each of their community aspects we will fail in building a truly safe environment.

2. Surveillance at the supermarket

Security and, the other side of the coin, surveillance, are inseparable. If security has to be at the centre of the network operating system it is impossible to consider it separately. Let us look at some facts concerning the ongoing phenomena ([Farmer, Mann, 2003, April], May):

- 26 million surveillance video cameras have already been installed worldwide. Of these 11 million are in the United States;

- by 2006 the U.S. will prescribe that each cell phone can transmit the exact caller position during emergency calls. Obviously, this feature will become available on a mass basis for other localization aims;

- the top three U.S. automobile manufacturers will install in every vehicle an RFI system (Radio Frequency Identification system)[9];

- Telesurveillance now counts for less than 1% of the global surveillance phenomenon;

There are, furthermore, trends forecast on some new surveillance devices like the mounted-wall surveillance camera Nokia is going to introduce on the U.S. market by summer 2003. The cost will be under $500 and it will be capable of sending images to mobile devices. It is expected that the market value of such devices will be about 28 billion dollars in four years from now (Source: Wireless Data Research Group [Charny, 2003]). So there will be several dozens millions of items of personal video surveillance systems in a few years.

This is only the tip of the iceberg, the only visible one. The biggest part is hidden from the eyes of the common citizen: it is the weaving of the data which comes from the above systems, governmental and marketing databases. In spite of all the dependability related difficulties concerning the data collected ([Farmer, Mann, 2003, April], May), it is possible to estimate that twenty years from now, in 2023, the equivalent of today's normal personal computer will suffice to monitor every single citizen, of the 330 million living in the United States at that time. In 2001 46.5% of companies were monitoring workers' emails and 36.1% were even monitoring organizations' computer files [Farmer, Mann, 2003, April].

Are we facing a hyper tech version of Big Brother [Mazoyer, 2001]? The answer to this question contains the security/surveillance paradox. Even if the process started with the big burocratic organizations (governmental and private) now it is the individuals and small organizations who are making it evolve in society.

If society *embeds* technology, then the technology we are producing today is embedding such values as fears and withdrawals, inside and amongst human beings. Such surveillance is not developing as in the Big Brother model, but rather it is something that emerges/happens every time we gain access to resources on the net.

Therefore, the collective emergent properties are generated starting from individual behavior, that then produces a dual relationship between the concepts of needs/rejection and security/surveillance.

In other words, our security needs take us toward a system that involves some special characteristics that most of us reject. This rejection produces some worrisome effects related to the global economic system's efficiency. For example individual productivity is reduced: in a working environment where the worker knows he or she is being monitored, the same worker is less open to sharing knowledge in a horizontal way. On the contrary, sharing is pursued by horizontal organizations and their knowledge management systems [10].

As individuals we can try to boycott the surveillance system if we are aware of being monitored. At the same time we are the same people who go to buy millions of video cameras or global positioning systems in order to know in every instant where our wife, husband, son or daughter is.

Do you remember the virtuous circle economics? This is exactly the reverse: a vicious circle that initially may cause a social block and then to follow an economic one. But what kind of economy is possible in a socially blocked system?

3. Security as control or community infrastructure?

As David Lyon [Lyon, 2001] suggests surveillance infrastructure is produced by the weaving of one to one marketing technologies with governmental agencies' improvements in tracking citizens[11]. This permits several subjects to track and influence each individual, simply by putting together the various pieces of the puzzle that, globally, represent his or her digital image: his or her own *body data* [Lyon, 2001].

However this is only the beginning of the story. Today surveillance has become a mass phenomenon that crosses, and sometimes drives, the institutional side of it. The market dimensions are too big and too granular to place all the blame on the institutional infrastructure alone.

One hypothesis, that will be an interesting research path, would be to verify if this process may facilitate the diffusion of the sense of connection as a substitute for the sense of loss of community membership in our postmodern society. As some authors suggest [Carboni, 2002; De Kerckhove, 1991] we are on the way to finding a *connection sense* - as the membership sense incomer - that, ipso facto, seems to be a weak tie. Maybe this concept could find a stronger dimension within a network communications system which has been founded, as it seems to be, on surveillance.

4. Towards 'Surveillance Computing'

Despite what our opinion may be, the surveillance building system has started and it is irreversible. The surveillance infrastructure will be the ring which will connect the real world with the cyber world. Surveillance, in fact, is exerting its influence through the *body data* located in the cyber world of databases: its effects are very real indeed. Surveillance acts on real physical bodies: ours.

Allowing individuals to gain control of surveillance is perhaps the only way for this system to be accepted and to be maintained inside the democratic space as we know it.

As Whitfield Diffie asserts [Merritt]:

> 'To risk sloganeering, I say you need to hold the keys of your own computer'.

Actually this is a slogan and like most slogans it does not contain the whole story. The second part of the story, in fact, is that what we need are the keys to our own computer AND the permission to gain access (potentially) to the log files where every part of our *body data* lies [12].

> In other words we need to know who is doing what and when with our own *body data* and to do this we need to have access to the log files.

This possibility may allow us to again have the right to be in control of our *body data.* Obviously this is just the beginning, and by itself it is not enough. What is necessary is to translate this assertion into technical specifications that can prove it is a real aim. These technical specifications can be compared with those of various 'Controlled Computing' organizations (TCPA, TCG, etc..)[13].

This principle is based upon two facts:

1 the surveillance process belongs both to society and technology in a reciprocal manner;

2 it is possible to define technical specifications which will embed faith as a value within the technological systems our society is producing. These specifications are based on the right to gain access to ourselves: we want to own the property of our *body data* and to know the reputation of who, apart from us, has the right to gain this access.

The first point belongs to the continuous feedback that exists at every moment between society and technology. The second, on the contrary, belongs to what is possible. From a technical point of view this means that the cryptographer scientists decide to define the technical specification that makes it possible to pursue the second aim. This will stop criticism[14] about how bad 'Control Computing' is and help the action to start[15].

Here the important aspect is to prove that a 'Surveillance Computing' model is possible and that it can cope on equal terms with the 'Controlled Computing' model.

This vision recognizes the surveillance stream which is flowing inside society, but does not fight it, rather it simply offers new ways to express itself. In this way we can see how an infrastructure which embeds the values of faith and sharing builds up an open social system in which, perhaps, some new economic movements may start again.

In this scenario there is no more static control over each *body data* as privacy rights supporters claimed in the past with no results.

A passive attitude has been transformed into an active one: concrete surveillance on our own *body data* that are available to our environment, but whoever gains access to them needs to give proof, in every instant, of his own reputation. This builds up, furthermore, a public responsibility process.

> To allow someone else to gain access under surveillance to our *body data* means there is no withdrawal. Data is still available but everybody holds the surveillance key, in person and through the community[16]. The

possibility of sharing still exists and an economy based upon knowledge sharing is still possible, actually it finds a truly *secure* environment in which to grow.

The steps we can highlight are:

1 The definitions of the technical specifications needed to gain access to the *body data* log files.

2 The creation of a consortium which is capable of assembling this specification and which constitutes a first group of companies at hand to implement it.

3 The lobbying of legislators and positive actions through consumer associations.

To proceed towards 'Surveillance Computing' it is necessary to establish specifications and organizations. It is necessary to set up a technoeconomical institution that creates technical specifications and lobbying, coping face to face with TCPA or TCG etc.

5. Beyond Privacy. Think different

If we really want to go towards a new concept of surveillance it is not possible to remain with archaic concepts like privacy[17]. Furthermore privacy takes with it the idea of distrust that goes exactly in the opposite direction in respect to what we have said till now. We need to overcome the traditional privacy borders inventing a new way to allow access to shared data in an open economy. This is why even some strong privacy rules, like in the EU[18], are not aimed in this direction.

The main principle is to define specifications of small groups of data, we can call it *body data core* that embeds an owner's digital signature. The possibility of gaining access to the log files has to be through this signature. Introducing a *body data core* simplifies the process because the log files need to be recorded only when external data are linked with someone of the core. For example: it is not necessary to gain access to the license plate image archive, but it has to be possible to have access to log files when the digital information embedded in the license plate image is used to gain access to some other core data. The *body data core* are in a process where every access to them triggers a record (embedding the owner's digital signature) in a log file. Obviously this is not a solution but just a very short example on the direction we can go if we decide to use the 'Trusted Computing' available technologies and use them in a different way in order to build a 'Society's Communications System' that embeds values rather different from today's concepts. This is not Utopia, unless you consider standards, protocols and specifications as Utopia [Moore, 1516].

These ideas are simple proposals for approaching the upcoming scenario, the network operating system. At the moment we are at a crossroads, in one direction there is only technology and in the other, there is the issue of privacy. These two directions lead on one hand to 'Controlled Computing' and on the other the old way of safeguarding privacy. Neither is fertile by itself: opportunities come from both sides. Considering them in such a way may generate, perhaps, a new developing path rich in consequences that up to now have not been possible to predict.

Notes

1. To all intents and purposes the network operating system is going to build up an important layer of the 'society communications system', i.e. a system that we, as a society, are continuously producing. In this work, that is only the starting point of a wider one, we will refer to the 'technological structure' of this complex communication system and we will call it a 'network operating system'.

2. Usually record companies, film studios and software houses. In fact the same representatives are the main promoters of the Trusted Computing Public Alliance consortium, now called the Trusted Computing Group consortium. For more details see [Anderson, 2003].

3. Henceforth we will refer to various denominations as well as to 'Trusted computing', 'Trustworthy computing' etc. for what they are in reality: 'Controlled Computing' as suggested by Ross Anderson in [Anderson, 2003].

4. For example see how the record companies have basically not registered falls in profits as a result of the net file sharing communities. See S. Lewis [Lewis, 2003].

5. There are several studies that aim at understanding Open Source economic process within the traditional economic framework [Lerner, 2000]. In this way, as they assert, it is possible to explain *almost* all of what is happening. The reality indeed is that 'almost' in one complex evolutive phenomenon may become a big difference in the final result.

6. This is evident in our economic situation that in recent times seems to have postponed the economic recovery until a near future that has not yet come.

7. This is very similar to how scientific research was before it has been infested by patent's anxiety. The difference here lies in the fact that this pressure towards open knowledge comes from a wide social force instead of from an intellectual elite.

8. For example recently Kevin Mitnick, The art of deception [Mitnick, 2003].

9. An RFI is a small device which will be inserted into a product destined for the end consumer and that is capable, in the beginning, of optimizing the production process in transmitting to the producer data of various kinds. Recently Benetton tried to embed such a device in each item of clothing. At the moment this decision has been abandoned due to the protest campaign led by customer associations around the globe. See [Albrecht, 2002; Krane, 2003].

10. It will be interesting to investigate the real effects of such systems and the oppositions they have triggered off. Every knowledge management system is, by definition, a documental and process surveillance system.

11. There are many titles about this subjects. For example see Peppers & Rogers [Peppers, Rogers, 1997].

12. See Carl S. Kaplan in [Farmer, Mann, 2003, May].

13. To know all the story related to the 'Controlled Computing' consortiums and their evolution see [Anderson, 2003].

14. However revealing what lies down this trend has been truly important indeed. Many of the changes which have taken place from last year to date have been caused by such revelations about TCPA and Palladium. See [Anderson, 2002].

15. One possible path of research could be to embed a personal backdoor, inside each one separate piece of body data. At least of the most important of the puzzle. One backdoor that starting from the principle at the root of digital signature connects each document to its real owner and allows one to gain access to the log files of the process in which it is involved by third parties.

16. Reputation is a social process.

17. Privacy, as we know it, is historically defined: it has not always existed and, furthermore, is strongly influenced by the social-cultural context in which we consider it. Actually, today, it does not exist anymore. Thanks to Dr. Andrea Glorioso for this contribution.

18. This is a general consideration that, obviously, is not related to the various legislation within each individual EU country.

References

Albrecht Katherine, Auto-ID: Tracking everything, everywhere, June 2002, at http://seattlepi.nwsource.com/business/116508_smarttags09.shtml

Anderson Ross, Cryptography and Competition Policy - Issues with 'Trusted Computing', 2nd Annual Workshop on Economics and Information Security, May29th-30th, 2003

Anderson Ross, 'Tcpa/Palladium Faq', at http://www.cl.cam.ac.uk/~rja14/tcpa-faq.html

Anderson Ross, Security Engineering - a Guide to Building Dependable Distributed Systems, Wiley, 2001

Betts Mitch, The future of business intelligence, April 14 2003, at http://www.computerworld.com/databasetopics/data/story/0,10801,80243,00.html

Buckendorff,J. *An interview with Tim O'Reilly*, from The O'Reilly Network, 12/07/2002, at http://www.open2p.com/lpt/a/2920

Hawken Paul, Amory Lovins and Hunter L. Lovins, Natural Capitalism. Creating the next industrial revolution, Little Brown an Co., Boston, 1999

Capra Fritjof, The Hidden Connections, Integrating The Biological, Cognitive, And Social Dimensions Of Life Into A Science Of Sustainability, Random House Inc, 2002

Carboni Carlo, La Nuova Societa, Laterza, Bari, Italy, 2002

Charny Bern, Nokia camera send a cell message, at http://www.businessweek.com/technology/cnet/stories/997228.htm

De Kerckhove Derrick, Brainframes, Technology, Mind and Business, Bosch & Keuning, 1991

Farmer Dan and Mann Charles C., Surveillance Nation part 1, April 2003, MIT Technology review, at www.techreview.com

Farmer Dan and Mann Charles C., Surveillance Nation part 1, May 2003, MIT Technology review, at http://www.techreview.com

Krane Jim, Benetton rethinks using 'smart tags' in clothes, Associated Press, April 9, 2003, at http://seattlepi.nwsource.com/business/116508_smarttags09.shtml

Locke Christopher, Gonzo Marketing. Winning through worst practices, Perseus Publishing, 2001

Lessig Lawrence, The Future of Ideas, Random House, NY, 2001

Lewis S., 'How Much is Stronger DRM Worth?', 2nd Annual Workshop on Economics and Information Security, May29th-30th, 2003

Luhmann Niklas, Vertrauen. Ein Mechanism der Reduktion sozialer Komplexitat, IV ed. Stuttgart, Lucius & Lucius, 2000.

Lyon David, The Electronic Eye: the rise of surveillance society, Polity Press, Cambridge 1994.

Lyon David, Surveillance society: monitoring everyday life, Polity Press, Milton Keynes, 2001.

Mazoyer Frank, Il lucroso mercato della sorveglianza, Le Monde Diplomatique (Italian Ed.), 2001, september

Maturana H., Varela F., The tree of knowledge, Shambala, Revised Edition, 1992

Merritt Rick, Cryptographers sound warnings on Microsoft security plan, EE Tiimes, April 16, 2003, at `http://www.techweb.com/wire/story/TWB20030416S0002`

Mitnick Kevin, The art of deception, Wiley Publishing, 2002

Moore Thomas, Utopia, 1516, Penguin Classics, 1965 Ed.

Ozzie Ray, Perspective: a mosaic of new opportunities, April 22, 2003, Cnet at `http://news.com.com/2010-1071-997725.html`

Pena Charles V., Targetting terrorism or... privacy?, The Whashington Times, 25/11/2002, at `http://www.whashtimes.com`

Peppers Don & Rogers Martha, The One to One Future: Building Relationships One Customer at a Time, Doubleday, 1997

Searls Doc, Weinberger David, Worlds of Ends, at `http://worldofends.com`, downloaded march 10th 2003

Lerner Josh, Tirole Jean, The Simple economics of Open Source, National Bureau of Economic Research, 2000, at `http://opensource.mit.edu/papers/`

Wood Robin, Managing Complexity, The Economist Books, 2000

Chapter 17

SECURITY AND LOCK-IN

Tom Lookabaugh
University of Colorado at Boulder

Douglas C. Sicker
University of Colorado at Boulder

Here we first develop a framework for security based lock-in before describing three important recent cases: set-top boxes in the US cable industry and cartridges in the video game and printer industries.

A customer experiences "lock-in" when the extra value it might obtain from a new supplier's products or services is exceeded by the cost of switching from its current vendor[1]. Customers may regret this state of affairs if they would have been better off having secured the alternative product from the start, or more simply, if the switching costs are substantially lower than the incremental value of the alternative supplier's product (in which case, the customer will switch and capture the difference). Conversely, an incumbent supplier might appreciate and indeed encourage this state of affairs to the extent it can realize additional profit. These two interact in the sense that a supplier would likely forego additional profit (and a customer would receive lower prices) if switching costs were lower, even if the customer does not actually switch. Less apparently, though potentially more importantly, lock-in may have substantial impact on the types of product innovation a customer accesses, both directly from its supplier and indirectly through innovation in complementary products.

Computer and communication security (hereafter simply security) seems particularly suited as a locus of lock-in by virtue of several fac-

[1]A very related concept is "lock-out", the extent to which a competitor is precluded from serving an incumbent provider's customer. The perspective of lock-out suggests framing the issue from a monopolistic behavior and anti-trust perspective (the relationship between competitors) as opposed to the emphasis on customer-supplier relationship of lock-in [Cohen, 1995].

tors: (i) it can be manifested as a technical compatibility requirement that must be met by a variety of applications and pieces of equipment communicating locally or across a network, and reverse engineering of the interface may in some cases be made equivalent to breaking a strong encryption system, (ii) suppliers may explicitly or implicitly suggest that proprietary security is better than open security since the supplier can control access to information about the system, (iii) it may be difficult to segregate legally permissible competitive reverse engineering from efforts to enable illegitimate piracy.

The *possibility* of security induced lock-in is not, by itself, that interesting. It becomes interesting if it actually occurs, it has non-trivial consequences, and there exists at least one other feasible state of affairs that would be preferable to some party. All three of these are important points that require both a theoretical framework and empirical evidence. They are challenging to tackle as they span technical, economic, business, and legal domains.

In fact, a number of candidate examples of security based lock-in exist. Here we first develop a framework for security based lock-in before describing three important recent cases: set-top boxes in the US cable industry and cartridges in the video game and printer industries. Finally, we describe security lock-in motivated tactics for suppliers, customers, and government.

1. Theoretical Framework

The Role of Security in Lock-In

Many security systems include protocols that describe how messages are to be transmitted securely or how various components of a system (local or distributed) are to interact to perform a secure action. Conformance to such protocols creates a compatibility requirement across system components. A supplier that wishes to sell a system component will either need to be compatible with the necessary security protocols, or must provide sufficient additional value to motivate a customer to replace all other system components that require those security protocols. In this latter case, the cost of replacing other system components becomes a switching cost and a source of lock-in. If the installed base that must be replaced is large, the cost can be prohibitive.

New suppliers attempting to circumvent security based lock-in without requiring wholesale replacement of compatible components by a customer will typically look to implement the necessary existing protocols. If the necessary protocols are not publicly known (they are proprietary), the new supplier may attempt to do so without the permission of those that originated, own, or otherwise control the required protocols. This may be technically feasible, but can be stymied by intellectual property law: the necessary information may be protected by various copyright and patent rights. This is, in fact, also true for the general case of technical compatibility based lock-in, but the effect is sharpened in the case of security because of the potential difficulty in distinguishing what might be considered legally protected reverse engineering activities for competition reasons from attempts to foster piracy for reasons of illegitimate access to messages or content. This particular effect has been manifested recently in controversy around application of the Digital Millennium Copyright Act. Originally created to outlaw circumvention by pirates of technology to protect intellectual property, the act is seeing broader application in preventing reverse engineering, such as a recent case in which an injunction was secured by Lexmark against a developer of chips that enable "clone" printer cartridges [Nowell, 2003].

Alternatively, a new supplier may seek to license the necessary security protocols from the owner. If the owner is the incumbent supplier, this should be feasible providing the incumbent supplier can extract the profit it forgoes for each product not sold from the new supplier through a license fee or equivalent compensation. But, it may be difficult to achieve this solution. If, for example, the new supplier's advantage is more efficient manufacturing and it can offer the product to the customer for a lower price than the incumbent, the manufacturing efficiency cost improvement must exceed the sum of the incumbent supplier's required unit profit *plus* the new supplier's required unit profit. Anything short of this will not present a solution as the licensed new supplier's product would, in fact, be more expensive than the original incumbent's product and hence not salable (rendering a licensing agreement moot). A second problem is that the incumbent supplier may correctly calculate the cost of profit foregone as larger than the apparent difference between product price and product cost by taking into account other costs such as reduced economies of scale and learning, effects on cross-subsidization among the suppliers products (for example, in the printer industry, low printer margins are offset by high cartridge margins), reduced marketing and sales effects that are driven by market share, and increased costs in terms of supporting licensees (for example, restricted ability to unilaterally make system changes that involve security protocols). Importantly, even if a licensing arrangement is feasible, the full cost of lock-in is still borne, now by the customer and the new supplier jointly, and continues to accrue as profit to the incumbent supplier.

In some cases, security protocols are not secret at all but are openly available (e.g., based on an open standard like the Data Encryption Standard or Advanced Encryption Standard [Burr, 2003]) or licensing is available at a sufficiently low cost. Lock-in may still occur, though, if successful interaction across the interface requires information (e.g., a cryptographic key) that is only available with the permission of another party, such as a competing vendor. In this case, although the protocol has been implemented, successful interoperation without permission of a hostile party may be equivalen to the problem of breaking a cryptographically strong system. A well designed cryptographic algorithm can be quite secure against such attacks making it economically infeasible to interoperate.

Security also has the potential to play an enhanced role in lock-in by virtue of the perceived value of system secrecy. Suppliers may explicitly or more discretely claim that their proprietary system is more secure than, say, a potential or actually openly available alternative, since the supplier can control access to information about the system itself. This has the virtue of appealing to a common sense proposition that for a system of a given security level, reduced knowledge about the system will not help and could reasonably be expected to hinder an attacker (at a minimum, by increasing the cost of attack by the amount required to learn about the system). Notwithstanding the potential effectiveness of this position in sales calls, it is one of the most controversial points of philosophy in security system design, designated by its critics as "security by obscurity."

The case against security by obscurity derives from original design principles of Auguste Kerchoffs, a 19th century French military cryptographer who maintained that good security system design means relying only on the secrecy of the key and the strength of the algorithm and not the fact that the algorithm itself is secret [Kerchoffs]. From the military cryptography perspective, this reasonably accounts for the likelihood that security devices will eventually fall into enemy hands (either by capture or treason). Interestingly, this eventuality also arises in the case of current commercial information technology security: a temporary worker at a document processing firm published the details of DirecTV's security system on the web after seeing them as part of DirecTV's litigation with its security supplier [AP, 2003]. But, more recent arguments against security by obscurity tend to rest on two related points: (1) security inventors who rely on secrecy tend to over rely on it, making mistakes in security implementation that are later discovered by attackers, often resulting in catastrophic security failure and (2) there is a large community of peer experts who are willing to review security protocols if made public and who are likely to uncover critical flaws prior to use of a system (and perhaps even recommend appropriate fixes) [Schneier, 1999].

The arguments for and against the beneficial role of system secrecy in security do not appear to be resolvable in any universal fashion. The debate has been sharpened recently by discussions of the relative security of open source and closed source software development. While many treatments take a position of orthodoxy (almost every one cites Kerchoffs) or speak to the experience of the community, treatments that attempt to delve deeper into whether obscurity never helps or whether open peer review is always superior (or even usually superior) tend to come up ambivalent citelk-anderson02,lk-lipner,lk-neumann,lk-schneider. The lack of a simple and compelling argument that "proves" Kerchoffs means that we can expect "security by obscurity" to continue to play a role in security induced lock-in.

Implications of Lock-In

The economic theory of lock-in has been playing an increasing role in economic, business, and policy thought, particularly since the 1980's. The key impetus for this interest comes from explicit consideration of increasing returns to scale, in which each increment of economic activity is increased in value by the amount that has already occurred, resulting in the potential of positive feedback. Much traditional economics relies on diminishing marginal returns to scale, resulting in negative feedback, and reasonably associated with limited resources; as production increases, the price of inputs ultimately is bid up, resulting inevitably in declining marginal returns. But two phenomena particularly important in the information age have the potential to show unbounded increasing returns: information or knowledge itself and network effects in which the value of access to a product increases with the number of other users of that product.

Modeling of economic processes with positive feedback deviates from traditional analysis of declining marginal returns; in particular, the usual and powerful proofs that market based systems converge to unique and globally optimal equilibrium no longer apply. It is conceivable, in the presence of positive feedback, that more than one stable equilibrium may exist, and that an economic system will tend to get locked-in to only one of them, not necessarily the globally optimal one [Arthur, 1994].

While the theoretical possibility of such lock-in is not contestable, the empirical evidence and the practical importance of lock-in is. Liebowitz and Margolis, for example, question first whether popular examples of lock-in actually demonstrate a non-trivial penalty between the locked-in state and a feasible alternative state, and secondly whether the effect is in fact important if there is a tendency for switching costs to ultimately be overcome regardless, typically by technological upheaval, leading to a more benign process of serial lock-in [Liebowitz, 2000]. Their critique is a strong argument for the necessity of careful collection and analysis of data to support the potential theoretical consequences of lock-in.

Beyond the need for empirical evidence of lock-in and its significant and detrimental effects, we also need to consider the possibility that customers and suppliers correctly anticipate the effect of lock-in and negotiate offsetting compensation [Shapiro, 1998]. This seems particularly feasible when customers are concentrated and so can more easily internalize the effects of decisions across the customer set (importantly, internalizing network externalities). A customer and a supplier, anticipating the cost of lock-in before it has occurred might simply negotiate a compensating up front discount that is sufficient to compensate for the lock-in. Of course, they may be wrong (in either direction) as to the cost of lock-in, but this is equivalent to the normal uncertainty in negotiating current contracts intended to cover future eventualities.

An effect that may be substantially more difficult to correctly anticipate, though, and one that has been less examined in the literature in spite of is important to the premise of serial lock-in (but see [Redding]), is the impact of lock-in on access to innovation. A locked-in customer will not access the potential benefit of an innovation that is not compatible with its supplier's product unless that benefit exceeds the necessary switching costs. This occurs whether the innovation is a direct product innovation or one that arises in complementary products.

Does lock-in, or more generally, a lack of competition retard innovation? The oldest hypothesis here is the neo-Schumpeterian thesis that innovation is optimal in firms with monopoly power. However, empirical work over the last several decades suggests that monopoly power is not strongly beneficial to innovation, that a mixture of competition and limited monopoly power maximizes innovation, and that both larger firms and smaller firms have innovative strengths [Kamien, 1982; Scherer, 1991]. We would not want, then, that security lock-in is so strong as to result in an effective monopoly; although a locked-in customer can reasonably expect some important types of innovation to be executed by its supplier, there is also a high likelihood that other potentially interesting innovations will not, so that the cost of denied access to innovation via lock-in could be substantial up to the point that such costs exceed the switching costs. Even harder to gauge but, again, potentially quite significant, is the possibility that useful innovations will never be pursued at all because of the perceived low likelihood of exceeding substantial switching costs in the customer base.

Classifying Security Lock-In

To better understand the potential types of lock-in and its consequence, we can classify types of security lock-in into several broad categories:

- Proprietary Security Protocols
- Open Security Protocols
- Proprietary Extensions to Open Security Protocol
- Intellectual Property Rights and Other Legal Constructs

Proprietary Security Protocols. In this type, a proprietary security protocol (or architecture) is a potential source of lock-in. There are numerous examples of this class, including set-top boxes in the cable industry (further developed in a subsequent section), wireless communication protocols, and hardware and software rights management for the PC.

In the case of wireless access devices, Cisco's LEAP products make use of proprietary security extensions applied to 802.11 (an open and very successful wireless LAN standard also known as Wi-Fi). The argument put forth for this proprietary development was that the existing wireless LAN security mechanisms were far too weak to promote adoption by security concerned consumers. There is the obvious argument that speaks to the need to address an immediate problem (in this case the insecurity of Wi-Fi) and later work to standardize the approach [Wexler]. It should be mentioned that Cisco eventually did make this technology available under free licensing agreements.

The Trusted Computing Platform Alliance (TCPA), recently succeeded by the Trusted Computing Group (TCG), an initiative led by Intel and assisted by Microsoft, proposes to create "a new computing platform for the next century that will provide for improved trust in the PC platform". [TCPA] However, critics claim that it is the application of hardware and software security technologies to not only restrict the distribution of copyright materials, but also to lock users into software and hardware suppliers. While the Digital Rights Management (DRM) issue is a clear and specified goal, it is the potential for this technology to restrict or limit users from deploying competing software that raises some concern. Avoiding the detail, the argument is that a supplier would have to comply with a certification process potentially developed by Microsoft, which might be burdensome or potentially anticompetitive.

The use of proprietary security to preclude manufacturing of low cost clone components is particularly relevant in industries which adopt a "razor and blades" pricing strategy. In these cases a central component may be provided at unusually low margins, even at a loss, with the expectation that a customer will become locked-in via the purchase and subsequently buy a sufficient quantity of higher margin "blades" to make the overall relationship profitable to the supplier. Apparent examples of the use of encryption in these cases to enhance lock-in include the printer and the video game industries, both discussed in more detail below.

Open Security Protocols. A supplier might make use of standard (open) security protocols to prevent competitors from developing interoperable software or hardware components. As with the case of proprietary security protocols, the video game industry also uses open security protocols to prevent unauthorized game cartridges – for example, the use of private key cryptography to sign cartridge software in the Microsoft X-box. The cable industry also uses public key cryptography so that set top boxes require authentication mechanisms provide via PKI certificates to operate. These certificates are obtained after verification testing by a supplier, a potentially lengthy and costly procedure. [Xbox]

Proprietary Extensions to Open Security Protocols. Proprietary extensions of an existing open security protocol may prevent interoperability with other standard compliant software and become a source of lock-in. Microsoft, for example, has had a stated objective of 'embracing, extending and extinguishing' (to paraphrase Paul Maritz) standardized protocols in this manner[2]. In the case of security protocols, in the late 1990s, Microsoft created a proprietary extension to the Kerberos authentication protocol. This extension tied the Kerberos client software to the Windows 2000 Server and integrated an authorization process into the mechanism, thereby making it difficult to interoperate with other servers. Microsoft pursued a similar extension in its development of Passport, its solution for single sign-on web based services. Here again, Microsoft proposed extensions to existing protocols, but in this case to tie the customer to a web services platform. This mechanism also created much debate in the privacy community, with concerns surrounding one entity potentially being aware of a user's web behavior and shopping history. [Passport] Other suppliers have extended protocols such as Secure Shell (SSH) and security related Session Initiation Protocols (SIP).

It may be that this is becoming a defining characteristic of competition in high technology industries with strong network effects – as these can lead to high concentration among suppliers (and hence substantial market power) yet exhibit high interest in compatibility to drive the overall growth of such industries (hence an interest in standardization). A standard tactic of market dominant players would be, when embracing open standards, to extend a protocol just sufficiently to preclude certain aspects of interoperability with competitors. Security protocols may not be privileged over other technologies in this respect but can be expected to play a role.

Intellectual Property Rights and Other Legal Constructs. This is a rather abstract case, in that it is not the security protocol itself that creates the lock-in, but rather the application of intellectual property rights around this technology. To illustrate this class, consider a company that establishes a security technology and then charges a licensing fee for its use. A prime example is that of the RSA algorithm. For many years, RSA (the company) charged fees for the use of RSA technology, but recently released this requirement ahead of the patent expiration. Recent IPR debates surrounding web services technology such as Shibboleth suggests that these relatively pure intellectual property versions of security based lock-in will likely continue.

[2]This particular phrase came up in testimony of Intel Senior Vice President Steve McGeady at the Microsoft antitrust trial in 1998 regarding a meeting in 1995 in which Microsoft Vice President Paul Maritz was describing his company's strategy relative to HTTP and HTML web standards and the Java programming language [Goodin, 1998].

As the above classifications suggest, suppliers have long benefited from security as a lock-in measure. Many of these measures have been rooted in legitimate security mechanisms (or, more skeptically, may have been disguised as such) developed for such needs as authentication, authorization and privacy. Our classification can be related back to the particular characteristics that privilege security technology as a source of lock-in, as shown in Table 17.1.

Table 17.1. Types of security based lock-in and ways in which security is privileged over other aspects of technology as a basis for lock-in

	Compatibility across interfaces that may be cryptographically strong	Argument that security is increased by keeping a system secret ("security by obscurity")	Inability to separate legally permissible reverse engineering from enabling of piracy
Proprietary Security Protocols and Proprietary Extensions to Open Security Protocols	•	•	•
Open Security Protocols	•		•
Intellectual Property Rights and other Legal Constructs	•		•

2. The US Cable Industry

The US cable industry's purchase of set-top boxes represents a particularly rich example of security based lock-in.

The US cable industry purchases set-top boxes and uses them to provide its subscribers with access to programming. Over the last decade, the industry has increasingly been deploying digitally based set-top boxes to replace analog ones. The cable operators buy their set-top boxes almost exclusively from two suppliers, Motorola (which purchased the former General Instrument) and Scientific Atlanta. Each supplier maintains a proprietary conditional access (rights management) system and the programming provided in each cable operators' cities is compatible with the conditional access system of one or the other supplier. Interestingly, the case can be considered as a proprietary extension of an open standard, since the underlying scrambling is the openly available triple-DES standard [NIST, 1999], but the mechanism for managing and distributing the necessary keys to each set-top box is proprietary to each vendor. Consequently, the cable operators (called multiple system operators or MSOs) are locked-in in each city to one of the two suppliers; the switching cost for a non-compatible alternative would include replacing all currently deployed set-top boxes in that city plus a substantial portion of the network equipment that processes programming (typically called "head end" equipment).

An alternative set-top box vendor attempting to create a compatible set-top box without the agreement of the incumbment set-top box supplier is confronted with the expected barreirs: the overall security protocol is not known; even if it is known, using a secure stream requries access to cryptographic information (keys) controlled by the incumbent supplier, the incumbent suppliers hold patents covering the security technology, and intentionally breaking the security system would likely be prosecutible as a violaiton of the Digital Millenium Copyright Act. Thus, even if an MSO customer were interested in enabling another supplier for price or innovation purposes, security technology makes the incumbent set-top box vendor's lock-in potent.

In this case, the customers exhibit substantial market power: a handful of large MSOs control most of the cable systems in the United States and represent a substantial fraction of sales for their suppliers.[3] Consequently, we would expect the MSOs to be sophisticated about the potential for lock-in and to negotiate some compensation at the beginning of each major lock-in cycle. Indeed, one of the most celebrated deals in the cable industry represents a creative way to extract just such compensation. In 1997, John Malone, then CEO of the largest MSO, TCI, led a buying consortium to commit to the purchase of 15 million set-top boxes from General Instrument (GI) (10 million for TCI) at a cost of $300 each. Committing to a large multi-year purchase at an attractive price is consistent with effort to reflect the cost of a lock-in cycle in an up front discount. But, the compensation was more sophisticated than a simple discount. In the deal, TCI (and the other MSOs) also received warrants to purchase shares of GI at a price set before the deal was announced, totaling 16% of the shares of GI, with warrants vesting as set-top boxes were purchased. And Liberty Media (controlled by Malone) received a further 10% of GI in return for ownership of a digital television transmission service. The deal had a substantial affect on GI's perceived market position – "in a single day, GI looked like the new dominant manufacturer of set-top boxes" [Robichaux, 2002], p.221 – but through their equity posiitions in GI, TCI and the other cable

[3]For example, Scientific Atlanta's top three customers, all MSOs, have accounted for well over half of its total sales in each of the fiscal years 2000, 2001, and 2002 [Scientific Atlanta].

operators were able to re-capture a portion of the present value of profit transferred to GI via lock-in. TCI and Liberty Media in particular had acquired rights to more than 20% of GI through the deal.

A second manner in which MSO customers can manage lock-in is by causing the two vendors to compete for new cities that are as yet uncommitted. Not only can an MSO use negotiation for purchases for the new city as the beginning of a new lock-in cycle for which it can hope to recover some of the cost to if of lock-in through discounts or other concessions, but the likelihood of important future competitions can be used to discipline the supplier to a degree in cities in which the MSO is already locked-in. However, although the dual vendor competition may provide important advantages relative to lock-in by a monopoly supplier, the structure represents a tradeoff between the cost to an MSO customer of working with multiple suppliers and the limits to competitive pricing and innovation possible in a duopoly.

The particular role of security in lock-in of set-top boxes is fairly easy to trace by examining both standardization of technology components and regulatory action. Although both General Instrument's and Scientific Atlanta's first digital set-top box offerings included a number of proprietary technologies, components other than security have migrated to industry standards and third party technologies, including video format (now MPEG-2, an open standard), audio format (now Dolby AC-3, licensed from a neutral third party), modulation (now follows the International Telecommunication Union's J.83 standard), signaling (currently migrating to an IP system based on the DOCSIS standard) and so on. Security maintains its position in both vendors' products as proprietary.[4]

The special role of security can also be seen in the partitioning specified by the FCC in its effort to enable retail distribution of set-top boxes. The FCC has mandated that technology that is uniquely required to enable the functions of a set-top box (that is, beyond openly available standards or technology licensable from third parties that could be implemented, for example, by a television manufacturer or other consumer electronics manufacturer not currently supplying the cable market) be captured in a "point of deployment" module separately available from an MSO, and that this technology be limited to security,[5] with implementation by the beginning of 2005. The FCC's point-of-deployment

[4]A position recently confirmed at the Consumer Communications and Networking Conference, Las Vegas, January 2004, where a Motorola (purchaser of General Instrument) representative on a panel stated that security will uniquely continue as a proprietary technology, albeit subject to some cross-licensing by different security technology providers.

[5]In Section 47 of Implementation of Section 304 of the Telecommunications Act of 1996, Commercial Availability of Navigation Devices, Order on Reconsideration, CS Docket No. 97-80, May 13, 1999, the FCC states "We clarify that Section 76.1204(a) regarding the components of the security module allows for inclusion of circuitry used for conditional access functions. We agree with Circuit City that, were the security modules to contain features and functions not related to security, commercial availability of navigation devices could be impaired."

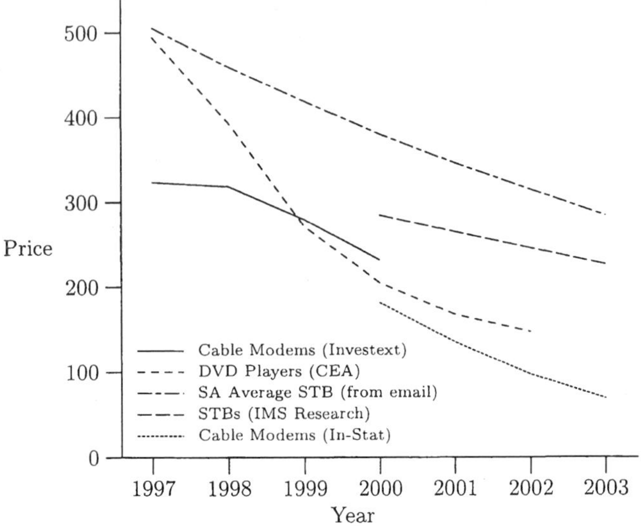

Figure 17.1. Prices of Set-top Boxes, DVDs, and Cable Modems

module ruling could have an important impact on the consequences of lock-in albeit without eliminating the lock-in itself. Since the price of the module is not regulated, the original manufacturer can continue to extract profit due to the lock-in of an MSO in a particular city. However, the consequences of lock-in on innovation can be weakened since the remainder of the set-top box functionality (anything that doesn't interact with security) can be competitively innovated and manufactured by a number of different suppliers.

Evidence that lock-in of set-top boxes (via security as argued in the previous paragraph) has had effect on pricing can be seen by comparing prices for cable set-top boxes with those of Digital Versatile Disk (DVD) and Cable Modems. The latter two devices contain between them essentially all the components that would be found in a cable set-top box with the exception of security. Yet, as shown in Figure 1, both have been experiencing substantially faster rates of decline (25% a year over the last several years) compared to set-top boxes (10% a year or less during a period in which the vast majority of set-top boxes sold continued to be "basic" in function).[6]

The effect of lock-in on innovation is less easily observed than pricing, beyond industry anecdotal and trade press discussions of MSO frustration at the relative rate of innovation in the direct broadcast satellite

[6]Indeed, in a rare public disclosure of pricing, Motorola notes in its 2002 annual report that set-top box average selling price declined by 4% in the preceding year.

industry, the consumer electronics industry overall, and the cable industry. However, a glimpse of frustration is occasionally available in public announcements.[7]

3. The Video Gaming and Printer Cartridge Industries

The video gaming and printer cartridge industries provide particular evidence of how open and proprietary security protocols and legal constructs (such as patent and copyright law) can all be employed to enable lock-in, particularly when conflated with efforts to outlaw piracy.

To understand the key issues, we first need to understand the process by which competitors attempt to defeat lock-in and the potential legal consequence of these actions. When most software manufacturers release their software products they do not make the source code (the code readable by humans) available. This means that competitors cannot readily understand how the code operates without attempting to reconstruct the source code from the computer readable code (the code that is made publicly available). This reverse engineering process, referred to as disassembly, may be the only way a competitor can get access to the functional elements and the interface specifications of the program.[8] Without knowing how the software operates, a competitor will have difficulty in interoperating with the original product. However, the degree to which reverse engineering may be applied to interoperate with a competitor intersects with copyright law.

The Digital Millennium Copyright Act (DMCA) added an "anti-circumvention" provision to the Copyright Act. The original intention of this provision was to prevent individuals from circumventing anti-piracy protection placed on copyrighted material; however, a consequence of this provision has been its use by vendors to lock-out legitimate competitors. Such consequences include the stifling of free speech, scientific research and fair use, as well as (and most relevant to this work) the impediment of competition and innovation. The DMCA includes two aspects specifically related to anti-circumvention; banning acts of circumvention and distribution of technology for circumvention. The violation of this provision carries substantial civil and potentially criminal penalties.

The argument against anti-circumvention technology typically states that reverse engineering for reasons of functional interoperability is not illegal and is in fact protected under the DMCA, which permits circumvention for reasons of interoperability. Further, such reverse engineering techniques are generally necessary to determine the operational and

[7]For example, John Malone, frustrated at the availability of advanced set-top boxes from General Instrument, made a colorful public joke at GI's expense before a large crowd at a Cable industry trade show in 1996 ([Robichaux, 2002], p. 171).

[8]This of course assumes that the competitor does not make it available through such means as open source and licensing.

functional character of a system and that such measure are not in violation of access control provisions contained within the DMCA. Lastly, it is generally held that applying copyright law to the issue of circumvention is a misuse and is only intended to thwart competition.

In a recent white paper, the Electronics Frontiers Foundation (EFF) described a number of interesting cases wherein provisions from copyright law have been used to thwart competitors from breach security based lock-ins. [EFF, 2003] The following paragraphs capture the ongoing legal battles in both the video gaming and printer cartridge industries. Note that these examples are fundamentally different from the previous cable industry example as most customers for video games and printers individually have very limited market power; it is not possible, therefore, for them to attempt to negotiate compensation for lock-in at the beginning of each lock-in cycle and they are limited to relying on the effects of competition (albeit such effects are clear through the way that competing suppliers will competitively discount the initial platform in order to secure locked-in customers for the later sale of profitable cartridges).

Video game cartridges: Within the video gaming industry, there exists a long history of using security lock-in to preclude competitors. The following includes a survey of the more interesting cases.

1 To preclude competitors from developing compatible game cartridges, Sega included a "trademark security system". This system essentially was a handshake between the console and the cartridge. When a game was inserted into the console, the console would look for an initialization code within the cartridge. This code was intended to verify that the game was valid (a game manufactured by Sega) and served no other purpose to the operation of the game. Interestingly, this initialization code was simply the letter sequence "SEGA". Therefore it was not actually encrypted, although it was object code and so not immediately readable without reverse engineering.

   Sega sued Accolade for deriving the source code via decompilation of the object code contained within cartridges designed for the Sega Genesis Console. In order to do so, Accolade had copied the object code of these cartridges, which was patented. The console was not patented, however, and the courts ruled that because this reverse engineering process was the only possible way of obtaining the information necessary to construct game cartridges compatible with the genesis console (outside of expensive licensing agreements, of course), it represented 'fair use' and sided with Accolade.

2 Nintendo also enacted a security based lock-in by implementing a security handshake between the console and cartridge. Nintendo would manufacture games from approved developers, and add the

security portion during the manufacturing process. This gave Nintendo the ability to lock out game developers similar to those that had commoditized the cartridge market while Atari was the console leader. Ironically, Atari broke Nintendo's security mechanism and Nintendo brought suit against Atari.

In this case, Atari fraudulently obtained the complete patented code needed to build NES compatible games by misleading the patent office, though their own engineers had already reverse engineered most of necessary code. In addition, Nintendo had obtained a patent on the game-console security system known as 10NES. This system consisted of two chips, a master in the console and a slave in the cartridge, both of which contained the 10NES program. When the cartridge is inserted into the console, the programs exchange a series of values according to an understood security algorithm. When agreement on these values is reached the console is unlocked and the game can proceed. The intention of the program is to exclude unauthorized programs. Nintendo also designed the program in such a way to make the process of reserve engineering difficult.

However, Atari developed Rabbit, a program that interacted with the console upon insertion of the cartridge in generating a code that, when matched with the code of the console, would allow the game to play. Rabbit was judged by the courts to contain components identical to that within the 10NES program that were unnecessary for game play, and therefore infringed on the patent of the 10NES. And because of the fraudulent behavior involved, Atari could not claim 'fair use' under copyright law.

3 Sony has made use of DMCA to litigate against several competitors. Fisrt, Sony used DMCA to sue the maker of Virtual Game Station, Connectix. VGS allowed users to play Sony Playstation games on Apple computers. In a similar case, Sony sued Bleem, a company that created software that allowed users to run Playstation games on a Windows platform. While both companies ultimately withdraw their products (due to high litigation costs), eventually, Connectix won a ruling in the Ninth Circuit Court that established its application of reverse engineering as 'fair use'.

4 Vivendi-Universal Blizzard Entertainment filed a law suite against a group of game enthusiast who reverse engineered Blizzard games. This group created a server, bnetd, which allowed users to play Blizzard games over the Internet rather than relying on Vivendi-Universal Blizzard online server. The group claimed that the Blizzard software did not provide the feature that they desired and so decided to create their own. Blizzard eventually withdrew its suite.

5 There are two interesting reverse engineering efforts that have been applied to the Microsoft Xbox. First, Andrew Huang published a book that described security flaws contained within the X-box gaming console. Huang discovered these flaws through reverse engineering techniques. Fearing possible legal repercussions, the initial publisher Wiley, decided not to publish this work. Eventually, Huang was able to publish with No Starch Press in July 2003. [Huang, 2003] The second group, the Xbox Linux Project, is an online group that demonstrated how to run Linux on Microsoft's Xbox. Their efforts allowed users to utilize the console as a PC, with somewhat expansive utility including, but not limited to, gaming. It is not clear what legal actions will come of this group work.

Printer cartridges: The US printer industry's battle between original-equipment and after-market manufacturers represents another interesting example of security based lock-in. For years Lexmark has been battling against after market competition in the area of laser printer cartridges. To prevent competitor from manufacturing compatible cartridges Lexmark implemented an authentication process between the printer and the cartridge. Static Control Components (SCC) developed a chip that enabled aftermarket cartridge providers to interoperate with Lexmark printers by bypassing the authentication process. SCC developed this chip by reverse engineering Lexmark authentication process. Lexmark filed for an injunction to bar SCC from selling the chip and in response SCC appealed and filed an antitrust law suite against Lexmark. This battle is still being fought in the courts today.

What should be clear from the above examples is that there is a rich set of examples that demonstrate how security has been used as a lock-in mechanism. The implication of such a security lock-in mechanism is to essentially tie the system (in this case the console or printer) to the cartridge in such a way to eliminate competition. The question remains is the implications of such mechanisms.

4. Implications

The previous section suggests that many aspects of security induced lock-in actually do occur in practice, though the specific mechanisms and their import substantially vary by case. Nonetheless, the existence of security induced lock-in suggests a number of possible initiatives depending on the role a party plays: customer, supplier, or government policy maker or regulator.

Customers

Lock-in can arise as a mutually beneficial state for both customer and supplier. Some types of lock-in (such as a customer investment in supplier specific training) do increase switching costs but at the same time may increase customer profit via improved efficiency even more than the implied shift in profit to the supplier. In other cases, particularly where customers and suppliers are both concentrated, bi-lateral lock-in may occur in which the supplier is also locked-in to the customer, would experience substantial switching costs in pursuing another customer, and is therefore induced to make concessions to the customer. Bi-lateral lock-in may be a less colorful but more precise statement of what it really means for a customer and supplier to "partner."

Nonetheless, Shapiro and Varian advance a simple but useful rule of thumb that the customer's switching cost equals the net present value of a supplier's profit in excess of what they could earn on the basis of the competitive strength of its product in the absence of lock-in [Shapiro, 1998]. So, a customer is normally interested in reducing switching cost and a supplier in increasing them. Here we suggest a number of customer strategies, some specific to security.

1 Estimate impact of lock-in on access to innovation and include it in negotiated up front concessions. There is no particular recipe to how to do this but rather an admonition to try. More practically, it may be feasible to negotiate clauses that will force access to innovation if such innovation occurs, e.g., by triggering licensing of security protocols to other suppliers on pre-negotiated terms. For example, the future modularization of set-top boxes in the cable industry required by the FCC could successfully open up set-top functionality (other than security or security-dependent functions) for broader innovation; a customer that simultaneously negotiated the pricing of security functionality as well as opening up this kind of modularization at an appropriate time might better be able to manage the impact of lock-in on innovation[9].

2 Consider open security systems. This amounts to rejecting the "security by obscurity" argument. Customers may be able to find existing open security standards that one or more suppliers will implement, or if sufficiently concentrated may be able to leverage an industry consortium to establish such a standard. Examples of security standards setting in the context of multimedia include the OpenCable interface standardization activity in CableLabs [Cable Labs], MPEG-4 and MPEG-21 Intellectual Property Management and Protection [MPEG-4], and the Digital Rights Reference Model of MPEG LA [MPEG LA]. A next best alternative would be to cause suppliers to license security technology from a third party. Of course, this creates lock-in to the third party, but if that supplier

[9]In fact, the role of modularization in effecting industry structure and the relative profitability at each stage of an industry's value chain is increasingly recognized as a key to competitive strategy [?; ?]

has less ability to use security in tying sales of products together, this may be a less expensive proposition. A related initiative in the case where a customer has a great deal of market power would be to attempt to restructure the supplier industry so that security is captured in a third party organization, for example, by requiring a potential equipment supplier to divest its security technology component into a separate company.

3 Develop credible commercial alternatives. This is a normal attack on lock-in. Investing in enabling another supplier implicitly lowers switching costs. The critical question is whether switching costs are lowered more than the investment, and whether the value can be realized reasonably quickly through continuing negotiations with the incumbent supplier. Simultaneously, the interest of an alternative supplier in participating, particularly if it is also making its own investments in support of the process, will be dampened if it perceived that it is only being used as a stalking horse (i.e., although the customer may realize a commercial advantage from the strategy, the alternative supplier never does).

4 Developing or selecting technical and architectural alternatives that weaken the effect of lock-in. There may be options that are different from adoption of an open standard. For example, selective encryption has been proposed as a technological solution in the US cable industry. It allows the introduction of as second conditional access system overlaid on an existing one without requiring replacement of the installed base of set-top boxes, albeit at some overhead in transmission bandwidth. [Lookabaugh, 2003]

Suppliers

Since suppliers typically benefit from lock-in, most strategies should either aim to increase it or decrease the incentive for customers to attempt to reduce it.

1 Enhancing arguments for the added value of proprietariness in security systems. This implies supporting the "security by obscurity" argument. A reasonable variant to advance (and one that is frequently used in conditional access systems) is "defense in depth." In this approach, a security system has multiple "fall backs" that are used to increase the cost or reduce the impact of breaches [Anderson, 2001]; the fall backs must necessarily be kept secret so the can be incrementally rolled out and must be attacked in turn.

2 Embedding security as a component in a rich collection of lock-in devices (e.g., other proprietary technologies, customer training investments, relationships) so that it is difficult to isolate it and

reduce its impact. Particularly potent in information technology is lock-in that derives from network effects. Security based lock-in that enhances network effects is desirable; an example might be creating a digital rights management system in which content providers are encouraged to purchase an encryption system and users are encouraged to purchase (or given for free) a compatible client. As content providers discover that most clients use the particular system, they are more incented to purchase that system's encryptor, and as users discover that most content is encrypted under that system, they are increasingly incented to obtain the matching client. The previously described privileged role of security technology in inhibiting reverse engineering by competitors (either technically or through the law) can now come into play.

3 Seek a compromise in which some potential lock-in profit is reduced but access to innovation is increased, in particular:

- Increased internal spending on innovation.
- Voluntary and attractive licensing terms or integration efforts to provide customers with access to innovations developed by others.

The goal here is to spend less on these initiatives than would be lost if the customer seriously incubated alternative suppliers in order to access innovation, and in particular to avoid the worst case of replacement as part of a process of serial lock-in[10].

Government

Policy makers have a number of options. To the extent security induced lock-in has resulted in convergence to a stable equilibrium that is not the globally optimal one (from the perspective of the public interest), policy makers should be interested in strategies to weaken the lock-in, providing, of course, that the medicine prescribed is not worse than the disease. Options include:

1 Law and Regulation. Policy makers can directly regulate the use of security technologies with a goal to avoiding their use in lock-in, as, for example in the case of the FCC's rulemaking on navigation devices for cable television. [FCC, 1999] Conversely, they may, intentionally or not, increase the role of security in lock-in, as arguably has occurred with the Digital Millennium Copyright Act. [DMCA]

[10] This strategy is consistent with an aggressive implementation of "open innovation" on the part of a supplier, in which external sources of innovation are systematically tapped through partnerships, licensing, and acquisitions [Chesbrough, 2003].

2 Antitrust Actions. Some versions of lock-in are caused by or associated with activities that are illegal under antitrust law and the use of security technology may be involved (for example, if it facilitates illegal tying). In these cases, policy makers can pursue antitrust remedies.

3 Support for Standards. The government has a successful history of supporting certain key security standards (e.g., DES and AES). Some challenges exist, though, in internal tensions between desire to promulgate good security, and the concerns of military intelligence and law enforcement branches that would prefer that security not be too strong to preclude wiretapping. A broadened role in either directly driving security technology standards or in creating a favorable environment for consortia and other bodies to develop security standards will tend to reduce the role of security in lock-in.

4 Nothing. Under the "first do no harm" maxim, government can rely on the sophistication of customers to correctly anticipate security based lock-in and either secure the appropriate compensation or themselves develop initiatives to reduce the lock-in. This seems more practical when customers have substantial market power (as in our cable example) than when they don't (as in the case of consumers, particularly if competition among vendors at the beginning of lock-in cycles abates).

5. Conclusion

The cases of set-top boxes in the U. S. cable industry, video games and their cartridges, and printers and their cartridges all illustrate ways in which security technology can play an enhanced role in lock-in of customers by their suppliers through creation of substantial switching costs. Openness of technology, normally an inhibitor of lock-in, can be argued against in the case of security on the basis of a presumed increase in security by keeping details of the security system secret and proprietary. Whether open or not, security technology can be used to make permissible reverse engineering equivalent to an infeasible problem of breaking a cryptographically strong algorithm. And what might appear to be permissible reverse engineering may be conflated with an effort to enable illegitimate piracy and rendered illegal. The extra potential for security technology as a locus of lock-in raises its importance in the strategic considerations of both customers and vendors and for legislators and regulators. Customers will want to consider how to reduce the effect of lock-in, particularly on access to innovation; vendors will want to consider how to increase lock-in where possible, and policy makers will want to consider where the public interest motivates efforts to intervene to mitigate lock-in.

Acknowledgements

The authors would like to acknowledge Brian McMurray for his work on gathering data for the cases studied here and the participants in the Second Annual Workshop on Economics and Information Security for their insightful comments on an earlier version of this work.

References

Anderson, R. Security Engineering: A Guide to Building Dependable Distributed Systems. John Wiley & Sons, Inc., New York, 2001.

Anderson, R., Security in Open versus Closed Systems - The Dance of Boltzmann, Coase, and Moore. in Open Source Software: Economics, Law and Policy, (Toulouse, France, 2002).

Student pleads guilty in DirecTV data case Associated Press, 2003.

Arthur, W.B. Increasing Returns and Path Dependence in the Economy. The University of Michigan Press, Ann Arbor, MI, 1994.

Baldwin, C. and Clark, K. Design Rules, vol. 1: The Power of Modularity. Boston, MA: The MIT Press, 2000.

Burr, William E.., "Selecting the Advanced Encryption Standard," IEEE Security & Privacy Magazine, vol. 1, issue 2, Mar-Apr 2003, pp. 43-52

Cable Labs, `http://www.opencable.com/`

Clayton Christensen and Michael Raynor, The Innovator's Solution, Boston, MA: Harvard Business School Press, 2003.

Julie E. Cohen Reverse Engineering and the Rise of Electronic Vigilantism: Intellectual Property Implications of "Lock-Out" Programs in 68 S. Cal. L. Rev. 1091 (1995).

DMCA. See `http://www.eff.org/IP/DMCA`

EFF. Unintended Consequences: Five Years Under the DMCA v.3, September 24, 2003, available at `http://www.eff.org/IP/DRM/DMCA/unintended_consequences.php`

FCC. Commercial Availability of Navigation Devices, Order On Reconsideration, Section 304 of the Telecommunications Act of 1996, CS Docket No. 97-80, May 13, 1999.

Dan Goodin, "Microsoft, Intel wage war of words," `cnet.news.com`, Nov. 12, 1998, at: `http://news.com.com/2100-1023\_3-217848.html`

Andrew Huang, Hacking the Xbox: An Introduction to Reverse Engineering, No Starch Press, July 2003.

Kamien, M. and Schwartz, N. Market Structure and Innovation. Cambridge University Press, Cambridge, UK, 1982.

Kerchoffs, A. La crytpographie militaire. Journal des sciences militaires, IX. 5-38.

T. Lookabaugh, D.C. Sicker, D.M. Keaton, Y.G. Wang, and I. Vedula, "Security Analysis of Selectively Encrypted MPEG-2 Streams," in *Multimedia Systems and Applications VI*, Proceedings of the SPIE, vol. 5241, Orlando, FL, 8-9 September 2003.

Henry Chresbrough, Open Innovation, Boston, MA: Harvard Business School Press, 2003.

Liebowitz, S.J. and Margolis, S.E. Winners, Losers & Microsoft. The Independent Institute, Oakland, CA, 1999.

Lipner, S.B., Security and source code access: issues and realities. in IEEE Symposium on Security and Privacy, (Oakland, CA, 2000).

MPEG-4. http://www.chiariglione.org/mpeg/standards/mpeg-21/mpeg-21.htm

MPEG LA. http://www.mpegla.com/news/n_03-10-02_drm.html

Neumann, P.G., Robust Nonproprietary Software. in IEEE Symposium on Security and Privacy, (Oakland, CA, 2000).

NIST. Federal Information Processing Standard 46-3, Data Encryption Standard, US Nat'l Inst. Standards and Technology, 1999, http://csrc.nist.gov/publications/fips/fips46-3/fips46-3.pdf

Nowell, P. Small firm irks printer giant; cartridges at center of legal tussle The Seattle Times, Seattle, WA, 2003.

Passport. See http://www.epic.org/privacy/consumer/microsoft/

Redding, S. Path Dependence, Endogenous Innovation, and Growth. International Economic Review, 43 (4). 1215-1248.

Mark Robichaux, Cable Cowboy: John Malone and the Rise of the Modern Cable Business, Hoboken, NJ: John Wiley & Sons, 2002.

Scherer, F. Changing perspectives on the firm size problem. in Acs, Z. and Audretsch, D. eds. Innovation and Technological Change: An International Comparison, The University of Michigan Press, Ann Arbor, MI, 1991, 24-38.

Schneider, F.B., Open source in security: visiting the bizarre. in IEEE Symposium on Security and Privacy, (Oakland, CA, 2000).

Schneier, B. Open Source and Security Crypto-Gram Newsletter, 1999.

Scientific Atlanta, Form 10-K for Fiscal Year Ended June 27, 2003, filed with US Securities and Exchange Commission, September 23, 2003, available at http://www.sec.gov/Archives/edgar/data/87777/000119312503052976/d10k.htm.

Shapiro, C. and Varian, H. Information Rules: A Strategic Guide to the Network Economy. Harvard Business School Press, Boston, MA, 1998.

TCPA. See http://www.trustedcomputing.org/, and for a different perspective see http://www.schneier.com/crypto-gram-0208.html

Joanie Wexler, Is Cisco LEAP-frogging the Standards Process? Available at http://www.nwfusion.com/newsletters/wireless/2003/0303wireless2.html

Xbox. For a description of the certification process see http://www.wimedia.org/events/docs/02012r0WM_PUB-GEN-0_Certification_Program_USB__Xbox_WiMedia_Oct_2002.pdf

Chapter 18

HOW AND WHY MORE SECURE TECHNOLOGIES SUCCEED IN LEGACY MARKETS

Lessons from the Success of SSH

Nicholas Rosasco
University of Maryland Baltimore County

David Larochelle
University of Virginia

How and why SSH did succeed despite the existence of an entrenched legacy tool, while similar technologies such as secure file transfer protocols have been far less successful?

Secure shell (SSH) can safely be called one of the rare successes in which a more secure technology has largely replaced a less secure but entrenched tool: telnet. Since the early commercial and later open source versions in the mid '90s, the tool, created as a replacement for telnet and the rsh/rlogin/rcp trio, has become the method of choice for remote login and X tunneling and is a rapidly becoming one of the most pervasive applications for encryption technology outside of embedded systems, particularly after being freed from RSA related patent complications [Bertrand, 1999].

It is a non-trivial task for an installed base to be brought to a new client, no matter how similar it is. The size of a system's login user base with a need for interactive OS access can be large, especially for large ISPs and development projects. Even with the necessary technically savvy; inertia and a preference for known tools must be overcome no matter how beneficial the software change is perceived to be. We perform a market analysis to determine how and why SSH succeeded despite the existence of an entrenched legacy tool while secure file transfer technologies have failed to displace FTP.

1. Background

SSH was developed by Tatu Ylönen after his university was the victim of a password sniffing attack [Barrett, 2001, 9]. SSH was first released in July of 1995. The initial version was designed as a drop in replacement for the rcp/rsh/rlogin trio, and offered similar interface functionality to the current version, including X tunneling [Ylönen, 1995]. Many in the security community responded positively to the release, and by the end of the year around 20,000 users were using SSH. Ylönen was also receiving around 150 email messages a day requesting support. He founded SSH Communications, Ltd. to commercialize the software [Miller, 2002] and handle the flow of email [Barrett, 2001, 10]. After SSH Communications began to release versions of SSH under increasingly restrictive licenses, OpenSSH, an open source version based on a liberally licensed earlier release of SSH, was created. This, combined with the expiration of the RSA algorithm patent and the relaxation of export rules regarding cryptography by the United States, has allowed OpenSSH to be freely distributed on the distribution media for many Unix distributions [Bertrand, 1999]. The growth of SSH has continued. It was estimated that by the end of 2000 there were 2,000,000 users of SSH [Barrett, 2001, 12]. Though OpenSSH is now the most widely used SSH server, the SSH Communications product still has significant market share [OpenBSD, 2003].

The creation of the OpenSSH project has no doubt contributed to the popularity of SSH. But it was SSH's early popularity in the security community that prompted the development of OpenSSH. Theo de Raadt, the founder of both OpenBSD and OpenSSH, claimed that for the two years before the release of OpenSSH in 1999, the first thing many users did after installing OpenBSD was to install SSH [Bertrand, 1999].

While SSH servers primarily run on Unix systems, many users need to connect to these servers from non-Unix systems. It is worth noting that SSH succeeded as a cross platform tool for interactive login – numerous clients are available for many operating systems – without the help of Microsoft. Microsoft continues to distribute a telnet client with Windows but does not distribute an SSH client.[1]

2. Analysis

We can view technical staff and their management as rational actors with an interest in the efficient achievement of security for their organization. Removing telnet entirely can be seen as promoting a socially optimal outcome by preventing careless users from placing others at risk.

[1]We were told that Microsoft decided not to include SSH in Windows XP because of legal complications involved with cryptography and because there were many freely available SSH clients for Windows [Moore, 2001].

In their rationality, we see them balancing the needs of functionality and ease of use with their desire to achieve security.

Network externalities are often a factor in technology driven products [Shapiro, 1999; Katz, 1994]. Metcalf's law states that the benefit each user gets from a network is proportional to the square of the number of users [Shapiro, 1999, 184]. This makes it difficult for new technologies to get established but can result in exponential growth curves for technologies that are becoming established. At first glance, network effects appear to be a significant impediment to widespread adoption of SSH. SSH clients are only useful if there are SSH servers, and servers are only useful if there are clients – the traditional "chicken and egg" problem. However, most users only have shell accounts on a few systems – and many have only one shell account. The utility a user derives from using an SSH client is determined by whether the few systems she accesses have SSH servers, not by the total number of SSH servers. Positive feedback still exists to an extent. For example, as expertise in SSH becomes more wide spread, this adds value to SSH. Additionally, after SSH reached the point where installing it was considered a standard best practice, its adoption increased further.

The cost of a security failure is borne by both the users and the owner/administrator of a system. On multi-user UNIX systems, once an attacker is able to obtain user-level access, it is often possible to obtain root privileges relatively easily – witness, as a classic example, the Emacs exploitation made famous by Stoll in *The Cuckoo's Egg* [Stoll, 1989]. It is therefore entirely possible that system administrators and other users on the system will suffer because of a single sniffed password. Even in the absence of extensive system damage or theft of information, they are deeply inconvenienced by the ensuing efforts necessary to restore faith in the system. At the corporate or institutional level, the entire organization suffers – particularly since the compromised system could have become a beachhead for further penetrations. System administrators and their managers had an incentive to install and promote SSH, but faced the challenges not just of software replacement, but also user training [Hatch, 2002]. However, a desire to increase accountability may have provided a further incentive to use SSH. In the event that a user account was compromised, SSH made it possible to push more culpability to the user for her password behavior. Without SSH, it was difficult to determine if the user was careless with her password, or if it was sniffed over the network.

Since SSH required both a client and a server, the existence of multiple clients, especially open source clients, helped limit the risks of a switch to SSH. To some extent, the existence of multiple clients was facilitated by the open nature of the protocol (a simple search reveals more than a dozen clients available from a wide range of sources [Google, 2003]), which permitted multiple versions of the server application as well. Through the eventual absence of patent or other intellectual property protection what began as a technology only available through a single commercial product became a no-license-cost option [Bertrand, 1999][2].

While password sniffing was not necessarily a common occurrence, and the processor capacity necessary to support the encryption not always trivial, the security advantages of SSH over telnet could be specified precisely. This avoided the customary imperfect information problem, which remains significant in information security. The software development community – particularly developers of open solutions, but also proprietary developers – should view this type of easy-to-compare situation as an invitation to an opportunity to compete. If a competitor has a solution that is known to be insecure, developers should aim to create a drop-in alternative. This is particularly the case if the developer can achieve a point of minimal added cost, such as most of the current popular incarnations of SSH over the equally free telnet solutions.

Aside from the security issues involved in the decision to install SSH, functionality was the same though communication and system performance were impacted by the overhead of encryption. The principal life cycle cost was installing SSH and replacing telnet-only clients at the user's end. This was more significant when cryptographic export and intellectual property issues made installation more of a hassle. For users of X Windows, functionality was enhanced: SSH could automatically handle the display of remote programs on a local desktop. The existing protocols required the user to manually adjust the settings each session. This feature of SSH constituted a major convenience and usability improvement, making SSH a powerful tool for remote applications. This is another important point for the developers of a potential competitor to an insecure legacy program, and an equally significant point for an advocate of creating security conscious consumers. "Secure" can, and perhaps should, be easily advocated when it comes with greater functionality.[3]

3. Secure File Transfer

The several technologies for secure FTP replacement are "also-ran" solutions that never achieved the same level of acceptance as SSH. Secure file transfer solutions are implemented by a wide selection of server and client applications but lack a single distinct standard. The various secure file transfer options include two semi-distinct protocols supported by tools within the OpenSSH and commercial SSH tool suites: secure copy(scp), a relative of the remote copy system, and sftp, which

[2]telnet was also unencumbered intellectual property restrictions.

[3]See [Larochelle, 2003] for a discussion of the interaction between security and functionality.

is loosely based on the tradition FTP protocol[4]. Both of these protocols rely on SSH[5] to provide an encrypted stream [Barrett, 2001].[6] scp was designed to be a drop-in replacement for rcp and was included with the UNIX version of SSH[7]. It has largely supplanted rcp. However, scp does not provide the power and ease of use of ftp. With early versions of scp there were widespread compatibility problems (significantly more so than those between the implementations of SSH1 and SSH2 protocols). sftp, which is included with SSH2, provides an ftp-like interface for secure file transfer. In addition to these two standards, there is also competition from products offering similar file transfer functionality, including various commercial entities that create "secure FTP" products that include security extensions to the existing FTP protocol and are often not compatible with either scp or sftp [Barrett, 2001, 379]. These solutions represented the best efforts of several companies and groups to provide secure authentication and transmission of files from one system to another.

The failure of the practitioners, system administrators and their employers, to adopt these as alternatives to the widely used clear-text FTP protocol provides a striking contrast to the near universal acceptance of SSH. This disparity can be easily confirmed by examining some current commercial practices. Unix based remote hosting providers nearly always offer remote access through SSH but rarely allow telnet access. By contrast, a significant number of these hosting providers allow FTP access [Jupitermedia, 2004; WebHostingRank.com, 2004]. Indeed, the cPanel control software [cPanel, 2004], a popular tool suite for remote website management, includes SSH access but not telnet access. However, it allows clear text FTP access. It is particularly noteworthy that despite the potential damage in terms of lost of reputation and revenue for both the hosting provider and the client from an account compromise, the market still demands clear text FTP access.

We see the inclusion of secure file transfer options into SSH as both facilitating and inhibiting the spread of secure file transfer programs. These tools are now available on many Unix systems. However, these protocols have not been widely implemented by other SSH clients. The

[4]These protocol standards are documented at: `http://www.ietf.org/proceedings/01aug/I-D/draft-ietf-secsh-filexfer-00.txt` and `http://www.openSSH.com/txt/draft-ietf-secsh-filexfer-02.txt`.

[5]SSH provides the ability to establish secure connections between arbitrary ports on different systems. However, the idiosyncrasies of FTP prevent this feature from being used to effectively secure the protocol. ([Barrett, 2001] includes a lengthy section describing methods to establish a fully encrypted FTP session using SSH. But their methods will not work on all systems. The authors acknowledge that because of the complexity, their solution is more of a "parlor trick [to use] at geek parties" than a practical means of obtaining secure file transfer.)

[6]Technically, these protocols will provide secure file transfer over any encrypted stream, but we are not aware of any implementation that does not use SSH for encryption and authentication.

[7]The version of scp included with SSH2 is actually implemented using sftp internally; however, this version still presents the same rcp-like interface as the version in SSH1.

relatively small number of graphical clients supporting these protocols is particularly problematic. Ironically, the success of early versions of SSH may have actually hurt the adoption of secure alternatives to FTP by providing some security functionality to technically savvy security conscious users through scp, which is an adequate replacement for rcp but lacks the functionality of FTP. The fact that an SSH server is required to run these tools may have also limited their appeal and prevented their emergence as first-class Internet services. Additionally, while SSH was intended to supplant the rlogin/rcp/rsh trio, these tools cannot be seen as true drop in replacements since they are not backwards compatible with FTP.

Key to the deafening silence facing scp and sftp, as opposed to the chorus of approval for secure interactive logins, is the lack of a "killer" functionality such as simplified X tunneling offered by SSH. For many systems, the perceived need for secure file transfer was significantly less than the perceived need for secure interactive login. Many users had FTP accounts on systems on which they did not also have shell accounts.[8] Unlike a sniffed telnet password, the damage from a compromised FTP password was often largely limited to the individual user. Additionally higher cost versus functionality (particularly the transfer speed impact of adding encryption), no doubt also hindered the selection of any of the secure alternatives to the sniffable FTP protocol. Without a compelling selling point, managers and system maintainers alike were loathe to take a lengthy and unpleasant client and server application plunge, especially when given the blurry availability and industry picture evident in the early days. While the confusion was certainly not unique to secure file transfer applications, the additional murkiness of the end-user choices also clouded the chance of acceptance by users and system operators alike.

Early adoption of the secure file transfer options was also complicated by insufficient "open" availability, consumer confusion over availability, and commercial versus open implementation questions. The welter of difficult to distinguish options and their relatively recent entry into the Internet protocol environment no doubt also hindered the displacement of clear-text protocols with encrypted communications. The absence of a broad selection of clients, particularly those geared for general users, for the early releases of the secure transfer protocols no doubt also made adoption more sluggish.

It is easy to think what might have been (the gradual supplanting of a clear text password network application), but also easy to spot where the various secure file transfer options did and did not offer the advantages of SSH: no increased functionality, even higher cost (far fewer client options) to switch, and a serious set of difficulties over the standard

[8]It is difficult to configure SSH to allow a user sftp access but not shell access [Barrett, 2000].

and complications with non-cooperative versions. However, we remain optimistic about the future of secure file transfer. With the growing acceptance of a standard and easier management implicit in the growing adoption of the OpenBSD team's implementations of the SSH2 suite, secure file transfer may achieve broader acceptance. The advent of a full-fledged secure FTP-like program (versus the less familiar rcp and scp) is relatively recent. The new application has yet to have a chance to achieve the same acceptance as the supplanter of telnet. Though we expect that many systems will continue to run FTP into the foreseeable future even with complementary secure alternatives, the spread of this new application is likely to be a bellwether for the acceptance of secure alternatives, and serve as a focal point in the overly fragmented area of secure file transfer protocols.

4. Conclusion

SSH provided superior security while maintaining current functionality. SSH's acceptance is demonstrated by the fact that installing SSH as an alternative to telnet is now widely considered to be a minimal security practice. The removal of telnet clients is now seen as a best practice [Fenzi, 2002], and this view has further increased the adoption of SSH.

Similar technologies such as secure file transfer protocols provide similar benefits but have not achieved nearly the same level of acceptance as SSH. We have performed an economic analysis to determine why telnet has been largely supplanted by SSH but FTP remains widely used. The consequences of a security breach exploiting clear text passwords is far reaching – the entire system is placed at risk. In many cases the risks posed by telnet and FTP were the same, but the perception of the costs to change obviously differs. An organization that provides shell accounts is likely to have an interest in the integrity of user data that extends beyond concerns for reputation and liability alone, and is also likely to be more willing to accept the difficulties and costs of the switch. How and more importantly why, does the market view one security solution as achievable, and yet ignore the other? We have attempted to find lessons to be learned about the tradeoffs that are made, and how the secure option can be made more attractive. We have shown that network externalities, usually a first order effect, were not a significant factor impeding the adoption of SSH, and that SSH offered equivalent functionality and greater ease of use. These factors were the primary consideration in the willingness to change. Additionally, we believe the openness of the standard, which facilitated the creation of numerous compatible implementations, was a key element in the economic decision made by system administrators.

Acknowledgements

We would like to thank Joel Winstead, Nicolas Christin, Anthony Wood, Shiva Prasad and the anonymous reviewers of the 2003 Workshop on Economics and Information Security for their helpful and insightful comments.

References

Daniel Barrett and Richard E. Silverman, SSH, the Secure Shell: The Definitive Guide, USA: O'Reilly & Associates, (2001).

Daniel Barrett and Richard E. Silverman, SSH Frequently Asked Questions, (Oct. 2000), http://www.snailbook.com/faq/restricted-scp.auto.html

Louis Bertrand, "How SSH was freed", Daemon News (Dec. 1999), http://www.daemonnews.org/199912/openSSH.html

cPanel, Inc., cPanel, http://www.cpanel.net

Kevin Fenzi and Dave Wreski. "Linux Security HOWTO", (June 2002), http://www.tldp.org/HOWTO/Security-HOWTO/index.html

Google, Inc. "Google Directory: SSH Clients", (2003), http://directory.google.com/Top/Computers/Security/Products_and_Tools/Cryptography/SSH/Clients/

Brian Hatch, "Greasing the Squeaky Wheels", ITWorld.com, (September 2002), http://www.itworld.com/nl/lnx_sec/09172002/

Jupitermedia Corporation, List of Web Hosts, (2004), http://webhosts.thelist.com/

Michael L. Katz and Carl Shapiro, "Systems Competition and Network Effects", The Journal of Economic Perspectives, Vol 8, (Spring 1994).

David Larochelle and Nicholas Rosasco, Towards a Model of the Costs of Security, (May 2003), http://www.cs.virginia.edu/larochelle/securitycosts

Damien Miller, SSH tips, tricks, and protocol tutorial, (August 2002), http://www.mindrot.org/~djm/auug2002/ssh-tutorial.pdf

Jason Moore, personal communication, (February 2001).

OpenBSD, SSH usage profiling, http://www.openssh.org/usage/, statistics listed as of May 2003.

Carl Shapiro and Hal R. Varian, Information Rules: a Strategic Guide to the Network Economy, Harvard Business School Press, (1999).

Clifford Stoll, The Cuckoo's Egg: Tracking a Spy through the Maze of Computer Espionage, New York : Doubleday, (1989).

WebHostingRank.com, Web Hosting directory list guide, http://www.webhostingrank.com/cgi-bin/search/basic.cgi statistics listed as of January 2004.

Tatu Ylönen, Usenet posting of the SSH release announcement, (July 1995), message archived at http://groups.google.com/groups?hl=en\&lr=\&ie=UTF-\&selm=YLO.95Jul12234021\%40shadows.cs.hut.fi

Chapter 19

COGNITIVE HACKING

Paul Thompson, George Cybenko and Annarita Giani
Dartmouth College

A cognitive hacker manipulates the victim's perception of the likelihood of winning a high payoff.

Misinformation, however it arises, can have a significant effect on the economic actions of individuals, organizations, and nations. In this chapter we focus on the deliberate use of misinformation to influence the actions of: a) an individual human user of information system technology, b) autonomous agents, and c) corporations and nations in the context of tactical and strategic information warfare. We also discuss automated countermeasures to these attacks. In section 1 we define cognitive and semantic hacking and discuss the related issues of perception management, deception detection, information warfare, and the role of cognitive, or semantic, hacking in intelligence and security informatics. In section 2 we discuss several recent examples of cognitive hacking on the Internet and then give a more detailed discussion of the problems of insider misuse, digital government, and of attacks on the financial infrastructure. In section 3 we discuss cognitive hacking in terms of several economic models, including information-theoretic models of the value of information, and the theory of the firm. In section 4 we discuss a variety of cognitive hacking countermeasures. Section 5 describes our plans for future work in this area, while section 6 provides a summary and conclusions.

1. Background

Computer and network security present great challenges to our evolving information society and economy. The variety and complexity of cyber security attacks that have been developed parallel the variety and complexity of the information technologies that have been deployed. Physical and syntactic attacks operate totally within the fabric of the computing and networking infrastructures. For example, the well-know

Unicode attack against older, unpatched versions of Microsoft's Internet Information Server (IIS) can lead to root/administrator access. Once such access is obtained, any number of undesired activities by the attacker is possible. For example, files containing private information such as credit card numbers can be downloaded and used by an attacker. Such an attack does not require any intervention by users of the attacked system. By contrast, a *cognitive* attack requires some change in users' behavior, accomplished by manipulating their perception of reality. The attack's desired outcome cannot be achieved unless human users change their behaviors in some way. Users' modified actions are a critical link in the sequencing of a cognitive attack.

Cognitive attacks can be overt or covert. No attempt is made to conceal overt cognitive attacks, e. g., website defacements. Provision of misinformation, the intentional distribution or insertion of false or misleading information intended to influence reader's decisions and / or activities, is covert cognitive hacking. The Internet's open nature makes it an ideal arena for dissemination of misinformation. Cognitive hacking differs from social engineering, which, in the computer domain, involves a hacker's psychological tricking of legitimate computer system users to gain information, e.g., passwords, in order to launch an autonomous attack on the system.

Most analyses of computer security focus on the time before misinformation is posted, i.e., on preventing unauthorized use of the system. A cognitive hack takes place when a user's behavior is influenced by misinformation. At that point the focus is on detecting that a cognitive hack has occurred and on possible legal action. Our concern is with developing tools to prevent cognitive hacking, that is, tools that can recognize and respond to misinformation before a user acts based on the misinformation.

By contrast, a *cognitive* attack requires some change in users' behavior, effected by manipulating their perceptions of reality. The attack's desired outcome cannot be achieved unless human users change their behaviors in some way. Users' modified actions are a critical link in a cognitive attack's sequencing. To illustrate what we mean by a cognitive attack, consider the following news report (Mann, 2000):

> Friday morning, just as the trading day began, a shocking company press release from **Emulex** (Nasdaq: EMLX) hit the media waves. The release claimed that Emulex was suffering the corporate version of a nuclear holocaust. It stated that the most recent quarter's earnings would be revised from a \$0.25 per share gain to a \$0.15 loss in order to comply with Generally Accepted Accounting Principles (GAAP), and that net earnings from 1998 and 1999 would also be revised. It also said Emulex's CEO, Paul Folino, had resigned and that the company was under investigation by the Securities and Exchange Commission. Trouble is, none of it was true.The real trouble was that Emulex shares plummeted from their Thursday close of \$113 per share to \$43 – a rapid 61% haircut that took more than \$2.5 billion off of the company's hide

> – before the shares were halted an hour later. The damage had been done: More than 3 million shares had traded hands at the artificially low rates. Emulex vociferously refuted the authenticity of the press release, and by the end of the day the company's shares closed within a few percentage points of where they had opened.

Mark Jacob, 23 years old, fraudulently posted the bogus release on Internet Wire, a Los Angeles press-release distribution firm. The release was picked up by several business news services and widely redistributed scale without independent verification. The speed, scale and subtlety with which networked information propagates have created a new challenge for society, outside the domain of classical computer security which has traditionally been concerned with ensuring that all use of a computer and network system is authorized.

The use of information to affect the behavior of humans is not new. Language, or more generally communication, is used by one person to influence another. Propaganda has long been used by governments, or by other groups, particularly in time of war, to influence populations (Coombs and Nimmo, 1993; Doob, 1935; Ellul, 1966). Although the message conveyed by propaganda, or other communication intended to influence, may be believed to be true by the propagator, it usually is presented in a distorted manner, so as to have maximum persuasive power, and, often, is deliberately misleading, or untrue. Propaganda is a form of perception management. Other types of perception management include psychological operations in warfare (Information Warfare, 2001), consumer fraud, and advertising (Coombs and Nimmo, 1993; Pratkanis and Aronson, 1992). As described in section 1.3, deception detection has long been a significant area of research in the disciplines of psychology and communications.

Perception Management

As noted by many authors, e.g. (Coombs and Nimmo, 1993; Denning, 1999; Ellul, 1966; Pratkanis and Aronson, 1992) perception management is pervasive in contemporary society. Its manifestation on the Internet is one aspect of the broader phenomenon. Not all perception management is negative, e.g., education can be considered a form of perception management; nor is all use of perception management on the Internet cognitive hacking (see definition in the next section). Clearly the line between commercial uses of the Internet such as advertising, which would not be considered cognitive hacking, and manipulation of stock prices by the posting of misinformation in news groups, which would be so considered, is a difficult one to distinguish.

Cognitive hacking is defined here as gaining access to, or breaking into, a computer information system for the purpose of modifying certain behaviors of a human user in a way that violates the integrity of the overall user-information system. The integrity of such a system would for example include correctness or validity of the information the user gets from such a system. In this context, the integrity of a computer system can be defined more broadly than the definition implicit in Landwehr's classic definition of computer security in terms of confidentiality, integrity, and accessibility (Landwehr, 1981). Smith (2001) refers to breaches in computer security as violations of the semantics of the computer system, i.e., the intended operation of the system. Wing (1998) argues a similar view. In this sense the World Wide Web itself can be seen as a computer system used for communication, e-commerce, and so on. As such, activities conducted over the Web that violate the norms of communication or commerce, for example, fraud and propaganda, are considered to be instances of cognitive hacking, even if they do not involve illegitimate access to, or breaking into, a computer. For example, a person might maintain a website that presents misinformation with the intent of influencing viewers of the information to engage in fraudulent commercial transactions with the owner of the website.

Semantic Attacks and Information Warfare

A definition of semantic attacks closely related to our discussion of cognitive hacking has been described by Schneier (2000), who attributes the earliest conceptualization of computer system attacks as physical, syntactic, and semantic to Martin Libicki (1994), who describes semantic attacks in terms of misinformation being inserted into interactions among intelligent agents on the Internet. Schneier (2000), by contrast, characterizes semantic attacks as "...attacks that target the way we, as humans, assign meaning to content." He goes on to note, "Semantic attacks directly target the human/computer interface, the most insecure interface on the Internet".

Denning's (1999) discussion of information warfare overlaps our concept of cognitive hacking. Denning describes information warfare as a struggle over an information resource by an offensive and a defensive player. The resource has an exchange and an operational value. The value of the resource to each player can differ depending on factors related to each player's circumstances. The outcomes of offensive information warfare are: increased availability of the resource to the offense, decreased availability to the defense, and decreased integrity of the resource. Applied to the Emulex example, described below, Jakob is the offensive player and Internet Wire and the other newswire services are the defensive players. The outcome is decreased integrity of the newswires' content. From the perspective of cognitive hacking, while the above analysis would still hold, the main victims of the cognitive hacking would be the investors who were misled. In addition to the decreased integrity of the information, an additional outcome would be the money the investors lost.

Deception Detection

Deception of detection in interpersonal communication has long been a topic of study in the fields of psychology and communications Buller and Burgoon, 1996; Cornetto, 2001; Cao, Burgoon, and Nunamaker, 2003). The majority of interpersonal communications are found to have involved some level of deception. Psychology and communications researchers have identified many cues that are characteristic of deceptive interpersonal communication. Most of the this research has focused on the rich communication medium of face to face communication, but more recently other forms of communication have been studied such as telephone communication and computer-mediated communication (Zhou, Twitchell, Qin, Burgoon, and Nunamaker, 2003). A large study is underway Cao, Burgoon, and Nunamaker, 2003; George, Biros, Burgoon, and Nunamaker, 2003) to train people to detect deception in communication. Some of this training is computer-based. Most recently a study has begun to determine whether psychological cues indicative of deception can be automatically detected in computer-mediated communication, e.g., e-mail, so that an automated deception detection tool might be built (Zhou, Burgoon, and Twitchell, 2003; Zhou, Twitchell, Qin, Burgoon, and Nunamaker, 2003).

Cognitive Hacking and Intelligence and Security Informatics

Intelligence and security informatics (Chen, Zeng, Schroeder, Miranda, Demchak, and Madhusdan, 2003) will be supported by data mining, visualization, and link analysis technology, but intelligence and security analysts should also be provided with an analysis environment supporting mixed-initiative interaction with both raw and aggregated data sets (Thompson, 2003). Since analysts will need to defend against semantic attacks, this environment should include a toolkit of cognitive hacking countermeasures. For example, if faced with a potentially deceptive news item from FBIS, an automated countermeasure might provide an alert using adaptive fraud detection algorithms (Fawcett and Provost, 2002) or through a retrieval mechanism allow the analyst to quickly assemble and interactively analyze related documents bearing on the potential misinformation. The author is currently developing both of these countermeasures.

Information retrieval, or document retrieval, developed historically to serve the needs of scientists and legal researchers, among others. Despite occasional hoaxes and falsifications of data in these domains, the overwhelming expectation is that documents retrieved are honest representations of attempts to discover scientific truths, or to make a sound legal argument. This assumption does not hold for intelligence and security informatics. Most information retrieval systems are based either on:

a) an exact match Boolean logic by which the system divides the document collection into those documents matching the logic of the request and those that do not, or b) ranked retrieval. With ranked retrieval a score is derived for each document in the collection based on a measure of similarity between the query and the document's representation, as in the vector space model (Salton and McGill, 1983), or based on a probability of relevance (Maron and Kuhns, 1960; Rijsbergen, 1979).

Although not implemented in existing systems, a utility theoretic approach to information retrieval (Cooper and Maron, 1978) shows promise for a theory of intelligence and security informatics. In information retrieval predicting relevance is hard enough. Predicting utility, although harder, would be more useful. When information contained in, say, a FBIS document, may be misinformation, then the notion of utility theoretic retrieval, becomes more important. The provider of the content may have believed the information to be true or false, aside from whether it was true or false in some objective sense. The content may be of great value to the intelligence analyst, whether it is true or false, but, in general, it would be important to know not only whether it was true or false, but also whether the provider believed it to be true or false. Current information retrieval algorithms would not take any of these complexities into account in calculating a probability of relevance.

Predictive modeling using the concepts of cognitive hacking and utility-theoretic information retrieval can be applied in two intelligence and security informatics settings which are mirror images of each other, i.e., the user's model of the system's document content and the systems model of the user as a potential malicious insider. Consider an environment where an intelligence analyst accesses sensitive and classified information from intelligence databases. The accessed information itself may represent cognitive attacks coming from the sources from which it has been gathered, e.g., FBIS documents. As discussed above, each of these documents will have a certain utility for the analyst, based on the analyst's situation, based on whether or not the documents contain misinformation, and, if the documents do contain misinformation, whether, or not, the analyst can determine that the misinformation is present. On the other hand, the analyst might be a malicious insider engaged in espionage. The document system will need to have a cost model for each of its documents and will need to build a model of each user, based on the user's transactions with the document system and other external actions.

Denning's theory of information warfare (1999) and an information theoretic approach to the value of information (Cover and Thomas, 1991) can be used to rank potential risks given the value of each document held by the system. Particular attention should be paid to deception on the part of the trusted insider to evade detection. Modeling the value of information to adversaries will enable prediction of which documents are likely espionage targets and will enable development of hypotheses for opportunistic periods and scenarios for compromise. These models will be able to detect unauthorized activity and to predict the course of a multi-stage attack so as to inform appropriate defensive actions.

Misinformation, or cognitive hacking, plays a much more prominent role in intelligence and security informatics than it has played in traditional scientific informatics. The status of content as information, or misinformation, in turn, influences its utility for users. Cognitive hacking countermeasures are needed to detect and defend against cognitive hacking.

2. Examples of Cognitive Hacking

This section summarizes several documented examples of cognitive hacking on the Internet and provides a more detailed discussion of the problem of insider misuse.

Internet Examples

NEI Webworld case. In November 1999 two UCLA graduates students and one of their associates purchased almost all of the shares of the bankrupt company NEI Webworld at a price ranging from 0.05 to 0.17 per share. They opened many Internet message board accounts using a computer at the UCLA BioMedical Library and posted more than 500 messages on hot web sites to pump up the stock of the company, stating false information about the company with the purpose of convincing others to buy stock in the company. They claimed that the company was being taken over and that the target price per share was between 5 and 10 dollars. Using other accounts they also pretended to be an imaginary third party, a wireless telecommunications company, interested in acquiring NEI Webworld. What the three men did not post was the fact that NEI, formerly a Dallas, Texas-based commercial printer, was bankrupt and had liquidated assets in May 1999. The stock price rose from $0.13 to $15 in less then one day, and they realized about $364,000 in profits. The men were accused of selling their shares incrementally, setting target prices along the way as the stock rose. On one day the stock opened at $8 and soared to $15 5/16 a share by 9:45 a.m. ET and by 10:14 a.m. ET, when the men no longer had any shares, the stock was worth a mere 25 cents a share.

On Wednesday, December 15, 1999, the U.S. Securities and Exchange Commission (SEC) and the United States Attorney for the Central District of California charged the three men with manipulating the price of NEI Webworld, Inc (Securities and Exchange Commission, 1999). On 6 July 2000, the SEC filed an amended complaint against two of the previously charged individuals, charging them with similar fraudulent manipulation of the stock of eleven other companies during the time period of April to October 1999 (Securities and Exchange Commission, 2000).

In late January 2001, two of the individuals agreed to gave up their illegal trading profits (approximately $211,000). The Commission also filed a new action naming a fourth individual, as participating in the NEI Webworld and other Internet manipulations. Two of the men were sentenced on January 22, 2001 to 15 months incarceration and 10 months in a community corrections center. In addition to the incarcerations, Judge Feess ordered the men to pay restitution of between $566,000 and $724,000. The judge was to hold a hearing on Feb. 26 to set a specific figure (Securities and Exchange Commission, 2001). On 13 March 2003, the fourth individual was permanently enjoined from violations of the antifraud provisions of the federal securities laws and ordered to pay a disgorgement of $339,393, as well as prejudgment interest of $82,696.44 (Securities and Exchange Commission, 2003).

Anyone with access to a computer can use as many screen names as desired to spread rumors in an effort to pump up stock prices by posting false information about a particular company so that they can dump their own shares and give the impression that their own action has been above board.

The Jonathan Lebed case. A 15 years old student using only AOL accounts with several fictitious names was able to change the behavior of many people around the world making them act to his advantage (Lewis, 2001a). In six months he gained between $12,000 and $74,000 daily each time he posted his messages and, according to the US Security Exchange Commission, he did that 11 times increasing the daily trading volume from 60,000 shares to more that a million. His messages sounded similar to the following one (Lewis, 2001b):

```
DATE: 2/03/00 3:43pm Pacific Standard Time
FROM: LebedTG1

FTEC is starting to break out! Next week, this thing will EXPLODE...
Currently FTEC is trading for just $21/2. I am expecting to see FTEC
at $20 VERYSOON... Let me explain why...

Revenues for the year should very conservatively be around $20
million. The average company in the industry trades with a price/sales
ratio of 3.45. With 1.57 million shares outstanding, this will value
FTEC at... $44. It is very possible that FTEC will see $44, but
since I would like to remain very conservative... my short term price
target on FTEC is still $20! The FTEC offices are extremely busy...
I am hearing that a number of HUGE deals are being worked on. Once we
get some news from FTEC and the word gets out about the company... it
will take-off to MUCH HIGHER LEVELS! I see little risk when
purchasing FTEC at these DIRT-CHEAP PRICES. FTEC is making TREMENDOUS
PROFITS and is trading UNDER BOOK VALUE!!! This is the #1 INDUSTRY
you can POSSIBLY be in RIGHT NOW. There are thousands of schools
nationwide who need FTEC to install security systems... You can't find
a better positioned company than FTEC! These prices are GROUND-FLOOR!
My prediction is that this will be the #1 performing stock on the
NASDAQ in 2000. I am loading up with all of the shares of FTEC I
possibly can before it makes a run to $20. Be sure to take the time
```

```
to do your research on FTEC! You will probably never come across an
opportunity this HUGE ever again in your entire life.
```

He sent this kind of message after having bought a block of stocks. The purpose was to influence people and let them behave to pump up the price by recommending the stock. The messages looked credible and people did not even think to investigate the source of the messages before making decisions about their money. Jonathan gained $800,000 in six months. Initially the SEC forced him to give up everything, but he fought the ruling and was able to keep part of what he gained. The question is whether he did something wrong, in which case the SEC should have kept everything. The fact that the SEC allowed Jonathan to keep a certain amount of money shows that it is not clear whether or not the teenager is guilty from a legal perspective. Certainly, he made people believe that the same message was post by 200 different people.

Richard Walker, the SEC's director of enforcement, referring to similar cases, stated that on the Internet there is no clearly defined border between reliable and unreliable information, investors must exercise extreme caution when they receive investment pitches online.

On Jan. 1, 2004 Lebed launched StockSpot.com (2004). A typical message is

By: jmiddleman (12-12) | IP logged
Date: 3/30/2004 1:39:30 PM

```
What a day in TTTP. 17x.185, last trade.185. Was.10 x.12 with
only 40k shares of vol when I mentioned it here. Looks like we'll do
real well on this one fellow stockspotters, :)
```

Since members can rate other members on the quality of their postings, Jonathan Lebed is optimistic that people are encouraged to post valuable information. He is also operating Lebed.biz (2004), a subscription-only site that entitles users to daily stock picks from Jonathan Lebed, email alerts throughout the trading day, and the privilege of submitting your picks to Lebed for him to review. The price is $50 a month.

Fast-Trade.com website pump and dump. In February and March 1999, Douglas Colt, a Georgetown University law student, manipulated four traded stocks using the web site Fast-trade.com. Together with a group of friends he posted hundreds of false or misleading messages on Internet message boards such as Yahoo! Finance Raging Bull with the purpose of encouraging people to follow Fast-trade.com advice. The site offered a trial subscription and in less then two months more than 9,000 users signed up. The group was able to gain more than $345,000.

PayPal.com.

```
We regret to inform you that your username and password have been lost
in our database. To help resolve this matter, we request that you
supply your login information at the following website.
```

Many customers of PayPal received this kind of email and subsequently gave personal information about their PayPal account to the site linked by the message (`http://paypalsecure.com` not `http://www.paypal.com`) (Krebs, 2001). The alleged perpetrators apparently used their access to PayPal accounts in order to purchase items on eBay.

Emulex Corporation. Mark S. Jakob, after having sold 3,000 shares of Emulex Corporation in a "short sale" at prices of $72 and $92, realized that, since the price rose to $100, he lost almost $100,000 (Mann, 2000). This kind of speculation is realized by borrowing shares from a broker and selling them in hope that the price will fall. Once this happens, the shares are purchased back and the stock is returned to the broker with the short seller keeping the difference.

On August 25th 2000, when he realized the loss, he decided to do something against the company. The easiest and most effective action was to send a false press release to Internet Wire Inc. with the goal of influencing the stock price. He claimed that Emulex Corporation was being investigated by the Security and Exchange Commission (SEC) and that the company was forced to restate 1998 and 1999 earnings. The story quickly spread, and half an hour later other news services such as Dow Jones, Bloomberg and CBS Marketwatch picked up the hoax. Due to this false information, in a few hours Emulex Corporation lost over $2 billion dollars. After sending misinformation about the company, Jakob executed trades so that he earned $236,000. Jakob was arrested and charged with disseminating a false press release and with security fraud. He is subject to a maximum of 25 years in prison, a maximum fine of $220 million, two times investor losses, and an order of restitution up to $110 million to the victims of his action.

Non-financial fraud – web search engine optimization. Con artists have defrauded consumers for many years over the telephone and via other means of communication, including direct personal interaction. Such financially-motivated fraud continues over the Internet, as described above. Some cognitive hacking uses misinformation in a fraudulent way that does not directly attack the end user.

One such use of misinformation is a practice (Lynch 2001) that has been called "search engine optimization", or "index spamming". Because many users of the Internet find pages through use of web search engines, owners of web sites seek to trick web search engines to rank their sites more highly when searched by web search engines. Many techniques, for example inaccurate metadata, printing white text on white background (invisible to a viewer of the page, but not to a search engine) are used. While this practice does not directly extort money from a user, it does prevent the user from seeing the search results that the user's search would have returned based on the content of the web site. Thus the primary attack is on the search engine, but the ultimate target of the attack is the end user. Developers at web search engines are aware of this practice by web site promoters and attempt to defeat it, but it is an on-going skirmish between the two camps.

Non-financial fraud – CartoonNetwork.com. Another common misinformation practice is to register misleading web site names, e.g., a name that might be expected to belong to a known company, or a close variant of it, such as a slight misspelling. In October 2001, the FTC (Washtech.com, 2001) sought to close thousands of web sites that allegedly trap web users after they go to a site with a misleading name. According to the FTC, John Zuccarini registered slight misspelling of hundreds of popular Internet domain names. When a user goes to one of these sites a series of windows advertising various products opens rapidly, despite user attempts to back out of the original site. Zuccarini allegedly made $800,000 to $1,000,000 annually in advertising fees for such attacks.

Bogus virus patch report. Although computer viruses are syntactic attacks, they can be spread through cognitive attacks. The W32/Redesi-B virus (Sophos, 2001) is a worm which is spread through Microsoft Outlook. The worm is contained in an e-mail message that comes with a subject chosen randomly from 10 possible subjects, e.g., "FW: Security Update by Microsoft". The text of the e-mail reads "Just received this in my email I have contacted Microsoft and they say it's real" and then provides a forwarded message describing a new e-mail spread virus for which Microsoft has released a security patch which is to be applied by executing the attached file. The attached file is the virus. Thus a virus is spread by tricking the user into taking action thought to prevent the spread of a virus.

Usenet perception management. Since the Internet is an open system where everybody can put his or her opinion and data, it is easy to make this kind of attack. Each user is able to influence the whole system or only a part of it in many different ways, for example by building a personal web site or signing up for a Newsgroup. Blocking the complete freedom to do these activities, or even checking what people post on the web, goes against the current philosophy of the system. For this reason technologies for preventing, detecting and recovering from this kind of attack are difficult to implement (Chez.com, 1997).

Political Web site defacements – Ariel Sharon site. Web site defacements are usually overt cognitive attacks. For example, in January 2001, during an Israeli election campaign, the web site of Likud leader Ariel Sharon was attacked (BBC News Online, 2001b). In this attack, and in the retaliatory attack described in example 11, no attempt was made to deceive viewers into thinking that the real site was being viewed. Rather the real site was replaced by another site with an opposing message. The Sharon site had included a service for viewers that allowed them to determine the location of their voting stations. The replacement site had slogans opposing Sharon and praising Palestinians. It also had a feature directing viewers to Hezbollah "polling stations".

Political Web site Defacements – Hamas site. Following the January attack on the Sharon web site, the web site of the militant group Hamas was attacked in March 2001 (BBC News Online, 2001a). When the Hamas website was hacked, viewers were redirected to a hard-core pornography site.

New York Times site. In February 2001 the New York Times web site was defaced by a hacker identified as "splurge" from a group called "Sm0ked Crew", which had a few days previously defaced sites belonging to Hewlett-Packard, Compaq, and Intel (Register, 2001a; Register, 2001b). The New York Times defacement included html, a.MID audio file, and graphics. The message stated, among other things, "Well, admin I'm sorry to say by you have just got sm0ked by splurge. Don't be scared though, everything will be all right, first fire your current security advisor..." Rather than being politically motivated, such defacements as these appear to be motivated by self-aggrandizement.

Yahoo site. In September of 2001 Yahoo's news web site was edited by a hacker (MSNBC, 2001). This cognitive hacking episode, unlike the defacements discussed above, was more subtle. While not as covert as hacking with the intent to engage in fraud or perception management, neither were the changes made to the website as obvious as those of a typical defacement. A 20-year old researcher confessed that he altered a Reuters news article about Dmitry Sklyarov, a hacker facing criminal charges. The altered story stated that Skylarov was facing the death penalty and attributed a false quote to President Bush with respect to the trial.

Web site defacements since 11 September terrorist incident. Since the 11 September terrorist incident, there have been numerous examples of web site defacements directed against web sites related to Afghanistan (Latimes.com, 2001). While official Taliban sites have been defaced, often sites in any way linked with Afghanistan were defaced indiscriminately, regardless of which sides they represented in the conflict.

Fluffi Bunni declares Jihad. Another type of politically motivated cognitive hacking attack has been perpetrated by "Fluffi Bunni", who has redirected numerous websites to a page in which Bunni's opinion on current events is presented. This redirection appears to have been accomplished through a hacking of the Domain Name System Server of NetNames (Hacktivist, 2001).

Web site spoofing – CNN site. On 7 October 2001, the day that the military campaign against Afghanistan began, the top-ranked news story on CNN's most popular list was a hoax, "Singer Britney Spears Killed in Car Accident". The chain of events which led to this listing started with a web site spoofing of CNN.com (Newsbytes, 2001). Then, due to a bug in CNN's software, when people at the spoofed site clicked on the "E-mail This" link, the real CNN system distributed a real CNN e-mail to recipients with a link to the spoofed page. At the same time with each click on "E-mail This" at the bogus site, the real site's tally of most popular stories was incremented for the bogus story. Allegedly this hoax was started by a researcher who sent the spoofed story to three users of AOL's Instant Messenger chat software. Within 12 hours more than 150,000 people had viewed the spoofed page.

In 1997 Felton and his colleagues showed that very realistic website spoofings could be readily made. More recently, Yuan, Ye, and Smith (2001) showed that these types of website spoofs could be done just as easily with more contemporary web technologies.

Web site spoofing – WTO site. Use of misleading domain names can also be political and more covert. Since 1999, a site, `www.gatt.org`, has existed which is a parody of the World Trade Organization site, `www.wto.org` (NetworkWorldFusion, 2001). Again, as in the case of the spoofing of the Yahoo new site mentioned above, the parody can be seen through fairly easily, but still could mislead some viewers.

Insider Threat

Trusted insiders who have historically caused the most damage to national security were caught only after prolonged counterintelligence operations. These insiders carried out their illegal activities for many years without raising suspicion. Even when it was evident that an insider was misusing information, and even when attention began to focus on the insider in question as a suspect, it took more years before the insider was caught. Traditionally apprehension of trusted insiders has been possible only after events in the outside world had taken place, e.g., a high rate of double agents being apprehended and executed that led to an analysis eventually focusing on the insider. Once it was clear that there was likely a problem with insider misuse of information, it was eventually possible to determine the identity of the insider by considering who had access to the information and by considering other factors such as results of polygraph tests.

The insider threat, is much more pervasive, however, than a small number of high profile national security cases. It has been estimated that the majority of all computer security breeches are due to insider attacks, rather than to external hacking (Anderson et al., 2000).

As organizations move to more and more automated information processing environments, it becomes potentially possible to detect signs of insider misuse much earlier than has previously been possible. Information systems can be instrumented to record all uses of the system, down to the monitoring of individual keystrokes and mouse movements. Commercial organizations have made use of such clickstream mining, as well as analysis of transactions to build profiles of individual users. Credit card companies build models of individuals' purchase patterns to detect fraudulent usage. Companies such as Amazon.com analyze purchase behavior of individual users to make recommendations for the purchase of additional products, likely to match the individual user's profile.

A technologically adept insider, however, may be aware of countermeasures deployed against him, or her, and operate in such a way as to neutralize the countermeasures. In other words, an insider can engage in cognitive hacking against the network and system administrators. A similar situation arises with Web search engines, where what has been referred to as a cold war exists between Web search engines and search engine optimizers, i.e., marketers who manipulate Web search engine rankings on behalf of their clients.

Models of insiders can be built based on: a) known past examples of insider misuse, b) the insider's work role in the organization, c) the insider's transactions with the information system, and d) the content of the insider's work product. This approach to the analysis of the behavior of the insider is analogous to that suggested for analyzing the behavior of software programs by Munson and Wimer (2001). One aspect of this approach is to look for known signatures of insider misuse, or for anomalies in each of the behavioral models individually. Another aspect is to look for discrepancies among the models. For example, if an insider is disguising the true intent of his, or her, transactions by making deceptive transactions that disguise the true nature of what the insider is doing, then this cognitive hacking might be uncovered by comparing the transactions to the other models described above, e.g., to the insider's work product.

User models have long been of interest to researchers in artificial intelligence and in information retrieval (Rich, 1983; Daniels, Brooks, and Daniels, 1997). Several on-going research programs have been actively involved in user modeling for information retrieval. The Language Modeling approach to probabilistic information retrieval has begun to consider query (user) models (Lafferty and Chengziang, 2001). The Haystack project at MIT is building models of users based on their interactions with a document retrieval system and the user's collections of documents. The current focus of this project, however, seems to be more on overall system architecture issues, rather than on user modeling as such (Huynh, Karger, and Quan, 2003).

The current type of user modeling that might provide the best basis for cognitive hacking countermeasures is recommender system technology (Varian, 1996, 1997; Hofmann, 2001). One of the themes of the recommender systems workshop held at the 1999 SIGIR conference (Herlocker, 2001) was the concern to make recommender systems applicable to problems of more importance than selling products. Since then, recommender systems technology has developed, but applications are generally still largely commercial. Researchers are concerned with developing techniques that work well with sparse amounts of data (Drineas, Kerendis, and Raghavan, 2002) and with scaling up to searching tens of millions of potential neighbors, as opposed to the tens of thousands of today's commercial systems (Sarwar, Karypis, Konstan, and Riedl, 2001). Related to this type of user modeling, Anderson and Khattak (1998) described preliminary results with the use of an information retrieval system to query an indexed audit trail database, but this work was never completed (Anderson, 2002).

Digital Government and Cognitive Hacking

The National Center for Digital Government is exploring issues related to the transition from traditional person-to-person provision of government services to the provision of such services over the Internet. As excerpted from the Center's mission statement:

> Government has entered a period of deep transformation heralded by rapid developments in information technologies. The promise of digital government lies in the potential of the Internet to connect government actors and the public in entirely new ways. The outcomes of fundamentally new modes of coordination, control, and communication in government offer great benefits and equally great peril.
> (National Center for Digital Government, 2003a)

A digital government workshop held in 2003 (National Center for Digital Government, 2003b), focused on five scenarios for future authentication policies with respect to digital identity:

- Adoption of a single national identifier
- Sets of attributes
- Business as usual, i.e., continuing growth of the use of ad-hoc identifiers
- Ubiquitous anonymity
- Ubiquitous identify theft.

The underlying technologies considered for authentication were: biometrics; cryptography, with a focus on digital signatures; secure processing/computation; and reputation systems.

Most of the discussion at the workshop focused on issues related to authentication of users of digital government, but, as the scenario related to ubiquitous identity theft implies, there was also consideration of problems related to misinformation, including cognitive hacking.

In the face to face interaction with other people associated with traditional provision of government services, there is normally some context in which to evaluate the reliability of information being conveyed. As we have seen, this type of evaluation cannot be directly transferred to digital government. The Internet's open nature makes it an ideal arena for dissemination of misinformation. What happens if a user makes a decision based on information found on the Web that turns out to be misinformation, even if the information appears to come from a government website? In reality, the information might be coming from a spoofed version of a government website. Furthermore, the insider threat is a serious concern for digital government.

3. Value of Information – Information Theoretic and Economic Models

Information theory has been used to analyze the value of information in horse races and in optimal portfolio strategies for the stock market (Cover and Thomas 1991). We have begun to investigate the applicability of this analysis to cognitive hacking. So far we have considered the simplest case, that of a horse race with two horses.

An Information Theoretic Model of Cognitive Hacking

Sophisticated hackers can use information theoretic models of a system to define a gain function and conduct a sensitivity analysis of its parameters. The idea is to identify and target the most sensitive variables of the system, since even slight alterations of their value may influence people's behavior. For example, specific information on the health of a company might help stock brokers predict fluctuations in the value of its shares. A cognitive hacker manipulates the victim's perception of the likelihood of winning a high payoff in a game. Once the victim has decided to play, the cognitive hacker influences which strategy the victim chooses.

A Horse Race. Here is a simple model illustrating this kind of exploit. A horse race is a system defined by the following elements (Cover and Thomas 1991)

- There are m horses running in a race
- each horse i is assigned a probability p_i of winning the race

- each horse i is assigned an odds o_i signifying that a gambler that bet b_i dollars on horse i would win $b_i o_i$ dollars in case of victory (and suffer a total loss in case of defeat).

If we consider a sequence of n independent races, it can be shown that the average rate of the wealth gained at each race is given by

$$W(b,p,o) = \sum_{i=1}^{m} p_i \log b_i o_i \tag{19.1}$$

where b_i is the percentage of the available wealth invested on horse i at each race. So the betting strategy that maximizes the total wealth gained is obtained by solving the following optimization problem

$$W(p,o) = \max_b W(b,p,o) = \max_b \sum_{i=1}^{m} p_i \log b_i o_i \tag{19.2}$$

subject to the constraint that the b_i's add up to 1. It can be shown that this solution turns out to be simply $b = p$ (proportional betting) and so $W(p,o) = \sum_{i=1}^{m} p_i \log p_i o_i$.

Thus, a hacker can predict the strategy of a systematic gambler and make an attack with the goal of deluding the gambler on his/her future gains. For example, a hacker might lure an indecisive gambler to invest money on false prospects. In this case it would be useful to understand how sensitive the function W is to p and o and tamper with the data in order to convince a gambler that it is worth playing (because W appears illusionary larger than it actually is).

To study the sensitivity of W to its domain variables we consider the partial derivatives of W with respect to p_i and o_i and see where they assume the highest values. This gives us information on how steep the function W is on subsets of its domain.

If we consider the special case of races involving only two horses ($m = 2$), then we have

$$W(p,o_1,o_2) = p \log p o_1 + (1-p)\log(1-p)o_2 \tag{19.3}$$

- $\frac{\partial W}{\partial p}(p,o_1,o_2) = \log\left(\frac{p}{1-p}\frac{o_1}{o_2}\right)$
- $\frac{\partial W}{\partial o_1}(p,o_1,o_2) = \frac{p}{o_1}$
- $\frac{\partial W}{\partial o_2}(p,o_1,o_2) = \frac{1-p}{o_2}$

Thus, if we fix one of the variables then we can conduct a graphic analysis of those functions with a 3D plot.

Case 1 o_1 is constant. This is the doubling rate function. The most sensitive parameter to let W increase is o_2. Increasing this variable W grows at a fast rate for low values of p and grows with a smaller rate for higher values of p.

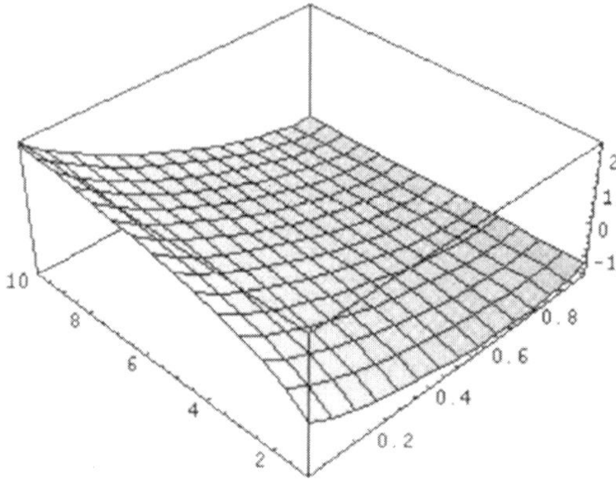

Applying the Horse Race Example to the Internet. Misinformation was used by Mark Jakob in a cognitive attack (Mann, 2002). Jacob posted a bogus release regarding the company Emulex on Internet Wire, a Los Angeles press-release distribution firm. The release was picked up by several business news services and widely redistributed without independent verification. Jakob sold Emulex short and profited, while other investors lost large sums of money selling the stock as its value fell sharply in response to the misinformation.

In this example the two horses are: horse 1, Emulex stock goes up; and horse 2, Emulex stock goes down. First the cognitive hacker makes the victim want to play the game by making the victim think that he can make a large profit through Emulex stock transactions. This is done by spreading misinformation about Emulex, whether positive or negative, but news that, if true would likely cause the stock's value to either sharply increase, or decrease, respectively. Positive misinformation might be the news that Emulex had just been granted a patent that could lead to a cure for AIDS. Negative misinformation might be that Emulex was being investigated by the Securities and Exchange Commission (SEC) and that the company was forced to restate 1998 and 1999 earnings. This fraudulent negative information was in fact posted by Jakob.

Theories of the Firm and Cognitive Hacking

Much attention in economics has been devoted to theories of the market. The economic actor has been modeled as enjoying perfect, costless information. Such analyses, however, are not adequate to explain the operation of firms. Theories of the firm provide a complementary economic analysis taking into account transaction and organizing costs, hierarchies, and other factors left out of idealized market models. It has been argued that information technology will transform the firm, such that "...the fundamental building blocks of the new economy will one day be 'virtual firms', ever-changing networks of subcontractors and freelancers, managed by a core of people with a good idea" (Economist, 2002). Others argue that more efficient information flows not only lower transaction costs, thereby encouraging more outsourcing, but also lower organization costs, thereby encouraging the growth of larger companies (Agre, 2001). More efficient information flow implies a more standardized, automated processing of information, which is susceptible to cognitive attack. Schneier (2000) attributes the earliest conceptualization of computer system attacks as physical, syntactic, and semantic to Martin Libicki, who describes semantic attacks in terms of misinformation being inserted into interactions among intelligent software agents (1994). Libicki was describing information warfare, but semantic, or cognitive, attacks can be directed against business systems, as well.

4. Cognitive Hacking Countermeasures

Cognitive hacking on the internet is an evolving and growing activity, often criminal and prosecutable. Technologies for preventing, detecting and prosecuting cognitive hacking are still in their infancies. Given the variety of approaches to and the very nature of cognitive hacking, *preventing* cognitive hacking reduces either to preventing unauthorized access to information assets (such as in web defacements) in the first place or detecting posted misinformation before user behavior is affected (that is, before behavior is changed but possibly after the misinformation has been disseminated). The latter may not involve unauthorized access to information, as for instance in "pump and dump" schemes that use newsgroups and chat rooms. By definition, *detecting* a successful cognitive hack would involve detecting that the user behavior has already been changed. We are not considering detection in that sense at this time.

Our discussion of methods for preventing cognitive hacking will be restricted to approaches that could automatically alert users of problems with their information source or sources (information on a web page, newsgroup, chat room and so on). Techniques for preventing unauthorized access to information assets fall under the general category of computer and network security and will not be considered here. Similarly, detecting that users have already modified their behaviors as a result of the misinformation, namely that a cognitive hack has been successful, can be reduced to detecting misinformation and correlating it with user behavior.

The cognitive hacking countermeasures discussed here will be primarily mathematical and linguistic in nature. The use of linguistic techniques in computer security has been pioneered by Raskin and colleagues at Purdue University's Center for Education and Research in Information Assurance and Security (Atallah, McDonough, Raskin, and Nirenburg, 2001). Their work, however, has not addressed cognitive hacking countermeasures.

Single Source Cognitive Hacking

In this section, we develop a few possible approaches for the single source problem. By single source, we mean situations in which redundant, independent sources of information about the same topic are not available. An authoritative corporate personnel database would be an example.

Authentication of Source. This technique involves due diligence in authenticating the information source and ascertaining its reliability. Various relatively mature certification and PKI technologies can be used to detect spoofing of an information server. Additionally, reliability metrics can be established for an information server or service by scoring its accuracy over repeated trials and different users. In this spirit, Lynch (2001) describes a framework in which trust can be established on an individual user basis based on both the identity of a source of information, through PKI techniques for example, and in the behavior of the source, such as could be determined through rating systems. Such an approach will take time and social or corporate consensus to evolve.

Information "Trajectory" Modeling. This approach requires building a model of a source based on statistical historical data or some sort of analytic understanding of how the information relates to the real world. For example, weather data coming from a single source (website or environmental sensor) could be calibrated against historical database (from previous years) or predictive model (extrapolating from previous measurements). A large deviation would give reason for hesitation before committing to a behavior or response.

As an interesting aside, consider the story lines of many well-scripted mystery novels or films. We believe that the most satisfying and successful stories involve s sequence of small deviations from what is expected. Each twist in the story is believable but when aggregated, the reader or viewer has reached a conclusion quite far from the truth. In the context of cognitive hacking, this is achieved by making a sequence of small deviations from the truth, not one of which fails a credibility test on it own. The accumulated deviations are however significant and surprise the reader or viewer who was not paying much attention to the small deviations one by one. However, a small number of major "leaps of faith" would be noticed and such stories are typically not very satisfying. Modeling information sources is something that can be done on a case-by-case basis as determined by the availability of historical data and the suitability of analytic modeling.

Ulam Games. Stanislaw Ulam (1991).in his autobiography *Adventure of a Mathematician* posed the following question

> "Someone thinks of a number between one and one million (which is just less than 2^{20}). Another person is allowed to ask up to twenty questions, to which the first person is supposed to answer only yes or no. Obviously, the number can be guessed by asking first: 'Is the number in the first half-million?' and then again reduce the reservoir of numbers in the next question by one-half, and so on. Finally, the number is obtained in less than $\log_2(1000000)$. Now suppose one were allowed to lie once or twice, then how many questions would one need to get the right answer?"

Of course, if an unbounded number of lies are allowed, no finite number of questions can determine the truth. On the other hand, if say k lies are allowed, each binary search question can be repeatedly asked $2k + 1$ times which is easily seen to be extremely inefficient. Several researchers have investigated this problem, using ideas from error-correcting codes and other areas (Mundici and Trombetta, 1997).

This framework involves a sequence of questions and a bounded number of lies, known a priori. For these reasons, we suspect that this kind of model and solution approach may not be useful in dealing with the kinds of cognitive hacking we have documented, although it will clearly be useful in cognitive hacking applications that involve a sequence of interactions between a user and an information service, as in a negotiation or multi-stage handshake protocol.

Linguistic Countermeasures with Single Sources. **Genre Detection and Authority Analysis** A careful human reader of some types of misinformation, e.g., exaggerated pump-and-dump scheme postings on the Web about a company's expected stock performance, can often detect the misinforming posting from other legitimate postings, even if these legitimate postings are also somewhat hyperbolic. Since Mosteller and Wallace's (1964) seminal work on authorship attribution, statistical linguistics approaches have been used to recognize the style of different writings. In Mosteller and Wallace's work this stylistic analysis was done to determine the true author of anonymous Federalist papers, where the authorship was disputed. Since then Biber and others (Biber, 1986, 1995; Karlgren and Cutting, 1994) have analyzed the register and genre of linguistic corpora using similar stylistic analysis. Kessler, Nunberg, and Schultze (1997) have developed and tested algorithms based on this work to automatically detect the genre of text.

Psychological Deception Cues. The approach to genre analysis taken, e.g., by Biber and Kessler et al., is within the framework of corpus linguistics, i.e., based on a statistical analysis of general word usage in large bodies of text. The work on deception detection in the psychology and communications fields (see section 19.2.0) is based on a more fine-grained analysis of linguistic features, or cues. Psychological experiments have been conducted to determine which cues are indicative of deception. To date this work has not led to the development of software tools to automatically detect deception in computer-mediated communication, but researchers see the development of such tools as one of the next steps in this line of research (Zhou, Twitchell, Qin, Burgoon, and Nunamaker, 2003).

Multiple Source Cognitive Hacking

In this section, we discuss possible approaches to preventing cognitive hacking when multiple, presumably redundant, sources of information are available about the same subject of interest. This is clearly the case with financial, political and other types of current event news coverage.

Several aspects of information dissemination through digital, network media, such as the Internet and World Wide Web, make cognitive hacking possible and in fact relatively easy to perform. Obviously, there are enormous market pressures on the news media and on newsgroups to quickly disseminate as much information as possible. In the area of financial news, in particular, competing news services strive to be to the first to give reliable news about breaking stories that impact the business environment. Such pressures are at odds with the time consuming process of verifying accuracy. A compromise between the need to quickly disseminate information and the need to investigate its accuracy is not easy to achieve in general.

Automated software tools could in principle help people make decisions about the veracity of information they obtain from multiple networked information systems. A discussion of such tools, which could operate at high speeds compared with human analysis, follows.

Source Reliability via Collaborative Filtering & Reliability Reporting. The problem of detecting misinformation on the Internet is much like that of detecting other forms of misinformation, for example in newsprint or verbal discussion. Reliability, redundancy, pedigree and authenticity of the information being considered are key indicators of the overall "trustworthiness" of the information. The technologies of collaborative filtering and reputation reporting mechanisms have been receiving more attention recently, especially in the area of on-line retail sales (Yaholom, Klein, and Beth; Dellarocas, 2001). This is commonly used by the many on-line price comparison services to inform potential customers about vendor reliability. The reliability rating is computed from customer reports. Another technology, closely related to reliability reporting is collaborative filtering (Thornton, 2001). This can be useful in cognitive hacking situations that involve opinions rather than hard objective facts.

Both of these approaches involve user feedback about information that they receive from a particular information service, building up a community notion of reliability and usefulness of a resource. The automation in this case is in the processing of the user feedback, not the evaluation of the actual information itself.

Consider the following scenario. An end user is examining a posting to the business section of Google News (Google News beta, 2003). The document purports to provide valuable news about a publicly traded company that the user would like to act on quickly by purchasing, or selling stock. Although this news item might be reliable, it might also be misinformation being fed to unwary users by a cognitive hacker as part of a pump-and-dump scheme, i.e., a cognitive hacker's hyping of a company by the spread of false, or misleading information about the company and the hacker's subsequent selling of the stock as the price of its shares rise, due to the misinformation. The end user would like to act quickly to optimize his or her gains, but could pay a heavy price, if this quick action is taken based on misinformation.

News Verifier, a prototype cognitive hacking countermeasure, allows an end user to effectively retrieve and analyze documents from the Web that are similar to the original news item. When the end user receives a news item that he, or she, suspects, may represent a cognitive attack, i.e., contain deliberate misinformation, the user can run the News Verifier. First, a query is automatically generated from the text of the news item. This query is then sent automatically to an API for Google News. Then, a set of documents is retrieved by the Google News clustering algorithm. The Google News ranking of the clustered documents is generic, not necessarily optimized as a countermeasure for cognitive attacks. News Verifier uses a combination process in which several different search engines are used to provide alternative rankings of the documents initially retrieved by Google News. The ranked lists from each of these search engines, along with the original ranking from Google News, are combined using the Combination of Expert Opinion algorithm (Mateescu, Sosonkina, and Thompson, 2002) to provide a more optimal ranking. Relevance feedback judgments from the end user are used to train the constituent search engines. It is expected that this combination and training process will yield a better ranking than the initial Google News ranking. This is an important feature in a countermeasure for cognitive hacking, because a victim of cognitive hacking will want to detect misinformation as soon as possible in real time.

Byzantine Generals Models. Chandy and Misra (1988) define the Byzantine General's Problem as follows:

> A message-communicating system has two kinds of processes, *reliable* and *unreliable*. There is a process, called *general*, that may or may not be reliable. Each process x has a local variable *byz[x]*. It is required to design an algorithm, to be followed by all reliable processes, such that every reliable process x eventually sets its local variable *byz[x]*, to a common value. Furthermore, if *general* is reliable, this common value is *d0[g]*, the initial value of one of *general*'s variables. The solution is

> complicated by the fact that unreliable processes send arbitrary messages. Since reliable processes cannot be distinguished from the unreliable ones, the straightforward algorithm – *general* transmits its initial value to all processes and every reliable process u assigns this value to *byz[u]* – does not work, because *general* itself may be unreliable, and hence may transmit different values to different processes.

This problem models a group of generals plotting a coup. Some generals are reliable and intend to go through with the conspiracy while others are feigning support and in fact will support the incumbent ruler when the action starts. The problem is to determine which generals are reliable and which are not.

Just as with the Ulam game model for a single information source, this model assumes a sequence of interactions according to a protocol, something that is not presently applicable to the cognitive hacking examples we have considered, although this model is clearly relevant to the more sophisticated information sources that might arise in the future.

Detection of Collusion by Information Sources. Collusion between multiple information sources can take several forms. In pump and dump schemes, a group may hatch a scheme and agree to post misleading stories on several websites and newsgroups. In this case, several people are posting information that will have common facts or opinions, typically in contradiction to the consensus.

Automated tools for preventing this form of cognitive hack would require natural language processing to extract the meaning of the various available information sources and then compare their statistical distributions in some way. For example, in stock market discussion groups, a tool would try to estimate the "position" of a poster, from "strong buy" to "strong sell" and a variety of gradations in between. Some sort of averaging or weighting could be applied to the various positions to determine a "mean" or expected value, flagging large deviations from that expected value as suspicious.

Similarly, the tool could look for tightly clustered groups of messages, which would suggest some form of collusion. Such a group might be posted by the one person or by a group in collusion, having agreed to the form of a cognitive hack beforehand.

Interestingly, there are many statistical tests for detecting outliers but much less is known about detecting collusion which may not be manifest in outliers but in unlikely clusters that may not be outliers at all. For example, if too many eyewitnesses agree to very specific details of a suspect's appearance (height, weight, and so on), this might suggest collusion to an investigator. For some interesting technology dealing with corporate insider threats due to collusion, see (SRD, 2003).

Automated software tools that can do natural language analysis of multiple documents, extract some quantitative representation of a "position" based on that document and then perform some sort of statistical analysis of the representations are in principle possible, but we are not aware of any efforts working at developing such a capability at this time.

Linguistic Countermeasures with Multiple Sources. Authorship attribution using stylometry is a field of study within statistics and computational linguistics with a long history. Mosteller and Wallace (1964) resolved a longstanding debate on the authorship of certain of the Federalist Papers. More recently, principal components analysis approach has been pioneered by Burrows (1987) in the field of literary and linguistic computing, while Rao and Rhatgi (2000) have shown that Burrows' techniques can be employed even more successfully with text taken from the Internet. A recent account of research on authorship attribution is given by Harold Love (2002); while works on forensic linguistics include Rieber and Stewart (1990), McMenamin and Choi (2002), Shuy (1998), and Grant (2004).

Stylometry techniques can be used to determine the likelihood that two documents of uncertain authorship are written by the same author, or that a document of unknown authorship is written by an author from whom sample writings are available. Similarly, given a set of documents with several authors, it is possible to partition the documents into subsets of documents all written by the same author. There are two parameters in such techniques: a) the data requirements per pseudonym, and b) the discriminating power of the technique. Using only semantic features, Rao and Rhatgi demonstrated that anonymity and pseudonymity cannot preserve privacy. Rao and Rhatagi did some exploratory research to confirm that inclusion of syntactic features, e.g., misspellings or other idiosyncratic features much more prevalent in web, as opposed to published, documents, could provide stronger results.

5. Future Work

In this chapter a variety of cognitive hacking countermeasures have been described, but implementation has begun on only a few of them. Our future work lies in implementation of the remaining countermeasures and in the development of countermeasures that can be used not only against cognitive attacks, but against semantic attacks more broadly, such as the attacks with misinformation against autonomous agents, as described in Libicki's original definition of semantic hacking.

6. Summary and Conclusions

This chapter has defined a new concept in computer network security, cognitive hacking. Cognitive hacking is related to other concepts, such as semantic attacks, information warfare, and persuasive technologies, but is unique in its focus on attacks via a computer network against the mind of a user. Psychology and Communications researchers have investigated the closely related area of deception detection in interpersonal communication, but have not yet begun to develop automated countermeasures for computer-mediated communication. We have argued that cognitive hacking is one of the main features which distinguishes intelligence and security informatics from traditional scientific, medical, or legal informatics. If, as claimed by psychologists studying interpersonal deception, most interpersonal communication involves some level of deception, then perhaps communication via the Internet exhibits a level of deception somewhere between that of face to face interpersonal communication, on the one hand, and scientific communication on the other. As the examples from this chapter show, the level of deception on the Internet and in other computer networked settings is significant, and the economic losses due to cognitive hacking are substantial. The development of countermeasures against cognitive hacking is an important priority. In this chapter we have discussed cognitive hacking countermeasures suitable for situations where there is a single source of information and for situations where there are multiple sources of information. We have discussed several examples of possible countermeasures fore each of these situations and described our initial prototype countermeasure, the News Verifer.

Acknowledgments

Support for this research was provided by a Department of Defense Critical Infrastructure Protection Fellowship grant with the Air Force Office of Scientific Research, F49620-01-1-0272; Defense Advanced Research Projects Agency projects F30602-00-2-0585 and F30602-98-2-0107; and the Office of Justice Programs, National Institute of Justice, Department of Justice award 2000-DT-CX-K001 (S-1). The views in this document are those of the authors and do not necessarily represent the official position of the sponsoring agencies or of the US Government.

References

Abel, S. (1998). "Trademark issues in cyberspace: The brave new frontier" `http://library.lp.findlaw.com/scripts/getfile.pl?file=/firms/fenwick/fw000023.html`

Agre, P. (2001). "The market logic of information". *Knowledge, Technology, and Policy* vol. 13, no. 1, p. 67-77.

Anderson, R. (2002). Personal Communication

Anderson, R. H., Bozek, T., Longstaff, T., Meitzler, W., Skroch, M. and Wyk, K. Van. (2000). Research on Mitigating the Insider Threat to Information Systems - #2: Proceedings of a Workshop Held August 2000. RAND Technical Report CF163, Santa Monica, CA: RAND.

Anderson, R. and Khattak, A. (1998). "The Use of Information Retrieval Techniques for Intrusion Detection" *First International Workshop on Recent Advances in Intrusion Detection (RAID)*

Atallah, M, J., McDonough, C. J., Raskin, V., and Nirenburg, S. (2001). "Natural Language Processing for Information Assurance and Security: An Overview and Implementations" *Proceedings of the 2000 Workshop on New Security Paradigms.*

BBC News Online. (2001). "Hamas hit by porn attack" `http://news.bbc.co.uk/low/english/world/middle_east/newsid_1207000/1207551.stm`

BBC News Online. (2001). "Sharon's website hacked" `http://news.bbc.co.uk/low/english/world/middle_east/newsid_1146000/1146436.stm`

Biber, D. (1995). "Dimensions of Register Variation: A Cross-Linguistic Comparison" *Cambridge University Press.* Cambridge, England

Biber, D. (1986). "Spoken and written textual dimensions in English: Resolving the contradictory findings" *Language* vol. 62, no. 2, p. 384-413.

Buchanan, Ingersoll, P.C. (2001). "Avoiding web site liability—Online and on the hook?" `http://library.lp.findlaw.com/scripts/getfile.pl?file=/articles/bipc/bipc000056.html.`

Buller, D.B. and Burgoon, J.K. (1996). "Interpersonal deception theory" *Communication Theory* vol. 6 no. 3, p. 203-242

Burgoon, J. K., Blair, J.P., Qin, T and Nunamaker, J.F. (2003). "Detecting Deception through Linguistic Analysis" *NSF / NIJ Symposium on Intelligence and Security Informatics, Lecture Notes in Computer Science,* Berlin: Springer-Verlag, June 1–3, 2003, Tucson, Arizona, 2003, p. 91–101.

Burrows, J.F. 1987. "Word Patterns and Story Shapes: The Statistical Analysis of Narrative Style" *Literary and Linguistic Computing,* vol. 2, p. 61–70.

Cao, J, Crews, J. M., Lin, M., Burgoon, J. K. and Nunamaker, J. F. (2003). "Designing Agent99 Trainer: A Learner-Centered, Web-Based Training System for Deception Detection" *NSF / NIJ Symposium on Intelligence and Security Informatics, Lecture Notes in Computer Science,* Berlin: Springer-Verlag, June 1-3, 2003, Tucson, Arizona, 2003, p. 358-365.

Chandy, K. M. and Misra, J. (1988). *Parallel Program Design: A Foundation.* Addison Wesley.

Chen, H., Zeng, D.D., Schroeder, J., Miranda, R., Demchak, C. and Madhusudan, T. (eds.). (2003). Intelligence *and Security Informatics: First NSF/NIJ Symposium ISI 2003 Tucson, AZ, USA, June 2003 Proceedings,* Berlin: Springer-Verlag.

Chez.com. (1997). "Disinformation on the Internet." `http://www.chez.com/loran/art_danger/art_danger_on_internet.htm`

Cignoli, R. L.O., D'Ottaviano, I. M.L. and Mundici, D. (1999). *Algebraic Foundations of Many-Valued Reasoning* Boston: Kluwer Academic

Combs, J. E. and Nimmo, D. (1993). *The new propaganda: The dictatorship of palaver in contemporary politics.* New York: Longman.

Cooper, W. S. and Maron, M.E. "Foundations of Probabilistic and Utility-Theoretic Indexing". *Journal of the Association for Computing Machinery* vol. 25, no. 1, 1978, p. 67-80.

Cornetto, K. M. (2001). "Identity and Illusion on the Internet: Interpersonal deception and detection in interactive Internet environments" Ph.D.Thesis. University of Texas at Austin.

Cover, T. A. and Thomas, J. A. (1991). *Elements of Information Theory.* New York: Wiley

Cybenko, G., Giani, A. and Thompson, P. "Cognitive Hacking: A Battle for the Mind" *IEEE Computer, 35*(8), 2002, 50-56.

Cybenko, G., Giani, A., Heckman, C. and Thompson, P. "Cognitive Hacking: Technological and Legal Issues", *Law Tech 2002* November 7-9, 2002.

Daniels, P., Brooks, H.M. and Belkin, N.J. (1997). *"Using problem structures for driving human-computer dialogues"* In Sparck Jones, Karen and Willett, Peter (eds.) *Readings in Information Retrieval San Francisco*: Morgan Kaufmann, p. 135-142, reprinted from RIAO-85 Actes: Recherche d'Informations Assistee par Ordinateur, Grenoble, France: IMAG, p. 645-660.

Dellarocas, C. (2001). "Building trust on-line: The design of reliable reputation reporting mechanisms for online trading communities" Center *for eBusiness@MIT* paper 101.

Denning, D. (1999). *Information warfare and security.* Reading, Mass.: Addison-Wesley.

Denning, D. (1999). "The limits of formal security models". *National Computer Systems Security Award Acceptance Speech.*

Doob, L. (1935). *Propaganda, Its psychology and technique* New York: Holt.

Drineas, P., Kerendis, I. and Raghavan, P. Competitive recommendation systems STOC'02, May 19-21 2002.

Ebay Inc. v. Bidder's Edge, Inc., 100 F. Supp. 2d 1058 (N.D. Cal., 2000)

Economist. (2002). "Re-engineering in real time" 31 January. `http://www.economist.com/surveys/PrinterFriendly.cfm?Story_ID=949093`.

Ellul, J. (1966). *Propaganda* translated from the French by Konrad Kellen and Jean Lerner New York: Knopf.

Farahat, A., Nunberg, G. and Chen, F. (2002). "AuGEAS (Authoritativeness Grading, Estimation, and Sorting)" *Proceedings of the International Conference on Knowledge Management CIKM'02* 4-9 November, McLean, Virginia.

Fawcett, T. and Provost, F. in W. Kloesgen and J. Zytkow (eds.). (2002) *Handbook of Data Mining and Knowledge Discovery,* Oxford University Press.

Felton, E. W., Balfanz, D., Dean, D., and Wallach, D. (1997). "Web spoofing: An Internet con game". Technical Report 54-96 (revised) Department of Computer Science, Princeton University.

George, J., Biros, D. P., Burgoon, J. K. and Nunamaker, J. F. Jr. (2003). "Training Professionals to Detect Deception". *NSF / NIJ Symposium on Intelligence and Security Informatics, Lecture Notes in Computer Science*, Berlin: Springer-Verlag, June 1-3, 2003, Tucson, Arizona, 2003, p. 366-370.

Gertz v. Robert Welch, Inc., 428 U.S. 323, 94 S.Ct. 2997, 41 L.Ed.2d 789 (1974).

Google News beta. (2003). `http://news.google.com/`.

Grant, Tim. 2004. Ph. D. thesis, Forensic Section, School of Psychology University of Leicester (upcoming publication).

Hacktivist, The. (2001). "Fluffi Bunni hacker declares Jihad" `http://thehacktivist.com/article.php?sid=40`

Heckman, C. and J. Wobbrock , J. (2000)"Put Your Best Face Forward: Anthropomorphic Agents, E-Commerce Consumers, and the Law". *Fourth International Conference on Autonomous Agents,* June 3-7, Barcelona, Spain.

Herlocker, J. (ed.). (2001). "Recommender Systems: Papers and Notes from the 2001 Workshop" *In conjunction with the ACM SIGIR Conference on Research and Development in Information Retrieval.* New Orleans.

Hofmann, T. (2001). "What People (Don't) Want". *European Conference on Machine Learning (ECML).*

Hunt, A. (2001). "Web defacement analysis". ISTS.

Huynh, D., Karger, D. and Quan, D. (2003). "Haystack: A Platform for Creating, Organizing and Visualizing Information using RDF". *Intelligent User Interfaces (IUI)*

Information Warfare Site. (2001). `http://www.iwar.org.uk/psyops/index.htm`

"Interpersonal Deception: Theory and Critique" Special Issue *Communication Theory* vol 6. no. 3.

Johansson, P. (2002). "User Modeling in Dialog Systems". St. Anna Report SAR 02-2.

Karlgren, J. and Cutting, D. (1994). "Recognizing text genres with simple metrics using discriminant analysis"

Kessler, B., Nunberg, G. and Schütze, H. (1997). "Automatic Detection of Genre" *Proceedings of the Thirty-Fifth Annual Meeting of the Association for Computational Linguistics and Eighth Conference of the European Chapter of the Association for Computational Linguistics*

Krebs, B. (2001). "E-Mail Scam Sought To Defraud PayPal Customers" *Newsbytes* 19 December,
`http://www.newsbytes.com/news/01/173120.html`

Lafferty, J. and Chengxiang, Z. (2001) Document language models, query models, and risk minimization for information retrieval. *2001 ACM*

SIGIR Conference on Research and Development in Information Retrieval (SIGIR).

Lafferty, J. and Chengxiang, Z. (2001). "Probabilistic relevance models based on document and query generation" Proceedings of the *Workshop on Language Modeling and Information Retrieval*, Carnegie Mellon University.(Kluwer volume to appear PT reviewing).

Landwehr, C. E. (1984). "A security model for military message systems" *ACM Transactions on Computer Systems.* vol. 9, no. 3.

Landwehr, C. E. (1981). "Formal models of computer security". *Computing Surveys*, vol. 13, no. 3.

Latimes.com. (2001). "'Hacktivists', caught in web of hate, deface Afghan sites" `http://www.latimes.com/technology/la-000077258sep27.story?coll=la\%2Dheadlines\%2Dtechnology`

Lebed.biz (2004). `http://www.lebed.biz/`

Lewis, M. "Jonathan Lebed: Stock Manipulator", S.E.C. Nemesis – and 15 *New York Times Magazine* 25 February 2001

Lewis, M. (2001). *Next: The Future Just Happened* New York: W. W. Norton p. 35-36.

Libicki, M. (1994). "The mesh and the Net: Speculations on armed conflict in an age of free silicon". National Defense University McNair Paper 28 `http://www.ndu.edu/ndu/inss/macnair/mcnair28/m028cont.html`

Love, Harold. 2002. *Attributing Authorship: An Introduction* Cambridge, UK: Cambridge University Press.

Lynch, C. (2001). "When Documents Deceive: Trust and Provenance as New Factors for Information Retrieval in a Tangled Web" *Journal of the American Society for Information Science & Technology*, vol. 52, no. 1, p. 12-17.

McMenamin, Gerald R. and Choi, Dongdoo (eds.). 2002. *Forensic Linguistics: Advances in Forensic Stylistics* Boca Raton, Florida: CRC.

Mann, B. (2000). "Emulex fraud hurts all". *The Motley Fool.* `http://www.fool.com/news/foolplate/2000/foolplate000828.htm`

Maron, M.E. and Kuhns, J.L. "On relevance, probabilistic indexing and information retrieval". *Journal of the ACM* vol. 7 no. 3, 1960, p. 216-244.

Mateescu, G.; Sosonkina, M.; and Thompson, P. "A New Model for Probabilistic Information Retrieval on the Web" *Second SIAM International Conference on Data Mining (SDM 2002) Workshop on Web Analytic*

Matthew Bender and Company. (2001). Title 15.Commerce and Trade. Chapter 22. Trademarks General Provisions. *United States Code Service.* `http://web.lexis-nexis.com/congcomp/document?_m=46a301efb7693acc36c35058bee8e97d&_docnum=1&wchp=dGLStS-1Sl_md5=5929f8114e1a7b40bbe0a7a7ca9d7dea`

Mensik, M. and Fresen, G. (1996). "Vulnerabilities of the Internet: An introduction to the basic legal issues that impact your organization" http://library.lp.findlaw.com/scripts/getfile.pl?file=/firms/bm/bm000007.html

Mosteller, F. and Wallace, D. L. 1964. *Inference and Disputed Authorship: The Federalist* Reading, MA: Addison-Wesley.

MSNBC. (2001). "Hacker alters news stories on Yahoo" http://stacks.msnbc.com/news/631231.asp.

Mundici, D. and Trombetta, A. (1997). "Optimal Comparison Strategies in Ulam's Searching Game with Two Errors", *Theoretical Computer Science*, vol. 182, nos 1-2, 15 August.

Munson, J. C. and Wimer, S. "Watcher: the Missing Piece of the Security Puzzle" 17th Annual Computer Security Applications Conference (ACSAC'01). December 10 - 14, 2001 New Orleans, Louisiana

National Center for Digital Government. (2003). Integrating Information and Government John F. Kennedy School of Government Harvard University. http://www.ksg.harvard.edu/digitalcenter/

National Center for Digital Government: Integrating Information and Government "Identity: The Digital Government Civic Scenario Workshop" Cambridge, MA 28-29 April 2003 John F. Kennedy School of Government Harvard University. http://www.ksg.harvard.edu/digitalcenter/conference/

NetworkWorldFusion. (2001). "Clever fake of WTO web site harvests e-mail addresses" http://www.nwfusion.com/news/2001/1031wto.htm

New York v. Vinolas, 667 N.Y.S.2d 198 (N.Y. Crim. Ct. 1997).

Newsbytes. (2001). "Pop singer's death a hoax a top story at CNN" http://www.newsbytes.com/cgi-bin/udt/im.display.printable?client.id=newsbytes&story.id=170973

Pratkanis, A. R. and Aronson, E. (1992). *Age of propaganda: The everyday use and abuse of persuasion* New York: Freeman.

Rao, J. R. and Rohatgi, P. (2000). "Can pseudonymity really guarantee privacy?" *Proceedings of the 9th USENIX Security Symposium* Denver, Colorado August 14-17.

R.A.V. v. City of St. Paul, 505 U.S. 377, 112 S.Ct. 2538, 120 L.Ed.2d 305 (1992)

Register, The. (2001). "Intel hacker talks to The Reg" http://www.theregister.co.uk/content/archive/17000.html

Register, The. (2001). "New York Times web site sm0ked" http://www.theregister.co.uk/content/6/16964.html

Rich, E. (1983). "Users are individuals: individualizing user models" International Journal of Man-Machine Studies vol. 18 no. 3, p. 199-214.

Rieber, Robert W. and Stewart, William A. (eds.) 1990. *The Language Scientist as Expert in the Legal Setting*, Annals of the New York Academy of Sciences vol. 606, New York: The New York Academy of Sciences.

Rijsbergen, C.J van. *Information Retrieval* 2d. edition, London: Buttersworth, 1979.

Salton, G. and McGill, M. (1983). *Introduction to Modern Information Retrieval* New York: McGraw-Hill.

Sarwar, B., Karypis, G., Konstan, J. and Reidl, J. "Item-based collaborative filtering recommendation algorithms." *WWW10* May 1-5, 2001 Hong Kong.

Schneier, B. (2000). "Semantic attacks: The third wave of network attacks" *Crypto-gram Newsletter* October 15, 2000. http://www.counterpane.com/crypto-gram-0010.html.

Securities and Exchange Commission. (1999). Litigation Release No. 16391. http://www.sec.gov/litigation/litreleases/lr16391.htm.

Securities and Exchange Commission. (2000). Litigation Release No. 16620. http://www.sec.gov/litigation/litreleases/lr16620.htm.

Securities and Exchange Commission. (2001). Litigation Release No. 16867. http://www.sec.gov/litigation/litreleases/lr16867.htm.

Securities and Exchange Commission. (2003). Litigation Release No. 18043. http://www.sec.gov/litigation/litreleases/lr18043.htm

Shuy, Roger W. 1998. *The Language of Confession, Interrogation, and Deception* Thousand Oaks, California: SAGE Publications.

Smith, A.K. "Trading in False Tips Exacts a Price", *U.S. News & World Report*, February 5, 2001, p.40

Smith, S. (2001). Personal communication.

Sophos. (2001). "W32/Redesi-B" http://www.sophos.com/virusinfo/analyses/w32redesib.html

SRD (2003). http://www.the3dcorp.com/prod_nora.html

Stockspot.com (2004). http://www.stockspot.com

Thompson, P. "Semantic Hacking and Intelligence and Security Informatics" *NSF / NIJ Symposium on Intelligence and Security Informatics, Lecture Notes in Computer Science*, Berlin: Springer-Verlag, June 1-3, 2003, Tucson, Arizona, 2003.

Thornton, J. (2001). "Collaborative Filtering Research Papers". http://jamesthornton.com/cf/.

Ulam, S.M. (1991). *Adventures of a Mathematician* Berkeley, CA: University of California Press.

Varian, H. R. (1996). "Resources on collaborative filtering" http://www.sims.berkeley.edu/resources/collab/

Varian, H. R. and Resnik, P. eds. *CACM* Special issue on recommender systems, *CACM* vol. 40, no. 3, 1997.

WallStreetNewscast.com. (2004). "You've Made Your Lebed, Now Sleep in It" http://www.wallstreetnewscast.net/news/01172004.html

Washtech.com. (2001). "FTC shuts down thousands of deceptive web sites" http://www.washtech.com/news/regulation/12829-1.html

Wing, J. M. (1998). "A Symbiotic Relationship Between Formal Methods and Security" *Proceedings from Workshops on Computer Security, Fault Tolerance, and Software Assurance.*

Yahalom, R., Klein, B., and Beth, Th. (1993). "Trust relationships in secure systems – A distributed authentication perspective. In *Proceedings of the IEEE Symposium on Research in Security and Privacy*, Oakland.

Yuan, Y.; Ye, E. Z.; and Smith, S. (2001). "Web spoofing 2001" Department of Computer Science/Institute for Security Technology Studies Technical Report TR2001-409

Zhou, L., Burgoon, J. K. and Twitchell, D. P. (2003). "A Longitudinal Analysis of Language Behavior of Deception in E-mail". *NSF / NIJ Symposium on Intelligence and Security Informatics, Lecture Notes in Computer Science*, Berlin: Springer-Verlag, June 1-3, 2003, Tucson, Arizona, 2003, p. 102-110

Zhou, L., Twitchell, D.P., Qin, T., Burgoon, J.K. and Nunamaker, J.F. (2003). "An exploratory study into deception in text-based computer-mediated communications" *Proceedings of the 36th Hawaii International Conference on Systems Science*

Chapter 20

EVALUATING SECURITY SYSTEMS: A FIVE-STEP PROCESS

Bruce Schneier
Counterpane Internet Security, Inc
www.schneier.com

I propose a five-step process to analyze and evaluate security systems, technologies, and practices. Each of these five steps contains a question that is intended to help you focus on a particular security system or security countermeasure.

Most computer security researchers seem so focused on the details of technology that they miss the forest for the trees. They build security systems that, while technically sound, fail operationally. The result are a seemingly endless stream of good security products that are badly implemented and misused, cause more problems then they solve or fail in the marketplace.

I propose a five-step process to analyze and evaluate security systems, technologies, and practices. Each of these five steps contains a question that is intended to help you focus on a particular security system or security countermeasure. The questions may seem, at first, to be obvious, even trivial. But if you bear with me, and take them seriously, I believe you will find they will help you determine–in context–which kinds of security make sense and which don't.

- *Step 1: What assets are you trying to protect?* This might seem basic, but a surprising number of people never ask this question. It involves understanding the scope of the problem. For example, securing a computer program, a computer, a local network, a distributed application, and the Internet are all different security problems, and require different solutions.

- *Step 2: What are the risks to these assets?* Here we consider the need for security. Answering it involves understanding what is being defended, what the consequences are if it is successfully attacked, who wants to attack it, how they might attack it, and why.

- *Step 3: How well does the security solution mitigate those risks?* Another seemingly obvious question, but one that is frequently ignored. If the security solution doesn't solve the problem, it's no good. This is not as simple as looking at the security solution and seeing how well it works. It involves looking at how the security interacts with everything around it, evaluating both its operation and its failures.

- *Step 4: What other risks does the security solution cause?* This might be called the problem of unintended consequences. Security solutions have ripple effects, and most cause new security problems. The trick is to understand the new problems and make sure they are smaller than the old ones.

- *Step 5: What costs and trade-offs does the security solution impose?* Every security system has costs and requires trade-offs. Most security costs money, sometimes substantial amounts; but other trade-offs may be more important, ranging from matters of convenience and comfort to issues involving basic freedoms like privacy. Understanding these trade-offs is essential.

These five steps don't lead to an answer, but rather provide the mechanism to evaluate a proposed answer. They lead to another question: Is the security solution worth it? In other words, is the benefit of mitigating the risks (Step 3) worth the additional risks (Step 4) plus the other trade-offs (Step 5)? It is not enough for a security measure to be effective. We don't have limitless resources or infinite patience. As individuals and a society, we need to do the things that make the most sense, that are the most effective use of our security dollar. But subjective (and sometimes arbitrary) economic incentives make an enormous difference as to which security solutions are cost-effective and which aren't.

...

One of the reasons security is so hard to get right is that it inevitably involves different parties–let's call them *players* (from game theory)–with subjective perceptions of risk, tolerances for living with risk, and willingnesses to make various trade-offs. It should come as no surprise, then, that there is a strong tendency for a player involved in a security system to approach security subjectively, making those trade-offs based on both his own analysis of the security problem, and his own internal and external non-security considerations: collectively, his *agenda*.

Think back to the week after 9/11, and imagine that all the players involved in airline security were in a room trying to figure out what to do. Some members of the public are scared to fly (each person to his own degree), and need to be reassured that everything is going to be okay. The airlines are desperate to get more of the public flying, but are leery of security systems that are expensive or play havoc with their flight schedules. They are happy to let the government take over the job of airport screening because then it won't be their fault if there's a problem in the future. Many pilots like the idea of carrying guns, as they now fear for their lives. Flight attendants are less happy with the idea, afraid that they could be left in danger while the pilots defend themselves. Elected government officials are concerned about re-election, and need to be seen by the public as doing *something* to improve security. And the FAA is torn between its friends in the airlines and its friends in government. Confiscating nail files and tweezers from passengers seems like a good idea all around: the airlines don't mind because it doesn't cost them anything, and the government doesn't mind because it looks like they're doing something. The passengers haven't been invited to comment, although most seasoned travelers simply roll their eyes.

As a security expert reviewing this imaginary scenario, I am struck by the fact that no one is trying to figure out what the optimal level of risk is, how much cost and inconvenience is acceptable, and then what security countermeasures achieve those trade-offs most efficiently. Instead, everyone is looking at the security problem from his own perspective.

And there are many more players, with their own agendas, involved in airline security. Did you ever wonder why tweezers were confiscated at security checkpoints, but matches and cigarette lighters–actual combustible materials–were not? It's because the cigarette lobby interjected their agenda into the negotiations by pressuring the government. If the tweezers lobby had more power, I'm sure they would have been allowed on board as well. Because there are power imbalances among the different parties, the eventual security system will work better for some than for others.

Self-interest has profound effects on the way a player views a security problem. Except for the inconvenience, credit card fraud is not much of a security problem to the cardholder, because in the U.S. the banks shoulder all but $50 of the liability. That $50 is a token liability: enough to make you concerned about the loss, but not so much that you'd be afraid to carry your credit card with you when you shop. Change the individual cardholder's liability to $500, for example, and her attitude toward the seriousness of the credit card fraud problem will certainly change overnight. It might even call into question the value of having a credit card.

...

This notion of agenda–personal and corporate and bureaucratic–explains a lot about how security *really* works in the real world, as opposed to how people might expect, and wish, it to work. For example:

- Think about the money in your wallet. You have an overriding agenda to be able to spend your money, and therefore have a powerful vested interest in believing that the money you have is not counterfeit. A security system that relies on you checking for counterfeit money won't work because you won't do your part. Preventing counterfeiting is the government's agenda, and they're the ones that need to expend effort to detect and combat forgery.

- When ATM cardholders in the U.S. complained about phantom withdrawals from their accounts, the courts generally held that the bank had to prove fraud. Hence, the banks' agenda was to improve security and keep fraud low, because they paid the costs of any fraud. In the UK, the reverse was true: The courts generally sided with the bank and assumed that any attempts to repudiate withdrawals were cardholder fraud, and the cardholder had to prove otherwise. This caused the banks to have the opposite agenda; they didn't care about improving security, because they were content to blame the problems on the customers and send them to jail for complaining. The result was that in the U.S., the banks improved ATM security to forestall additional losses–most of the fraud actually was not the cardholder's fault–while in the UK the banks did nothing.

- The airline industry has a long history of fighting improvements in airplane safety. International treaties limited the amount of damages airlines had to pay families of international airplane crash victims, which artificially changed the economics of airplane safety. It actually made more economic sense for airlines to resist many airplane safety measures, and airplane safety improvements came only after military development contracts and then government regulation. Notice that the agendas of governments–increased passenger safety–was forced onto the airlines, because the governments had the power to regulate the industry.

- Through 2002, the U.S. government tried to convince corporations to improve their own security: at nuclear power plants, chemical factories, oil refineries, software companies, and so on. Officials appealed to the CEOs' sense of patriotism, reminding them that improving security would help their country. That this had little real effect should surprise no one. If the CEO of a major company announced that he was going to reduce corporate earnings by 25 percent in order to improve security for the good of the nation, he would almost certainly be fired. If I were on the company's board of directors, I would fire him. Sure, the corporation has to be concerned about national security, but only to the point where its cost is not substantial.

- Sometimes individual agendas are a harrowing matter of life and death: On 1 September 1983, Korean Air Lines flight 007, on its way from Anchorage, Alaska to Seoul, Korea, carrying 269 passengers and crew, strayed off its intended course and entered into

Soviet airspace. It was destroyed in midair because the Soviet general in charge of air defense knew that the last time a plane violated their airspace, the general in charge that night was shot. The general didn't care about getting the risks right, whether the plane was civilian or military, or anything else. His agenda was his own neck.

In all of these stories, each player is making security trade-offs based on his own subjective agenda, and often it's the non-security concerns are more important. This means is that you have to evaluate security opinions based on the positions of the players. When a pharmaceutical manufacturer says that tamper-resistant packaging doesn't add much to security and would be inconvenient for the consumer, it's because he does not want to pay for the security countermeasure. Tamper-resistant packaging is not worth the expense *to him*. When the software industry lobbying groups say that applying liability laws to software would not improve software quality and would be a disaster for the public, it's because the affected companies don't want the expense. Liability laws are not worth the expense to *them*. When the U.S. government says that security against terrorism is worth curtailing individual civil liberties, it's because the cost of that decision is not borne by those making it. Extra security is worth the civil liberty losses because *someone else* is going to suffer for it. Security decisions are always about more than security. Understanding a player's negotiating position requires you to understand their personal agenda and trade-offs.

In economics this is called an externality; it occurs when one player makes a decision that affects another player, one not involved in the decision. It's the kind of problem that surfaces when a company can save substantial money by dumping toxic waste into the river, and everyone in the community suffers because of less healthy water. The community is the player that gets stuck with the externality because they're not involved in the company's decision. In terms of overall good to society, it is a bad decision to dump toxic waste into the river. But it's a good decision for the company because it doesn't bear the cost of the effects. Unless you understand the players and their agendas, you will never understand why some security systems end up as they are.

The ideas in this brief chapter have been developed more fully in *Beyond Fear: Thinking Sensibly About Security in an Uncertain World*, Copernicus Books, 2003.

Index